THE OXFORD REFERENCE GRAMMAR

Edmund Weiner is Principal Philologist of the *Oxford English Dictionary* (2nd edn), and is the author of *The Oxford Dictionary of English Grammar* (with Sylvia Chalker) and *The Oxford Guide to English Usage* (with Andrew Delahunty).

The Oxford
Reference
Grammar

SIDNEY GREENBAUM

Edited by EDMUND WEINER

OXFORD
UNIVERSITY PRESS

OXFORD
UNIVERSITY PRESS

Great Clarendon Street, Oxford OX2 6DP

Oxford University Press is a department of the University of Oxford.
It furthers the University's objective of excellence in research, scholarship,
and education by publishing worldwide in

Oxford New York

Auckland Bangkok Buenos Aires Cape Town Chennai
Dar es Salaam Delhi Hong Kong Istanbul Karachi Kolkata
Kuala Lumpur Madrid Melbourne Mexico City Mumbai Nairobi
São Paulo Taipei Tokyo Toronto

Oxford is a registered trade mark of Oxford University Press
in the UK and in certain other countries

Published in the United States
by Oxford University Press Inc., New York

British Library Cataloguing in Publication Data

Data available

Library of Congress Cataloging in Publication Data

Data available

ISBN 0-19-860044-5

5 7 9 10 8 6

Designed by Jane Stevenson
Typeset in Minion and Franklin Gothic
by Alliance Phototypesetters, India
Printed in Great Britain by
Biddles Ltd, King's Lynn

Preface

This book is addressed primarily to native speakers of English and others who use English as their first language. It is a comprehensive account of the syntax of present-day English that is chiefly focused on the standard varieties of American and British English, but it also refers frequently to non-standard varieties and it draws on the history of the language to illuminate and explain features of English of today. It offers a description of the language and is not intended to prescribe or proscribe.

This work is written to be accessible to non-specialists, but is organized with the needs of students of the English language and related subjects especially in mind. It serves as a reference work and can also be used as a textbook. Each chapter is prefaced by a list of contents and a summary of the chapter. The text of each chapter is subdivided into smaller sections in order to keep the user orientated at all times. Cross-references link topics mentioned to the places where they are discussed in more detail. All grammatical terms used in the book are highlighted in the text on their first occurrence in each chapter, apart from very frequent, well-known terms such as *noun*, *verb*, etc. All terms are defined in the Glossary at the end of the book, which also provides more discursive explanations of the most important terms.

Numerous citations (quotations from actual spoken or written English) appear in this book. These are important because they show that the grammatical analysis corresponds with real language use and is not based solely on the intuition of the grammarian. Many of them come from American and British newspapers, magazines, and books. Most are taken from two sources: ICE-GB (the British million-word component of the International Corpus of English) and the *Wall Street Journal* (about three million words from issues of this American newspaper published in 1989, provided in a CD-ROM by the Association for Computational Linguistics Data Collection Initiative). Citations from ICE-GB are for language used during the years 1990–3. There are 500 texts (samples) in ICE-GB, each text containing about 2,000 words, for a total of about one million words. The spoken texts number 300. Fifty of the spoken texts are scripted (written down and read aloud); the scripted texts are transcribed from the spoken recordings. Many of the texts are composite; that is, they are composed of several subtexts (shorter samples), such as a text comprising a number of personal letters. (For a further explanation of the use of corpora in grammatical study, see 1.11.1.)

All citations preserve the original wording. If anything is omitted (to avoid irrelevant distractions), the omission is indicated by [...]. Pauses are indicated by ... Citations from published material are usually followed by the author and work in the case of a book, or simply the title of the periodical. Citations from unpublished material (essays, examination scripts, and letters), and from administrative regulations, government leaflets, etc. are followed by '[W]'. All other citations are from spoken texts.

This book is based on chapters 1–6 of *The Oxford English Grammar* (1996). The text follows that of the parent volume but has been broken up into smaller subsections; this has sometimes occasioned the reordering and rewriting of material. Some citations have been rearranged, a few have been omitted, and a few have been shortened; precise references to the textual corpora have been omitted or replaced by author and title or periodical title. All footnotes have been moved into the main text as panels (labelled 'Note'), except for those suggesting further reading, which have been given a section of their own at the end of the book. Some paragraphs that give detailed syntactic information and are to some extent parenthetic have been set off distinctively from the main text in panels with headings that explain their function. The Glossary has been expanded to cover all the technical terms used in the main text.

The revision follows the outline plan drawn up by the author of *The Oxford English Grammar*, Sidney Greenbaum. It is a matter of great regret that he did not live to edit the book himself and the editor's earnest wish is that it may serve the purposes for which he intended it.

Contents

List of Tables

List of Figures

Pronunciation Table

Consonants

voiceless

p	pen	s	sit
t	top	ʃ	she
k	cat	tʃ	chip
f	few	h	he
θ	thin		

voiced

b	but	m	man
d	dog	n	no
g	get	ŋ	ring
v	van	l	leg
ð	this	r	red
z	zoo	w	we
ʒ	vision	j	yes
dʒ	jar		

Vowels

a	cat	ə	ago
ɑ:	arm (RP) arm (GA)	ʌɪ	my
ɛ	bed	aʊ	how
ə: (RP)	her	eɪ (RP) e: (GA)	day
ɜ (GA)	her	əʊ (RP) o: (GA)	no
ɪ	sit	ɛ:	hair (RP) hair (GA)
i:	see	ɪə (RP) ɪ (GA)	near (RP) near (GA)
ɒ (RP) ɑ: (GA)	hot	ɔɪ	boy
ɔ:	saw	ʊə (RP) ʊ (GA)	poor (RP) poor (GA)
ʌ	run	ʌɪə (RP) ʌɪ (GA)	tire (RP) tire (GA)
ʊ	put	aʊə (RP) aʊ (GA)	sour (RP) sour (GA)
u:	too		

The pronunciation symbols follow those used in *The New Shorter Oxford English Dictionary*.

RP (Received Pronunciation) is an accent that is typical of educated speakers of British English, though by no means all educated speakers use it. GA (General American) is an abstraction from what is typical of English pronunciation in the United States in contrast to RP. Most of the differences for vowels between RP and GA are due to the [r] being separately pronounced in GA after a vowel. Syllabic consonants (consonants that constitute a syllable by themselves) are marked by a subscript vertical line: ḷ, ṇ.

Primary stress is marked by (') before the syllable, and secondary stress by (,) before the syllable: 'capita,lize.

Abbreviations and Symbols

A	adverbial
GA	General American
ICE-GB	British corpus of ICE (International Corpus of English)
M	main clause
NP	noun phrase
O	object
P	predicative
PP	prepositional phrase
RP	Received Pronunciation
S	subject
sub	subordinate clause
V	verb
( )	comment or explanation after citation; optional letter(s) or word(s)
[ ]	comment or explanation within citation; phonetic transcription
/ /	phonemic transcription

Part 1
Introduction

Chapter 1
The English Language and its Grammar

Summary

English is essentially a Germanic language introduced by invading tribes from the European continent into what later became known as England. It is used in most countries of the world as a first language, a second language (for communication between inhabitants), or a foreign language. Since the end of the Second World War English has been the foremost language for international communication. The standard varieties of American and British English have influenced those of other countries where English is a first language and they have generally been the models taught to foreign learners. In the past they have also been the models for English as a second language, but in recent decades some second-language countries have begun to develop their own standard varieties.

Standard English is remarkably homogeneous across national boundaries, particularly in the written language. It admits less variation than non-standard varieties. Its repertoire offers choices according to type of activity engaged in through language, medium of communication, and degree of formality. Correct English is conformity to the norms of standard English. Good English is good use of the resources of the language: language used effectively and ethically. Sensitivity to the feelings of others requires avoidance of offensive and discriminatory language.

The word *grammar* is used variously, both in everyday language and as a technical term. It may refer to a book or to the contents of a book. Its scope may be restricted to syntax (the ways in which words combine into structures of phrases, clauses, and sentences) or it may include many other aspects of language. Grammars may be primarily intended as reference works or as textbooks; they may be aimed at native speakers or foreign learners. Descriptive grammar describes the rules of the language objectively whereas prescriptive grammar evaluates and advises.

In one technical sense, a grammar is a theory of language description that can be applied to individual languages. Universal grammar concerns the properties that are common to all human languages. Traditional grammar adopts terms and approaches to language description, derived from Latin grammars, that were common in previous centuries.

Sentences may be unacceptable for various reasons; for example, because they are factually or logically nonsensical or because they are stylistically clumsy. Technically, a sentence is ungrammatical only in relation to a particular model of grammar; it is ungrammatical if that grammar does not account for it as a grammatical sentence of the language.

For their data, linguists may draw on samples of actual use of the language, their own knowledge of the language, and judgements about the language elicited from native speakers. Theoretical linguists have tended to rely solely on introspection and their own evaluations.

The study of language has a strong claim to be included in the curriculum as part of general knowledge. There are also applications for the study of language generally and for the study of syntax in particular.

The tradition of English grammatical writing is based on the Latin grammars that were produced in the medieval and renaissance periods. Their influence persists in current terminology and approaches to grammar.

1.1 The spread of English

1.1.1 The spread of English in the British Isles

From the middle of the fifth century and for the next hundred years, waves of invading tribes from the European continent—Angles, Saxons, Jutes, and Frisians—brought their Germanic dialects to Britain, settling in the country and driving the Celtic-speaking Britons westward to Wales and Cornwall. Isolated from other Germanic speakers, the settlers came to acknowledge their dialects as belonging to a separate common language that they called English.

Germanic is a branch of the Indo-European family of languages, from which have descended—among others—Latin and its Romance derivatives, Greek, Celtic, and Sanskrit. The Germanic dialects of the settlers belonged to West Germanic, the parent language also of modern German, Dutch, Flemish, and Frisian. From the middle of the ninth century England suffered large incursions by Danish Vikings, intent on settling as well as plundering. Their Scandinavian language belonged to North Germanic. The Danes came close to capturing the whole country, but were defeated overwhelmingly by the English under the leadership of King Alfred the Great. The Treaty of Wedmore signed in the same year (878) confined the Danes to the east of a line roughly from London to Chester, an area known as the Danelaw. There were further Danish invasions in the late ninth century, and finally from 1014 to 1042 the whole of England was ruled by Danish kings. The Scandinavian language introduced a considerable number of common loanwords into English and contributed to present dialectal differences in the north and east of the country. Much of the population in those areas must have been bilingual and it has been suggested that bilingualism may have hastened the reduction of inflections in English since the stems of words were often similar in the two Germanic languages.

In 1066 William the Conqueror, Duke of Normandy, invaded England and became its king. The Norman conquest established a French-speaking ruling class. French was the language of the royal court, the nobility, the church leaders, parliament, the law courts, and the schools. Most of the population continued to speak English, but bilingualism became common. Bilingualism resulted in an enormous influx of French words into English. From the late fourteenth century English displaced French for most purposes, and during the next century a standard English language emerged to meet the needs of the central bureaucracy, the printers, and the educators. Latin, however, was the language of learning throughout the Middle Ages—as in the rest of Europe—and remained so in England as late as the seventeenth century.

1.1.2 The spread of English internationally

The geographical spread of English is unique among the languages of the world, not only in our time but throughout history. English is the majority first language in twenty-three countries. It is an official language or a joint official language in about fifty other countries, where it is used in addition to the indigenous first languages for a variety of public and personal functions. It is also used as a second language, though without official status, in countries such as Bangladesh and Malaysia. Countries where English is a first or second language are located in all five continents. The total population of these countries amounts to around 2.5 billion, about 49 per cent of the world's population. Where English is a first or second language, it is used internally for communication between nationals of the same country. In addition, English is used extensively as a foreign language for international communication by people who do not ordinarily employ it when speaking or writing to their compatriots.

1.1.2.1 English as a first language

The number of first-language speakers of English has been estimated at well over 300 million, of whom over 216 million live in the United States. The United Kingdom has about 53 million, Canada over 17 million, and Australia about 14 million. Countries where English is a majority first language may have large percentages of bilingual speakers and speakers for whom English is a second language. For example, Canada has a large minority of unilingual French speakers (nearly 17 per cent) as well as an almost equal percentage of speakers who are bilingual in French and English.

1.1.2.2 English as a second language

Most countries with second-language speakers of English are former British colonies, such as India and Nigeria. English has been retained as an official language in the majority of these countries after independence because none of the indigenous languages was accepted by all citizens as the sole national language. As an official second language, English is used in a variety of public functions: in government, in the law courts, in broadcasting, in the press, and in education. In many African and Asian countries it serves as the means of interpersonal communication between speakers of different indigenous languages. Because of both its national and its international reach, English is often used for literature, sometimes in forms that draw heavily on local colloquial forms of English. Writers and politicians in some African and Asian countries are ambivalent about the role of English: English may be viewed as an imperialist language, imposed by colonial oppressors and impeding the role of indigenous languages, or as the language of liberation and nationalism in countries divided by tribal loyalties.

The problem in calculating the numbers of second-language speakers is how to decide who counts as a speaker of the language. Should we include in our totals those who have a rudimentary knowledge of vocabulary and grammar but can make themselves understood only in certain types of exchanges—for example, giving street directions or offering goods for sale? If so, we might recognize as second-language speakers perhaps most of the 2.5 billion that live in countries where English is used as a second language. On the other hand, conservative estimates, requiring much greater competence in the language, tend to put the number at about 300 million.

1.1.2.3 English as a foreign language

A similar problem arises in calculating the numbers of users of English as a foreign language. Estimates have ranged wildly—from 100 million to 600 million. English is extensively studied as a foreign language. It is a compulsory subject or the preferred optional language in most countries where it is not a first or second language. It has been estimated that over 150 million children are studying English as a foreign language in primary or secondary schools. Many millions of foreigners listen to BBC broadcasts in English, and many millions follow the BBC English lessons on radio and television. 'Follow Me', the BBC English by Television 60-programme course for beginners, produced in 1979 with a consortium of European television stations, has been shown in over 80 countries. It attracted vast audiences in countries throughout the world in the 1980s, and in China alone it had an estimated audience of over 50 million. Over half a million visitors, mostly from the European continent, currently visit the United Kingdom each year to study English as a foreign language. A poll conducted in December 1992 showed that English is the most popular language in the European Union (then called the European Community) among young people (aged 15 to 24), and while 34 per cent of that age group spoke English in 1987 the figure in 1990 had risen to 42 per cent. A European Commission report for 1994–5 showed that 89 per cent of secondary school students in the European Union were learning English as a second language, compared with just 32 per cent learning French, the nearest competitor.

1.2 English as an international language

The pre-eminence of English for international communication is in part indebted to the spread of English as a first or second language for internal communication in numerous countries that were once part of the British Empire. The role of English as an international language has gathered momentum since the end of the Second World War through the economic and military global dominance of the United States and the resources it deploys for scientific and technological progress. The United States remains by far the richest country in the world as measured by gross domestic product, which amounted in 1998 to 8,083 billion dollars, compared with 4,186 billion for Japan, its nearest rival.

1.2.1 The international uses of English

In developing countries, English is regarded as the language of modernization and technological advancement. Most of the world's scientific and technical journals are in English. It is commonly required for international trade and at international conferences, and is the official medium for communication at sea and in the air. Television programmes in English are viewed in many countries where English is a foreign language, and when demonstrators wish to achieve the maximum international impact they chant and display their slogans in English.

> **NOTE**
>
> The international presence of English has not been welcomed everywhere. In some countries English has been viewed as having a malign influence on local languages, contaminating their purity by infiltrating large numbers of foreign words. Official resistance to English loanwords is fiercest in France, where there have been moves by the government to bar their use in the media, advertising, and official documents. Most media reaction in France has declared the restrictions unenforceable. More generally, French officialdom has been concerned with the preservation of French as an international language and the threats from English and other languages to the retention of French by the francophone countries in Africa and the Americas.

1.2.2 First-language varieties of English

The English taught to foreign learners is generally British or American English in their standard varieties. Except for pronunciation the differences between the two are relatively minor, as indeed they are between the standard varieties in any of the countries where English is the majority first language. The mass media are ensuring, if anything, the smoothing of differences and are encouraging reciprocal influences, though the influence of American English is predominant. Despite some trivial variation in spelling and punctuation, and some more important variation in vocabulary, the standard first-language varieties of written English are remarkably homogeneous. Predictions that they will diverge to become mutually unintelligible are implausible. It is reasonable to speak of an international standard written English. It is also reasonable to speak of an international standard spoken English if we limit ourselves to the more formal levels and if we ignore pronunciation differences. Even pronunciation differences—which of course exist within each national variety—do not constitute a major obstacle, once speakers have tuned into each other's system of pronunciation.

1.2.3 Second-language varieties of English

The situation in countries where English is primarily a second language is fluid and varies. In the past these countries have looked to British or American English for language norms. But there are indications that in some countries—such as India, Nigeria, and Singapore—local models of English are being sought that are based on their own educated varieties. This indigenization of English augurs well for the continued use of English for internal functions in those countries.

At present, there are no established and generally acknowledged standard varieties in second-language countries. As a result, teachers and examiners are uncertain as to the norms towards which teaching should be geared: those of the evolving local standard or those of some external standard. In some areas the insecurity of teachers is exacerbated by inadequacies in their acquisition of English. Institutionalization of national standards will require research by grammarians and lexicographers into the language of educated speakers and the agreement of educational and governmental authorities. (A notable example of such a research project is the International Corpus of English, co-ordinated by the staff of the Survey of English Usage, University College London, covering standard varieties in some fifteen countries, half of which have English as a second language.)

The standard will then be codified in dictionaries, grammars, and usage guides, and incorporated in textbooks and in school and college examinations. The likelihood is that, as in Britain and the United States, only a minority will be fully competent in the national standard and that there will be a continuum of non-standard variation linked to it. We may hope that the new national standards will take their place as constituents of an International Standard English, preserving the essential unity of English as an international language and therefore its continuing value for that role.

1.2.4 English as a second language versus local languages

The continuance of English as a second language or its demotion to a foreign language depends on government policies. In some countries the decision has been taken to promote a local language as the national language to the detriment of the role of English in administration and education. Thus, Swahili is being promoted in Tanzania, Bahasa Malaysia in Malaysia, Burmese in Burma, and Filipino in the Philippines. But governmental policies can change, as they have in some countries—at least for higher education—where the decline of English has been viewed with concern and the need has been accepted for an élite that is proficient in English. It is likely, however, that in some countries English will no longer be used for internal purposes. The lack of a legal official status need not in itself affect all the uses to which English is put within second-language countries. After all, English is not an official language in the United States, though there are current moves to designate it as such.

1.2.5 **Reasons for the international role of English**

The present role of English as an international language derives from its geographical spread and the prestige and practical value it has acquired through the United States in the last few decades. It cannot be attributed to the intrinsic superiority of English over potential other candidates. It is possible to point to some features that appear to make English easier to learn than some other languages. English has few inflections, so foreign learners do not have to memorize declensions and conjugations. It has natural rather than grammatical gender, so learners do not need to memorize the gender of each noun and do not have to cope with ensuring gender agreement between the noun and an accompanying article or adjective. For most Europeans at least, the Germanic and Romance elements that constitute the bulk of English vocabulary provide welcome help. On the other hand, the absence of inflections has increased the importance of prepositions and the burden of memorizing the preposition that goes with a particular verb, noun, or adjective in a particular meaning: *look at* and *look to, pride in* and *proud of, afraid of* and *alarmed at*. English also confronts the learner with a multitude of idiomatic combinations, particularly verbs with adverbs; *get by, do in, turn up, make out*. The frequent absence of correlation between pronunciation and spelling is a serious obstacle for learning to read and write. There is no method of weighing the advantages and disadvantages of English in comparison with other languages for foreign learners. Ultimately their motivation for learning English is pragmatic, depending on the value they expect to gain from doing so.

1.3 Standard English

In Great Britain, standard English is the national variety of the language inasmuch as it is not restricted to any region within the country. It is taught throughout the education system, and is identified with educated English. It is the public language of official communication—in central and local government, in parliament and the law courts, and generally in the mass media. It is pre-eminently the language of printed matter; indeed, only the standard language has an established orthography. It is the variety that is taught to foreign learners.

No English-speaking country has a language academy to monitor changes in the standard language and to pronounce on their acceptability. To some extent the functions of an academy have been adopted by writers on usage in newspaper columns or in guides to usage. Grammars of English focus on the standard language, paying minimal attention to differences in non-standard varieties—partly because there has been less research in those varieties and partly because grammars of the standard language have applications in the teaching of English to foreigners. Except for specialized dictionaries of dialect and slang, dictionaries too encode the standard language. Although they generally proclaim themselves to be descriptive, in practice they evaluate through their usage labels and they often include notes on usage problems.

National standard varieties in countries where English is a first language are remarkably homogeneous, particularly in written English. The homogeneity is explained by their common descent from the British English of the seventeenth century. It is only in the late eighteenth century that the United States—the first of the states originally settled by British colonists—began to develop its own language norms. The influence of print, and more recently of radio, television, and film, have contributed to prevent the national standards of English-speaking countries from drifting far apart. If anything, under these influences and the ease of international travel the national standards have tended to converge.

1.4 Variation in standard English

1.4.1 **Variation in 'usage'**

A major characteristic of standard varieties is that they admit relatively less variation than non-standard varieties. Nevertheless, their uniformity should not be overstated. There are of course the well-known usage disputes: *Whom do you want?* and *Who do you want?*; *It is I* and *It is me*; *hopefully* in the sense 'I hope that'; *different from, different to,* and *different than.* Such variants represent changes in progress within the standard variety that have not been accepted by all speakers or that have not spread across the informal–formal continuum. But most variants are noticed only by English language specialists. In the following pairs, the [a] sentence is probably satisfactory for all English speakers, whereas the [b] sentence may be considered odd by some:

[1a] Who (*or* whom) did they give the prize to?

[1b] Who (*or* whom) did they give the prize?

[2a] I want you to say nothing about it.

[2b] I want that you should say nothing about it.

[3a] They're keeping an open mind on the appointment.

[3b] They're keeping open minds on the appointment.

[4a] That looks like being the best solution.

[4b] That looks to be the best solution.

[5a] My family donated to the college a well-equipped gymnasium.

[5b] My family donated the college a well-equipped gymnasium.

1.4.2 **Variation according to use**

A different kind of variation within standard English relates to the choices available for different uses.

1.4.2.1 **Variation according to type of activity**

One dimension of use is the type of activity engaged in through language. Varieties defined by this dimension are sometimes termed registers, though the term is also extended to use varieties of all dimensions. Instructions typically resort to imperatives, as in cooking recipes: *Bring to the boil, then pour over the meat* rather than *You should bring* … Also typical is the omission of the direct object: *Bring to the boil* rather than *Bring the gravy to the boil.* Such omissions are also usual for instructions on labels: *Do not freeze; Stand upright; Keep out of reach of children.* We can immediately recognize as legal language the following sentence extracted from the instructions accompanying the issue of a credit card:

> *No delay by the Bank in debiting the Account for any Card Use or part thereof*
> *shall affect or prejudice the Bank's right to do so subsequently.*

The sentence illustrates prescriptive *shall*, archaic *thereof*, and the legal sense of *prejudice*. The unusual capitalization of *Account* and *Card Use* is conspicuous. The vocabulary items convey unmistakably the provenance of the sentence.

Many registers have been recognized apart from the language of recipes and the language of legal documents. For example: literary language, religious language, academic prose (including scientific writing), technical writing, business writing, the language of advertising, the language of newspaper headlines, journalistic writing. When such specialized registers irritate non-specialists by their obscurity, they are sometimes referred to by pejoratives such as journalese, officialese, gobbledygook, legalese, computerese. More generally, they are disparagingly called jargons.

1.4.2.2 **Variation according to medium**
Another dimension is the medium: whether the communication is in speech or in writing. Most speech is in the form of dialogue, an instantaneous interaction not occurring in writing. Most dialogue is spontaneous conversation, contrasting with the planning and revision that is usually possible in writing. Speech communicates also through intonation and paralinguistic features and when the participants are visible to each other also through body language. On the other hand, there are some punctuation and graphic features that are unique to the written language.

1.4.2.3 **Variation in degree of formality**
A third dimension is the formality of the language. The appropriate choices depend on the attitude of the speaker (or writer) to the listener (or reader), to the topic, and to the purpose of the communication. Much vocabulary is neutral in this dimension. Here is an opening sentence of a formal, coldly distant letter:

> *Further to my letter of 10 December 1993, the Interest Review Unit have*
> *considered your representations.*

A more friendly and more informal letter would have begun:

> *Thank you very much for your reply to my letter of 10 December 1993. The*
> *Interest Review Unit have taken account of what you have written.*

Contrast the casualness of *Sorry about what I said* with the more formal and polite *I apologize for my remarks.*

The three dimensions—type of activity, medium, and level of formality—overlap. Most speech tends to the less formal end of the formality continuum. Legal documents are necessarily in writing and are generally formal. Scientific articles in learned journals are formal, though popular scientific articles are much less so. The young discipline of computer science is happier with greater informality.

1.5 Correct English

Correct English is the notion of correctness applied to standard English. It is legitimate to speak of mistakes in the use of standard English affecting spelling, punctuation, vocabulary choice, and grammar. At the same time, there are a relatively few disputed usages, and about those there may be legitimate disagreements on which variant is correct.

1.5.1 **Pronunciation**

More controversial are views that would extend the notion of correctness to pronunciation. Standard English in the sense of the term used in this book may be pronounced by a variety of accents. The nearest to a non-localizable British accent is Received Pronunciation or RP (also known more popularly as BBC English, Oxford English, or the Queen's English), an accent with some variability used by those in the upper socioeconomic ranges in England. All English-speaking countries have accents that are indicative of the socio-economic class of the speakers. In some countries, these vary regionally. For example, in the United States there is no non-localizable upper-class accent, but presenters in the major networks use a homogenized accent (Network English) that avoids regional associations.

Also controversial is the view that children should be taught to speak standard English as well as write it. Most educationists—though not all those in authority over education—advocate tolerance of non-standard dialects and all accents in speech while encouraging the acquisition of written standard English. They similarly support the maintenance of bilingualism, viewing the retention of an immigrant language as a valuable asset.

1.5.2 **Dialect**

Just as English cannot claim intrinsic superiority as the reason for its international role, so the choice of the dialect that developed into our present standard English was not motivated by its superiority over other dialects of the period. It originated in the dialect that was common in London in the fifteenth century. London educated speech was a mixture of dialects among which predominated the East Midlands dialect, which was spoken by more people than any other dialect. The London dialect was a supra-regional dialect that reflected the status of London as the seat of the royal court and the political, judicial, and commercial capital of the country. Had it not been for the Norman Conquest, the standard language might have arisen from the Wessex dialect, which because of the dominance of the West Saxon kingdom under King Alfred and his successors had become the literary language.

The London dialect was not intrinsically superior to other dialects of the fifteenth century, and any other dialect or mixture of dialects might have suited just as well as the basis from which the standard language emerged. However, because of the functions it has been required to fulfil, standard English has become elaborated in grammar and vocabulary to an extent far beyond any of the non-standard dialects. In particular it alone can be used for the range of writing that is essential in a modern society.

1.6 Good English

Good English is sometimes equated with correct English, but the two concepts should be differentiated. Correct English is conformity to the norms of the standard language. Good English is good use of the resources available in the language. In that sense we can use a non-standard dialect well and we can use the standard language badly.

1.6.1 **Effective, pleasing use of language**

By good English we may mean language used effectively or aesthetically: language that conveys clearly and appropriately what is intended and language that is pleasing to the listener or reader. In the last few decades, lack of clarity in government writing and legal documents has been the target of movements for plain English in several English-speaking countries and they have achieved some successes in promoting legislation and in changing the attitudes of governments and businesses.

1.6.2 **Ethical use of language**

By good English we may also mean language used ethically. Commentators have highlighted and criticized doublespeak, the dishonest language employed by some political and military leaders to conceal their actions by obfuscations or to manipulate their followers in explaining away their policies. Protection is in some instances offered through legislation or overseeing agencies to prevent advertisers from lying about products or services.

1.6.3 **Swearing**

Bad language is usually equated with swearing, which violates taboos against certain expressions referring (in the main) to sex and excretion. The use of swear-words and tolerance of their use have varied across time, region, and social class. In most countries where English is a majority first language greater tolerance has been extended in recent decades to swearing and obscenities when they occur in realistic portrayals of characters in literature, film, and television drama. But the taboos generally remain in force for at least their use by children as well as by adults where both sexes are present, particularly in middle-class society or on public formal occasions. Swearing by politicians and sports celebrities still evokes scandalized comments, even when not intended for public hearing.

1.6.4 **Offensive and discriminatory language**

Recent decades have seen a heightened awareness of another aspect of bad language. Attention has been drawn to language that is likely to give offence to particular groups and that might result in discrimination against them. As a result, positive or neutral expressions have been offered to replace language considered sexist or racist and nomenclature considered hurtful to those with physical or psychological disabilities. Excesses in the advocacy of such replacements have given rise to the disparaging terms *political correctness* and *politically correct*. The politically correct movement—particularly strong in American universities—has been viewed by many outside it as repressive and punitive and has evoked protest and ridicule.

There is now a vocabulary of terms in *-ism* and *-ist* to denote behaviour and attitudes that are considered to be offensively discriminatory and that refer to people who are thought to be prejudiced or to discriminate. In addition to the well-established terms *racism* and *sexism*, we can find designations such as *ableism* (discrimination in favour of able-bodied people), *ageism* (discrimination on grounds of age), *animalism* (discrimination against animals), *classism* (discrimination on grounds of social class), *handism* (discrimination against the left-handed), *heterosexism* (discrimination against homosexuals), *lookism* (discrimination because of a person's looks), *sizism* (discrimination because of a person's size).

1.6.4.1 **Non-discriminatory language in general**

Among expressions that have been coined, or given greater currency, to avoid language that was thought to be prejudicial are *humankind* ('mankind'), *humans* or *human beings* (generic 'man'), *chair* or *chairperson* ('chairman'), *flight attendant* ('steward' or 'stewardess'), *supervisor* ('foreman'), *gender reassignment* ('sex change'), *differently abled* ('handicapped'). Compounds with *challenged*—such as *physically challenged* ('crippled') and *intellectually challenged* ('unintelligent')—have been created to denote people who suffer from disabilities or to refer to the disabilities themselves, since *disabled* and *handicapped* were felt to be objectionable. This compounding has given rise to jocular inventions, such as *sartorially challenged* applied to a British politician who is notorious for slovenly clothing.

1.6.4.2 **Non-sexist language**

The perception, promoted by the feminist movement, that English has an in-built bias against women has had the most repercussions, and some of the proposals for change have won wide acceptance in several of the countries where English is a majority first language. In particular, the generic use of *man* and *men* to include women is now avoided. Whereas the American Declaration of Independence asserted in 1776 that 'all men are created equal', as far back as 1948 the Universal Declaration of Human Rights declared unambiguously that 'All human beings are born free and equal in dignity and rights'.

One major target for attack has been a feature in grammar. English has a gender distinction for the third person singular pronoun: masculine *he* and feminine *she*. It does not have a gender-neutral singular pronoun when generic reference is intended to include both men and women. Numerous proposals, reaching back more than a hundred years, have been offered for an epicene pronoun; for example: *thon, tey, en*. None has gained acceptance. The present fluidity of usage may be seen in extracts from the 1990 regulations of a School in the University of London. The first citation follows the traditional prescription to use the masculine:

[1]   No student will be admitted to any course until *he* has paid the requisite fees.

This use has been denounced as reinforcing the stereotype of men as dominant and in some contexts (for example, job advertisements) it may be interpreted as excluding women. The alternatives *he or she* (sometimes written *s/he, him/her, his/her*) may serve as a satisfactory substitute:

[2]   No student is allowed to register or study concurrently for more than one examination of the University of London or of the School unless *he or she* has previously obtained in writing the permission of the Director of the School.

If alternative forms are needed more than once, the result can be clumsy:

[3]   A candidate who wishes to enter the School before *his or her* eighteenth birthday may be asked to write to state *his or her* reasons.

Resort can be had instead to *they, them*, or *their* as generic singulars, a common usage in speech:

[4]   This certificate lists the four courses for which the student was registered, showing letter grade assessments of *their* work over the year and grades for *their* examination performance.

Some people object to this use of the *they*-pronouns as singulars, despite the convenience. Another method is to use the plural throughout, thereby sanctioning the use of *they*:

[5]   *Students* failing to disclose this fact are liable to have *their* registration cancelled.

Or to avoid using pronoun forms:

[6]   Every student is allocated a tutor, who will advise in the selection of courses and act throughout the session as supervisor.

In [6] the direct object pronoun has been omitted after *advise*, and possessive pronouns have been omitted before *courses* and *supervisor*.

Some writers—usually women writers—have employed a mixture of stratagems, including the use of *she* as a generic. Professor Jean Aitchison, a linguist, explicitly mentions this in the preface to a recent book:

[7]   One further point: in this edition, I have tried to avoid the sexist linguistic usages found in the earlier versions, which misleadingly implied in places that only males of our species could talk. I have done this partly by using the plural (*people* instead of *he*), partly by using indefinites (*a person, anyone*) followed by a plural pronoun (*if anyone is surprised, they should see how increasingly common this usage is*), and partly by interchanging *he* and *she* in places where a neutral between sexes pronoun is required. [Jean Aitchison *Teach Yourself Linguistics* (London: Hodder & Stoughton, 1992), p. viii.]

The previous edition was published in 1987, only five years earlier. It is likely that people will continue to choose from the existing variants rather than adopt a new pronoun and that *they* will increasingly become acceptable as the generic singular even in formal style.

1.7 Types of grammar book

The word *grammar* is used in a number of ways. It may refer to a book, in which case a grammar is analogous to a dictionary. And just as we have many English dictionaries, which vary in the number of their entries and the quality of their definitions, so we have many English grammars (or grammar books), which vary in their coverage and their accuracy. The largest English dictionary is the scholarly twenty-volume *Oxford English Dictionary*, which traces the history of words and their meanings. Similarly, there are large scholarly grammars, notably Otto Jespersen's seven-volume *Modern English Grammar on Historical Principles*, published at intervals between 1909 and 1949 and still consulted by scholars, and the more recent *Comprehensive Grammar of the English Language* by Randolph Quirk et al., published in 1985, that extends to nearly 1,800 pages.

In the concrete sense of the word *grammar*, a grammar is a book of one or more volumes. We of course also use *grammar* for the contents of the book. When we compare grammars for their coverage and accuracy, we are referring to the contents of the book: a grammar is a book on grammar, just as a history is a book on history.

Grammars vary in their coverage. Some, like this book, are restricted to syntax, the ways in which words combine into structures of phrases, clauses, and sentences. But grammars may also include descriptions of one or more other aspects of language: morphology (the internal structure of words), word-formation (how new words are formed from more basic elements), phonetics (the possible sounds and sound patterns), phonology (the distinctive sounds and sound patterns), orthography (the conventional spellings), vocabulary, semantics (the meanings of words and sentences), and pragmatics (the interpretation of utterances in their contexts). In most of this book, the term *grammar* is used in a common popular and technical usage as a synonym of *syntax.*

A distinction is often made between a reference grammar and a pedagogical grammar. Like a dictionary, a reference grammar is intended for individual consultation; it is not expected to be read or studied from beginning to end. Some reference grammars resemble dictionaries closely in being organized alphabetically rather than (as is usual) thematically.

Pedagogical grammars, on the other hand, are textbooks, chiefly intended for class use under the guidance of a teacher. The material in pedagogical grammars is graded according to the level and ability of the expected users and is generally presented in sections that can reasonably be absorbed within a class period. A topic is usually revisited in later sections in greater detail. It is assumed that sections will be studied in consecutive order.

In practice, the distinction between these two types of grammar is not always clear-cut. Reference grammars—or chapters from them—are sometimes used in class, and the more advanced pedagogical grammars may explicitly aim to serve also as reference works. Some pedagogical grammars are intended additionally—or chiefly—for self-study.

Further distinctions can be drawn that apply to both pedagogical and reference grammars. Some English grammars are primarily intended for native speakers and others primarily for non-native learners. And just as there are bilingual dictionaries, so there are grammars of English that point out problems for (say) German or Swedish speakers or interesting contrasts with what occurs in their own language.

Finally, grammars have different general objectives and their readers differ in their interests. Some readers study grammar because they wish to improve their use of the language. Others feel themselves competent in the language and are interested in learning about the language—in studying grammar for its own sake and not necessarily for practical applications.

1.8 Descriptive and prescriptive grammar

A distinction is often made between descriptive grammar and prescriptive grammar. **Descriptive grammar** attempts to describe the rules of the language objectively, accounting for what actually occurs. **Prescriptive grammar** is evaluative, guiding readers as to what is correct or incorrect. For example, a prescriptive grammar may prescribe that *none* takes a singular verb or it may allow either singular or plural; it may proscribe the adverb *badly* after a copula verb as in *We feel badly about it* (insisting on the adjective *bad*), *can* in the permission sense as *Can I leave now?* (requiring *may* instead), and *like* as a conjunction in *They behaved like they know me* (prescribing *as if*). Prescriptive grammar focuses on phenomena that are in divided usage in standard English, such as whether *data* is to be treated as singular or plural, or features that occur chiefly in non-standard usage, such as the multiple negation in *I didn't say nothing about nobody* (corresponding to *I didn't say anything about anybody* in standard English).

Evaluations as to what is correct or incorrect are intended for those who want to use standard English and are unsure about particular points. Evaluations may vary, since prescriptive writers rely largely on their own feelings. They do not necessarily accept evidence of what most educated people use or even of the usage of those considered to be the best writers or speakers.

Guides to usage are predominantly prescriptive. Many grammars contain both descriptive and prescriptive rules. The most sensitive guides and grammars point to stylistic variation, noting (for example) that the conjunction *like* is common in speech in standard English but not in writing. Pedagogical grammars are inherently prescriptive when their purpose is to tell their users—for example, foreign learners of English—what to say or write, but the best are based on accurate descriptions of current uses.

Descriptive grammars that are concerned with stylistic variation sometimes refer to prescriptive rulings, since the rulings reflect attitudes to usages that may result in stylistic restrictions; for example, confinement of the usages to speech or to formal writing. Descriptive grammars generally describe the standard variety, though some may occasionally refer to different practices in non-standard varieties. In recent decades, major reference grammars of English have dealt with both the American and the British national standards, sometimes noting differences in other national standards. Descriptive grammars that are restricted to descriptions of standard varieties may be viewed as covertly prescriptive in that by ignoring non-standard varieties they implicitly downgrade their value. It is possible to formulate grammars of non-standard varieties, though there is greater variation in these varieties.

1.9 Theories of grammar

Every grammatical description presupposes an underlying theory, though many descriptions do not make their theoretical basis explicit and some are eclectic in drawing on more than one theory. In one technical sense, a grammar is a theory of language description. Grammatical theories make assumptions about the nature of natural languages (the languages that human beings acquire naturally, as opposed to artificial languages, such as computer languages), present goals for describing them, and develop methods of argumentation, formulation, and explanation. Among the many current general theories of language are Transformational-Generative Grammar, Tagmemic Grammar, Systemic Grammar, and Word Grammar. Some designations refer to a set of theories that share objectives but differ in many important respects. For example, generative grammars include Government and Binding Theory, Generalized Phrase Structure Grammar, and Lexical-Functional Grammar.

Grammatical theories are applied to the descriptions of individual languages. Sometimes the purpose of the application is to develop the theory, to demonstrate how the theoretical framework can cope with the language data and to investigate what changes in the theory are required for it to be successful.

Universal grammar concerns the properties that are common to all human languages (including potential languages) and that may therefore be taken to be defining and necessary properties of human language. In another approach, requiring studies of large numbers of languages, language universals may be absolute without exceptions (for example, that all languages have nouns), or there may be universal tendencies that admit relatively few exceptions (for example, that the basic word order is for the subject to appear before the object in a sentence, in the sequences subject–verb–object or subject–object–verb or verb–subject–object). Typological linguistics is the study of the characteristics shared by groups of languages (for example, that in one language type the subject normally precedes the verb whereas in another type it normally follows the verb) even though the languages are not necessarily related historically. On the other hand, historical linguistics (also called comparative grammar) deals with the characteristics of languages that are related historically, and traces the development of families of languages from a common source or traces the development of individual languages.

Traditional grammar adopts the approaches and descriptive categories used, particularly in school grammars, in the eighteenth and nineteenth centuries. Traditional grammars describe solely, or chiefly, the written language and are indebted to Latin grammars for some of their analyses of English. Scholarly reference grammars of the first half of the twentieth century, such as the *Modern English Grammar on Historical Principles* by Otto Jespersen, have also been considered traditional grammars. Traditional grammars typically make use of notional criteria; for example, defining a noun as the name of a person, place, or thing rather than by formal criteria such as that nouns typically take plural inflections or that they typically may be introduced by *the*. Grammars that make frequent use of notional definitions are notional grammars.

A distinction is sometimes drawn between formal grammars and functional grammars. Formal grammars describe the formal rules and structures of the language. Functional grammars also describe how the language is used, taking account of communicative purposes and of stylistic and social factors.

1.10 Grammatical and acceptable

In everyday use, a sentence is said to be grammatical when it conforms to what are thought to be the norms of the language. Critics may condemn *Tell it like it is* as ungrammatical or not correct because *like* is being used as a conjunction, contrary to what they think is correct or proper in standard English. They may similarly condemn constructions such as *people what live in this neighbourhood* and *It ain't right*.

As a technical term in linguistics, **grammatical** is used to designate conformity to the rules of a grammar based on a particular grammatical theory. Such a grammar applied to a non-standard dialect of English may include *people what live in this neighbourhood* as a grammatical construction.

A generative grammar attempts in its formulations an explicit account of the rules that differentiate grammatical or well-formed sentences from ungrammatical, ill-formed, or deviant sentences. The boundaries between the well-formed and the ill-formed are fuzzy. It is obvious that *Little a boy the ran street up* is not an English sentence, but judgements among both linguists and non-linguists have differed on the status of sentences such as *The talking about the problem saved her* and *I didn't believe it, although Sid asserted that Max left*. In their eagerness to reach the boundaries of the language, some generative linguists have discussed extremely clumsy sentences they thought should be included, such as *Max wanted Ted to persuade Alex to get lost, and Walt, Ira*.

Judgements on whether sentences are well-formed or not are judgements on their acceptability. In a generative grammar, sentences are either grammatical or ungrammatical—either included by the rules or excluded. Acceptability, however, is scalar:

not only are there disagreements among native speakers, but also they may evaluate certain sentences as neither completely acceptable nor completely unacceptable.

It can be maintained that grammaticality and acceptability are distinct concepts: grammaticality relates to competence (underlying knowledge of the language), whereas acceptability relates to performance (actual use made of that knowledge). A sentence may be unacceptable because of its length or complexity, reasons having to do with style or limitations on human memory. But such sentences are to be treated as grammatical because they cannot be excluded from the set of grammatical sentences without excluding acceptable sentences. For example, certain rules apply recursively and there is no obvious limit to the recursion. Examples of recursion are coordination in [1] and relative clauses in [2]:

[1]   Peter is happy and Joan is tired and Carol is angry and Norman is cold and . . .

[2]   This is the man that hit the dog that bit the cat that ate the mouse that frightened the child that . . .

Since there is no definable limit to the number of coordinate or relative clauses, the grammar will allow an infinite number, but in practice nobody would continue to produce them indefinitely or be happy with sentences that went on too long. In certain types of embedding of relative clauses within other relative clauses, the degree of unacceptability increases with each recursion, but generative grammars may find it inappropriate or uneconomical to handle the increase in terms of grammaticality. Compare the differences in acceptability in [3], [4], and [5]:

[3]   The woman who(m) the detective questioned lives in my apartment building and is an old friend of mine.

[4]   The woman who(m) the detective who(m) the students recognized questioned lives in my apartment building and is an old friend of mine.

[5]   The woman who(m) the detective who(m) the students who(m) I teach recognized questioned lives in my apartment building and is an old friend of mine.

Grammars vary in what types of unacceptability they can account for or want to account for. They tend to exclude types for which it is difficult or impossible to generalize. Sentences may be factually nonsensical, as in [6], or logically nonsensical, as in [7]:

[6]   The earth is flat.

[7]   Two and two are five.

Unacceptability may depend on one's beliefs:

[8]   His parents are atheists, and mine are eccentric too.

We may reject a sentence because it seems implausible or absurd:

[9]   Your daughter has just swallowed a whale.

But it is often possible to imagine contexts or interpretations where a sentence such as [9] makes sense; for example, the whale was a toy or cake in the form of a whale. Metaphorical uses override absurd literal interpretations. Sentences that are nonsensical under a normal interpretation are commonly found in children's literature, fables, and poetry. We might dismiss [10] as ridiculous, but a recent work of fiction fits the sentence into a plausible context:

[10]   Give the lad a happy story to drink (Salman Rushdie *Haroun and the Sea of Stories*)

1.11 The study of grammar

1.11.1 **The data for grammar**

Scholars researching into grammar can draw on a number of sources for their data. One obvious source is examples of actual use of the language. The examples may be collected to investigate a particular point; for instance, negative constructions in English (*I don't have any money, I have no money, I think it's not right, I don't think it's right*). These may be collected systematically (for example by reading through a set of newspapers) or casually (by noting examples that one reads or hears) or by a combination of these two approaches. For the first edition of the voluminous *Oxford English Dictionary* some 800 voluntary readers supplied citations on slips from their casual reading, which were added to the citations that were more systematically collected from specified early works. Scholarly grammarians in the first half of this century (such as Otto Jespersen, cf. 1.7) amassed enormous numbers of citation slips for their research.

The recent availability of increasingly powerful small computers has promoted the creation of large **corpora** (collections of electronic texts) that are distributed internationally, providing data for researchers that were not involved in their compilation. A corpus may be limited in its scope (say, to dramatic texts or runs of particular newspapers) or it may attempt a wide coverage. Some English corpora now run into many millions of words. A few contain transcriptions of the spoken language, material that is not easily obtainable by individual researchers. Some corpora are annotated for grammatical or other features of the language, enabling researchers to retrieve such information as well as specified words or combinations of words. Corpus linguistics has become a major area of linguistic research. Studies in computer corpora have resulted in numerous publications.

Corpus studies have obvious attractions for linguists who are not native speakers of the language, since they can be confident that their material is reliable. Those who are native speakers still find it useful to check corpora for their generalizations. Corpora are essential for studies of varieties of language, since differences between varieties are generally exhibited in the relative frequencies with which particular linguistic features occur.

It may be a matter of chance whether relatively uncommon constructions or language features appear in even a very large corpus in sufficient quantities—or at all—to provide adequate evidence. Linguists can supplement corpus data by drawing on their own knowledge of the language. Indeed, it has been common practice among theoretical linguists in the last thirty years to rely solely on data drawn from introspection. They use their knowledge of the language to create a set of samples for their own investigation, and evaluate the samples for acceptability, similarities of meaning, and ambiguities, and draw on their intuitions for decisions on grammatical structure.

Linguists may be biased or unsure in their judgements. It has been a common practice to consult the judgements of others, often native informants who would not know the purpose of the investigations. Some linguists have devised elaborate elicitation procedures under controlled conditions, asking large groups of informants for their judgements or requiring them to perform specified tasks. For example, when 175 British informants were asked to complete a sentence beginning *I badly*, most of them used either *need* (65 per cent) or *want* (28 per cent), indicating that these were the favourite verbs when the intensifier *badly* was in pre-verb position. In another experiment, eighty-five American informants were asked to use *probably* with the sentence *He can not drive a car,* 70 per cent of them positioned it before the auxiliary *can,* evidence that this is its normal position in a negative sentence.

1.11.2 Reasons for studying grammar

From time to time there are public debates about the teaching of grammar in schools. Educational fashions change, and after a period of over twenty-five years since the formal teaching of grammar was abandoned in most state schools there have been recent calls in both Britain and the United States for the reintroduction of grammar teaching as part of 'a return to basics'.

There are sound arguments for teaching about language in general and the English language in particular. An understanding of the nature and functioning of language is a part of the general knowledge that we should have about ourselves and the world we live in. In this respect, linguistics deserves a place at all levels of the curriculum at least as much as (say) history, geography, or biology. For language is the major means by which we communicate with others and interact with them, and our attitudes to our own variety and the varieties of others affect our image of ourselves and of others. Linguistics is a central discipline that has bearings on many other disciplines: psychology, sociology, anthropology, philosophy, literature, and computer science. Vocational applications are found in areas as diverse as the teaching of foreign languages, speech therapy, and information technology.

Study of the English language can help students develop their ability to adjust their language appropriately to different contexts. They should be aware of the expectations that standard English is the norm for public writing, and they will need to learn to adopt the conventions for public writing in grammar, vocabulary, spelling, and punctuation.

Grammar (in the sense of 'syntax') is generally regarded as central to linguistics, and it should therefore be included in a linguistic curriculum on its own terms. Many educationists have denied that a study of grammar can improve the ability to write English correctly and effectively, but (as with all subjects) it depends on what is taught and how it is taught. It would seem reasonable to suppose that written style can be improved through learning about the resources for grammatical structures, word order, and the devices for connecting sentences and paragraphs. Certainly, that kind of knowledge would be helpful at the editing stages to improve the style of earlier drafts and to correct grammatical errors.

There are other applications of a knowledge of grammar both in and out of the classroom: the interpretation of texts—literary or non-literary—sometimes depends on grammatical analysis; recognition of grammatical structures is often required for punctuation; and a study of one's own grammar is helpful in studying the grammar of a foreign language.

1.11.3 The tradition of English grammatical writing

The Western tradition for the study of grammar derives from the Greek philosophers, who treated it in their discussions of logic and rhetoric, and the study was taken up by Roman scholars. This tradition continued in the works on Latin grammar that were produced in the medieval and renaissance periods, when Latin was the language of learning. The grammar that was taught in the early grammar schools in England was Latin grammar, not English grammar.

The earliest known grammar of English was by William Bullokar, published in 1580, who wanted to show that English was as capable of grammatical analysis as was Latin. By 1800, a total of 112 grammars were published, excluding later editions. Most of these were slight, containing lists of letters and syllables and their pronunciation, definitions of parts of speech with their inflections, and treatments of punctuation and versification, and a very little on syntax. The traditional analyses for Latin grammar were generally applied to English grammar, including the Latin case names for nouns and the tenses for verbs, even though English does not have analogous inflections. There were exceptional authors such as John Wallis (one of the founders of the Royal Society), who treated English in its own terms in his 1653 grammar.

Most of the eighteenth- and nineteenth-century grammarians were prescriptive, setting out rules for correct speech and writing. By the twentieth century, both scholarly grammarians and textbook writers focused on the analysis of clauses. The emphasis on historical linguistics by the late nineteenth century added a new dimension, mainly in scholarly grammars: the writing of grammars of English that traced the history of forms and constructions. The most influential contemporary approach is exemplified in *A Comprehensive Grammar of the English Language* published in 1985 (cf. 1.7), an eclectic work drawing on the scholarly traditional grammars and on various recent linguistic theories. It is restricted to the two major national standards of American and British English in their present state, and has taken account of the spoken as well as the written language and of other types of stylistic variation. A notable feature is that it goes beyond the sentence to incorporate the influence of the context, both the linguistic context and the situational context.

Part 2
An Outline of Grammar

Chapter 2
Sentences

Summary

Words, phrases, clauses, and sentences are grammatical units that constitute a hierarchy in which the sentence is at the highest level, though exceptions are common in the hierarchical relationship. Some grammatical phenomena apply across sentences, and some morphemes (constituents of words), such as inflections, need to be treated in the grammar.

Sentences can be classified in various ways: (1) simple, compound, complex; (2) declarative, interrogative, imperative, exclamative; (3) statement, question, directive, exclamative; (4) assertion, request, offer, apology, and other kinds of speech act; (5) positive, negative; (6) active, passive.

2.1 The grammatical hierarchy

2.1.1 **Words, phrases, clauses, and sentences**

Words combine into the structures of phrases, clauses, and sentences. These four grammatical units—words, phrases, clauses, and sentences—constitute a hierarchy. The sentence is at the highest level in the hierarchy, the word is at the lowest level. Within the hierarchy:

> a sentence consists of one or more clauses
> a clause consists of one or more phrases
> a phrase consists of one or more words

2.1.1.1 **Sentence and clause**

In **[1]** the sentence consists of just one clause:

[1]   His account contains many historical solecisms

We can divide that sentence into three phrases:

[2]   His account
contains
many historical solecisms

2.1.1.2 **Phrase and word**

The phrases in **[2]** consist of one or more words. Each phrase has a **head** (or principal word). The three heads are the noun *account*, the verb *contains* (the only word in the phrase), and the noun *solecisms*. The three phrases are named after their heads:

[2a]   His account   **noun phrase**
contains   **verb phrase**
many solecisms   **noun phrase**

Each phrase can be assigned a grammatical function in the clause:

[2b]   His account   **subject**: noun phrase
contains   **verb**: verb phrase
many solecisms   **direct object**: noun phrase

As we can see from **[2b]**, a noun phrase can function as either the subject or the direct object. However, a verb phrase can function only as the verb of the clause or sentence.

> **NOTE**
>
> Caution is necessary in the use of the term *verb*. In traditional practice, it is applied in two ways: (1) for a part of speech (*contains* is a verb in the verb phrase *contains* and *given* in the verb phrase *has been given*) and (2) for a major constituent in a sentence or clause (*contains* in **[1]**; '*ve been given, have,* and *may be reduced* in **[4]**.

Just as a sentence may consist of only one clause so a phrase may consist of only one word. This may seem peculiar, since in everyday usage we think of phrases as having more than one word. The reason for the grammatical usage is economy. Rules that apply to a phrase apply equally whether the phrase consists of one word or more than one word. By allowing one-word phrases, grammarians can avoid having to repeat the same rules for one-word phrases and multi-word phrases. We can see that this is so, since we can reduce each phrase in **[2b]** to one word and preserve its grammatical functions.

[2c]	It	subject: noun phrase
	contains	verb: verb phrase
	solecisms	direct object: noun phrase

You will notice that in **[2c]** the pronoun *it* is taken as the head of a noun phrase. That is because pronouns are essentially a subcategory of nouns.

2.1.2 Subversion of the grammatical hierarchy

The grammatical hierarchy is subverted in two ways: at the same level and across levels.

2.1.2.1 Unit nested within same unit
A grammatical unit can contain other units at the same level in the hierarchy.

Compounds are words composed of more than one word (usually only two words), e.g. the noun *headache* and the verb *babysit*.

Phrases commonly contain other phrases. To take a simple example, the subject of **[3]** is the noun phrase *the title of the course*:

[3]   *The title of the course* was Woodland Ecology

The noun phrase (**NP**) contains within it the **prepositional phrase** (**PP**) *of the course* (headed by the preposition *of*), which in turn contains the noun phrase *the course*. These relationships are expressed schematically in **[3a]**:

[3a]	the title	of	the course	NP
		of	the course	PP
			the course	NP

A clause can also contain another clause:

[4]   If you've been given a voucher because you have a low income, the value of your voucher may be reduced.

The *if*-clause ends at *income*, and the *because*-clause is within the *if*-clause ('if you've been given a voucher for that reason').

Finally, a sentence can be **embedded** within a sentence in direct speech, as in the sentence marked off by quotation marks in **[5]**:

[5]   Prince Charles duly walked down the line, shook hands with who was there, and then, showing a rather splendid sense of humour said 'You know, I could have commanded him to be here tonight.' [Graham Stark *Remembering Peter Sellars*]

2.1.2.2 Higher-level unit within lower-level unit

Units at a higher level in the grammatical hierarchy can function within units at a lower level. For example, the clause *pay as you earn* can be embedded in the noun phrase *the pay-as-you-earn policy*. More commonly, the embedded clause follows the head noun; for example, the *that*-clause in [6], which modifies the noun *things*:

[6]   I had *a whole list of things that I wanted to buy eventually*

2.2 Above the sentence and below the word

2.2.1 **Above the sentence**

The sentence is the highest unit that is normally treated in grammar. However, some grammatical phenomena apply equally across sentences. For example, pronouns may refer to words in a preceding sentence, as in [1]:

[1]   *Organic farming* takes its cue from traditional agriculture. *It* makes use of the best ideas from the past and grafts onto them a scientific approach coupled with modern techniques that were unheard of in our grandfather's day. [David Mabey et al. *Thorson's Organic Consumer Guide*]

The initial pronoun *it* in the second sentence refers back to the initial phrase *organic farming* in the first sentence, and the choice of *it* rather than (say) *she* or *they* is determined by the reference to that phrase. If we were to combine the two sentences by introducing the **subordinating conjunction** *since* between them, the same reference of *it* to *organic farming* would be across clauses but within one sentence. This type of reference also occurs within a clause: in the first sentence of [1] *its* also refers back to *organic farming*. Here is an example with *it*:

[2]   *Moussaka*'s got aubergines in *it*

2.2.2 **Below the word**

The unit below the word is the **morpheme**. Words consist of one or more morphemes; for example, we can divide the word *grandfather* into the morphemes *grand* and *father*. For most purposes, the word is the lowest unit that is treated in grammar. However, there is one important respect in which the grammar needs to refer to morphemes. **Inflections** are morphemes that signal the grammatical variants of a word; the inflectional *-s* at the end of *ideas* indicates that the noun is plural; the inflectional *-s* at the end of *makes* indicates that the verb is the third person singular, so that we say *she makes* but *I make* and *they make*. In addition, some **affixes** signal the part of speech to which a word belongs: the prefix *en-* in *enslave* converts the noun *slave* into a verb, and the suffix *-ize* converts the adjective *modern* into the verb *modernize*.

2.3 Simple, compound, and complex sentences

Traditionally, sentences are classified as simple, compound, or complex according to their internal clause composition.

2.3.1 **Simple sentences**

A sentence consisting of one clause is a **simple sentence**. Hence, [1] is a simple sentence, and so is the much longer [2], which has phrases that are more complex than those in [1]:

[1]   I went there last week

[2]   My Right Honourable Friend the Secretary of State met health authority chairmen on the tenth of July and more recently at a briefing seminar in Cardiff on the nineteenth of October

Clauses are units that, like sentences, can be analysed in terms of **constituents** functioning as subject, verb, direct object, etc.

2.3.2 **Compound sentences**

A **compound sentence** consists of two or more clauses at the same grammatical level. Each of the clauses is a **main clause**, and typically each could be an independent sentence:

[3]   It has only been a week *and* I feel lonesome without you. [W]

In [3] the two main clauses are linked by the coordinator *and*.

2.3.3 **Complex sentences**

A **complex sentence** contains a **subordinate clause** as one of its constituents. In the complex sentence [4] the subordinate clause functions as a direct object of the verb *understood*. The clause is introduced by the subordinator *that*:

[4]   Men of rank and education in the provinces understood that the preponderance of Roman strength doomed resistance or revolt to failure. [P. A. Brunt *Roman Imperial Themes*]

It is perhaps easier to see that the *that*-clause is a direct object if we replace it with the pronoun *that*, as in [4a]:

[4a]   Men of rank and education in the provinces understood that.

Unlike [4], [4a] is a simple sentence, since it consists of only one clause.

2.3.4 **More complicated clausal patterns**

The traditional classification of sentences into simple, compound, and complex is a simplification of the clausal patterns in sentences, since it does not take into account frequent clause relations such as the coordination of subordinate clauses and subordination within one or more of the main clauses in a compound sentence. In addition, the spoken language in particular commonly contains utterances that cannot be analysed in terms of clauses. These issues are discussed in 13.1–7.

2.4 Declarative sentences

We can distinguish four types of sentences with respect to their major uses in communication:

1. **declaratives**, or declarative sentences, for statements
2. **interrogatives**, or interrogative sentences, for questions
3. **imperatives**, or imperative sentences, for directives
4. **exclamatives**, or exclamative sentences, for exclamations

Declaratives are the most common type. They are also the basic type, in that the others can be most easily described by their differences from declaratives.

The four sentence types are illustrated by the following four related simple sentences:

[1]   They work hard. (declarative)
[1a] Do they work hard? (interrogative)
[1b] Work hard. (imperative)
[1c] How hard they work! (exclamative)

2.5 Interrogative sentences

The two major types of interrogatives are *yes–no* questions and *wh*-questions.

> **NOTE**
> *Yes–no* questions have also been called polarity questions, polarity being the system of positive/negative contrast. *Wh*-questions have also been called information questions.

2.5.1 *Yes–no* questions

Yes–no questions are generally intended to elicit the reply *yes* or *no*:

[1]   Do you always work very quickly?
[2]   Have you got an Uncle Victor?
[3]   Would you quarrel with that?
[4]   Can you remember how you felt when you heard that she died?
[5]   Are there any other matters arising?
[6]   Is this call for maturity amongst our politicians and communicators naïve? [W]

The response may be more informative than a simple *yes* or *no*:

[7]   A: Do you drink quite a lot of it?
      B: Use it as a mixer for my uhm … lemonade … and lime lemon lime and someone introduced it to me the other day

YES–NO QUESTIONS IN DETAIL

The word order in *yes–no* questions differs from that in declaratives. In declaratives the subject comes before the verb, as in the declarative corresponding to **[2]**:

[2a]   You have got an Uncle Victor.

In the *yes–no* question **[2]** the auxiliary verb is placed before the subject *you*. This change is **subject–operator inversion**, the **operator** generally being the first or only **auxiliary**. If the question does not have an auxiliary, *do* is inserted as a **dummy** auxiliary, as in **[1]**. For example, the *yes–no* question in **[8a]** corresponds to the declarative in **[8]**:

[8]   It interferes with your life.

[8a]   Does it interfere with your life?

Does in **[8a]** has the appropriate inflection (3rd person singular present tense) corresponding to the inflection of the verb *interferes* in **[8]**. The insertion of *do* in **[1]** and *does* in **[8a]** ensures that the question begins with the sequence verb followed by subject.

NOTE

In earlier periods of English, questions such as **[8a]** would have been formed by subject–verb inversion, without the support of the auxiliary *do*; thus Shakespeare's Hamlet asks:

[N1]   Stay'd it long?

The present-day equivalent is:

[N1a] Did it stay long?

The main verb *be* has continued to follow the earlier pattern of subject–verb inversion without *do*-support, if no auxiliary is present:

[N2]   Are they naughty?

But if an auxiliary accompanies, there is subject-operator inversion:

[N2a] Have they been naughty?

British English allows both options for the main verb *have*, but American English generally follows the regular pattern with *do*-support:

[N3]   Have you enough to eat?

[N3a] Do you have enough to eat?

Analogous uses of *do*-support apply elsewhere when present-day English requires an auxiliary, as in verb negation (cf. 2.11).

The older forms of questions and verb negation without *do*-support are occasionally found in present-day English either in solemn oration or in jocular style. The oratorical use is exemplified in John Kennedy's often-quoted words in his 1961 inaugural address:

[N4]   And so, my fellow Americans, *ask not* what your country can do for you; ask what you can do for your country.

Negative questions generally convey the speaker's expectation that the response should be positive:

[9]   Isn't that a little irregular? [W] ('Surely it is')

[10]   Haven't they got that the wrong way round?

[11] Can't you wait until everybody's finished having their lunch?

[12] Am I not allowed friends any more? [W]

2.5.2 *Wh*-questions

Wh-questions expect a reply that supplies the information that the *wh*-word indicates as required. They are called *wh*-questions because the **wh-words** generally begin with *wh*-, the exception being *how*. The *wh*-word may be a pronoun [13]–[15], an adverb [16]–[21], or a determiner (introducing a noun phrase) [22]:

[13] *What* made you write them?

[14] *What* did he mean?

[15] *Who*'s next?

[16] Uhm but *why* isn't it in French?

[17] *Where* did it all begin? [W]

[18] *How* will this embarrassing confrontation end? [W]

[19] *When* should the allies according to you cease hostilities?

[20] *How* deep is the snow?

[21] And uh … *how* long did that go on for?

[22] *Which* bit do you want to start with first?

WH-QUESTIONS IN DETAIL

The *wh*-word is generally at the beginning of the question. If the *wh*-word or the phrase it is part of is the complement of a preposition, in formal style the preposition moves to the front together with its complement:

[23] First of all *to what companies* does that scheme apply?

In less formal style, the preposition remains at the end:

[23a] First of all *what companies* does that scheme apply *to*?

The rule of subject–operator inversion applies generally to *wh*-questions. For example in [24] the direct object *what* begins the question and is followed by the dummy operator *do* and the subject *you*:

[24] What do you think? [W]

However, if the *wh*-expression is the subject of the sentence, there is no inversion. The normal declarative subject–verb order is retained:

[25] The crucial and fundamental question then arises: Who communicates about the threat and for what purposes? [W]

If the question seeks more than one piece of information, it may contain more than one *wh*-expression:

[26] Who is sampling who?

In the spoken language, the normal subject–verb order is sometimes retained even when the *wh*-expression is not the subject:

[27] You took which car?

[28] You did what next?

These may occur in an interview in a sequence of abrupt questions, they may be simple requests to repeat information, or they may express disbelief.

> **NOTE**
>
> Not all prepositions can be **fronted** in *wh*-questions. For example, the prepositions that follow the verb *be* are retained in final position:
>
> **[N1]** *What* was the food *like?*
>
> So also:
>
> **[N2]** *What* did you say that *for?*

2.5.3 Alternative questions

In addition to *yes–no* questions and *wh*-questions there are alternative questions. **Alternative questions** offer two or more options for the responses. One type of alternative question resembles a *yes–no* question **[29]–[31]** and the other type a *wh*-question **[32]–[33]**:

[29] But is that a reflection on them … or on us?

[30] Do we ask too much or too little of our police?

[31] And, that extrusion, would it take place on a flexion injury or an extension injury or could it take place on either?

[32] What are you doing for the summer, staying in Paris or going home? [W]

[33] Which you ask is the more authentic the more mandated by tradition religious moderation … or religious extremism?

2.6 Tag questions

Tag questions are attached to clauses that are not interrogatives. The most common type of tag question is the abbreviated *yes–no* question:

[1] Your heroines are very much of a type *aren't they*

[2] I can't be sure, *can I?* [W]

The tag may occur in the middle of a sentence:

[3] So on going back to your to your childhood it was your mother *wasn't it* who was the driving force behind all of this behind this sort of intellectual rigour?

> **TAG QUESTIONS IN DETAIL**
>
> Tag questions generally consist of an operator followed by a pronoun. The operator echoes the previous auxiliary and the pronoun is co-referential with the previous subject. If there is no previous auxiliary, the **dummy operator** *do* is introduced, as with all *yes–no* questions (cf. 2.5.1).
>
> **[4]** And I think your mum likes company *doesn't she* ?
>
> A positive declarative generally takes a negative tag question **[1]** and **[3]–[4]**, whereas a negative declarative generally takes a positive tag question **[2]**.
>
> The **nuclear tone** (distinct pitch movement) on the tag operator may be a **rise** or a **fall**. A rise is neutral in attitude, inviting the hearer to decide whether the preceding proposition is true. A fall invites the hearer to agree with the proposition.

Examples of tag questions with various operators:

[5]   But it's understated violence *isn't it* ?

[6]   Yes they're always thrown in at the deep end *aren't they* ?

[7]   He's not gone *has he* ? [W]

[8]   There's another story there, *isn't there* ? [W]

[9]   You don't mind, *do you* ? [W]

[10]   I can write *can't I* ?!! [W]

Innit is an occasional informal variant of *isn't it*:

[11]   It's good news for you though *innit*

[12]   Bit cheeky *innit*

Both the declarative and its tag question are sometimes positive:

[13]   So that's really unrealistic *is it* wanting to do to teach English?

[14]   What's this funny thing What's this thing It's a foil *is it* ?

[15]   You're going to be transcribing all this *are you* ?

[16]   You've marked it *have you* ?

This type of tag question points to a conclusion that the speaker has drawn on the basis of what was previously said or seen.

Tag questions may also be used with imperatives **[17]**–**[18]** and exclamatives **[19]**–**[20]**:

[17]   Take a seat, *won't you* ?

[18]   Let me have a look, *will you* ?

[19]   What a mess he was in, *wasn't he* ?

[20]   How well she played, *didn't she* ?

There are several tag questions that have the same form whatever appears in the previous declarative or exclamative. *Is it* appears to be a recently coined **fixed tag**:

[21]   You mean about Felicity and her achievements *is it* ?

[22]   She looks she looks Puerto Rican or something *is it* ?

[23]   So you put you put in the sedative *is it* ?

Some well-established fixed tags are exemplified below:

[24]   So you're not coming in *right* ?

[25]   Well what the hell *eh* ?

[26]   It must be peculiarly disconcerting, *don't you think*, to be left for someone entirely different from oneself? [Sarah Caudwell 'An Acquaintance with Mr Collins' in *A Suit of Diamonds*]

2.7 Imperative sentences

2.7.1 Second person imperatives

Second person imperatives—the typical and by far the most frequent imperatives—generally do not have a subject, but *you* is implied as subject:

[1]   Just look at the beautiful scenery here

[2] Never lecture with … animals or children and never ever try to do chemistry experiments live.

[3] As for whatever I said on the phone about our relationship, well if you can remember any of it still *please forget it*.

[4] Stir the spices into the meat, and season with salt and pepper.

You can be added either for contrast or for some kind of emphasis (entreaty or warning):

[5] You pay now and I'll pay next time.

[6] You tell me. [W]

Occasionally, third person subjects occur:

[7] Nobody say anything.

[8] Those without letters from their parents raise their hands.

2.7.2 First and third person imperatives

First and third person imperatives are formed with *let*. *Let* may be a main verb ('allow'), but *let's* must be the imperative auxiliary:

[9] Uhm let me find you something ethnic

[10] Let me put it this way

[11] Let's have a closer look at some of those manoeuvres

[12] Let's get really drunk

[13] Let us be clear, though, that a mature attitude to communications about national identity and international threat is possible. [W]

[14] Now … let me say again that is not a bad record by the police

[15] The motto of the market is 'Let the buyer beware' [W]

[16] In the long term, it is the replacement of Arab dictatorships by democracies that will be the best guarantee of freedom, stability and peace in the Middle East. Let Iraq be the first. [*Evening Standard*]

USE OF *DO* WITH IMPERATIVES

Do is placed before the imperative verb or auxiliary to make it less abrupt and more persuasive:

[17] Do bear in mind that unit values, and their income can fall as well as rise. [W]

[18] Do come in [W]

[19] Do let's have another game.

Don't or *do not* is placed initially to negate second person and third person imperative sentences:

[20] But don't underestimate the problems

[21] Don't be intimidated by vehicles following too close behind

[22] Do not hesitate to contact me if you need any more information. [W]

[23] Don't let anybody in except me

First person imperatives may be negated simply by inserting *not* after the pronoun:

[24] Oh let's not get touchy touchy

[25] Let me not fall into temptation.

Alternatively, *don't* is inserted before *let's* or *let me* (especially in British English) or after *let's* (especially in American English):

[26] Don't let's tell the police.

[27] Don't let me think about it.

[28] Let's don't tell anyone.

2.8 Exclamative sentences

Exclamative sentences begin with *what* or *how*. *What* introduces noun phrases. Otherwise, *how* is used.

[1] What strong words you use. [W]

[2] What an idea you've got

[3] And what an opportunity ... this is for the youngster [W]

[4] What a star you are—as you would say! [W]

[5] How she—how she talks

[6] How clever he is

[7] How sweet they were [W]

[8] How well she plays.

EXCLAMATIVE SENTENCES IN DETAIL

Like the interrogative *wh*-phrase, the exclamative phrase is fronted. Otherwise, the word order is that of declaratives. Unlike questions, there is no subject–operator inversion (cf. 2.5). For example, the declaratives corresponding to [1] and [6] are:

[1a] You use such strong words.

[6a] He is so clever.

Such in [1a] is a determiner introducing a noun phrase, and *so* in [6a] is a pre-modifier of an adjective and can also premodify an adverb. Like *such* in [1a] and *so* in [6a], *what* and *how* are **intensifiers**. In the absence of evaluative expressions in the context they may be interpreted as conveying either a high degree or a low degree. Thus, *what an idea* in [2] may be interpreted as 'an excellent idea' or as 'a terrible idea'. Similarly, *how she plays* may be interpreted as 'she plays excellently' or 'she plays badly'.

Exclamatives are often abbreviated to just the exclamative phrase:

[9] What a shame

[10] What an admission from an actor. [W]

[11] How stupid

[12] How nice for you

In the following example, the *that*-clause is subordinate to the abbreviated exclamatory phrase *How wonderful*:

[13] How wonderful that this man has gotten a position in a university to help undo all the silly things that secretaries do when arranging luncheons, meetings, etc. [*Wall Street Journal*]

2.9 Statements, questions, directives, exclamations

We have seen (cf. 2.4) that sentences fall into four main types that differ in form and that these four types are associated with four major uses in communication:

1. declaratives   statements
2. interrogatives   questions
3. imperatives   directives
4. exclamatives   exclamations

However, there is not a complete correlation between the sentence types and the communicative uses.

For example, **rhetorical questions** are interrogative in form but have the communicative function of a statement. If the rhetorical question is positive the implied statement is negative, and vice versa. The implied statement is the mental answer that the speaker intends the hearer to infer from the rhetorical question. Rhetorical questions are a persuasive device, and they are particularly common in persuasive discourse such as political speeches and newspaper editorials. They may take the form of *yes–no* questions **[1]–[2]** or *wh-*questions **[3]–[5]**:

> **[1]**   Don't I waffle on? ('I certainly waffle on') [W]
>
> **[2]**   My question is: is there any point in having a democracy when it can elect and keep on electing such a ludicrous government as we have had for the last ten years [Terry Jones in Ben Pimlott et al. *The Alternative*] ('There certainly isn't any point')
>
> **[3]**   What else is there to do? [W] ('There's nothing else to do')
>
> **[4]**   It has been a while since we spoke, but not too long for me to forget you—*how could I forget you.* [W] ('I couldn't possibly forget you')
>
> **[5]**   A: But sorry is this the right example Is this correct now
>   B: *Who knows* I really don't know.

Here is a series of rhetorical questions from an editorial:

> **[6]**   Even though the changes were more than he planned, we see no evidence that Mr Major's limited game of musical chairs is the shot in the arm his government badly needs. Does sending Gillian Shephard to agriculture make any more sense than sending John Gummer to environment? Where, apart from Mr Clarke's move, is the flair, the dash, the new blood and the supreme self-confidence the Tories need to sustain them through a troubled fourth term? Is John Redwood, the Thatcherite MP for Wokingham, really the man for Wales when his only link with the principality until now has been the M4? [*The Sunday Times*]

In contrast to rhetorical questions, **declarative questions** have the form of a declarative but the force of a question. In writing they end in a question mark and in speech—as in A's question in **[8]**—they end with a rising intonation.

> **[7]**   With all the bits of work you've done over the years, your CV must be full? [W]
>
> **[8]**   A: A gentleman from the bank came down to see you
>   B: That's right.

Exclamations may take the form of declaratives **[9]–[11]**, imperatives **[12]–[15]**, and interrogatives **[16]–[18]**:

> **[9]**   I've not had a permanent job for almost two years now! [W]

[10] You can only have showers on week-days after supper, and you have to pay 5 Francs each time—I couldn't believe it! [W]

[11] He is also the most unsexy Spaniard I have ever seen! [W]

[12] I don't mean to sound religious, *God forbid no!* [W]

[13] Don't think that for one minute

[14] Do something exotic, wet and wild! [W]

[15] Shoot him! [W]

[16] Have you managed to have time away from wife-to-be!?! [W]

[17] What the hell is this? [W]

[18] So isn't the weather gorgeous? [W]

The nearest non-exclamative sentences that have the same force as exclamatives are sentences with the intensifiers *such* and *so* (cf. 2.8).

[19] The country created *such* a strong impression on us! ('What a strong impression the country created on us') [W]

[20] Oh that was *so* funny ('How funny that was')

Directives can have the form of declaratives **[21]** or interrogatives **[22]**:

[21] You will apologize immediately

[22] Could you shut the door?

2.10 Speech acts

The four major communicative uses discussed in 2.9 distinguish uses at a very general level. We can make numerous more refined distinctions when we examine the utterance of sentences in actual contexts. When we utter a declarative, we generally do more than state something. We may simply inform somebody of something, as perhaps in this response of a patient to the doctor's query:

[1] A: Now uh the rest of your health is okay I mean are you generally well

B: *I feel fine*

But we use declaratives for numerous purposes. For example, we can use declaratives to praise **[2]**, to request **[3]**, to apologize [4], to advise **[5]**, to give permission **[6]**, and to make an offer **[7]**:

[2] I'm very happy with your work.

[3] I should like some sugar, please.

[4] I'm sorry for the interruption.

[5] You should use another route.

[6] You may have another piece.

[7] I can lend you a hand with the washing-up.

We can express similar kinds of communication by using other sentence forms:

[2a] How splendid your work is!

[3a] Pass the sugar, please.

[4a] Will you forgive my interruption?

[5a] Shouldn't you use another route?

[6a] Help yourself to another piece.

[7a] Can I lend you a hand with the washing-up?

At the same time, these utterances retain their general communicative force. For example, **[5a]** is more polite than **[5]** because it is framed as a question that more easily allows the hearer to reject the advice.

When we speak or write, we are performing communicative actions. These actions, expressed in words, are speech acts, which are intended to convey communicative purposes to the intended hearers or readers. The communicative purpose depends on the particular context. For example *It's going to rain* may be simply a prediction, or it may be intended as a warning to take an umbrella, or it may be intended to indicate that a projected excursion should be cancelled.

Speakers occasionally convey their purpose by using performative verbs, which explicitly denote their communicative purpose:

[8] I *apologize* for the interruption.

[9] I *predict* that it will rain this afternoon.

[10] Talking to the driver is *forbidden*.

[11] I must *inform* you that your time is up.

[12] I *sentence* you to three months' imprisonment.

[13] We *advise* you to avoid becoming involved.

> **NOTE**
>
> **[11]** is an example of a hedged performative, where a modal auxiliary is used to express (for example) the obligation, ability, or willingness to perform the speech act designated by the performative verb, but at the same time the speaker intends what he says to constitute the performance of that speech act.

A sentence may convey more than one communicative purpose:

[14] I'm sorry for the interruption, but I should like to use the phone.

The first clause conveys an apology, and the second a request.

2.11 Positive and negative clauses

Clauses are either positive or (less commonly) negative. The most frequent method of negating clauses is to insert *not* or the contracted form *n't* in the verb phrase:

[1] He would not stay long. [W]

[2] Such communication was not part of the proceedings. [W]

[3] The countries around the world do not fit into neat and precise categories of climate and weather. [Bill Giles *The Story of Weather*]

[4] Well, that bit wasn't true, but he certainly didn't go to the première. [W].

> **NEGATIVE CLAUSES IN DETAIL**
>
> Like questions (cf. 2.5), negative clauses require an operator. *Not* is positioned after the operator **[1]**–**[3]**, and *n't* is attached to the operator. In **[1]** the operator is the

---

first—and, in this instance, only—auxiliary (*would*); it is the main verb *was* in **[2]**; and it is the dummy operator *do* in **[3]**. In the two clauses of **[4]** *n't* is attached to the operators *was* and *did*. As **[4]** demonstrates, negation may apply to more than one clause in a sentence.

In negative questions, contracted *n't* is attached to the operator and therefore comes before the subject **[5]**, whereas *not* generally follows the subject **[6]**–**[8]**:

> **[5]** Listen can't we do this at some other time?
>
> **[6]** Can we not have his forecast of the underlying rate of inflation excluding mortgage interest at the end of next year the fourth quarter?
>
> **[7]** Does novel-writing not come easily to you?
>
> **[8]** Why did they not speak out? [W]

But *not* may also occasionally come between the operator and the subject:

> **[9]** Do not the police really remain ... as to many they appeared in nineteen eighty-one to have become ... a white male force encased in technology?

Clauses may be negative because of negative words other than *not*:

> **[10]** Things *never* work out the way we would like them to.
>
> **[11]** At the time of the original meeting *nobody* had any idea of what would happen
>
> **[12]** There's *no* surer way to lose a good friend than to marry her. [Mary Wesley *A Sensible Life*]
>
> **[13]** However, I have heard *nothing* formally.

In standard English, two negative words occasionally occur in the same clause, but in that case they make a positive:

> **[14]** None of the countries have no political prisoners. ('All the countries have some political prisoners.')

Non-standard dialects use more than one negative to emphasize the negation:

> **[15]** Nobody told me nothing.
>
> **[16]** We don't want none, neither.

The equivalents of **[15]** and **[16]** in standard English are:

> **[15a]** Nobody told me anything.
>
> **[16a]** We don't want any, either.

NOTE

Double or multiple negation was common in earlier English, but by the eighteenth century it was no longer acceptable in standard English.

Negation may affect a phrase, without making the clause negative:

> **[17]** They spent a not unpleasant time at my place, didn't they?
>
> **[18]** They were no doubt shocked to read some of the reports.
>
> **[19]** I was greeted by none other than the mayor, and so was my assistant.

A tag question accompanying a negative sentence or clause is typically positive, as in **[17a]**; *some* (or its compounds such as *somebody*) is typically replaced by *any* (or its compounds) in negative clauses, as in **[18a]**; *so* in **[19]** requires to be replaced by *nor* or *neither* in **[19a]**.

[17a] They didn't spend a pleasant time at my place, *did they?*

[18a] They were not shocked to read *any* of the reports.

[19a] I was not greeted by the mayor, *nor* was my assistant.

As speech acts, negative sentences are used to deny something that has been mentioned:

[20] A: I mean four of the five sabbaticals were missing
         B: That's irrelevant
         A: It *isn't* irrelevant

[21] But he was saying it as if it was my job to do it whereas of course it *isn't*

More commonly, what is denied is an assumption that is not made explicit:

[22] A: Rugby ... the girls are just treated like a few honorary girls but they're *not* integrated
         B: At King's Canterbury they are integrated but it *isn't* too free it's still quite academic.

Negative sentences are also used to reject an offer or invitation:

[23] A: Have some banana bread ...
         B: Look I'm not much of a banana bread eater.

Negative *yes–no* questions often convey an expectation of a positive response, though the expectation may be frustrated:

[24] 'Don't you know snails are a delicacy?'
         'I don't want to know anything,' I said, turning on my side and closing my eyes.
         [Agnes Owens 'Patience' in Alison Fell *The Seven Cardinal Virtues*]

They can also be used to mean 'is it the case that...not', expecting the answer *no*:

[25] Don't you want something to eat?

[26] Oh dear, can't they come?

Why don't you and the abbreviated *why not* convey advice or offers:

[27] So why don't you knock on his door?

[28] Other times you say hey look I mean there's no point in competing why don't you come in with us?

[29] Why don't you have some Guinness?

[30] We are happy to give a randomly selected jury power over the life or death of individuals, so why not give a similarly randomly selected panel power over the nation? [Terry Jones in Ben Pimlott et al. *The Alternative*]

2.12 Active and passive sentences

2.12.1 The passive

An **active** clause often contains an object as one of its constituents (cf. 3.4). Active clauses can sometimes be made **passive**. The changes required by the transformation of active to passive are illustrated in the contrast of active **[1]** with passive **[1a]**:

[1]   One of the lecturers recommended us to do this at the university.

[1a]   We were recommended to do this at the university by one of the lecturers

---

CHANGE OF ACTIVE TO PASSIVE IN DETAIL

Some of the changes affect the verb phrase. An additional auxiliary (generally the auxiliary *be*) is added, which in **[1a]** is *were*; and the main verb is made into a passive participle, which for *recommended* is the same form as the past. The active object *us* becomes the passive subject *we*; the active subject is moved to the end, where it is introduced by the preposition *by*.

Get is used less commonly as a passive auxiliary:

[2]   And just under half get invited to staff meetings

[3]   And that's why I got sent home the night when other people didn't turn up and ended up going … to Cambridge

---

2.12.2 **Use of the passive**

A valid reason for resorting to the passive is that it is then possible to omit any mention of the **agent** (or cause) of the action, which is expressed in the active by the subject. Indeed, the *by*-phrase referring to the agent is commonly omitted, as in **[2]** and **[3]** above and **[4]** below:

[4]   I'm not trained as a … as a therapist

The usual motivation for omitting mention of the agent is that identification of the agent is irrelevant or intended to appear so. The identity of the agent may also be unknown, as in **[5]**, or the agent may not be a specific person as in **[6]**; similarly in **[7]**, where *it* refers to a film:

[5]   Oh she's called Jennifer.

[6]   I think it's how you're introduced to them.

[7]   It's set in the future.

In scientific and technical writing it is quite common for writers to resort to the agentless passive to avoid frequent use of the personal pronouns *I* and *we* and thereby maintain a more impersonal style:

[8]   For observation by bright field and interference microscopy urediniospores scraped from erumpent pustules and macerated or hand-sectioned telia *were mounted* in lactic acid and *heated* to boiling point. [*Mycological Research*]

[9]   This approach *was* therefore *considered* and *found* to be far more attractive. [W]

The agentive passive can be used to good purpose, despite the availability of the more common active:

[10]   The story was inspired by a tip-off from an officer of the SB (the Polish secret police, which had been harassing Gowing for a few months), that Soviet hardliners, backed by the KGB, were trying to depose General Jaruzelski. [Donald McCormick and Katy Fletcher *Spy Fiction*]

The passive is preferable in **[10]** for two reasons. First, the active would produce a clumsy unbalanced sentence in which the part before the verb was much longer than the object (*the story*):

[10a] A tip-off from an officer of the SB (the Polish secret police, which had been harassing Gowing for a few months), that Soviet hardliners, backed by the KGB, were trying to depose General Jaruzelski inspired *the story*.

Secondly, *the story* refers to what has been mentioned before and comes naturally at the beginning of the sentence as a link to the new information about the tip-off. In **[11]** *Kim Philby* is placed at the end of the passive *which*-clause as the climax:

[11] It is noteworthy that the section in which Greene worked was that of the Iberian sub-section of Section V of the SIS, which was controlled by none other than Kim Philby. [Donald McCormick and Katy Fletcher *Spy Fiction*]

Chapter 3
The Constituents of Sentences

Summary

Summary

The basic structures of sentences always have a subject and a verb as constituents. The main verb may also require or permit one or two complements. The possible complements are direct object, indirect object, subject predicative, and object predicative. In addition, sentences usually have one or more adverbials, which are optional constituents. The constituents have semantic roles, indicating the part they play in the description of the situation. For example, the subject may be the agent of an action. The basic structures can be arranged in various ways.

Part of the structure of a sentence may be omitted without affecting the acceptability of the sentence or its interpretation. The interpretation of the ellipsis may depend on information in the situation as well as the words of the sentence. For textual ellipsis the interpretation depends solely on the words that come before the ellipsis (anaphoric ellipsis) or those that come after it (cataphoric ellipsis).

3.1 The basic sentence structures

A sentence consisting of just one clause is a **simple sentence**. The basic structures of a clause are therefore identical to those of a simple sentence.

3.1.1 Structure of the simple sentence

For a first approach to the grammar of the sentence and clause, it is sensible to examine the basic structures of simple sentences that are **declarative** (typically making a statement), positive (rather than **negative**), **active** (rather than **passive**), and complete (rather than **elliptical**). The **constituents** of the basic structures appear in their normal order, and they consist of phrases that do not themselves contain clauses. Each basic structure constitutes the nucleus of a simple sentence:

[1]   I'm sending you this card.

[2]   He shrugged his shoulders.

We can add one or more **adverbials**, which are optional constituents:

[1a]   I'm sending you this card *to stand in your bedroom*. [W]

[2a]   He *merely* shrugged his shoulders. [W]

In analysing the basic structures, we disregard adverbials.

3.1.2 Sentence structure: subject and verb

The basic structures have two obligatory constituents: a **subject** and a **verb**, denoted by the symbols **S** and **V**. Below are examples of sentences consisting of just a subject and a verb in that order. The two constituents are indicated by the parenthesized symbols that follow them.

[3]   All the flowers (S) have disappeared (V).

[4]   The enemy tanks (S) are retreating (V).

[5]   You (S) should be working (V).

[6]   All my friends (S) laughed (V).

The verb (V) of the sentence takes the form of a **verb phrase**. The verb phrase consists of one or more **auxiliaries** (or **auxiliary verbs**) plus the **main verb**, which is the head of the verb phrase.

NOTE

The term *verb phrase* is also used for the verb plus its complements (if any). *Predicate* may be similarly used, but may also be extended to include adverbials that are closely attached to the sentence. The verb of the sentence is sometimes called the predicator.

The main verbs in **[3]–[6]** are *disappeared, retreating, working,* and *laughed.* It is the main verb that determines which constituents may follow it, and these constituents are the **complements** of the verb. In **[3]–[6]** there are no complements.

3.1.3 **Sentence structure: complements**

The types of complement are:

direct object	O
indirect object	O
subject predicative	P
object predicative	P

The complements are discussed in later sections (3.2–8). They are exemplified in the sentences below:

[7]   I (S) hate (V) this noise (O).

[8]   The idea (S) could make (V) her (O) a fortune (O).

[9]   The party treasurer (S) is (V) very hospitable (P).

[10]   They (S) drove (V) us (O) crazy (P).

Complements may be obligatory, as in **[9]**, or at least obligatory in the intended sense of the verb, as in **[10]**. More important is the link between the complement and the verb. Only one instance of a particular complement type (direct object, indirect object, etc.) can occur in the same clause. This restriction does not exclude coordination of two phrases, since the coordinated unit as a whole functions as a complement:

[10a] They (S) drove (V) us and everybody else (O) crazy (P).

Some verbs allow more than one type of complementation. For example: the verb *drive* can have no complements, or just a direct object, or a combination of direct object with an object predicative:

[11]   He (S) is driving (V).

[11a] He (S) is driving (V) his father's car (O).

[11b] He (S) is driving (V) me (O) mad (P).

3.1.4 **Sentence structure: subject and predicate**

Traditionally, sentences have also been divided into two parts: the **subject** and the **predicate**. The predicate consists of the verb and its complements and also most adverbials. Excluded from the predicate are **sentence adverbials**, which point to logical links with what precedes **[11a1]** or express a comment by the speaker or writer **[11b1]**:

[11a1] Nevertheless (A), he is driving his father's car.

[11b1] Frankly (A), he is driving me mad.

> **NOTE**
>
> *Predicate* is not a constituent in the grammatical framework used in this grammar.

3.1.5 **Sentence structure: constituent realization**

As we have seen, the verb of the sentence takes the form of a verb phrase. The subject, direct object, and indirect object take the form of a noun phrase. The subject predicative and object predicative can be a noun phrase, adjective phrase, adverb phrase, or prepositional phrase. The adverbial can be a noun phrase, adverb phrase, or prepositional phrase.

3.2 Subject and verb

The verb is the easiest constituent to recognize, because of its formal characteristics. The verb of the sentence takes the form of a verb phrase, and the first or only word in the verb phrase indicates present or past **tense** (cf. 4.2.3). Thus, *like* is present in **[1]** and *liked* is past in **[1a]**:

[1]   I *like* the music.

[1a]   I *liked* the music.

In **[2]** *have* is present tense even though *have thanked* refers to past time:

[2]   I *have* thanked them for the gift.

In contrast, *had* is past tense:

[2a]   I *had* thanked them for the gift.

In **[2a]** *had thanked* is the verb phrase, and *thanked* is the main verb. The phrase can be replaced by the one word *thanked*, in which case *thanked* is past tense and its corresponding present is *thank*:

[2b]   I *thanked* them for the gift.

[2c]   I *thank* them for the gift.

We can identify the subject easily if we change a declarative into a *yes–no* **question**, since the change involves the movement of the subject (cf. 3.5). For example, the declarative **[3]** can be turned into the **interrogative [3a]**:

[3]   *His manner* was often intense.

[3a]   Was *his manner* often intense?

The subject is *his manner* in both **[3]** and **[3a]**. Similarly, the subject is *the education minister* in both **[4]** and **[4a]**:

[4]   *The education minister* managed the rare feat of antagonizing all the teaching unions.

[4a]   Did *the education minister* manage the rare feat of antagonizing all the teaching unions?

If an adverbial (A) is present at the beginning of the declarative it is often moved to a later position in the interrogative:

[5]   Last week (A) she (S) began (V) a campaign against journalistic clichés (O).

[5a] Did she begin a campaign against journalistic clichés last week?

But some types of adverbial generally occur initially:

[6]   Anyway (A), would you necessarily get the job

3.3 Subject

The subject has a number of characteristics, two of which we have seen in 3.2. The major characteristics of the subject are discussed in 3.3.1–3.3.8:

3.3.1 Position of subject in declaratives

In declaratives, the subject normally comes before the verb:

[1]   I (S) might go (V) back to Cambridge early.

It need not come immediately before the verb, since an adverbial may intervene:

[2]   I (S) just (A) remembered (V) the letter.

3.3.2 Position of subject in interrogatives

In interrogatives, the subject generally comes after the **operator**, the verb used for forming interrogatives (cf. 2.5); the rest of the verb phrase (if it consists of more than the operator) follows the subject. In the examples, the operator is indicated by 'v' and the rest of the verb phrase (if any) by 'V':

[3]   *Are* (v) *they* (S) aware of your views?

[4]   What *did* (v) *you* (S) *get* (V) out of it?

[5]   *Is* (v) *everything* (S) *being changed* (V)?

There is no change in the declarative order in *wh*-interrogatives if the interrogative *wh*-expression is itself the subject:

[6]   *Who* (S) *did* (V) most of the driving?

[7]   *What* (S) *made* (V) them angry?

[8]   *What sort of physical activities* (S) *were* (V) available?

3.3.3 Subject in second person imperatives

In second person **imperatives** (the most common type), the subject *you* is normally omitted:

[9]   *Turn* (V) it off.

3.3.4 **Verb agreement with subject**

The verb agrees in **number** (cf. 4.3.1.1) and **person** (cf. 4.2.6–7, 6.4.1) with the subject where the verb has distinctive forms in the present or past tense:

[10]   *I* (S) *am* (V) in sympathy with her position.

[11]   *We* (S) *are* (V) very concerned about you.

[12]   *All their children* (S) *were* (V) in good shape.

[13]   *He* (S) *seems* (V) nervous.

The agreement applies only to the first verb in the verb phrase if there is more than one:

[14]   *Your friends* (S) *are* being (V) bitchy.

3.3.5 **Subject and reflexive pronouns**

The subject decides the form of a **reflexive** pronoun (e.g. *myself, herself, themselves*) functioning as the object, when the subject and object refer to the same person or thing:

[15]   *You* (S) can cut *yourself*.

[16]   *They* (S) washed *themselves*.

3.3.6 **Pronoun as subject**

Some pronouns have a distinctive form when they function as subject (cf. 3.6, 6.4):

[17]   *She* (S) is at college, so you can't see *her* now.

[18]   *We* (S) very rarely worked with them, though they contact *us* sometimes.

She and *we* are subjective forms, contrasting with *her* and *us*.

3.3.7 **Effect of passivization on subject**

The transformation of an active sentence into a passive sentence (cf. 2.12), requires a change of subjects:

[19]   *The young producer* (S) proved all the critics wrong.

[19a] *All the critics* (S) were proved wrong by the young producer.

3.3.8 **Agentive role of subject**

In an active sentence that expresses the notion of an **agent** ('doer of the action'), the agentive role is taken by the subject:

[20]   *My aunt* (S) gave me a mower for my wedding.

3.4 Direct object

When a main verb that is not a **copular** verb (cf. 3.6) does not have a complement, it is **intransitive**. When it has a direct object (O), it is **transitive**. Many verbs can be either intransitive or transitive:

[1]   *I* (S) *am eating* (V).

[1a]   *I* (S) *am eating* (V) *my lunch* (O).

If a sentence has only one complement of the verb and that complement is a direct object, its basic structure is SVO.

We can identify the direct object in a declarative sentence if we can elicit it as a response to a question beginning with *who* or *what* followed by the operator (cf. 2.5) and the subject:

[2]   She (S) would have asked (V) her parents (O).

[2a]   Who (O) would (v) she (S) have asked (V)? [W]

[3]   They (S) speak (V) Welsh (O) at home.

[3a]   No but at home what (O) do (v) they (S) speak (V)

In formal style, *whom* is used as the direct object in place of *who*.

[2b]   *Whom* would she have asked?

Here are some major characteristics of the direct object.

3.4.1 **Position of direct object**

The direct object normally comes after the verb, as in **[1a]**, repeated below:

[1a]   *I* (S) *am eating* (V) *my lunch* (O).

The main exceptions to this rule occur in **wh-questions** (cf. 2.5) and in **relative clauses** (cf. 10.9). If the *wh*-expression in a question is a direct object, it is **fronted**:

[4]   *What sort of dance training* (O) *did* (v) *you* (S) *have* (V)

[5]   *Which car* (O) *did* (v) *you* (S) *take* (V)

Similarly, if the relative expression in a relative clause is a direct object it is fronted:

[6]   I had to meet this girl *who* (O) *I* (S) *haven't seen* (V) for ten years from my school

[7]   If you want a large black pencil ... that's a marker pencil *which* (O) *you* (S) *have* (V) there

3.4.2. **Pronoun as direct object**

Some pronouns have a distinctive form when they function as direct objects:

[8]   My shoes are killing *me*. *I* don't like them at all.

[9]   Nobody can catch *them*. *They* are hardened smugglers.

Contrast objective *me* and *them* with subjective *I* and *they*.

3.4.3 **Reflexive pronoun as direct object**

If the object and the subject refer to the same person or thing, the direct object is a reflexive pronoun (which ends in -*self* or -*selves*):

[10] *I* (S) could kick *myself* (O).

[11] *She* (S) has completely cut *herself* (O) off from me.

3.4.4 **Effect of passivization on direct object**

When we change an active sentence into a passive sentence, the active object becomes the passive subject:

[12] *The massive costs* (S) harm *the film industry* (O).

[12a] *The film industry* (S) is harmed by the massive costs.

3.5 Indirect object

BASIC STRUCTURES: RECAPITULATION

We have so far encountered two basic structures: SV and SVO, exemplified in **[1]** and **[2]**:

[1] My glasses (S) have disappeared (V).

[2] Our country (S) is absorbing (V) many refugees (O).

The verb *disappear* here is an intransitive verb, since it does not have a complement. The verb *absorb* is here a transitive verb, since it has a direct object as its complement.

Some transitive verbs can have two objects, an indirect object as well as a direct object. In **[3]** *sending* has just one complement, a direct object; in **[3a]** it has two complements, an indirect object followed by a direct object (O). Both objects are indicated by 'O':

[3] I am sending *an official letter of complaint* (O).

[3a] I am sending *you* (O) *an official letter of complaint* (O).

Here are some other examples of verbs with these two complements:

[4] We tell *each other* (O) *everything* (O)

[5] And what I would suggest is that we make *you* (O) *an appointment to go and see one and talk it through* (O)

[6] That teaches *one* (O) a *lesson about predicting things* (O)

[7] The public sector health service buys *you* (O) *free private care* (O)

[8] And that earns *United* (O) *a free kick* (O)

[9] 'Intelligence' permits *individual organisms* (O) *an increased capacity either to avoid change, or to track change, or both* (O). [W]

[10] And I wish *you* (O) *success in finding a suitable career opening* (O). [W]

The indirect object typically refers to a person or some other animate being that is the recipient or beneficiary of the action.

The indirect object can generally be paraphrased by a phrase introduced by *to* or *for*, but that phrase follows the direct object. For example:

[4a]   We tell everything (O) to each other.

[7a]   The public sector health service buys free private care (O) for you.

Sometimes the direct object is absent and the indirect object alone is the complement of the verb:

[11]   And we shall I promise you (O) ... bring our own forces back home just as soon as it is safe to do so

[12]   Only God knows if there is absolute truth, and God doesn't tell us (O). [W]

When there is one object, the basic structure is SVO; when there are two objects it is SVOO, the first object being indirect and the second direct. A verb taking one object is **monotransitive**, a verb taking two objects is **ditransitive**.

Like the direct object, the indirect object can be questioned by *who(m)* or *what*:

[13]   Easterly winds bring *us* (O) *this extreme cold* (O).

[13a] *What* (O) do easterly winds bring *us* (O)?

[13b] *Who* (O) do easterly winds bring *this extreme cold* (O)?

However, many people prefer to use the construction with a preposition in questions such as **[13b]**:

[13c] *Who* do easterly winds bring this extreme cold *to*?

[13d] *To whom* do easterly winds bring this extreme cold? [formal]

The indirect object shares characteristics with the direct object (a reason for calling both of them objects).

3.5.1. Position of indirect object

The indirect object comes after the verb:

[14]   The waiver clause *denied* (V) *them* (O) *their rights* (O).

When both objects are present, the indirect object comes before the direct object.

NOTE

British English also allows the direct object to come first if both objects are pronouns. The normal order—indirect object followed by direct object—occurs in this example:

Well if you give *me* (O) *it* (O) tomorrow I might be able to do some tomorrow morning.

The exceptional order—direct object followed by indirect object—is shown below:

Give *it* (O) *me* (O) tomorrow.

3.5.2 Pronoun as indirect object

As with the direct object, some pronouns have a distinctive form when they function as indirect object. The objective forms *me* in **[15]**, and *us* in **[16]** contrast with the subjective forms *I* and *we*.

[15] Well if you give *me* (O) *it* (O) tomorrow I might be able to do some tomorrow morning

[16] Can you pick a photograph that uh shows *us* (O) *the position* (O)

3.5.3 **Reflexive pronoun as indirect object**

If the indirect object and the subject refer to the same person or thing, the indirect object is a reflexive pronoun:

[17] *They* (S) asked *themselves* (O) the same question.

3.5.4 **Effect of passivization on indirect object**

When we change an active sentence into a passive sentence, the active indirect object can become the passive subject. Compare repeated **[3a]** with **[3b]**:

[3a] I am sending *you* (O) *an official letter of complaint* (O).

[3b] *You* (S) are being sent *an official letter of complaint* (O).

The active direct object (*an official letter of complaint*) is retained in the passive of **[3b]**. The direct object can also become the passive subject:

[3c] *An official letter of complaint* (S) is being sent *you* [O].

In **[3c]** the active indirect object (*you*) is retained in the passive. More commonly, the corresponding prepositional phrase replaces the passive indirect object:

[3d] An official letter of complaint is being sent *to you.*

3.6 Subject predicative

BASIC STRUCTURES: RECAPITULATION

So far we have seen three basic structures: SV, SVO, SVOO. They are exemplified in **[1]–[3]**:

[1] My glasses (S) have disappeared (V).

[2] Our country (S) is absorbing (V) many refugees (O).

[3] I (S) am sending (V) you (O) an official letter of complaint (O).

In **[1]** the main verb *disappeared* is intransitive, whereas in **[2]** and **[3]** the main verbs *absorbing* and *sending* are transitive. *Absorbing* in **[2]** has one complement: the direct object; *sending* in **[3]** has two complements: the indirect object and the direct object.

Some verbs are neither intransitive (without any complement), nor transitive (accompanied by one or two objects as complements). Such verbs are **copular** (or **linking**) verbs. The most common copular verb is *be*. The complement of a copular verb is the **subject predicative** (P).

[4]   *The water-bed* (S) *was* (V) *very comfortable* (P).

[5]   *The baby tortoise* (S) *was* (V) *the size of a large soup plate* (P).

The subject predicative typically characterizes the person or thing referred to by the subject. It also commonly identifies the subject or the location of the subject.

> **NOTE**
>
> Subject predicative has also been called subject complement and object predicative has also been called object complement. *Complement* has been replaced by *predicative* to avoid confusion, because *complement* has a more generalized sense. *Predicative* has been traditionally used for predicative adjectives and predicative nouns (or nominals) when these are functioning to complement a copular verb.

Copular verbs can refer to a current situation, e.g. *be*, or to a changed situation, e.g. *become*. Contrast:

[6]   The disastrous consequences *are* obvious.

[6a]   The disastrous consequences *became* obvious.

Here are examples of subject predicatives with the copular verb *be*:

[7]   My name is *Amanda* (P)

[8]   Yes you were *in Brunei* (P) that year

[9]   I remember I wasn't *there* (P)

[10]   'We have no useful information on whether users are *at risk* (P),' said James A. Talcott of Boston's Dana-Farber Cancer Institute. [*Wall Street Journal*]

[11]   Big mainframe computers for business had been *around* (P) for years. [W]

[12]   Some of his observations about Japanese management style are *on the mark* (P). [W]

Copular verbs other than *be* or *become* can be replaced by *be* or *become*, though the other verbs may contribute an additional element of meaning.

[13]   The Third World (3W) constitutes *most of Asia (excepting Japan) Africa and Latin America* (P) [W]

[14]   Neither we nor, almost certainly, President Bush and Mr Major know how much of Iraq's armoury remains *intact* (P) [W]

[15]   It seems *a pity* (P) to waste it on an unappreciative audience. [W]

[16]   The recent explosion of country funds mirrors the 'closed-end fund mania' of the 1920s, Mr. Foot says, when narrowly focused funds grew *wildly popular* (P). [*Wall Street Journal*]

Copular verbs often take an **adjective phrase** as their complement; for example:

[17]   It just sounds *a little affected* (P)

[18]   I feel *so self-conscious* (P) in high heels

[19]   I mean the audience used to go *mad* (P) as soon as he came on

[20]   And of course I always wax *poetic* (P) about it to you

[21]   They the owners were demanding payment of instalments as they fell *due* (P) or became *due* (P) up to the date of the award

The subject predicative is characterized in these ways:

3.6.1 **Position of subject predicative**

The subject predicative comes after the verb, as in all the above examples.

3.6.2 **Absence of passivization with subject predicative**

The subject predicative cannot become the passive subject of the sentence, unlike the direct and indirect objects, since the distinction between active and passive applies only to sentences with transitive verbs. If the copular verb is *be* and if the subject predicative identifies the subject, the subject and subject predicative can change places:

[22] *The president* (S) *was* (V) *Bill Clinton* (P).

[22a] *Bill Clinton* (S) *was* (V) *the president* (P).

3.6.3 **Pronoun as subject predicative**

If the subject predicative is a pronoun with distinctive subjective and objective forms, we have a choice. The subjective form tends to occur in formal style:

[23] It is *I* (P). [formal]

[23a] It's *me* (P).

3.7 Object predicative

BASIC STRUCTURES: RECAPITULATION

We have seen four basic structures: SV, SVO, SVOO, and SVP:

[1] My glasses (S) have disappeared (V).

[2] Our country (S) is absorbing (V) many refugees (O).

[3] I (S) am sending (V) you (O) an official letter of complaint (O).

[4] The water-bed (S) was (V) very comfortable (P)

In [1] the main verb is intransitive, in [2] and [3] transitive (in [2] monotransitive and in [3] ditransitive), and in [4] it is copular.

The fifth basic structure contains a transitive verb with two complements: a direct object (O) and an object predicative (P), normally in that order (cf. 3.10.8):

[5] *I* (S) *have made* (V) *my position* (O) *clear* (P).

A verb that has a direct object and an object predicative is a **complex-transitive** verb. Both complex-transitive verbs and ditransitive verbs have two complements.

COMPLEX-TRANSITIVE VERBS IN DETAIL

There are two important ways in which the complements of complex-transitive verbs differ from those of ditransitive verbs.

1. There is a predicative relationship between the direct object and the object predicative. The relationship is analogous to that between the subject and the subject predicative. Thus, for **[5]** the relationship is shown when we introduce a copular verb between the direct object and the object predicative **[5a]**, and similarly for **[6]** and **[6a]**:

[5a] My position (S) became (V) clear (P).

[6] They (S) called (V) it (O) freelance teaching (P).

[6a] It (S) was (V) freelance teaching (P).

2. Only the direct object in an SVOP structure can be made the subject of a passive sentence:

[5] I (S) have made (V) my position (O) clear (P).

[5b] My position (S) has been made (V) clear (P).

Since the object predicative is not an object, it cannot be made a passive subject. In contrast, both complements in an SVOO structure—the indirect object and the direct object—can be made passive subjects:

[3] I (S) am sending (V) you (O) an official letter of complaint (O).

[3a] You (S) are being sent (V) an official letter of complaint (O).

[3b] An official letter of complaint (S) is being sent (V) you (O).

Here are some further examples of the SVOP structure:

[7] But state courts upheld a challenge by consumer groups to the commission's rate increase and found *the rates* (O) *illegal* (P). [W]

[8] The department placed *a moratorium* (O) *on the research* (P), pending a review of scientific, legal and ethical issues. [W]

[9] They call *it* (O) '*photographic*' (P). [W]

[10] Many felt Hearst kept *the paper* (O) *alive* (P) as long as it did, if marginally, because of its place in family history. [W]

[11] She found *him* (O) *really frustrating* (P) because he didn't seem bothered

[12] You're driving *independents* (O) *out of business* (P)

[13] Police and customs kept *the Defiant* (O) *under observations* (P)

[14] The German press dubbed *him* (O) *honest John* (P) today

[15] The allies' ability to attack powerfully and accurately at night caught *the Iraqis* (O) *at a disadvantage* (P)

[16] He still thought *a leadership challenge* (O) *unlikely* (P)

If the object predicative is a prepositional phrase, it may not be possible to make a simple paraphrase of the relationship between the direct object and the predicative. The paraphrase, however, can be established by omitting the preposition **[17]**–**[18]** or replacing it by another preposition **[19]**:

[17] I first got *a millionaire* (O) *for my neighbour* (P) at twenty-four twenty-five years old ('A millionaire is my neighbour')

[18] Maybe I'll just treat *it* (O) *as a work of art* (P) ('It is a work of art')

[19] The French initiative threw *the United Nations Security Council* (O) *into confusion* (P) ('The United Nations Security Council is in confusion')

3.8 Complements and adverbials

We have so far encountered five basic structures: SV, SVO, SVOO, SVP, SVOP. The constant constituents are the subject and the verb. The other constituents are the complements of the verb: direct object, indirect object, subject predicative, and object predicative. Complements of the verb can be clauses as well as phrases (cf. 14.7).

The basic structures can be expanded by **adverbials**, which are optional constituents of the sentence. They are not complements, because their occurrence is not dependent on the main verb in the sentence. They are optional in the sense that the sentence remains well-formed when they are omitted. However, they usually provide information that is important in the context, and in that sense they cannot be omitted without damaging the communication. Here are some examples of adverbials (A) that show their informational value. The examples also illustrate the possibility for more than one adverbial to occur in a sentence.

[1]   It was quite a nice do *otherwise* (A)

[2]   I met a girl *on the train* (A) *today* (A)

[3]   *In the summer* (A) you can take a car and four people *for a hundred and twenty pounds* (A)

[4]   You need a lot of strength *in the right hand* (A)

[5]   *Well* (A) *presumably* (A) she called him

Adverbials are usually adverbs (e.g. *presumably* in **[5]**), prepositional phrases (e.g. *on the train* in **[2]**), or clauses (cf. 6.13f.). They may also be noun phrases:

[6]   I had a really good supper *last night* (A)

[7]   Give me a warning *next time* (A)

[8]   In the 'good old days' our great-great-grandmothers walked *several miles* (A) to the village [W]

[9]   Oh Cath was in *this afternoon* (A)

Some constituents resemble adverbials semantically but nevertheless are complements, since they are obligatory and are dependent on the main verb: these are predicatives (P). For example, *last night* in **[10]** is required to complete the sentence, unlike *last night* in **[6]**:

[10]   *Our committee meeting* (S) *was* (V) *last night* (P).

In **[10]**, the subject predicative completes a sentence beginning with a subject and a verb. The basic structure of the sentence is SVP. Similarly, in **[11]** the object predicative is an adverb:

[11]   Yeah you put *it* (O) *here* (P)

Elsewhere *here* may be an adverbial, but in **[11]** it is an object predicative that is required to complete the sentence. The basic structure of **[11]** is SVOP.

BASIC STRUCTURES: SUMMARY

The five basic structures are listed below in full:

SV	Subject + Verb
SVO	Subject + Verb + Direct or Indirect Object
SVOO	Subject + Verb + Indirect Object + Direct Object

> SVP   Subject + Verb + Subject Predicative
> SVOP   Subject + Verb + Direct Object + Object Predicative
>
> Here are examples of the five structures:
> **[12]** My glasses (S) have disappeared (V).
> **[13]** Our country (S) is absorbing (V) many refugees (O).
> **[14]** I (S) am sending (V) you (O) an official letter of complaint (O).
> **[15]** The water-bed (S) was (V) very comfortable (P).
> **[16]** I (S) have made (V) my position (O) clear (P).

There is one further element that is optionally added to the basic structure—the **vocative** (cf. 10.15):

[17] *Robin* what do you think

Agreement between the subject and verb in number and person is discussed in 10.14.

3.9 Semantic roles

Sentences—and the clauses within them—are used to describe situations. Each constituent of a sentence or clause plays a role in the description. It is not clear how many roles should be distinguished, nor is there space to discuss the roles in detail, but some indication is here given of the major roles that have been identified and of the verb types that are typically involved.

3.9.1 Roles of the subject

3.9.1.1 Agentive role
If the verb is transitive or intransitive the subject typically has the **agentive** role, referring to the doer of an action:

[1] Will *anyone* (S) congratulate me on my cooking
[2] *You* (S) picked her up
[3] Does *she* (S) play tennis

3.9.1.2 Identified and characterized role
If the verb is copular, the subject typically has the **identified** role (referring to someone or something identified through the subject predicative) **[4]**–**[5]** or it has the **characterized** role (referring to someone or something characterized by the subject predicative) **[6]**–**[7]**:

[4] *This* (S) is my daughter Felicity
[5] *The difficulty* (S) is the travel
[6] So *this one* (S) was … lower middle-class in that case
[7] *You* (S) 're not a neurotic wreck on the other hand uhm

3.9.1.3 **Experiencer role**
If the verb is transitive, the subject may have the **experiencer** role, referring to someone who has experienced a sensation, an emotion, or cognition:

[8] As he climbed *he* (S) smelled roasting lamb on the damp wind and heard harsh shouts above the cries of children. [Mary Wesley *A Sensible Life*]

[9] *I* (S) find him quite appealing

[10] Uhm … have *you* (S) considered until now the effects that having an absent father may have had on your childhood

3.9.1.4 **Affected role**
If the verb is intransitive, the subject may have the **affected** role, referring to the person or thing directly affected by the action:

[11] In the past few years *many dolphins* (S) have drowned in fishing nets. [*BBC Wildlife*]

[12] He clutched at it and *his trousers* (S) slipped onto his hips. [Ian Enters *Up to Scratch*]

The passive subject typically has the affected role:

[13] *My D H Lawrence* (S) was swept away

[14] *Some* (S) were drafted into the army if they were suitable for that

3.9.1.5 **Eventive role**
The subject sometimes has the eventive role, referring to an event:

[15] *The last meeting* (S) was in the European championship in nineteen eighty-eight

[16] *The crash of Polly Peck* (S) is the biggest in British corporate history, but only in nominal terms. [*Sunday Times*]

3.9.1.6 **No role: use of prop *it***
English grammar requires that a sentence or clause have a subject, though it may be absent in imperatives (cf. 2.7) or it may be **ellipted** (cf. 3.11). If there is no role to be assigned to the subject, *it* is added to serve as subject. This **prop** *it*, supporting the subject function, is used in particular with time and weather expressions (cf. 6.7.4):

[17] *It* (S)'s a bit late now

[18] But unfortunately both Saturday and Sunday *it* (S) was really foggy

---

3.9.2 **Roles of the direct object**

3.9.2.1 **Affected role**
The direct object typically has the affected role, noted above for the subject:

[19] And someone came and locked *the gate* (O) after us

[20] Now put *him* (O) outside nicely … and then brush *him* (O) out

3.9.2.2 **Eventive role**
Like the subject, it may have the eventive role. Typically, the noun in the object is derived from a verb and carries the main meaning, while the verb has a general meaning (e.g. *do, have, make, take*).

[21] He had *a stroke* (O), didn't he

[22] We did *some good praying* (O)

[23] I made *a note* (O) at the time and afterwards

[24] From the start our College took *a conscious decision that it would not resort to compulsory redundancies.* [W]

3.9.2.3 **Resultant role**

The direct object sometimes has the **resultant** role, referring to something that comes into existence as a result of the action of the verb:

[25] Well ... uhm ... I wrote *my thesis* (O) in such a way that it's ... considerably more accessible than most people's

[26] So they built themselves *a magnificent amphitheatre for popular sporting activities*

3.9.3 **Roles of the indirect object**

The indirect object typically has the roles of **recipient [27]** or **beneficiary [28]**:

[27] That reminds us Tom hasn't paid *us* (O) yet ('Tom hasn't paid money *to us*')

[28] The people we were staying with they ... uh cooked *us* (O) a traditional Normandy dinner (O) ('They cooked a traditional Normandy dinner *for us*')

In **[28]** *us* is the indirect object and *a traditional Normandy dinner* is the direct object. Where the indirect object comes before an eventive direct object, it is likely to have the affected role (cf. **[21]–[24]** above):

[29] Stephen straightened unsteadily and gave *him* (O) *a push.* [W] ('Stephen pushed *him*')

[30] Give *me* (O) *a fright* (O) ('Frighten *me*')

3.9.4 **Roles of the predicative**

3.9.4.1 **Characterizing role**

Predicatives typically characterize the subject **[31]–[32]** or object **[33]–[34]**:

[31] I was *lucky* (P)

[32] That was *a bit sad* (P)

[33] I find *it* (O) *fascinating* (P)

[34] The iron castings and the cast steel hour and declination axles were in sound condition and I considered *its restoration* (O) *a worthwhile challenge* (P) [*Journal of the British Astronomical Association*]

3.9.4.2 **Identifying role**

They may also identify the subject **[35]–[36]** or object **[37]**:

[35] He was *the first person in a wheelchair that I'd ever met* (P)

[36] It was the gauge that was *the killer* (P) in the first place

[37] The college paper published something on my work and called *it* (O) *Psychotherapy* (P)

3.9.4.3 **Locative role**

Another common role is **locative**, designating the place of the subject **[38]** or object **[39]**:

[38] This was *in America*

[39] She put *her hand* (O) *on Dee's arm* (P) [Marion Babson *Past Regret*]

3.9.5. **Roles of the verb**

The major distinction in verbs is between those that are stative and those that are dynamic.

3.9.5.1 **Stative verbs**

Stative verbs are used in referring to a state of affairs:

[40] It *is* quite popular of course
[41] It still *sounds* ridiculous
[42] And parents *have* different expectations about boys from girls
[43] Every war *possesses* a grim rhythm. [*Daily Telegraph*]
[44] He may not even have *liked* his brother [W]

3.9.5.2 **Dynamic verbs**

Dynamic verbs are used in referring to a happening:

[45] He *walked* through the town *giving* out blessings and absolution to all sinners
[46] We *discussed* extensively our needs for computing
[47] The last few days haven't been quite so hot and on Friday night it actually *rained*. [W]
[48] I *paid* it off in one large lump
[49] One eye-witness I *spoke* to said six people had *died*

3.9.5.3 **Verbs that can be either stative or dynamic**

Some verbs can be used both statively and dynamically. For example, the verb *be* is usually stative, but in **[50]** it is dynamic:

[50] I hope life is *being* kind to you and you kind to yourself. [W]

Similarly, whereas *taste* in **[51]** and **[52]** is stative, in **[53]** and **[54]** it is dynamic:

[51] He could *taste* warm blood in his mouth from the lip he had just bitten. [W]
[52] The hamburgers *taste* good.
[53] *Taste* the fish.
[54] Do you want to *taste* the soup?

3.10 Rearranging the basic structures

We have noted several instances where the basic declarative structures are rearranged: the focused element is fronted in **wh-questions** (cf. 2.5), **exclamatives** (cf. 2.8), passives (cf. 2.12), and relatives (cf. 3.4, 10.9).

There are three types of drastic rearrangement:

1. cleft sentences
2. sentences with extraposed subjects
3. existential sentences

Another kind of rearrangement involves the use of pronouns. There are two types (cf. 5.11):

4. left dislocation
5. right dislocation

There are two types of inversion, which result from the fronting of a sentence constituent:

6. subject–verb inversion
7. subject–operator inversion

And lastly

8. Exchanged positions of direct object and object predicative

3.10.1 Cleft sentences

Cleft sentences, as the term suggests, involve a split. It is the basic structure that is split. The previous sentence is itself a cleft sentence. Its basic structure is **[1]**:

[1]   *The basic structure* (S) is split.

The cleft sentence begins with *it* and a copular verb, generally *be*. The focused part comes next and then the rest of the sentence, which is introduced by a relative such as *that*, *which*, or *who*. In **[1a]** the focus is the subject of **[1]**:

[1a]   It is *the basic structure* that is split.

Here is a further example:

[2]   He felt a sharp pain *then*.

[2a]   It was *then* that he felt a sharp pain

For more on the cleft sentence, see 6.7.3 on cleft *it*.

3.10.2 Sentences with extraposed subjects

Clauses that are functioning as subject are commonly moved to the end and replaced by *it*. In **[3]** the *that*-clause is subject. In **[3a]** the clause is **extraposed** and replaced by *it*:

[3]   That anything can be proved is hardly probable.

[3a]   It is hardly probable that anything can be proved [Ian Enters *Up to Scratch*]

For more on extraposed subjects and objects, see 6.7.2 on **anticipatory *it*.**

3.10.3 Existential sentences

Existential sentences are introduced by *there*. **[4a]** shows the effect of this rearrangement on the basic structure **[4]**:

[4]   *Other telecommunications companies* are in this country.

[4a]   *There* are *other telecommunications companies* in this country

For more on existential sentences, see 6.8.

3.10.4 Left dislocation

In **left dislocation**, an introductory noun phrase is not integrated into the sentence structure and a pronoun appears in the position that the noun phrase might have occupied:

[5]   *Nuclear reactors they*'re not environmentally friendly

[6]   *My ex-boyfriend Phil he* got me interested

3.10.5 **Right dislocation**

In **right dislocation**, the noun phrase appears at the end:

[7]   *They*'ve got a pet rabbit ... *Laura and her boyfriend Simon*

[8]   *That*'s a nice area isn't it *Leatherhead*

3.10.6 **Subject–verb inversion**

Subject–verb inversion occurs in some types of sentence when a complement is fronted:

[9]   *At the back of the house* (P), overlooking the garden, *was* the large room Eleanor used as her study. [Christopher Priest *The Quiet Woman*]

[10] *Far worse* (P) *was* the spectre of youth unemployment looming on the horizon. [W]

Complements can sometimes be fronted without inversion:

[11] *A royal wedding British-style* (P), it is not [W]

[12] *Tea* (O) he makes *tea* (O) he makes *phone calls* (O) he makes gets me lollipops

Subject–verb inversion is an option, generally in fiction writing, for reporting clauses used with direct speech (cf. 15.1):

[13] 'We are not celebrating anything,' *said* the woman in the chair. [Mary Wesley *A Sensible Life*]

3.10.7 **Subject–operator inversion**

Subject–operator inversion is common in questions (cf. 2.5). Otherwise, it mainly occurs (a) when negative expressions are fronted **[14]–[15]**, (b) when the conjunctive adverbs *nor* and *neither*, and the additive adverb *so* introduce a clause **[16]–[17]**:

[14] *No more did* they speak of the importance of reducing public expenditure [W]

[15] *Never were* slaves so numerous as in Italy during the first century B.C. [P. A. Brunt *Roman Imperial Themes*]

[16] *Nor would* she mention her discovery to a soul, not even Mrs Staples. [James Lees-Milne *The Fool of Love*]

[17] Social attitudes, such as the desire for insurance in one's old age, encourage this. *So too does* the teaching of the dominant Catholic Church. [Peter Calvert and Susan Calvert *Latin America in the Twentieth Century*]

3.10.8 **Exchanged positions of direct object and object predicative**

The direct object may follow the object predicative if the object is long, so that the SVOP structure changes to a SVPO order:

[18] Let me first *make clear* (P) ... *certain important points on which I have ... no disagreement ... with my right honourable friend* (O)

On the postponement of the **postmodification** in a noun phrase, see 10.7.

3.11 Ellipsis

Ellipsis is the omission of part of the structure of a sentence. We can interpret the sentence despite the omission because we know what has been ellipted either from the situational context or from the textual context, though in some cases the distinction between these two sources may be blurred.

3.11.1 Situational ellipsis

Situational ellipsis is typical of conversation, but it also occurs in informal writing or in written dialogue. Here are some examples, with the position of the ellipsis indicated by a caret:

[1]   A: They can't uh … keep tracks on everybody
      B: ^ Shouldn't think so

[2]   Oh we'll find something I mean a quid ^ Doesn't matter if it's really crap,… ^ Haven't wasted much cash

[3]   What do you think anamnesis means ^ Got any idea

[4]   ^ Just spoken to you on the phone and heard your news [W]

[5]   ^ Really looking forward to seeing you my dear [W]

[6]   How are you? ^ Looking forward to your move to Cambridge? [W]

The first three examples come from conversations and the last three from social letters. The situational context as a whole (including the structure and content of the sentences) provides the clues to the interpretation of the ellipsis. All six sentences have deficiencies in their structure because of the ellipsis. In [1] and [2], subjects are missing; in [3]–[6] both subjects and auxiliaries are missing. Yet the sentences are quite normal and are easily understood.

3.11.2 Textual ellipsis

In **textual ellipsis**, the interpretation is crucially dependent on the words that precede or follow the ellipsis.

In [7] the interpretation depends on what comes beforehand:

[7]   A: I'd just wondered if you'd seen it
      B: Yes I have ^

We understand B's response as 'Yes I have seen it'. The **antecedent** of the ellipsis—the part of the linguistic context that determines the interpretation—is 'you'd seen it' in A's query.

3.11.2.1 Anaphoric ellipsis

When the antecedent comes before the ellipsis, the ellipsis is **anaphoric**. Here are other examples of anaphoric ellipsis:

[8]   A: Didn't there used to be deer in Richmond Park
      B: Yeah there still are ^
      A: Are there ^

[9]   A: But I'll have to drive
      B: How far ^
      A: ^ About three miles probably

[10] A: We found the tiles ...
      B: What tiles ^

[11] A: When's your Mum coming back
      B: Uh, ^ Friday I think
      A: Uh huh ...
      B: ^ Friday very early morning

[12] Luke offers the excuse that they're worn out by grief Matthew and Mark don't ^

[13] A: I've never had one
      B: Who you ^ Nor've I ^

[14] Uh it may well be there's been a change in policy I think if there has ^ he owes to the House to make that clear

[15] A strange silence fell on the house and suddenly there was a big space and you weren't here and weren't going to be ^. [W]

One conspicuous though relatively infrequent kind of anaphoric ellipsis is **gapping**, where the verb is ellipted in coordinated clauses:

[16] All schools in the state system are being given budgetary freedom and their boards of governors ^ strengthened powers so that they can encourage the best and respond to local circumstances

3.11.2.2 **Cataphoric ellipsis**

In **cataphoric** ellipsis, the antecedent comes after the ellipsis, so that the interpretation is held in suspense until the antecedent is reached:

[17] If you don't want to ^, I'll prepare lunch.

[18] When they can ^, they will show us around.

Chapter 4
Phrases and Words

Summary

There are five types of phrase: noun phrases, verb phrases, adjective phrases, adverb phrases, prepositional phrases. The major division in word classes (or parts of speech) is into open classes (nouns, verbs, adjectives, adverbs) and closed classes (such as pronouns and auxiliaries). The open classes readily admit new words and therefore most words belong to the open classes.

Seven grammatical categories apply to verbs (main verbs and auxiliaries), affecting the forms that verbs can have: mood (indicative, imperative, subjunctive), modality (modal auxiliaries), tense (present, past), aspect (perfect, progressive), voice (active, passive), number (singular, plural), person (first, second, third).

Two categories apply to nouns: number (singular, plural) and case (common, genitive). Four categories apply to pronouns: number (singular, plural), person (first, second, third), case (subjective, objective, genitive), gender (masculine, feminine, non-personal).

The semantic category of comparison applies to adjectives and adverbs that are gradable. These may have inflections for comparatives (e.g. *taller*) and superlatives (e.g. *tallest*) or periphrastic forms (e.g. *more wealthy, most wealthy*).

Phrases may be linked by coordination or apposition.

4.1 Phrase types and word classes

4.1.1 **Phrase types**

There are five types of phrase, named after the head of the phrase:

1. noun phrase — *a weak government* (head: noun *government*)
2. verb phrase — *may have succeeded* (head: verb *succeeded*)
3. adjective phrase — *far more enjoyable* (head: adjective *enjoyable*)
4. adverb phrase — *too noisily* (head: adverb *noisily*)
5. prepositional phrase — *in a wine bar* (head: preposition *in*)

Chapters 10, 11, and 12 are devoted to phrases.

4.1.2 **Word classes**

Word classes, such as noun and verb, are traditionally called **parts of speech**. We can divide word classes into open classes and closed classes. **Open** classes readily admit new words, and therefore they contain most words in the language. **Closed** classes, on the other hand, rarely admit new words, so that it is possible to list all the words belonging to them. For example, we can list all the pronouns. However, it is impossible to list all the nouns, not only because they are so numerous but primarily because new nouns are being created all the time. The resistance to adding words to closed classes is highlighted in the failure of attempts to introduce a new personal pronoun that is neutral between *he* and *she* (cf. 1.6).

4.1.2.1 **Open classes**
There are four open classes:

noun	*Texas, freezer, hygiene*
verb (or main verb)	*remember, depend, become*

| adjective | *personal, afraid, mere* |
| adverb | *lavishly, luckily, consequently* |

4.1.2.2 Closed classes

Chapters 5–9, which deal in greater depth with word classes, recognize seven closed classes and distinguish their subclasses:

auxiliary (or auxiliary verb)	*will, have, be*
conjunction	*and, if, although*
preposition	*of, by, into*
determiner	*the, no, some*
pronoun	*she, none, some*
numeral	*five, twentieth, one-sixth*
interjection	*oh, ouch, wow*

In this chapter we will be looking just at auxiliaries and pronouns.

4.2 Verbs

Seven categories apply to verbs (main verbs and auxiliaries), affecting the forms that verbs take:

1. mood
2. modality
3. tense
4. aspect
5. voice
6. number
7. person

Verbs that function as operators (cf. 11.2) may be **contracted** and attached as **enclitics** to preceding words (e.g. *'s* from *is*, *'ll* from *will*) and they may have negative forms in which *n't* is attached or fused with them (e.g. *isn't, won't*).

4.2.1 Mood

Mood relates the action of the verb to conditions such as certainty, obligation, and possibility. Three **moods** are distinguished for English: indicative, imperative, and subjunctive. The **indicative** mood applies to most verbs used in declaratives, and to verbs used in interrogatives and exclamatives. **Imperatives** (cf. 2.7) and present **subjunctives** (cf. 11.9f.) have the same uninflected form of the verb, and the past subjunctive is confined to *were*. Here are examples of the three moods:

4.2.1.1 Indicative

[1]   Envy *is* deep and agonizing.

[2]   *Could* that be a joke?

[3]   How preposterous the poem *seemed*!

4.2.1.2 Imperative

[4]   *Pay* me next time.

4.2.1.3 **Subjunctive**

[5]   God *help* America

[6]   So *be* it!

[7]   If I *were* you, I would complain.

[8]   We insisted that she *be* in charge.

[9]   It is important that he *sign* the petition.

4.2.2 **Modality**

Modality, which is sometimes used to include mood, is a semantic category that deals with two types of judgement:

(1) those referring to the factuality of what is said (its certainty, probability, or possibility)

(2) those referring to human control over the situation (ability, permission, intention, obligation).

4.2.2.1 **Modality and modal auxiliaries**
These judgements are grammaticalized through the modal auxiliaries and marginal auxiliaries: *can, could, may, might, shall, should, will, would, must, ought to* (cf. 11.8). The same auxiliaries are used for the two types of judgements. Here are some examples:

[10]   This *may* come as a surprise to those who associate organic food with vegetarianism. [W] [possibility]

[11]   In the meanwhile, *may* I just confirm a few administrative details. [W] [permission]

[12]   You *must* have been a very fast driver [certainty]

[13]   I *must* remember to put that away [obligation]

[14]   There is still a long way to go before it *can* be said that the ethnic minorities are adequately represented in the membership of the police [possibility]

[15]   Not everybody has the time to foster but everyone *can* help [ability]

[16]   I was woken first by another relation who sounded like Pam's Mum and just kept saying '*Can* I speak to Pamela?' [W] [permission]

4.2.2.2 **Modality and other word classes**
Modality can also be expressed by means other than auxiliaries: nouns **[17]**, main verbs **[18]**, adjectives **[19]**, and adverbs **[20]**:

[17]   There may be cars passing you from behind … and the *possibility* of pedestrians too

[18]   Were this a Yoshizawa book, the designs would be yet more beautiful, but western writers are not usually *permitted* to publish the very best of his work. [Paul Jackson *Classic Origami*]

[19]   If it continues I'll be *able* to have my first shorts and burgers Bar-B-Q on my balcony in no time at all. [W]

[20]   Because they were giving away free wine it *probably* went on for a reasonable length of time

4.2.3 **Tense**

Tense is a grammatical category relating to the time at which the action of the verb is viewed as occurring. English has two tense categories indicated by the form of the verb: **present** and **past**. The tense distinction is made on the first or only verb in the verb phrase:

Present   *speaks, is* speaking, *has* been speaking
Past   *spoke, was* speaking, *had* been speaking

We also use auxiliaries for distinctions in time; for example, *will* and *be going to* (*I am going to write to you soon*) refer to future time. On tense, see 11.4–7.

4.2.4 Aspect

Aspect is a grammatical category referring to the way that the action expressed by the verb is viewed by the speaker or writer (e.g. as completed or in progress). English has two aspects: **perfect** and **progressive** (cf. 11.11–16). Aspect is indicated by a combination of an auxiliary and a following verb form. The perfect aspect requires the perfect auxiliary *have* and a following *-ed* **participle** (also called the **past participle** or the **perfect participle**):

| *has* called | may *have* called | could *have* been called |
| *had* written | will *have* written | should *have* been written |

The progressive (or continuous) aspect requires the progressive auxiliary *be* and a following *-ing* **participle** (also called the **present participle**):

| *is* calling | may *be* calling | *is* being called |
| *was* writing | will *be* writing | *was* being written |

A common use of the present perfect is to refer to a situation beginning in past time and extending to the present:

[21] They are gathered in a building which ... stands on a site where there *has been* worship for perhaps fifteen hundred years

The past perfect refers to a situation that precedes another past situation:

[22] He didn't know if Sally *had heard* him or not, but she went over to Anne and Tommy and encircled them with her arms. [Steve Harris *Adventureland*]

A common use of the progressive is to view the situation as in progress:

[23] A couple of months ago we reported how medical ethics *is being taught* at St Mary's Hospital Medical School in London

[24] The whole system makes it difficult to offer any assessment of what *is going* on in the Soviet economy

4.2.5 Voice

The grammatical category of **voice** distinguishes **active**, the basic type, from **passive**. The distinction, discussed earlier (cf. 2.12), affects other parts of the sentence as well as the verb. The passive requires the passive auxiliary *be* (or, less frequently, *get*) and a following *-ed* participle (also called the **passive participle**):

| *is* called | may *be* called | has *been* called |
| *was* written | will *be* written | had *been* written |

4.2.6–7 Number and person

For all verbs except *be* (whether *be* is a main verb or an auxiliary), **number** and **person** are categories that affect only the present tense. The *-s* form is used for the **third person singular** and the **base** or uninflected form is used for the rest:

[25] My children *write* letters home every day.

[26] My daughter *writes* to me regularly.

The base form *write* is used whether the subject is a plural noun phrase such as *my children* or one of the personal pronouns *I, we, you,* or *they.* The -*s* form *writes* is used when the subject is a singular noun phrase such as *my daughter* or one of the personal pronouns *he, she,* or *it.* The verb *be* makes a further distinction in the present tense—*am* for the **first person singular**:

am	1st person singular
is	3rd person singular
are	others

Be also has two forms in the past:

was	1st and 3rd person singular
were	others

4.3 Nouns and pronouns

Nouns (cf. 5.3) and pronouns (cf. 6.1) share certain distinctions.

4.3.1 Nouns: number and case

Two categories apply to nouns:

1. number
2. case

4.3.1.1 Number in nouns

The category of **number** distinguishes between **singular** and **plural** nouns (cf. 5.4f.). Number contrast does not ordinarily apply to **proper nouns**, such as *Caroline* or *the Netherlands*. **Common nouns** can be either **count** (or **countable**) or **non-count** (or **uncountable** or **mass**). Count nouns have number contrast: *house/houses, nurse/nurses.* Non-count nouns generally do not have a plural form: *wine, information;* but many of them are occasionally converted into count nouns to refer to kinds or quantities: *French wines, two teas* ('two cups of tea').

4.3.1.2 Case in nouns

Case is a grammatical category that distinguishes differences in grammatical function. Present-day English has only two cases for nouns: the **common** case and the **genitive** (or **possessive**) case (cf. 5.10). In irregular nouns such as *woman,* the combination of case with number yields four forms of the noun:

common singular	woman	the *woman* next door
genitive singular	woman's	the *woman's* husband
common plural	women	all the *women* in the family
genitive plural	women's	the *women's* grievances

Regular nouns make the four-way distinction only in writing:

common singular	nurse	the *nurse* in charge of the ward
genitive singular	nurse's	the *nurse's* patients

| common plural | nurses | the *nurses* in the hospital |
| genitive plural | nurses' | the *nurses'* pay |

In speech, the distinction is apparent only between *nurse* and the other three, since *nurse's*, *nurses*, and *nurses'* are pronounced identically.

4.3.2 Pronouns

Four categories apply to pronouns:

1. number
2. person
3. case
4. gender

4.3.2.1 Demonstratives
The demonstratives (cf. 6.14) have only a distinction in number:

singular *this, that*   plural *these, those*

4.3.2.2 Personal pronouns
All personal pronouns (cf. 6.3f.) have distinctions in person: first, second, and third. Most also have distinctions in number (singular and plural) and in case (subjective, objective, and genitive). The third person singular also has distinctions in **gender**: masculine, feminine, non-personal. Broadly speaking, the **subjective** case is used when the pronoun functions as the subject, and the **objective** case is used otherwise (but cf. 3.6). In general, *he* refers to males, *she* to females, and *it* to all else.

> **NOTE**
>
> It has been argued that gender as a grammatical category does not exist in English, since the only candidates for gender distinctions are a few pronouns, and their choice is overwhelmingly determined by sex reference, whereas choices in grammatical gender are determined by agreement with words according to their subclass (e.g. the noun agreeing with an adjective or verb). The choice of reflexive pronoun in the following two sentences depends on extralinguistic information, not on agreement with the noun *friend*:
>
> Your friend is washing herself.
> Your friend is washing himself.

She and (less commonly) *he* are occasionally used to refer to inanimate objects such as cars, boats, and computers. *It* is used for babies and animals where the sex is unknown or disregarded.

1st person	singular *I, me, my* plural *we, us, our*
2nd person	*you, your*
3rd person	masculine singular *he, him, his*
	feminine singular *she, her*
	non-personal *it, its*
	plural *they, them, their*

You may be singular or plural, and subjective or objective. *Her* may be either objective or genitive, and *it* may be either subjective or objective.

4.3.2.3 **Possessive pronouns**

The genitives of the personal pronouns are also called **possessive pronouns** (cf. 6.3f.). There is generally a distinction in form between those that are dependent on a noun and those that can function independently. The contrast between the **dependent** and the **independent** possessives is illustrated by the difference between dependent *my* in *my book* and independent *mine* in *That book is mine.* Here is the full set of contrasts:

1st person	*my, mine; our, ours*
2nd person	*your, yours*
3rd person	*his, her, hers; its; their, theirs*

There is no contrast between dependent and independent in the third person singular masculine *his* and the non-personal *its*. The independent function is rare for *its*.

4.3.2.4 **Reflexive pronouns**

Reflexive pronouns (cf. 6.3f.) generally parallel the personal pronouns in person and number:

1st person	*myself, ourselves*
2nd person	*yourself, yourselves*
3rd person	*himself, herself, itself, themselves*

However, unlike the personal and possessive pronouns, the reflexives make a distinction in number in the second person: singular *yourself,* plural *yourselves.*

4.3.2.5 **Relative pronouns**

The ***wh*-relative pronouns** (cf. 6.12) display distinctions in gender and case. The gender contrast is between **personal** *who* or *whom* and **non-personal** *which*:

> *the friends who give me advice*
> *the book which I have just read*

The case contrast applies only to subjective *who* and objective *whom*, though *whom* tends to be restricted to formal style:

> *the teacher who taught me English*
> *the teacher whom* (or *who*) *you met*

Relative *that* does not have distinctions in gender or case:

> *the friends that give me advice*
> *the book that I have just read*

Genitive *whose* is mainly used for personal reference, but it is also sometimes used for non-personal reference:

> *the friend whose daughter you know*
> *the house whose owners you know*

4.3.2.6 **Interrogative pronouns**

The personal **interrogatives** *who, whom,* and *whose* (cf. 6.12) also display distinctions in case:

> *Who taught you English?*
> *Who* (or *whom*) *did you interview?*
> *Whose is that book?*

4.4 Adjectives and adverbs

The semantic category of **comparison** applies to adjectives and adverbs that are gradable (cf. 8.4). They are **gradable** when we can view them as on a scale; for example, for the adjective *cold*: *a bit cold, somewhat cold, rather cold, very cold, extremely cold*. We can also express comparisons for gradable adjectives or adverbs: *as cold (as), less cold (than), more cold (than), (the) most cold*.

Comparison is a grammatical category that can be expressed by inflections in many gradable adjectives and in a few gradable adverbs. The inflectional forms end (usually) in *-er* and *-est*:

absolute	comparative	superlative
tall	*taller*	*tallest*
wealthy	*wealthier*	*wealthiest*

Comparatives are required in standard English for a comparison in which one member (or more) of a set is contrasted with one or more other members (*Sam and Pete are taller than Joe and Richard*) and superlatives for a comparison in which one member (or subset of members) is contrasted with the set to which it belongs (*Sam and Pete are the tallest in the family*).

COMPARISON: INFLECTIONAL AND PERIPHRASTIC FORMS

The inflectional comparatives and superlatives are used with monosyllabic words, such as *tall* and *young*, and some disyllabic words, such as *wealthy* and *clever*. Monosyllabic words generally take the inflectional forms, disyllabic words take either the inflectional forms or the periphrastic forms with *more* and *most* (*more wealthy, most wealthy*), and longer words take only the periphrastic forms (*more beautiful, most beautiful*). Adverbs that have the same forms as adjectives can also take inflectional forms: (work) *harder*, (work) *hardest*. A few common adjectives and adverbs have irregular forms:

good, better, best
badly, worse, worst

4.5 Coordination and apposition

4.5.1 Coordination

Coordination links items of equivalent grammatical status. In chapter 2 (cf. 2.3) we saw an example of coordination of clauses in a compound sentence:

[1] It has only been a week *and* I feel lonesome without you. [W]

The two clauses of **[1]** have equivalent grammatical status since each can stand alone as an independent sentence (cf. 13.2–8):

[1a] It has only been a week. I feel lonesome without you.

Phrases, including just the headwords, can also be coordinated. (For coordination of noun phrases, see 10.12f.) As with coordination of clauses, the central **coordinators** are *and, or,* and *but* (cf. 9.1.1), though only *and* and *or* can link more than two units:

[2] They've sort of got rice *and* carrots *and* things in there

[3] They work out a sum that they think is reasonable for you to pay back every week *or* every month

[4] When did you last have your teeth seen *and* cleaned

[5] It's turned upside down *and* back to front

[6] I knew that the fault lay not with our young people *but* the quality and type of education they had received. [Lord Young *The Enterprise Years*]

Units may be coordinated without a coordinator being present. In [7] *dingy* and *stagnant* are considered to be coordinated because the coordinator *and* is implied:

[7] They only thrive in *dingy* ... *stagnant* areas where the oxygen levels are fairly low

Coordination with a coordinator is **syndetic** coordination, coordination without a coordinator is **asyndetic** coordination.

The coordinated phrases must be identical in function, but they need not be identical in type of phrase. In [8] *themselves to themselves* (noun phrase plus prepositional phrase) is coordinated with *well away from the roads* (adverb phrase plus prepositional phrase); both are subject predicatives (cf. 3.6):

[8] They tend to keep themselves to themselves *and* well away from the roads

4.5.2 **Apposition**

Apposition (cf. 10.11) is similar to coordination in that it links items of equivalent grammatical status. The difference between them is that the linked **appositives** are identical in their reference (refer to the same person or same thing) or they overlap in their reference (one appositive included in the reference of the other). Typically, the units in apposition are noun phrases. Here are some examples:

[9] But in fact uhm most of us know it's really a version of *that huge robust plant the acanthus* ... which many of you may have in your gardens

[10] For the average property, the cistern should have a capacity of *230 litres (50 gallons)*. [W]

[11] Inside was *the engine his engine*. [E.V. Thompson *Lottie Trago*]

[12] *My sister Mary Jane* squeezed in beside me at the rail. [Agnes Owens 'Patience' in Alison Fell *The Seven Cardinal Virtues*]

Appositives may be linked by the coordinators *and* or (more usually) *or*:

[13] The single layer net can be seen as a crude emulation of a *neural cell, or neuron*, in the brain. [*British Telecom Journal*]

This is coordinative apposition, since *neural cell* and *neuron* refer to the same thing.

Part 3
Word Classes

Chapter 5
Nouns

Summary

Summary

Word classes (or parts of speech) are either open or closed. Open classes are by far the largest because they readily admit new words. The open classes are noun, verb, adjective, and adverb. The closed classes are auxiliary, conjunction, preposition, determiner, pronoun, numeral, and interjection. Many words belong to more than one class.

Word classes are established on the basis of three types of criteria: notional (meanings), morphological (forms), and grammatical (relations with other words and larger units).

Nouns by themselves or with determiners and modifiers typically function as subject and direct object. Nouns are either common or proper, count (having both singular and plural forms) or non-count. They may be in the common case or the genitive case, for which there is a corresponding *of*-phrase. Gender differences (masculine, feminine, non-personal) are signalled only through some associated pronouns.

5.1 Determination of word classes

Grammatical descriptions require reference to **word classes** (or parts of speech), such as noun and verb. Further distinctions may be made within word classes; for example, within nouns the distinction between common nouns and proper nouns. Grammarians have varied on the number of classes and subclasses. The more comprehensive and detailed their descriptions, the more classes and subclasses they require.

5.1.1 **Open and closed classes**

Word classes fall into two categories: open classes and closed classes. **Open** classes readily admit new members and therefore are by far the largest classes. There are four open classes:

> noun
> verb
> adjective
> adverb

The seven **closed** classes recognized in this grammar are:

> auxiliary
> conjunction
> preposition
> determiner
> pronoun
> numeral
> interjection

As with the open classes, the closed classes may be divided into subclasses. For example, conjunctions are subdivided into coordinators (or coordinating conjunctions) and subordinators (or subordinating conjunctions).

5.1.2 **Multiple class membership**

Items may belong to more than one class. In most instances we can only assign a word to a word class when we encounter it in context. *Looks* is a verb in 'It *looks* good', but a noun in 'She has good *looks*'; *that* is a conjunction in 'I know *that* they are abroad', but a pronoun in 'I know *that*' and a determiner in 'I know *that* man'; *one* is a generic pronoun in '*One* must be careful not to offend them', but a numeral in 'Give me *one* good reason'.

5.1.3 **Central and peripheral membership**

Some members of a class are **central** (or **prototypical**), whereas others are more **peripheral**. *Tall* is central to the class of adjectives, because it conforms to all the characteristics of adjectives; in particular it can be attributive (premodifying a noun) as in *that tall building* and predicative (functioning as subject predicative) as in *That building is tall*. *Afraid*, on the other hand, is peripheral, because it can only be predicative as in *He was afraid*.

5.1.4 **Multi-word class members**

Some members of a class consist of more than one word. *Book review* and *cable car* are **compound** nouns, *no one* and *one another* are compound pronouns, *because of* and *in spite of* are complex prepositions, *as well as* and *in order that* are complex conjunctions. Compounds may be written as orthographic words, either solid or hyphenated. The pronouns *nobody* and *yourself* are written solid (though *yourself* is separated in *your good self*), and *no one* is sometimes hyphenated as *no-one*.

5.1.5 **Lexical and grammatical words**

Roughly corresponding to the distinction between open-class and closed-class words is that between **lexical** or **content** words, on the one hand, and **grammatical** or **function** words, on the other. These terms acknowledge the importance of most of the closed-class words in the grammatical relations between words or higher units. It would be wrong, however, to think of closed-class words as lacking content. The preposition *into* contrasts with *out of* in the sentence 'He went *into* the kitchen and she went *out of* the kitchen', and the pronouns *nobody* and *everybody* are obviously different in their meaning.

5.1.6 **Anomalous words**

Some words do not fit well into any of the classes. Among them are:

5.1.6.1 The **negative particle** *not* and its contraction *n't*, which are used to form **negative** sentences (cf. 2.11);

5.1.6.2 The **infinitive particles** *to*, *so as to*, and *in order to*, which are followed by an **infinitive** verb;

5.1.6.3 The **infinitive particles** *for* and *in order for*, which introduce the subject of an **infinitive** clause (cf. 9.1):

   [1]   And I mean it's you know a bit difficult *for* people to get there

[2] *In order for* a closure to be carried ... there have to be a hundred honourable members for the closure

5.1.6.4 *With* and *without*, when they introduce the subject of a **non-finite** or **verbless** clause (cf. 9.1):

[3] I put it on *with* the zip done up

[4] You'll never get a word in *with* me talking

[5] We're riding here *with* our visors up as it was a very cold and humid day

5.1.6.5 **Existential *there*** (cf. 6.8):

[6] *There*'s a certain amount of academic snobbery attached to UNIX I always feel

5.2 Criteria for word classes

Word classes have been established on the basis of three types of criteria: notional, morphological, and grammatical.

5.2.1 Notional criteria

Notional (or **semantic**) criteria involve generalizations about the meaning of words in a class. Notional definitions have often been applied to English nouns and verbs. A common notional definition of the noun class is that nouns are names of persons, things, and places. To some extent it is a satisfactory notional definition in that many central nouns refer to persons, things, and places. But it is inadequate in that it excludes many words that we wish to place in the same class as *child*, *book*, and *city* because they behave in the same way grammatically. The notional definition of nouns excludes abstract nouns such as *action, destruction, morality, time, authorship, happiness, existence, contradiction*—to mention just a few. Verbs have been notionally defined as expressing an action or a state. The definition is undermined by the very words *action* and *state*: *action* is a noun, and so is *state* as used in the definition.

5.2.2 Morphological criteria

Morphological criteria refer to the forms of words that belong to one class. These may be **inflectional** forms of the same lexical item: plurals of nouns (*book/books, child/children*), variant forms of verbs (*steal/steals/stole/stealing/stolen*), comparatives and superlatives of adjectives (*happy/happier/happiest*). Or they may be **affixes**, usually suffixes, that identify particular classes. For example: *-ness* or *-ity* for nouns (*goodness, normality*), *-ize* or *-ify* for verbs (*specialize, dignify*), *-able* or *-less* for adjectives (*suitable, careless*), *-ly* for adverbs (*mostly*).

Morphological criteria are inadequate for differentiating word classes in English for several reasons.

First, many words are invariable in English, and do not admit inflections. This is so particularly for the closed classes.

Secondly, even with the classes that admit inflections, many words are invariable. Nouns such as *chess* and *information* do not have plural forms. Adjectives with more than two syllables (*beautiful, interesting*) do not have inflected forms, nor do many with two syllables (*famous, hopeful*). Most adverbs are not inflected for comparison. Only verbs are virtually always inflected.

> **NOTE**
>
> The exception is the main verb *beware*, which is not inflected. Among auxiliaries and semi-auxiliaries, there are no inflections for *must, ought to, had better* (or *better*), *had best* (or *best*). The uninflected *got to* (*gotta* in non-standard spelling) is an informal variant of '*s got to,* '*ve got to,* '*d got to.*

Thirdly, most words are not marked by affixes as belonging to particular classes. The forms of the words do not identify *speech* as a noun, *come* as a verb, *nice* as an adjective, or *here* as an adverb, though potentialities for inflections differentiate the first three words.

Finally, since it is often possible to convert words from one class to another, some affixes that are characteristic of a particular class remain when the words are converted to another class: the noun suffix -*tion* (*prevention, education*) remains when certain nouns are converted to verbs (*condition, proposition*); the adjectives *disposable* and *hopeful* are converted into the nouns *disposable/disposables* and *hopeful/hopefuls*. When they are in isolation, we cannot tell whether *look* and *looks* are nouns or verbs, though we know that *looked* and *looking* are verb forms.

Morphological criteria alone are generally insufficient to establish word classes or to identify the word-class membership of a word in isolation. However, in context the inflectional potential of a word is a guide to its word class, where inflectional variants are available. We know that *make* in [1] is a noun because we can add a plural inflection:

[1] How would you know what *make* it was

[1a] How would you know what *makes* they were?

And we know that *make* is a verb in [2] because we can inflect it as a verb:

[2] If you're a stone and a half it must *make* some difference.

[2a] If you're a stone and a half it must have *made* some difference.

[2b] If you're a stone and a half it must be *making* some difference.

[2c] If you're a stone and a half it *makes* some difference.

Since verbs are almost always inflected, inflectional potentiality is a useful criterion for verbs.

5.2.3 Grammatical criteria

Grammatical (or **syntactic**) criteria involve the grammatical functions of the word in its relation to other words. The criteria are invoked to establish the actual functions in context or the potential functions in isolation. As head of a noun phrase, a noun may function as subject, direct object, indirect object, etc. It may be introduced by determiners, premodified by adjectives, and postmodified by prepositional phrases and relative clauses. As head of an adjective phrase, an adjective may function as premodifier of a noun and as subject predicative and it may be premodified by adverbs. Similar criteria may be applied to all the word classes. Grammatical criteria are the most reliable criteria for establishing word classes, though peripheral members may not conform to all the criteria.

5.2.4 **Practical considerations**

In practice, morphological criteria are employed together with grammatical criteria where inflectional variants or affixal characteristics are available. Central members of the noun class can function as subject, be preceded by the determiner *the*, and take plural forms.

Notional criteria are often a useful entry to a recognition of a class, as indeed is simply a list of examples. Notional criteria are valid for establishing equivalences in word classes across unrelated languages, since morphological resemblances are likely to be absent and grammatical resemblances may sometimes be insecure.

5.3 Characteristics of nouns

5.3.1 **Functions as head of noun phrase**

As the head of a noun phrase, a noun has a range of functions (cf. 10.3). For example, the noun *teachers* is the head of the subject noun phrase of **[1]** and the noun *dinner* is the head of the object noun phrase in **[2]**:

[1]   *The teachers* aren't perhaps aware of how they can work with the disabled student

[2]   The people we were staying with they … cooked us *a traditional Normandy dinner*

5.3.2 **Determiners and modification**

Typically, nouns are introduced by a **determiner** (cf. 6.1ff.): the definite article *the* in **[1]** and the indefinite article *a* in **[2]**. They may be **premodified**: in **[2]** by the adjective *traditional* and the noun *Normandy*. They may also be **postmodified**: the relative clause *we were staying with* postmodifies *people* in **[2]** and the prepositional phrase *in the building* postmodifies *room* in **[3]**:

[3]   And they were saying wait until summer and you'll get the benefit then…because it's the coolest *room in the building*

5.3.3 **Singular and plural forms**

The typical noun has both singular and plural forms: *teacher/teachers, dinner/dinners, building/buildings*.

TYPICAL NOUN ENDINGS	
-*age*:	*postage, pilgrimage, patronage, savage, courage, beverage*
-*ation*, -*tion*, -*sion*, -*ion*:	*explanation, education, nation, division, invasion, objection*
-*er*, -*or*:	*writer, painter, player, actor, doctor*
-*ing*:	*building(s), saving(s), shaving(s), writing(s), gathering(s), wandering(s)*
-*ity*:	*reality, immunity, disparity, eternity*

-ment:	*appointment, deferment, experiment, establishment, embarrassment, ointment*
-ness:	*awkwardness, eagerness, giddiness, happiness, lawlessness, readiness*
-ist:	*atheist, soloist, apologist, biologist, capitalist, specialist, realist, dramatist*

Some of these endings were endings of the words when they were borrowed from other languages.

5.4 Proper nouns

Nouns are either common or proper.

Proper nouns name specific people, animals, institutions, places, times, etc. They have unique reference, and in writing they begin with a capital letter; *Bill Clinton, Jerusalem, Christmas, December*. Names may consist of a combination of a proper noun with other words (adjectives, common nouns, prepositional phrases), and it is usual for the initial letters of each open-class word in the name to be written in capitals, and also the definite article *the* if it is part of the name:

The Hague	*Queen Elizabeth*
The New York Times	*Scotland Yard*
Lake Michigan	*Great Britain*

Closed-class words, such as the definite article (when not part of the name) and prepositions, are generally in lower case:

the Pacific	*the United States of America*
the University of Michigan	*the King of Belgium*

Proper names are **non-count**: they have no contrast in number. Generally, they have only a singular form, but some place-names have only a plural form:

the Netherlands	*the Bahamas*
the Alps	*the Andes*
the United Nations	*the British Isles*

Proper names are treated as common nouns when they do not have unique references, though they retain capitals in writing. They can then be in the plural and take determiners that are confined to count nouns:

[1] I bet it's busy on *Sundays*

[2] I've got a lot of *Julians* in my class

[3] It's about a group of latterday *Rip Van Winkles* who in a Bronx hospital in 1969 were briefly awakened from a catatonic state in which they'd existed for 30 or even 40 years

[4] But you're *a bit of a Bertie Wooster* yourself

[5] So this is a very common sight ... on *a Saturday* at Paestum

5.5 Count and non-count nouns

Common nouns are either count (or countable) or non-count (or uncountable or mass).

5.5.1 Count nouns

Count nouns have both a singular and a plural and they can be introduced by determiners that accompany distinctions in number. For example:

$$\left.\begin{array}{l} a \\ one \\ every \\ either \\ this \end{array}\right\} picture \qquad \left.\begin{array}{l} two \\ several \\ few \\ many \\ these \end{array}\right\} pictures$$

5.5.2 Non-count nouns

Non-count nouns indicate entities that are viewed as uncountable. They are singular in form and are treated as singular for **subject–verb agreement** (cf. 10.14). They are introduced by a restricted set of determiners (cf. 6.1ff.). For example:

$$\left.\begin{array}{l} the \\ this \\ some \\ any \\ no \end{array}\right\} information \qquad \left.\begin{array}{l} my \\ whose \\ which \\ what \\ whatever \end{array}\right\} sugar$$

Like plural count nouns, non-count nouns may head a noun phrase without an overt determiner, the **zero article** (cf. 6.2):

[1] I think they're not too good on *music*

[2] She was an enthusiastic gardener, a collector of *old furniture* ('Not antiques,' Eleanor once said to her), a hoarder of books and records, photographs and silly mementoes. [Christopher Priest *The Quiet Woman*]

[3] *Honesty* is appreciated a lot

[4] You even have to pay extra if you want *bread* with your meal. [W]

5.5.3 Concrete and abstract nouns

The count/non-count distinction correlates to some extent with the distinction between concrete and abstract nouns. **Concrete** nouns are used to refer to entities that are typically perceptible and tangible, whereas **abstract** nouns refer to those that are not perceptible and tangible, such as qualities, states of mind, and events: *morality, happiness, belief, disgust, pursuit*. When concrete nouns are non-count, the entities they refer to are viewed as an undifferentiated mass: *furniture, bread, cheese, coffee, whisky*.

5.5.4 **Partitive expressions**

We can often achieve countability with non-count nouns (particularly concrete nouns) through **partitive** expressions. There are general partitive expressions, such as *a piece of*/*pieces of* and *a bit of*/*bits of*:

a piece of	bread
a bit of	sugar
some pieces of	cheese
two pieces of	information
	advice
	evidence
	news

There are also partitive expressions that tend to go only with certain non-count nouns:

> *two slices* of bread/cheese/cake/meat
> a *lump* of sugar/coal
> a *bar* of chocolate/soap/gold
> a *glass* of water/soda/whisky
> three *cups* of coffee/tea

We can also use measurements:

> *two pounds* of sugar/coffee/tea
> a *ton* of coal
> a *litre* of brandy

5.5.5 **Count/non-count nouns**

Some nouns can be either count or non-count, sometimes with a difference of meaning:

- **[5]** How would we do it if it was *paper* (non-count)
- **[6]** It's gonna be difficult cos all my *papers* are in a mess in my desk (count)
- **[7]** That's exactly what happens in our eyes and that's why the nasal retina actually sees *light*...from the lateral field (non-count)
- **[8]** At the beginning death was seen as a *light*, now he seems to be praising it as a darkness. [W] (count)
- **[9]** Do you want *cake* (non-count)
- **[10]** Mm that's a wonderful walnut *cake* (count)
- **[11]** Is that because you were having *difficulty* remembering things (non-count)
- **[12]** They might be in financial *difficulties*
- **[13]** One loses *interest* in everything when one has children (non-count)
- **[14]** I mean Thames and Hudson have expressed an *interest* and it's possible I would be able to publish something out of that but you know all that takes a very long time

5.5.6 **Concrete non-count nouns**

More generally, many concrete nouns that are normally non-count can be treated as count nouns in two uses:

5.5.6.1 When the noun refers to different kinds or qualities:

[15] I don't like *sparkling wines* all that much

[16] We bought *Italian cheeses*, fresh pasta and olives [W]

5.5.6.2 When the noun refers to quantities in a situation where the units are obvious:

[17] *One sugar* only, please.

[18] I'll have *two coffees*.

5.6 Regular plurals

5.6.1 Singular and plural

Count nouns make a distinction between singular and plural. **Singular** denotes one, and **plural** more than one:

[1] It weighs one *pound* exactly.

[1a] It weighs at least one and a half *pounds*.

In writing, the regular plural ends in -*s*:

> *cat/cats   book/books   house/houses*

5.6.2 Spelling changes

Some spelling rules affect the addition of the regular -*s* inflection:

5.6.2.1 If the singular ends in a sibilant (see 5.6.3.1) that is not followed by -*e*, add -*es*:

> *pass/passes   buzz/buzzes   bush/bushes   church/churches   box/boxes*

A few nouns ending in -*s* have a variant in which the consonant is doubled before the inflection:

> *bus/buses* or *busses   bias/biases* or *biasses   focus/focuses* or *focusses*
> *gas/gases* or *gasses*

If a sibilant is followed by -*e*, only -*s* is added:

> *cage/cages   disease/diseases   grudge/grudges*

5.6.2.2 If the singular ends in a consonant plus *y*, change the *y* to *i* and then add -*es*:

> *spy/spies   curry/curries   worry/worries*

Proper nouns are exceptions:

> *the Kennedys   Bloody Marys*

If a vowel precedes the final *y*, the plural is regular:

> *toy/toys   play/plays*

5.6.2.3 For some nouns ending in -*o*, add -*es*. Here are common examples:

> *echo/echoes   hero/heroes   potato/potatoes*
> *tomato/tomatoes   veto/vetoes*

In some instances there is variation between -*os* and -*oes*; for example:

> *cargo/cargos* or *cargoes*   *motto/mottos* or *mottoes*
> *volcano/volcanos* or *volcanoes*

5.6.3 **Pronunciation of the regular plural**

The regular -*s* plural inflection is pronounced as /ɪz/, /z/, or /s/ depending on the final sound of the singular.

5.6.3.1 /ɪz/ if the singular ends in a sibilant:

/s/	*bus/buses*	*box/boxes*
/z/	*buzz/buzzes*	
/ʃ/	*bush/bushes*	
/tʃ/	*church/churches*	
/ʒ/	*barrage/barrages*	
/dʒ/	*grudge/grudges*	

5.6.3.2 /z/ if the singular ends in a vowel or a voiced consonant other than a sibilant (/b/, /d/, /g/, /v/, /ð/, /m/, /n/, /ŋ/, /l/, or (American English) /r/):

> *ray/rays* *study/studies* *key/keys* *attitude/attitudes* *dog/dogs* *barn/barns*

5.6.3.3 /s/ if the singular ends in a voiceless consonant other than a sibilant:

> *cat/cats* *cake/cakes* *tramp/tramps* *tourist/tourists*

5.7 Irregular plurals, collective nouns, and compounds

5.7.1 **Voicing of final consonant**

Some nouns ending in -*f* or -*fe* form their plurals by changing the ending to -*ves*. They include:

calf/calves	*life/lives*
half/halves	*loaf/loaves*
knife/knives	*self/selves*
leaf/leaves	*thief/thieves*

Others have regular plurals as well:

> *dwarf/dwarves* or *dwarfs*
> *handkerchief/handkerchiefs* or *handkerchieves*
> *hoof/hooves* or *hoofs*
> *scarf/scarves* or *scarfs*
> *wharf/wharves* or *wharfs*

Some nouns ending in -*th* have the regular plural in spelling, but the pronunciation of *th* is voiced /ð/ and therefore followed by /z/. However, in most cases, the regular pronunciation /θs/ is a variant:

> *baths* *oaths* *paths* *sheaths* *truths* *wreaths* *youths*

A change of voicing also occurs from the voiceless /s/ ending in singular *house* to the voiced ending in /zɪz/ in plural *houses*.

5.7.2 Mutations

In a few nouns, the plural is formed by mutation (a change in the vowel):

man/men	*woman/women*	*tooth/teeth*
foot/feet	*goose/geese*	
mouse/mice	*louse/lice*	

Children, the plural of *child*, combines a vowel change and the irregular ending *-en* (a survival of an Old English plural inflection). A similar combination appears in *brethren*, a specialized plural of *brother*. The older plural ending is found without vowel change in *ox/oxen*. In American English there are also variant plurals of *ox*: regular *oxes* and the unchanged form *ox*.

5.7.3 Zero plurals

Count nouns that have the same form for singular and plural are said to have **zero plural**. These include the names of some animals, particularly *cod, deer, sheep*; nouns denoting quantity when they are premodified by a numeral or other quantifier and particularly when they are attached to a noun head: *two hundred (people), three dozen (plants), several thousand (dollars)*. The measure nouns *foot* (length unit), *pound* (unit of weight or of British currency), and *stone* (British weight unit) optionally take zero plurals: *six foot two, twenty pound, fifteen stone*.

5.7.4 Foreign plurals

5.7.4.1 Some nouns borrowed from other languages (in particular from Latin and Greek) may retain their foreign plurals, but generally only in technical usage. In nontechnical usage, the regular plural is normal in some of the instances listed below:

(a) nouns in *-us*, with plural in *-i*:
   alumnus/alumni   bacillus   locus   nucleus
(b) nouns in *-us*, with plural in *-a*:
   corpus/corpora   genus/genera
(c) nouns in *-a*, with plural in *-ae*:
   alga/algae   antenna   formula   vertebra
(d) nouns in *-um*, with plural in *-a*:
   addendum/addenda   bacterium   curriculum   erratum   ovum
(e) nouns in *-ex* or *-ix*, with plural in *-ices*:
   appendix/appendices   codex   index   matrix
(f) nouns in *-is*, with plural in *-es*:
   analysis/analyses   axis   basis   crisis   diagnosis   ellipsis   hypothesis   oasis   parenthesis   synopsis   thesis
(g) nouns in *-on*, with plural in *-a*:
   automaton/automata   criterion   phenomenon

(h) nouns in -*eau*, with plural in -*eaux*:
   bureau/bureaux

(i) nouns in -*o*, with plural in -*i*:
   tempo/tempi   virtuoso

NOTE

The regular plural is normal with *bureau* and other such words borrowed from French (e.g. *plateau, tableau*). Some French words ending in -*s* have the same spelling for their plural, but are pronounced regularly with /z/ (e.g. *corps, rendezvous*).

5.7.4.2 Certain nouns in -*a* are regularly treated as singular, though the ending represents an original plural: *agenda, insignia*. The use of other nouns in -*a* as singulars is controversial. They include *criteria, media, phenomena, strata*. *Media* in the sense 'mass media' is often treated as singular:

[1]   This is a call for a more mature leadership, a more mature *media* and a more mature constituency. [W]

[2]   And maybe the *media* plays a part in all this

[3]   The way-up *criteria* is a phenomenon used to establish which way the rocks were originally deposited. [W]

[4]   Many LA countries, including Brazil, Argentina and Chile, opted for import-substitution industrialization, a *phenomena* where manufactured goods are made in the country for a domestic market instead of importing them from abroad. [W]

[5]   Schmidt (1982) explained this *phenomena* by describing the motor program for walking—in animals—as being innate. [W]

Data is commonly used as a non-count noun in scientific discourse:

[6]   In this context inertia is … is a combination of how much *data* we've got and then how and how far away it is from the average

[7]   Uhm in order to contextualise what I want to say I just want to play you a little bit of *data*

[8]   Regression is commonly used by statisticians to calculate the best-fit through a set of data points in order to establish how close the *data* is to the ideal. [W]

[9]   Now the SPDIF link is a single channel, where all this *data* plus other information on subcodes, emphasis, etc, is encoded. [W]

5.7.5 Uninflected plurals, without singulars

cattle   livestock   people (as plural of *person*)
police   poultry   vermin

5.7.6 Binary plurals

Some nouns with plural inflection refer to instruments or articles of clothing that consist of two parts that are joined together. For example:

binoculars   clippers   glasses   scissors   spectacles
briefs   jeans   pants   shorts   trousers

They take a plural verb:

[10] If you need glasses because your sight has changed or because your *glasses* are worn out [W]

5.7.7 Inflected plurals, without singulars

Some nouns have the regular plural inflection but do not have a corresponding singular, at least in the relevant sense. For example:

> *arms* ('weapons')
> *clothes* ('garments')
> *customs* ('tax')
> *manners* ('behaviour')
> *premises* ('building')

5.7.8 Collective nouns

Singular **collective nouns** refer to a group of people or animals or to institutions. They may be treated as either singular or plural. They are treated as plural (more commonly in British English than in American English) when the focus is on the group as individuals rather than as a single entity. They may then take a plural verb, and plural pronouns may be co-referential with them (cf. 10.14):

[11] The Argentine *team are* in possession now inside *their* own half

Citation **[12]** illustrates a change in the treatment of the collective noun *class* from singular to plural. In the first two uses, *a class* is conceived of as an entity ('cohesive', 'which is made up of people'), whereas in the third use, *a class* refers to individuals ('who own most of the land'). There is a conspicuous switch from non-personal *which* for the singular to personal *who* for the plural:

[12] I was brought up in New Zealand and I've never forgotten how odd it seemed to me when I arrived in this country to find a society which is dominated by a ruling class *a class which is* cohesive and self-defining *a class which is* made up of people who look different often because they're actually taller and bigger and sound different because they speak in a different tone or accent who enjoy better health and longer life expectancy who live in different sorts of houses who send their children to different sorts of schools who are educated in different sorts of universities *a class who dominate* all the best jobs *who own* most of the land *control* most of the wealth *exercise* most of the power and *whose* dominant position is underpinned by a dense and complex class structure which effectively insulates *them* against challenge

SOME COMMON EXAMPLES OF COLLECTIVE NOUNS:		
administration	*enemy*	*majority*
army	*family*	*minority*
audience	*firm*	*mob*
class	*gang*	*nation*
committee	*government*	*public*
company	*group*	*swarm*
crew	*herd*	*team*
crowd	*jury*	

5.7.9 **Plurals of compounds**

Compounds generally follow the regular rule by adding the regular -s inflection to their last element:

> *gunfight/gunfights*
> *pop group/pop groups*
> *two-year-old/two-year-olds*
> *gin-and-tonic/gin-and-tonics*

Compounds ending in an adverb also generally follow the regular rule:

> *close-up/close-ups*
> *take-over/take-overs*
> *stand-in/stand-ins*

Though having the plural inflection at the end, these two break the spelling rule by retaining *y* before the inflection:

> *lay-by/lay-bys*
> *stand-by/stand-bys*

The following two compounds are exceptional in taking the inflection on the first element:

> *passer-by/passers-by*
> *listener-in/listeners-in*

A few compounds ending in -*ful* usually take the plural inflection on the last element, but have a less common plural with the inflection on the first element:

> *mouthful/mouthfuls* or *mouthsful*
> *spoonful/spoonfuls* or *spoonsful*

Compounds ending in -*in-law* allow the plural either on the first element or (informally) on the last element:

> *sister-in-law/sisters-in-law* or *sister-in-laws*

Some compounds consisting of a noun plus a postmodifying adjective also allow both alternatives:

> *court martial/courts martial* or *court martials*
> *attorney general/attorneys general* or *attorney generals*
> *poet laureate/poets laureate* or *poet laureates*

Other compounds with a postmodifying adjective or prepositional phrase have the plural inflection only on the first part:

> *heir apparent/heirs apparent*
> *notary public/notaries public*
> *commander-in-chief/commanders-in-chief*
> *right-of-way/rights-of-way*

5.8 Non-standard plurals

Non-standard dialects may differ from standard dialects in the plurals of nouns. Among the differences found in various non-standard dialects are:

5.8.1 **Zero plurals**

After numerals or quantifiers, a few count nouns may have a zero plural (the same form as in the singular) in standard English, e.g. *six foot, eleven stone.* Other nouns permit this in non-standard dialects:

> *thirty year, many mile*

5.8.2 **Regular plurals**

Nouns that have irregular plurals in standard dialects may take regular plurals:

> *mouses, louses, sheeps, swines, deers*

5.8.3 **Double plurals**

Nouns that have irregular plurals in standard dialects may have an added regular plural:

> *mens, childrens, mices*

Some regular plurals in standard dialects may take a second regular plural:

> *bellowses, beasteses* (with an intrusive /ɪ/)

5.8.4 **Mutation plurals**

Like standard *mice* is non-standard mutation plural *kye* ('cows'), a survival of an older plural. Double plurals of the same word are also found: *kyes* and (with older *-en* plural ending) *kine.*

5.8.5 **Plurals in *-(e)n***

The older plural ending in *-(e)n* found in standard *oxen* is also found in non-standard *een, eyen* ('eyes'); *shoon, shoen* ('shoes'); *flen* ('fleas'); *housen* ('houses').

5.8.6 **Plurals in *-(e)r***

The older plural ending in *-(e)r* found in the standard double plural *children* is found in non-standard regularly formed *childer.*

5.9 Gender

Gender is a grammatical category by which nouns are divided into two or more classes that require different agreement in inflection with determiners and adjectives, and perhaps also with words of other classes, such as verbs. There is often an association between gender classes and meaning contrasts such as in sex, animacy, and size.

> **NOTE**
>
> Old English had three genders: masculine, feminine, and neuter. Determiners, adjectives, and co-referring pronouns agreed with nouns in gender. For example, the determiner equivalent to present-day *the* and *that* assumes three different forms in agreement with singular nouns from different genders functioning as subject:
>
> | | |
> |---|---|
> | *se cyning* | ('king'—masculine) |
> | *seo lufu* | ('love'—feminine) |
> | *thæt land* | ('land'—neuter) |
>
> The assignment of nouns to gender classes in Old English cannot be predicted from their meaning. For example, *mere* ('lake') and *ham* ('home') are masculine, *miht* ('might') and *stow* ('place') are feminine, *folc* ('people') and *land* ('land') are neuter. Nor do they necessarily reflect contrasts in sex: *wif* ('woman', 'wife') is neuter, whereas *wif-mann* ('woman') is masculine.

5.9.1 Natural gender

English has no classes of nouns that signal gender differences through their inflections, nor do determiners or adjectives vary according to the gender of nouns. English no longer has grammatical gender. (See 4.3.2.2, note.) It can be said to have natural gender, in that certain pronouns expressing natural contrasts in gender are selected to refer to nouns in accordance with the meaning or reference of the nouns:

he, him, his, himself	masculine
she, her, hers, herself	feminine
who, whom, whoever, whomever	personal—either masculine or feminine
it, its, itself, which	non-personal

In **[1]** *hers* is chosen because it refers back to *Natalie* ('the same as Natalie's letter'), whereas in **[2]** *his* is chosen because it refers back to *Shakespeare* ('Shakespeare's plays'):

[1] Well, if you've seen *Natalie*, this letter will probably be very boring, as it will contain much the same as *hers*! [W]

[2] Who can remember who was Secretary of the Council when *Shakespeare* wrote *his* plays

The choice of pronouns does not depend on differences in the word classes of *Natalie* and *Shakespeare*. It relates to differences in the sex of Natalie and Shakespeare. We know that Natalie is a name applied to females and that the playwright Shakespeare was a male.

5.9.2 Gender: male and female noun pairs referring to persons

There are male and female pairs of nouns. Some of these are not marked morphologically:

father—mother	*boy—girl*
brother—sister	*man—woman*
son—daughter	*king—queen*
uncle—aunt	*monk—nun*
nephew—niece	*bachelor—spinster*

> **NOTE**
>
> *Spinster* is not generally used nowadays for young unmarried women, because of its connotation of a woman unlikely to be married. *Single* is preferred, and used for both women and men.

Some pairs are morphologically marked, usually with the suffix for the female noun:

host—hostess	*prince—princess*
waiter—waitress	*emperor—empress*
actor—actress	*hero—heroine*
god—goddess	*usher—usherette*

The male noun has the morphological marking in these two pairs:

>   *bride—bridegroom   widow—widower*

Since these endings are found in only a few nouns, they cannot be regarded as signalling gender classes. Furthermore, increasingly the male noun is used to refer to both sexes in some instances, e.g. *waiter, actor,* or a neutral noun replaces the pair, e.g. *attendant* for *usher—usherette*.

5.9.3 Gender: animals and children

Similar male and female pairs are found for some animals. For example:

bull—cow	*ram—ewe*
dog—bitch	*lion—lioness*
stallion—mare	*tiger—tigress*

Pet-owners and those who have close dealings with the animals may use *he* and *she* as appropriate and perhaps *who*, whereas others will use *it* and *which* for all animals. Similarly, *it* and *which* might be used to refer impersonally to a child or baby, particularly if the sex is not known or is irrelevant:

> **[3]**   He had fathered a child upon an unknown woman, for some reason it had been impossible for them to marry—or of course either he or she had not wanted to marry—and they got rid of *the baby* almost as soon as *it* was born. [Julian Symons *Death's Darkest Face*]

5.9.4 Gender: *she* referring to inanimates

The personal pronoun *she* may be used to refer to countries and also (though occasionally *he* occurs) to inanimate entities such as ships, cars, and planes:

> **[4]**   So *France* one of the world's biggest arms suppliers and by reputation the West's most promiscuous salesman will still allow *her* customers to buy secrecy along with their kit

> **[5]**   Within the last twenty years the *People's Republic of China* ... became so fearful of the population outstripping the means of subsistence within *her* frontiers ... that Peking if I can still call it like that ... decreed restraint of parenthood ... under penalty ... to one child for each couple

> **[6]**   In the predawn on Sept. 25, 1967, the Cunard Line's Queen Mary, outbound from New York, passed *her* sister ship the Queen Elizabeth heading west. [*Wall Street Journal*]

5.10 Case

Case is an inflected form of the noun that coincides with certain syntactic functions (such as subject) or semantic relations (such as possessor).

NOTE

In Old English, nouns distinguished five cases—nominative, accusative, genitive, dative, and instrumental—though the distinction between dative and instrumental was neutralized inflectionally and other distinctions were often neutralized in particular declensions (sets of nouns with the same inflections). For example, singular *cyning* ('king') has the same form for the nominative and accusative, as well as for the dative and instrumental:

nominative/accusative	*cyning*
genitive	*cyninges*
dative/instrumental	*cyninge*

In Old English, determiners and premodifying adjectives agreed with the noun in case as well as gender. All five cases of the noun are differentiated in the following examples of the singular masculine noun *cyning*. The differentiation is signalled by the different inflectional forms of the adjective *god* ('good'), though there are only three inflectional forms of the noun:

nominative	*god cyning*
accusative	*godne cyning*
genitive	*godes cyninges*
dative	*godum cyninge*
instrumental	*gode cyninge*

In the course of time, most case inflections were lost.

5.10.1 Common case and genitive case

The two remaining cases for nouns are the **common** case and the **genitive** case. The common case is the one that is used ordinarily, whenever the genitive case is not required.

NOTE

Apart from the -*es* inflection, Old English had other genitive singulars: -*e*, -*an*, -*a*, and an uninflected genitive. During the Middle English period, the -*es* or -*s* inflection became dominant, spreading to nouns which originally did not have this inflection. Similarly, the plural -*es* or -*s* inflection became the only inflection for the plural, including the genitive plural. In some non-standard dialects (e.g. Black English and in the north Midlands of England) the genitive is often not inflected: *your wife sister, that man coat.*

5.10.2 Pronunciation of the genitive inflection

In speech, the genitive is signalled in singular nouns by an inflection that has the same pronunciation variants as for plural nouns in the common case (cf. 5.6):

5.10.2.1 /ɪz/ if the singular ends in a sibilant (see 5.6.3.1)

> *the church's* membership

5.10.2.2 /z/ if the singular ends in a vowel or a voiced consonant other than a sibilant

　　the boy's father　my *dog's* lead

5.10.2.3 /s/ if the singular ends in a voiceless consonant other than a sibilant

　　the student's parents

5.10.3 **Spelling changes**

There is no difference in speech between the genitive singular, the common case plural, and the genitive plural for regular nouns, though they are differentiated by means of the apostrophe in writing:

	singular	plural
common case	*girl*	*girls*
genitive case	*girl's*	*girls'*

Nouns with irregular plurals are differentiated for all four possibilities:

	singular	plural
common case	*child*	*children*
genitive case	*child's*	*children's*

5.10.4 **Dependent and independent genitives**

Genitives may be dependent or independent. The **dependent** genitive is dependent on the head of the noun phrase. It functions like a possessive pronoun (cf. 6.3f.):

　　Estelle's eldest daughter (dependent genitive)
　　her eldest daughter　(possessive pronoun)

The **independent** genitive is not dependent on a following noun, but a noun is implied. The implied noun may be recovered from the context:

[1]　There's a possibility of giving up my car ... and taking on *my dad's* ('my dad's car')

[2]　Well ... uhm ... I wrote my thesis in such a way that it's ... considerably more accessible than *most people's* ('most people's theses')

Again, possessive pronouns may be used if their reference is clear: 'taking on *his*' in **[1]** and 'more accessible than *theirs*' in **[2]**.

The independent genitive is also used with reference to places. Possible place references are given in parentheses:

[3]　So you're not going to go back and work in *the publisher's* and serve tea...and stuff ('the publisher's office')

[4]　They are always singing in *the men's* ('the men's room')

[5]　And you can get them from Marks & Spencer's ('Marks & Spencer's store')

[6]　If they uh produce as good a cricketer as you and you took advantage of those nets at *Lord's* you'd put put the fear of God into a few of the players there ('Lord's cricket ground')

[7]　I stood on a pair of scales at *my cousin's* ('my cousin's home')

The dependent genitive usually corresponds to an *of*-phrase with the definite article *the* in the first noun phrase:

　　Estelle's eldest daughter
　　the eldest daughter of Estelle

The two constructions are occasionally combined:

a daughter of Estelle's

This **double genitive** construction—genitive plus *of*-phrase—generally has an indefinite first noun phrase, introduced (for example) by the indefinite article *a* or *an*. Sometimes, however, the demonstratives *this* or *that* are used:

[8]   *That hall of Martin's* is quite big actually

[9]   *That new film of Joey Jodie Foster's* looks quite good

5.10.5 The genitive as enclitic

The present-day English genitive is treated here traditionally as a case that is signalled by inflectional suffixes. In an alternative analysis, the genitive is regarded as an **enclitic**, a word joined on to a preceding word (as with contracted *n't* in *isn't*). The analysis is motivated by the fact that the genitive is not necessarily attached to one particular word. It may serve a coordinated phrase, as in [10]–[13]:

[10] Seven rounds of talks have already failed to produce an agreement mainly because of *France and Germany's* refusal to accept a proposal from the European Commission for cuts of thirty percent

[11] Three o'clock and Doctor Finley is up again after just *an hour and a half's* sleep

[12] For the last two years Joe's father has visited him regularly at *Peter and Sheila's* home and on Friday nights Joe goes to his father's for the weekend

[13] It's this kind of immediate help that enables *children and young people's* views to be heard and hard-pressed foster families to go on fostering

Paraphrases with an *of*-phrase show that the genitive applies to the coordinated noun phrases and not simply to the noun it is attached to. For [13], for example, the paraphrase is 'views of children and young people'.

Similarly, the genitive at the end of a postmodifying prepositional phrase may apply to the whole of the noun phrase and not just to the noun that comes before the genitive:

[14] Trevor Emms *the Duke of Norfolk's* agent and Sir Leslie Scott a land commissioner were level-headed men with a lifetime of land management behind them ('the Duke's agent', not 'Norfolk's agent')

[15] The cost of compensating dockers made compulsorily redundant by the Government's abolition of the Dock Labour Scheme is likely to be more than five times *the Department of Transport's* original estimate. [*The Independent*] ('the Department's original estimate', not 'Transport's original estimate')

The genitives in [10]–[15] are **group genitives**.

5.10.6 Genitive as noun phrase head

The genitive is the head of a genitive noun phrase and may therefore take its own determiners and modifiers:

a layperson's point of view ('the point of view of a layperson')
your mother's mother ('the mother of your mother')
the doctor's daughter ('the daughter of the doctor')
different people's experience ('the experience of different people')
my youngest child's computer ('the computer of my youngest child')

5.11 Genitive and *of*-phrase

5.11.1 **Genitive preferred**

The genitive is preferred to the corresponding *of*-phrase when the noun phrase denotes persons, animals, or human institutions:

[1] Each has its place in *the designer's* studio [W]

[2] The unions say they accept that a twenty percent drop in passenger traffic justifies *the management's* action

[3] Then he said they wanted to try and get to *the air defence system's* command

[4] Well now the Japanese are trying harder in the executive car market as well ... and *Mitsubishi's* new Sigma is priced directly to compete with *BMW's* five series

[5] In the dawn greyness she had listened to *the birds'* first brave cheepings. [Denise Robertson *Remember the Moment*]

The genitive is commonly used with noun phrases referring to time or place:

[6] And the first performance will be ... in about *a month's* time

[7] So I think from *today's* session you've realised I hope that you shouldn't start somebody on life-long anti-hypertensive therapy based upon one single blood pressure measurement

[8] This investment was intended to provide the infrastructure necessary to *Hong Kong's* continued economic development [W]

The genitive is also commonly used with noun phrases that denote entities, states, and activities associated with human beings:

[9] The Frenchman said *my heart's* desire is to be married to a woman so beautiful that everybody in the room is jealous of me

[10] The aim of the Corpus Definition sub-system is to enable the definition of a corpus structure to be entered by *the program's* user. [W]

[11] She's called the Alpha Challenge and the arbitrators were asked to decide questions of principle arising out of *the vessel's* arrest and detention

[12] Genesis also favoured *the meletron's* unique sound ... and they featured it heavily on many of their classic early seventies albums

[13] Different theorists dispute the role and relative importance of these factors in our feeling *an emotion's* intensity and differentiation of emotions. [W]

[14] To establish the soundness of a theory in principle, *the methods'* feasibility need be demonstrated just in principle. [W]

The genitive sometimes occurs with noun phrases where none of the above conditions applies:

[15] Chromosomes are made up of protein and DNA, and the latter comprises *the cell's* genetic material [W]

[16] They're not smooth like *an apple's* flesh

[17] That means you're not keeping it there but you'd rather do it for *simplicity's* sake

5.11.2 *Of*-phrase preferred

If the noun that might take the genitive has **restrictive** postmodification (cf. 10.8), the *of*-phrase is preferred to the group genitive (cf. 5.10.5):

[18] And they were all uh reproductions *of a … particular period in art history*

[19] Gaveston's … description of the King of England as being interested in plays and masques and poetry uh uh immediately makes him as far as I can uh see in the eyes *of most people who read that play* effeminate

The alternative group genitive construction would be clumsy: for **[18]** *a particular period in art history's reproductions* and for **[19]** *most people who read that play's eyes.*

The *of*-phrase may be preferred for reasons of communicative importance. The more important information tends to be placed last. In **[20]** the *of*-phrase is used in 'the head *of a cat*', when the noun *cat* is introduced, but the genitive is used in '*the cat's* head', since the new point being introduced is about the head:

[20] And he showed that he could in fact measure absorption changes across the head *of a cat* and *the cat's* head's about four or five centimetres diameter

5.12 Meanings of genitive and *of*-phrase

5.12.1 Possessive genitive

The genitive has also been called the possessive, since one of its meanings has been to denote the possessor of what is referred to by the second noun phrase, as in '*the couple's* home'. But possession has to be interpreted liberally if it is to cover many instances of the genitive and the *of*-phrase. In a liberal interpretation, we could count as possession any connections between the two nouns where the verbs *possess* or *have* can be used in a paraphrase; for example, family relationships: *Tom's son* ('the son that Tom has').

Here are other examples of the possessive genitive:

Mexico City's population
Tom's shock of blond hair
Napoleon's army
the local team's morale
hunger's most acute form
the world's food reserves
Peter's illness
the manufacturer's name and address
my son's bedroom
Japan's importance
the owner's privacy

5.12.2 Subjective and objective genitive

If the second noun is derived from a verb, the relationship between the genitive phrase and the second noun phrase may correspond to that between subject and verb or that between object and verb. The subjective relationship is more common for the genitive. For example, *the people's choice* corresponds to *The people chose*, where *The people* is subject, and hence *the people's* in *the people's choice* is a **subjective genitive**. On the other hand, *Kennedy's* in *Kennedy's assassination* is an **objective genitive** ('Somebody assassinated Kennedy').

The *of*-phrase may also be subjective or objective. But when the genitive and the *of*-phrase co-occur, the genitive phrase is subjective and the *of*-phrase is objective:

> *God's* choice *of Israel* ('God chose Israel')
> *the reviewer's* analysis *of the play* ('The reviewer analysed the play')
> *my neighbour's* criticism *of my children* ('My neighbour criticized my children')
> *the judge's* presentation *of the facts* ('The judge presented the facts')
> *the country's* abolition *of slavery* ('The country abolished slavery')
> *the Department's* acceptance *of the need for reform* ('The Department accepted the need for reform')

Although there may be ambiguity when constructions with the genitive or *of*-phrase are viewed in isolation, the context or general knowledge will resolve the ambiguity. Both factors contribute to interpreting *women's* in *women's subjection* as objective in [1]:

> [1]   In this novel, both sides to the question of women's rights and *women's subjection* are presented through various characters by the concealed narrator, and the reader can draw her own conclusions. [Jennifer Breen *In Her Own Write*]

A *by*-phrase will show that the genitive is objective, as in this sentence that appears earlier in the same text:

> [2]   Thus the narrator, through Baruch's simplistic exaggerations, is putting across one of the more neglected aspects of political feminism: how to make an analysis of *women's subjection by men* in relation to subjection according to class. [Jennifer Breen *In Her Own Write*]

The *by*-phrase corresponds to the *by*-phrase in passive sentences:

> *women's subjection by men* ('Women are subjected by men', 'Men subject women')

The subjective *by*-phrase therefore contrasts with the objective *of*-phrase:

> *women's subjection of men* ('Women subject men')

Compare:

> *the subjection of men by women*

5.12.3 Genitive with *-ing* clause

The genitive noun phrase may also be the subject of an ***-ing* participle** clause (cf. 14.1, 14.7), especially when the noun phrase is a pronoun or a proper noun. Here are some examples with proper nouns:

> [3]   There is something inherently suspect about *Congress's* prohibiting the executive from even studying whether public funds are being wasted in some favored program or other. [*Wall Street Journal*]

> [4]   If successful, the offer would result in *McCaw's* owning a total of slightly more than 50% of LIN's common shares on a fully diluted basis. [*Wall Street Journal*]

> [5]   The future depends on *Algeria's* finding more efficient ways to run its factories and farms, perhaps with the help of foreign companies it has largely rejected since independence. [*Wall Street Journal*]

> [6]   He said various 'normal investment banking fees' were discussed as part of *Shearson's* joining the KKR team. [*Wall Street Journal*]

The *-ing* participle in such constructions is called a **gerund**.

5.12.4 **Temporal genitive**

The genitive and *of*-phrase can have several other meanings. The **temporal** genitive denotes a period of time or a duration of time:

a session's legislation	('legislation passed during a session')
today's lower standards	('the lower standards that apply today')
this season's games	('the games during this season')

5.12.5 **Source genitive**

The **source** genitive denotes such relationships as authorship and origin:

Coleridge's poetry	('the poetry written by Coleridge')
the consultants' views	('the views expressed by the consultants')
Bill Clinton's speech	('the speech made by Bill Clinton')
Australia's exports	('the exports that come from Australia')
the sun's rays	('the rays emanating from the sun')

5.12.6 **Genitive and determiners**

In most of its uses, the dependent genitive phrase functions in the same way as determiners such as *the* and *her*:

her	*children*
Carol's	*children*
my daughter's	*children*

Central determiners cannot co-occur, so that we cannot say *the her children*. Similarly,
genitive phrases cannot co-occur with central determiners, so that we cannot say *the my
daughter's children*. However, the head of the noun phrase is implicitly definite: *my
daughter's children* corresponds to *the children of my daughter* and *a friend's children* to
the children of a friend. The central determiners *my* and *a* in those examples belong to the
genitive phrase and not to the head of the noun phrase, as the paraphrases show. And of
course *a* in *a friend's children* could not apply to *children* because *a* can only be a determiner with singular count nouns.

5.12.7 **Descriptive genitive**

The **descriptive** genitive differs grammatically from the other uses of the genitive. It is a
modifier. The determiner that precedes a descriptive genitive applies to the whole noun
phrase and not to the genitive. For example, *girls'* is a descriptive genitive in *a girls' school*
('a school for girls') and its function is equivalent to that of *local* in *a local school*. A
modifier that precedes the descriptive genitive may belong either to the genitive or to the
head of the noun phrase. *A good girls' school* is ambiguous between 'a school for good
girls' and its more plausible interpretation 'a good school for girls'.
    Here are some examples of descriptive genitives:

cow's milk	('milk produced by cows')
a warm *summer's* day	('a warm day in summer')

a *ten minutes'* walk   ('a walk lasting ten minutes')
the *lion's* share of the booty   ('the largest share')

Descriptive genitives may form part of an idiomatic phrase, as in *lion's share* above and in *dowager's hump* and *dog's dinner* below:

[7]   The typical bent spine of osteoporosis has been given the name of '*dowager's hump*'. [W]

[8]   Well the thing I'm worried about more than anything is having to go into his office dressed up like *a dog's dinner*

Some descriptive genitives can be replaced by nouns that are not in the genitive: *a warm summer day, a ten minute walk*. Nouns are regularly used to premodify other nouns, as in this noun phrase: *a plastic cat litter scoop*. Generally, the singular form of the noun is used in premodification.

Chapter 6
Determiners, Pronouns, and Numerals

Summary

Summary

Determiners (e.g. *the, your*) introduce noun phrases, whereas pronouns (e.g. *she, anybody*) function as noun phrases by themselves or with modifiers. Many words may be either determiners or pronouns. The definite article *the* and the indefinite article *a(n)* are only determiners. The major sets of pronouns/determiners are the primary pronouns (personal, possessive, reflexive), the *wh*-pronouns (interrogative, exclamative, relative, nominal relative, *wh*-conditional), and the indefinite pronouns (assertive, nonassertive, negative, universal, quantifying). Other sets of pronouns or determiners are demonstratives, reciprocals, pronoun *one*, existential *there*.

Numerals may function as pronouns or determiners. There are three types: cardinals (e.g. *two, ten thousand*), ordinals (e.g. *first, twentieth*), fractions (*a half, two-thirds*).

6.1 Characteristics of determiners and pronouns

Determiners introduce **noun phrases** (cf. 10.2). They express such notions as number or quantity and the kind of reference of the noun phrase. *This* and *any* may be determiners:

[1] So when was the sell-by date of *this* soup

[2] Programming the areas is relatively easy and, as the speech is digitised, *any* vocabulary in *any* language may be used. [W]

Pronouns are in effect closed sets of nouns. They are typically deictic, pointing to entities in the situation or pointing to linguistic units in the previous or following context. Typically they are not introduced by determiners and are not modified. *This* and *any* may be pronouns:

[3] Yes if the anterior ligament is intact and there's injury disruption to the posterior ligament ... then *this* is incurred in a flexion injury ... when the head is moving forward

[4] *Any* of these matters may serve as 'mitigating circumstances' reducing the defendant's moral responsibility and thus calling for a degree of leniency in fixing the appropriate sentence. [Sebastian Poulter *Asian Traditions and English Law*]

As examples [1]–[4] indicate, words that function as determiners may also function as pronouns. This combination of potential functions is sufficiently common that it is economical to set up one pronoun-determiner word class for most pronouns and determiners. Some pronouns in the pronoun-determiner class have only pronominal functions, e.g. *I, someone, themselves*; some have only determiner functions, e.g. *no, your, every*; most have both pronominal and determiner functions, e.g. *some, that, which*. Independent possessive pronouns, e.g. *mine, yours*, have dependent possessive pronouns (cf. 6.3.1), e.g. *my, your*, as their counterparts with determiner function.

The major sets of pronouns/determiners may be grouped as follows:

primary pronouns/ determiners (cf. 6.3f.)	{	personal	e.g. *I, you, she*
		possessive	e.g. *my/ mine, you/ yours*
		reflexive	e.g. *myself, herself, ourselves*

wh-pronouns/ determiners (cf. 6.12)	⎧ interrogative ⎪ exclamative ⎨ relative ⎪ nominal relative ⎩ *wh*-conditional	e.g. *what, whose* *what* e.g. *who/which* e.g. *who, whatever* e.g. *whatever, whichever*
indefinite pronouns/ determiners (cf. 6.13)	⎧ assertive ⎪ non-assertive ⎨ negative ⎪ quantifying ⎩ universal	e.g. *some, somebody* e.g. *any, anyone* e.g. *none, nothing* e.g. *few, many* e.g. *all, everyone*

In addition, there are smaller sets or individual items:

reciprocal pronouns/determiners: *each other, one another* (cf. 6.11)
demonstrative pronouns/determiners: *this, that, these, those* (cf. 6.14)
generic pronoun *one* (cf. 6.5)
substitute pronoun *one* (cf. 6.6)
existential *there* (cf. 6.8)

The numerals (cf. 6.15) also function as pronouns or determiners.

Finally, the important class of the definite and indefinite articles (cf. 6.2) function only as determiners.

6.2 Definite and indefinite articles

The definite and indefinite articles are determiners. The **definite article** is *the*, usually pronounced /ðə/ but pronounced /ði:/ when stressed. The indefinite article is represented by two variants: *a* (/ə/ or stressed /eɪ/) or *an* (/ən/ or stressed /an/).

USE OF *A* AND *AN* IN DETAIL

The choice between the variants of the indefinite article depends on the initial sound, not the spelling, of the following word. *A* is used before a consonant sound: *a way, a video, a huge house, a one-off event, a unit, a U-turn, a eunuch*. *An* is used before a vowel sound: *an idea, an architect, an hour, an honorary member, an MBA, an H-bomb, an x-ray*. There are a few words beginning with *h* that some people pronounce with an initial vowel sound (an older pronunciation): *an hotel, an historian*.

The definite article serves as a determiner with singular or plural **count nouns** and with **non-count nouns**:

the issue/issue   the information

The **indefinite article** can only be used with singular count nouns, reflecting its historical derivation from the numeral *one*:

an issue

The analogous indefinite reference for plurals and non-count nouns is conveyed through the absence of a determiner (sometimes termed the **zero article**) or through the presence of *some* (pronounced /səm/):

(some) *issues*   (some) *information*

The definite article is used when the speaker (or writer) assumes that the hearer (or reader) can identify the reference of a noun phrase:

[1]   Uhm ... a couple of people can't make *the performances* but *the majority of them* yes

The indefinite article is used when that assumption cannot be made:

[2]   It was *a fourteenth or thirteenth century chateau* and we just sort of wandered in

The distinction between the two articles is neutralized for generic noun phrases. For example, **[3]** could be replaced by **[3a]** without affecting the meaning:

[3]   *The sandflats* are regarded as the province of *marine biologists,* while *the dunes* are investigated by *terrestrial biologists.* [Colin Little *The Terrestrial Invasion*]

[3a]   *A sandflat* is regarded as the province of *the marine biologist,* while *a dune* is investigated by *the terrestrial biologist.*

As can be seen, the distinction between singular and plural is also neutralized in generic phrases. For further discussion of the definite and indefinite articles, see 10.16.

6.3 Forms of personal, possessive, and reflexive pronouns

The three **primary** sets of pronouns—personal, possessive, and reflexive—are interrelated. They exhibit contrasts in **person** (first, second, third), **number** (singular, plural), **gender** (masculine, feminine, non-personal), and **case** (subjective, objective). These contrasts are not available in all instances.

6.3.1 **Usual forms of the primary pronouns**

The usual forms of these sets of pronouns in standard English are displayed in Table 6.3.1. The possessive pronouns fall into two types: **dependent** (with determiner function) and **independent** (with pronominal function).

Table 6.3.1 Primary pronouns

person	number and gender	personal subjective	objective	possessive dependent	independent	reflexive
1st	singular	*I*	*me*	*my*	*mine*	*myself*
	plural	*we*	*us*	*our*	*ours*	*ourselves*
2nd	singular	*you*	*you*	*your*	*yours*	*yourself*
	plural	*you*	*you*	*your*	*yours*	*yourselves*
3rd	masc. singular	*he*	*him*	*his*	*his*	*himself*
	fem. singular	*she*	*her*	*her*	*hers*	*herself*
	non-pers. singular	*it*	*it*	*its*	*its*	*itself*
	plural	*they*	*them*	*their*	*theirs*	*themselves*

Some of the pronouns have stressed and unstressed pronunciations. Common unstressed pronunciations are given below, preceded by stressed pronunciations:

me	/miː/, /mɪ/	*her*	/həː/ or /həːr/, /hə/ or /hər/ or /ə/ or /ər/
my	/mʌɪ/, /mɪ/	*him*	/hɪm/, /hɪm/ or /ɪm/
we	/wiː/, /wɪ/	*his*	/hɪz/, /hɪz/ or /ɪz/
us	/ʌs/, /əs/	*she*	/ʃiː/, /ʃɪ/
you	/juː/, /jʊ/ or /jə/	*them*	/ðɛm/, /ðəm/
he	/hiː/, /hɪ/ or /ɪ/		

NOTE

The unstressed pronunciation of *my* is sometimes represented in fictional dialogue by the spelling *me*:

> **[N1]** '*Me* brother Sam gives it another twelvemonth, m'm.' [James Lees-Milne *The Fool of Love*]

The possessive pronouns were originally the genitives of the personal pronouns. During the Middle English period the two functions—dependent and independent—came to be distinguished in form. A genitive inflection *-(e)s* was attached to the possessive to yield *your(es), our(es)*, etc. In other areas, *-(e)n* was attached by analogy with *min* ('mine') and *thin* ('thine') to form *his(e)n, our(e)n, your(e)n*, etc. as independent possessives. On the other hand, the dropping of the final *-n* gave rise to the new forms *my* and *thy*, which were used as dependent possessives.

6.3.2 Possessive pronouns with *own*

The possessive pronouns can be emphasized by a following *own*. It functions as a determiner when it follows the dependent possessive pronoun within a noun phrase:

> **[1]** He showed my children love something that *their own* father hadn't shown them

Own can help to avoid ambiguity. In **[2]** *his own* emphasizes that Galiamin is in Galiamin's half, not in Chernishkov's half:

> **[2]** Chernishkov in the end plays the ball forward to Galiamin who's eight yards inside *his own* half

Own can be intensified by *very*: *my very own*, etc.

Own cannot combine with the independent possessive (*mine, theirs*, etc.), but it functions as a pronoun in combination with the dependent possessive:

> **[3]** But ... people who can converse in languages other than *their own* ... as I can not ... advance the cause of civilization

As in the **double genitive** construction (cf. 5.10), the combination of possessive and *own* can combine with the *of*-phrase:

> **[4]** Later I was surprised to be consulted by him on *a scheme of his own* an entirely original scheme for electronic scanning

Compare *a scheme of his own* with *his own scheme*, and the analogous comparison of *a scheme of his* with *his scheme*.

NOTE

Own in combination with the dependent possessive effectively functions as the genitive of the primary reflexive pronoun, since reflexive pronouns (cf. 6.9) have no genitives.

6.3.3 **Alternative pronoun forms**

There are alternative forms to those displayed in Table 6.3.1.

6.3.3.1 *'s* is a contracted form of *us* in *let's*, the combination with the **imperative auxiliary** *let*:

> **[5]** Well it's not that wonderful a film really … *let's* be honest
>
> **[6]** But before we look at the paintings *let's* look at the technique that the Egyptians used for decorating these tombs

6.3.3.2 *'em* is an informal alternative to *them*:

> **[7]** The previous year there had been a disc called 'Sock it to *'em*, J.B.' by Rex Garvin with Mighty Craven [Nigel Rees *Dictionary of Popular Phrases*]
>
> **[8]** 'He gets angry with Lottie and Jacob sometimes, but he wouldn't see *'em* without a roof over their heads, even though they've nothing to do with him.' [E.V. Thompson *Lottie Trago*]

NOTE

This is usually explained as a survival of a Middle English form *hem*, which was gradually replaced by *them*. The *th*-forms (*they, them, their*) derive from Scandinavian and fully ousted the older *h*-forms for the third personal plural. The objective *hem* was the last to give way, but has been preserved in contracted *'em*, which is now generally felt to be a contraction of *them*.

6.3.3.3 In some regions, there are informal combinations for the second personal plural: *you all* or *y'all* (genitive *y'all's*), *you guys* (American), *you lot* (British). These compensate for the absence of number contrast in present-day second personal forms.

6.3.3.4 *themself* has been introduced in recent decades as a singular **gender-neutral** pronoun, analogously to this use of *they, them,* and *their*, but it seems to be of rare occurrence so far.

> **[9]** Or the person who's trying not to drink so much and beats *themself* up when they slip back and get drunk! [Linda Stoker *Having It All*]

6.3.3.5 Archaic second personal forms sometimes appear in poetry and religious language, and are otherwise occasionally used facetiously. They are displayed in Table 6.3.2.

> **[10]** A: Can I create staff shortages please as well as snow
> B: Do as *thou* wills *thou* wilt please

Table 6.3.2 Archaic second person forms

	personal subjective	objective	possessive dependent	independent
singular	*thou*	*thee*	*thy*	*thine*
plural	*ye*	*you*	*your*	*yours*

6.3.4 **Pronouns in non-standard dialects**

Non-standard dialects exhibit many variants. In some dialects the objective forms of the personal pronouns (*me, us,* etc.) are commonly used as subject, and occasionally the reverse occurs (e.g. *I* and *he* as objects). The objective forms are common in all dialects when the subject consists of co-ordinated phrases, and they sometimes appear in the informal speech of speakers of standard English:

[11] Because *me and John* said

[12] *Xepe and me* have had about ten minutes yeah ten minutes over the last week or something

Masculine and feminine pronouns are used in some dialects to denote inanimate objects and to refer to inanimate noun phrases. *Youse* or *you'uns* are found in some dialects as the second personal plural.

The possessive *thy* and *thine* survive in some dialects for the second personal singular. Some dialects have preserved the older forms *hisn, hern, ourn, theirn* as independent possessives. Others have regularized *mine* to *mines* by analogy with *yours, ours,* etc. The dependent possessive pronoun *me* is commonly used in non-standard dialects.

Regularization has similarly affected the paradigm of reflexive pronouns in non-standard English. By analogy with *myself, yourself,* etc. (which combine the possessive with *self*) there are the widespread non-standard forms *hisself* and *theirselves. Thyself* has been preserved in some non-standard dialects together with the other second personal singular *th*-pronouns.

6.4 Person, number, gender, case

6.4.1 Person

Contrasts in person apply to all three primary sets of pronouns. The **first person** (e.g. *I, we, my, ourselves*) includes the speaker or speakers (in written language, the writer or writers). The **second person** (e.g. *you, your, yourselves*) includes the person or persons addressed but excludes the speaker. The **third person** (e.g. *he, her, themselves*) excludes the speaker and the person or persons addressed.

6.4.1.1 Coordinated phrases

Noun phrases other than pronouns are in the third person and are so treated for **subject–verb agreement** (cf. 10.14). In standard English, conventional politeness requires that in **coordinated phrases** the second person comes first and the first person last:

> *my husband and I*
> *you and your husband*
> *you, Mary, and me*
> *you and me*

In informal speech the first person is sometimes put first:

[1] This man suddenly fled past *me and Martin Meredith* and all these Falange started firing at him

In **[2]**, cited from fictional dialogue, the prior mention of *me* is motivated by the superior (parental) role of the speaker:

[2] I suppose he's right, but it don't make things any easier for *me and the kids* when there's no money coming in. [E. V. Thompson *Lottie Trago*]

Notice, however, the use of non-standard *don't* instead of standard *doesn't*.

6.4.1.2 Inclusive *we*

Inclusive *we* is the use of *we* to include also the person or persons addressed. It combines first and second persons.

[3] I'm saying I mean I could meet you here tomorrow night and then *we* could go off

The contracted pronoun *'s* is generally inclusive in *let's*:

[4] Right let*'s* see how many words *we* can think of beginning with D

Inclusive *we* is commonly used in writing to draw the reader into closer involvement with the written work:

[5] As *we* have seen, reassertion of identification with the Plantagenet past also took place at this time. [Malcolm Vale *The Angevin Legacy and the Hundred Years War 1250–1340*]

6.4.1.3 Exclusive *we*

Exclusive *we* excludes the person or persons addressed. It generally combines first and third persons:

[6] I was out with some friends and *we* got talking about books

[7] A: First of all … uh how do you see the future of the group
B: Uhm … well *we*'re sort of working towards our first performance

Exclusive *we* may also represent the speech or writing of more than one person, as in prayer or in joint authorship.

6.4.1.4 First-person equivalent *one*

In British English, *one* is sometimes used as the equivalent of the first person singular pronoun, usually by speakers of the upper social classes or in argumentative spoken or written contexts:

[8] It's been a mixture of … extreme pleasure I've had hundreds of letters from all sorts of people who have enjoyed the book … and considerable irritation because of being constantly interviewed And the phone never stops going And … people offer *one* goodies Not that *one* doesn't get offered nice things

[9] No I think I would certainly want to live with someone that could understand *one*'s own angst and anxieties

[10] And *one* has to say straightaway I won't say it again during this programme but all three … who've just spoken are active supporters of the Labour Party

---

6.4.2 Number: *we* and *us*

The plural personal pronoun *we* is sometimes used with singular reference. The authorial *we* may be preferred in formal lectures or learned writing by single authors to avoid using *I*, which is felt by some to be too intrusive. Citations **[11]** and **[12]** are excerpted from works by single authors:

[11] In this chapter *we* shall develop some of the issues dealt with in Chapter 2.1. [W]

[12] *We* are currently engaged in measuring these rates in Professor Shetty's subjects. [W]

We and the pronoun *us* or *'s* in combination with *let* can refer to a single speaker in situations of unequal relationship; for example, a doctor or dentist speaking to a patient or a teacher speaking to a student. The intention is to convey a friendly tone, although it is increasingly regarded by some as patronizing.

[13] Well *we*'ll just check your blood pressure

[14] There may be a little tartar build up as well which has cracked off so ... low levels of tartar which I'll just clean Yes *we* saw you in July about six months ago

[15] Let's have a look at your throat just now

In informal conversation, *us* is sometimes used in place of *me* between equals in certain expressions, especially with the verb *give*:

[16] Nigel you couldn't give *us* a hand could you

In a jocular use, the first personal plural can refer to a single hearer:

[17] A: God you really know how to put someone down don't you
B: Oh let's not get touchy touchy

6.4.3 Gender: the third person

The **gender** contrasts apply to the use of the third personal singular pronouns to refer to entities in the situation **[18]** or to an antecedent in the linguistic context **[19]**:

[18] Look at *him*!

[19] He married *a girl* from the Soviet Union and *she* followed him

In general, *he* refers to males, *she* to females, and *it* to all else. *She* and (less commonly) *he* are occasionally used to refer to inanimate objects such as cars, boats, and computers. *It* is used for babies and animals where their sex is unknown or disregarded:

[20] A: So I was left with the baby
B: How old is *it*

[21] But you couldn't have *a dog* leaving *it* all day could you

The absence of a gender-neutral singular personal pronoun has posed problems. On the various methods of dealing with the problem, see 1.6.

6.4.4 Case

The contrasts in **case** apply to the personal pronouns. In general, the **subjective case** is used for the subject of a sentence or finite clause and the **objective case** in all other instances, as in these contrasts between subjective *I* and objective *me*:

[22] Can *I* find out the computer data you hold about *me*? [W]

[23] *I'm* sure that you are expecting *me* to say something stimulating thought-provoking and original

[24] But *I* think really what made my mind up was when my husband Terry gave *me* an ultimatum

There is, however, variation in case when the pronoun is the **complement** of the verb *be*. The formal variant is the subjective form and the less formal variant is the objective form:

[25] His name was Trophemus and it was *he* who introduced Christianity to this land

[26] The reason that this is such a sacred place is because the two Marys remained in the Camargue with Sarah the servant and it is *she* who has become the most important person for the gypsies

[27] Hello it's *me* again

The objective form is also normal in abbreviated responses in the spoken language:

[28]   A: Well I don't suppose she knows how many people are living in the whole
property
B: *Me*

6.4.5 **Personal pronouns as determiners**

We and *you* function as determiners when in combination with a following noun or
nominal adjective:

[29]   We are an endangered species *we* men and *we* sportsmen

[30]   Jules was going around saying *you* bloody men *you* hypochondriacs

For the third person, demonstrative *those* is used in standard English, but non-standard
dialects use the third person pronouns *them* or *they* (cf. 6.14).

6.4.6 **Modification of personal pronouns**

Personal pronouns are sometimes **modified** by **relative clauses**:

[31]   And *we* who happen to be in a better position than the others to be able to send
any troops have sent some troops

Other possibilities (mainly for first person plural and second person) are modification
by adjectives in exclamatory phrases (*poor you*), and by adverbs (*we here*), and prepositional phrases (*you at the back*, mainly in vocative phrases). *It* and *they* are not modified
by adjectives or relative clauses. Demonstrative *those* is used instead of *they* with relative
clauses.

6.5 Generic pronouns

Generic reference may be conveyed by the **generic pronoun** *one* (genitive *one's*, reflexive
oneself or *one's self*) and the personal pronouns *we, you,* and *they*.

The generic pronoun *one* is **formal** and tends to be replaced by the personal pronouns
we, you, and *they* in less formal contexts. They all refer generally to people, though the
reference may be restricted by the context. Here are some examples of generic *one*:

[1]   *One* loses interest in everything when *one* has children

[2]   Or the stresses may be psychological ones uhm bereavement divorce or marriage
come to that ... loss of *one's* job

[3]   In other words, within the pluralist society, *one* is free to choose to be
unconfronted by choice; *one* may find *oneself* choosing from the variety to have no
variety. [W]

Generic *we* has the widest extent in that it must include the speaker as well as those
addressed. *You*, the most common generic pronoun in speech, generally includes the
person or persons addressed. *They* excludes the speaker and those addressed.

[4]   *We* don't have a constitution which says Congress shall pass no law restricting the
freedom of press or Congress shall pass no law uhm discriminating against
religions

[5] *We* should not underestimate the defence of honour or the realization of claims to certain titles, rights and privileges as motivating factors leading to the outbreak of open and public war during this period. [W]

[6] God *you* do have to be careful don't *you*

[7] When *you* select these modes, the Page up/down buttons allow *you* to step through their software pages, while the data entry controllers allow *you* to edit the parameters. [*Music Technology*]

[8] A: And is Japan the one that doesn't like beards or long hair
B: So *they* say

Here are examples of the alternative reflexive forms of *one*—*oneself* and the less frequent *one's self*:

[9] And will he take it from me and my own experience that it's a very satisfactory way of employing *oneself* and serving the customer

[10] It must be peculiarly disconcerting, don't you think, to be left for someone entirely different from *oneself*? [Sarah Caudwell 'An Acquaintance with Mr Collins' in *A Suit of Diamonds*]

[11] The solutions must involve a re-emphasis of the values that have helped many blacks succeed: respect for the family, for the community, for *one's self*. [*Wall Street Journal*]

To avoid repeating *one*, some speakers and writers switch to another generic pronoun, such as *you*:

[12] *One* feels that if *you* create too many if *you* secrete too many of *your* own endorphins ... *you* get addicted to *your* own ... home-made opiates and then have to keep producing them

In American English, *one* was traditionally followed by *he*:

[13] If *one* is wise, *he* should not put all *his* savings in one place.

However, many would now not use generic *he*, to avoid charges of sexism.

6.6 Substitute pronoun *one*

Apart from generic *one* (cf. 6.5) and the numeral *one*, there are two uses of *one* as a **substitute pronoun**.

6.6.1 *One* as substitute for an indefinite noun phrase

One may be a substitute for an **indefinite** noun phrase:

[1] Uhm ... the movement language that's being developed is *one* which involves different people with different skills to talk to each other

[2] A: Why are you looking at me Bobby ... I've never borrowed a hardback
B: You mean you've never borrowed *one* off me love never

[3] A: Well I could have parties and things
B: She's planning *one*

In **[1]** *one* substitutes for *a movement language*, in **[2]** for *a hardback*, and in **[3]** for *a party*. The plural of this use of *one* is the indefinite pronoun *some*.

6.6.2 *One* as substitute for the head of a noun phrase

In the second use, *one* substitutes for the **head** of a noun phrase and perhaps also one or more of its **modifiers**:

[4] A: Oh what sort of a park is it
B: It's quite a huge *one*

[5] And then the suitors will try for her hand and those who don't make it will be killed and the *one* who gets through will marry her

[6] A long-lived scar on the American psyche second only I suspect to the *one* marked Vietnam bore the name of Iran

In **[4]** *one* substitutes for *park*, in **[5]** for *suitor*, and in **[6]** for *scar on the American psyche* (the head with its **postmodifier**). The plural of this use of *one* is *ones*:

[7] The most commonly used model of psychopathology is the medical model as opposed to the dynamic, behavioural, phenomenological and ethical *ones*, for example. [W]

[8] A: Who are your favourite poets
B: Well...different *ones* for different times I think

[9] Consequently, all the early types of video recording, and most of the later *ones*, have attempted to achieve a high writing speed without an excessive actual tape speed. [David Cheshire *The Complete Book of Video*]

In **[7]** *ones* substitutes for *models* (the head only), in **[8]** for *favourite poets* (the head and its **premodifier**), and in **[9]** for *types of video recording* (the head and its postmodifier).

6.6.3 *One* used without reference to a noun phrase

One and *ones* may serve as pronouns without reference to any preceding noun phrase:

[10] In England it doesn't matter because ... he can get help as he's uh the only *one* allowed to drive that car

[11] Here too are the families of those who lost loved *ones* during the conflict

6.7 *It*

The pronoun *it* has four uses:

1. referring *it*
2. anticipatory *it*
3. cleft *it*
4. prop *it*

6.7.1 **Referring** *it*

Referring *it* is exemplified in **[1]**–**[3]**:

[1] A: How long did you do *English* for
B: Uh I did *it* for about half a term

[2] And so Bob drafted *this questionnaire* and gave *it* to Dick

[3] I had *a really really good supper* last night *It* was lovely

It can also refer to the whole or part of a sentence or clause:

[4]   *I was very alert* yesterday *It*'s a bit unlike me

[5]   I hope you don't mind my *rubbing my hands* I think perhaps *it*'s a nasty gesture but I find they get cold

[6]   I don't think *we can run A-REV on Apples* ... I think *it*'s unlikely

[7]   A: So *you're going tonight* then yeah
      B: I'm thinking about *it* uh

6.7.2 Anticipatory *it*

Anticipatory *it* is used when a clause (generally one that might have functioned as subject) is postponed to provide a more balanced sentence, a sentence where what precedes the verb is shorter than what follows it. Anticipatory *it* then serves in the position that might have been occupied by the clause. For example, anticipatory *it* is the subject in [8] and the **extraposed** clause (the clause taken out of its position and moved to the end) is *he's not going to be back here*:

[8]   *It*'s a shame *he's not going to be back here*

As a less common alternative, the clause could have been the subject, though in this instance the omitted conjunction *that* would have to be restored.

[8a]   *That he's not going to be back here* is a shame.

Extraposition is normal with clausal subjects. But subject *-ing* clauses usually occur in the initial position. Here is an example of an *-ing* clause that has been extraposed:

[9]   So a lot of my friends were in one-parent families as well so *it* didn't seem particularly odd *not having a father* ... I think

[9a]   *Not having a father* didn't seem particularly odd.

Here are some further examples of extraposed clauses:

[10]   *It*'s a funny thought isn't it *that I was embarrassed*

[11]   *It* is hardly probable *that anything can be proved*; *it* is even possible *that there is nothing to prove*; and unwarranted investigation might cause undeserved distress. [Ian Enters *Up to Scratch*]

[12]   *It* was extraordinary *what you went through to to get the picture in those circumstances*

[13]   *It* is physically impossible *to force myself to work* sometimes

[14]   *It* would be a waste of time *for people watching this programme to think that this is a party political split across the board*

[15]   How difficult is *it* going to be *for her to find employment*

If after a **complex-transitive** verb (one having both object and object predicative; cf. 3.7) the object clause is a *that*-clause, it is generally extraposed:

[16]   And did he make *it* clear *that he wasn't putting in any money*

Compare:

[16a] Did he make *his decision* clear?

To-infinitive object clauses are also generally extraposed. Here are other examples of extraposed object clauses:

[17] And will he take *it* from me and my own experience *that it's a very satisfactory way of employing oneself and serving the customer*

[18] But I have such a thin skin I'm always terribly easily hurt and I find *it* very hard *to forgive* although I do ... eventually

6.7.3 Cleft *it*

Cleft *it* serves as subject of a **cleft sentence** or cleft clause.

USE OF CLEFT *IT* IN DETAIL

The sentence is split to put the focus on some part of it. The cleft sentence is introduced by cleft *it* followed by a verb phrase whose main verb is a copular verb, generally *be*. The focused part comes next, followed by the rest of the sentence introduced by a relative item.

Here are examples of cleft *it*:

[19] *It* is *the ability to do the job* that matters not where you come from or what you are

[20] *It* uh looks like *Justin Channing* who's receiving treatment

[21] And *it* was *then* that he felt a sharp pain

[22] *It's this kind of routine work* where she says her concentration is most affected

[23] *It* was *not nominal electoral mass but political contacts* which gave clout

The focused part is occasionally **fronted** for additional emphasis:

[24] *Semione it* is who chips the ball in

The relative item may be a **zero relative** (omitted relative *that*):

[25] And *it's these motions* we're designing for

[26] *It's the young miner* I feel sorry for, especially one with a young family. [E. V. Thompson *Lottie Trago*]

Generally zero relative is not used when the focused part is the subject of the rest of the cleft sentence, but it is occasionally found in informal conversation:

[27] *It's his Mum* falls in love with him

The focused part may be a clause:

[28] *It* is *what you put in and what you achieve* which counts

[29] But *it* was *as we moved on to consider the crucial monetary issues ... in the European context ...* that I've come to feel increasing concern

[30] But *it's when the happy little game strays into the field of advertising* that hackles are bound to rise. [*The Scotsman*]

[31] *It* wasn't *till I was perhaps twenty-five or thirty* that I read them and enjoyed them

Standard English does not allow the focused part of a cleft sentence to be the subject predicative after copula *be* or to be a part of a verb phrase. Both these are allowed in non-standard dialects of Irish English:

[32] *It's lucky* she is.

[33] *It must have been smoking* they were.

6.7.4 **Prop *it***

Prop *it* (or **empty *it***) is used to fill the place of a required function—generally the subject —but has little or no meaning.

6.7.4.1 **Prop *it* as subject**
Prop *it* is particularly frequent in expressions referring to weather and time:

[34] Anyway if *it*'s really bad weather we'll just...you know stay in

[35] One day we went up on the chair-lift and *it* was bright sunshine

[36] I think *it*'s going to rain

[37] *It*'s a bit late now

[38] *It*'s so near Christmas

[39] No idea what time *it* is! [W]

[40] A: Sorry about this
B: *It*'s alright

[41] *It*'s just been all work and no play

[42] I may well be tempted into the party that Helen was talking about depending how much work I have to do, you know how *it* goes

6.7.4.2 **Prop *it* in other functions**
Prop *it* also occurs in functions other than as subject, including a variety of idiomatic expressions:

[43] Actually you probably wouldn't have enjoyed *it* here

[44] I'm not really in favour of boys' schools taking on girls in the sixth form and that's *it*

[45] Uh Rebecca can't make *it* tomorrow

[46] And when I started again in the September I said now if nothing comes you've had *it* chum

[47] The constraints on member governments would be purely political so in practice probably wouldn't prevent individual governments going *it* alone as they did in the Gulf

[48] Yes we are creating a classless Britain and a first-class Britain one which can compete and where everyone can make *it* wherever they come from whatever their backgrounds

[49] His ambition is not to make money but to play the Casanova but hasn't the confidence to hit *it* off with the streetwise town women. [W]

[50] I'm taking *it* easy myself, at least while the summer weather lasts. [W]

6.8 Existential *there*

Existential *there* is to be distinguished from the spatial adverb *there*. The two can co-occur. In [1] the first *there* is existential and the second *there* is spatial:

[1] When I went through Romania ... *there* were guards *there* as well

Existential *there* has some of the characteristics of a pronoun, as we will see later in this section.

6.8.1 **Functions of existential** *there*

Ordinarily, some of the information in a sentence (or clause) is known to the hearer or speaker, perhaps from the situation or linguistic context. The subject of the sentence or clause is usually known information. **Existential** *there* is used as a device for rearranging the sentence so as to present the subject (at least) as new information.

USE OF EXISTENTIAL *THERE* **IN DETAIL**

The rearrangement involves postponing the subject and replacing it by existential *there*, which is followed by a verb phrase (generally with *be* as the main verb):

[2]   *There* were *a lot of idiots* on the road

In [2] *there* is the grammatical subject and *a lot of idiots* is the notional subject. Without existential *there* the sentence would be:

[2a]   *A lot of idiots* were on the road

Since the notional subject is new information, it is commonly an indefinite noun phrase; that is to say, a noun phrase with an indefinite determiner (such as *a, some, any*) or no determiner, or an indefinite pronoun such as *someone, nobody, any*. But a definite noun phrase may occur if it is new information:

[3]   Uhm … there may be some funds that the department knows how to tap … *There* may be *the odd scholarship*

6.8.1.1 **Existential** *there* **with notional subject only**
The existential sentence sometimes has only the notional subject following the verb, as in [3] above. In that case, only the existential form of the sentence is possible if the verb is *be*. Here are some further examples:

[4]   *There* were *hundreds of cabins*

[5]   I don't think *there's anything quite like Toblerone*

[6]   Oh I think *there's a lot of that*

[7]   *There* are *various places where you can do that*

[8]   *There's too much of me talking*

[9]   *There's no problem*

[10]   *There's* still *time*

6.8.1.2 **Existential** *there* **with notional subject and other elements**
More usually, there are elements other than the notional subject in the existential sentence. They may precede or (more commonly) follow the notional subject:

[11]   But within the beech and oak woods *there* are *different kinds* ('Within the beech and oak woods are different kinds')

[12]   I thought *there* was *safety* in numbers ('Safety was in numbers')

[13]   I'll leave the bastard and then he'll realise that *there's something* wrong ('Something is wrong')

6.8.1.3 **Existential** *there* **with an** *-ing* **participle**
The notional subject may be followed by an *-ing* **participle** and perhaps its complements. The participle would be the main verb in the corresponding non-existential sentence.

[14]   *There's a road* going up the side ('A road is going up the side')

[15] Otherwise *there* would've been *two groups* sitting there waiting for me to lecture on Tuesday ('Two groups would've been sitting there ...')

[16] *There* should be *quite a few people* coming tomorrow ('Quite a few people should be coming tomorrow')

6.8.1.4 Existential *there* with noun phrase and relative clause

Another type of existential sentence has a noun phrase followed by a relative clause. As in the cleft sentence, the effect is to give greater prominence to the element preceding the relative clause:

[17] Well *there* are *five* who've got forms with me so far

[18] *There* is *one thing* that truly disturbs me, and I speak as a Methodist clergyman. [*Wall Street Journal*]

[19] And *there* were *these weird organisms* that are well preserved

In this construction, the noun phrase may have functions other than as notional subject:

[20] It's very flat and *there's* *a lot of things* I'm ignoring ('I'm ignoring a lot of things')

[21] And *there* are *weeks* when you can get struck down

[22] You notice that halfway down this trail *there's* *a line* I've drawn

In [23] there is a **zero relative** (omitted relative *that*). As with cleft sentences, the zero relative occurs in informal speech even though it is the subject of the relative clause (cf. 10.9):

[23] Uh ... so *there* was *something* happened at that boundary which is of significance although we don't know what it is ('Something that happened at that boundary ...')

6.8.2 Characteristics of existential *there*

Existential *there* has some of the characteristics of pronouns. It can occur as the subject of its sentence or clause. This is evident in questions where it is positioned after the operator (cf. 11.2):

[24] Is *there* anything else

[25] Are *there* any particular events that you can remember about your father

Similarly, like personal pronouns it acts as the subject of a tag question:

[26] There wouldn't be any point would *there*

[27] There's no problem is *there*

Like other grammatical subjects it often determines number concord, taking a singular verb even though the notional subject is plural. This usage is common in informal speech:

[28] *There* was elements of it that were fun

[29] No I mean *there's* no seats left on that day

[30] But honest to goodness *there's* all these numbers that you can dial for all ... all the different sexual pleasures that you want

The alternative plural concord with a plural notional subject also occurs frequently:

[31] But it shouldn't be too difficult because *there* are always loads of jobs going

6.9 Primary reflexive pronouns

Reflexives (*myself, yourself,* etc.) have two uses:

1. The **primary reflexive** is used in place of a personal pronoun to signal that it **co-refers** with another **nominal** in the same sentence or clause; that is to say, they both refer to the same entity. Primary reflexives may be either obligatory or optional.

2. The **emphatic reflexive** is used in addition to another nominal to emphasize that nominal. The addition is always optional.

6.9.1 **Co-reference with subject**

6.9.1.1 **Reflexive co-referring with explicit subject**

The primary reflexive usually co-refers with the subject. The reflexive may be the **direct object [1]**, the **indirect object [2]**, the **subject predicative [3]**, the object of a **prepositional verb [4]**, or the **agent** in a *by*-phrase **[5]**:

[1]   U.S. trade negotiators argue that *countries with inadequate protections for intellectual-property rights* could be hurting *themselves* by discouraging their own scientists and authors and by deterring U.S. high-technology firms from investing or marketing their best products there. [*Wall Street Journal*]

[2]   The first chapter asks about your daydreams and then as an exercise *you* have to write *yourself* an obituary one which in your wildest dreams you would love to have. [W]

[3]   One of the great motifs of moral thought in the last century … has been the crucial importance of private space the territory in which *we*'re simply free to be *ourselves*

[4]   *The word dissemination,* I decided, referred only to *itself.*

[5]   Takeover experts said they doubted *the financier* would make a bid by *himself.* [*Wall Street Journal*]

6.9.1.2 **Reflexive co-referring with implied subject**

The subject with which the reflexive co-refers may be implied from a **host clause**. This commonly occurs in subordinate **non-finite clauses** without a subject:

[6]   After your first three weeks of sleep deprivation, you are scarcely in touch with reality; without psychiatric treatment, *you* may well be unable to fend for *yourself* ever again. [*Wall Street Journal*]

[7]   Following the acquisition of R.P. Scherer by a buy-out group led by Shearson Lehman Hutton earlier this year, *the maker of gelatin capsules* decided to divest *itself* of certain of its non-encapsulating businesses. [*Wall Street Journal*]

[8]   *He* also charged that the utility lobby was attempting to all but buy votes with heavy campaign contributions to *himself* and his colleagues. [*Wall Street Journal*]

[9]   Starting in late November, *the Conservative government* intends to raise about $20 billion from divesting *itself* of most of Britain's massive water and electricity utilities. [*Wall Street Journal*]

In **[10]** the subordinate clause is initial, so that the reflexive is **cataphoric** since it precedes the pronoun (*she*) with which it co-refers:

[10]   Believing *herself* to be by nature unbusiness-like—for her husband deals with all the household bills, investments and tax demands—*she* does her best to suggest efficiency by her appearance. [Anne Melville 'Portrait of a Woman' in *Snapshots*]

The subject may be implied in a subordinate clause even when there is no co-referring noun phrase in a **host clause:**

[11] It is physically impossible to force *myself* to work sometimes

[12] And will he take it from me and my own experience that it's a very satisfactory way of employing *oneself* and serving the customer

[13] He and I share a belief that walking is not simply therapeutic for *oneself* but is a poetic activity that can cure the world of its ills. [*Wall Street Journal*]

Similarly, the subject may be implied in subjectless independent sentences:

[14] Why not do it for *ourselves*?

It is implied regularly in second personal imperatives:

[15] Don't compare *yourself* with anyone else

[16] So stir *yourselves* tonight. [*The Guardian*]

6.9.2 **Reflexive co-referring with nominal other than subject**

Less commonly, the reflexive may co-refer with a nominal other than the subject; for example, the direct object **[17]–[19]** and the subject predicative **[20]–[21]:**

[17] You've neither judged or encouraged me but you have allowed *me* to be *myself* and make my choices. [W]

[18] 'Learn what the white man has to teach *us*—then do it for *ourselves,*' says Derrick Malloy, eight minutes older than his brother. [*Wall Street Journal*]

[19] Will not someone out there save *him* from *himself*? [W]

[20] They were very much in the shadows ... and it was *him* ... all by *himself* on this stage you know

[21] It is *every man* for *himself*. [W]

6.9.3 **Required reflexive**

6.9.3.1 **Required reflexive as object or complement of verb**

When there is co-reference with a subject, the reflexive is required if it functions as an object (including **prepositional object,** cf. 11.20) or complement of the verb. Hence, the subject and the direct object refer to two different people in **[22]** but to the same person in **[23]:**

[22] *He* taught *him* to play the piano.

[23] *He* taught *himself* to play the piano.

Exceptionally the personal pronoun is used instead, to convey the impression of two aspects of a person—in **[24]** the giver and what is given:

[24] *You* have given me *you* and you have restored to me myself. [W]

6.9.3.2 **Required reflexive in the complement of preposition**

The reflexive is also required in many instances in the complement of a preposition. These include instances where the prepositional phrase modifies a noun that denotes a picture, work of literature, etc.:

[25] The princess is drawing a *picture of herself* and it's going to be pinned on the palace door

[26] Two Dallas schoolteachers sent him a *videotape of themselves* and told him, 'If you do not like what you see, pass it along to your buddies.' [*Wall Street Journal*]

[27] You could commission *prints of yourself*

[28] All the same, he gives an extremely good *account of himself* [*Wall Street Journal*]

The reflexive is also required in a prepositional phrase that is a part of an idiomatic expression [29]–[33]:

[29] Could the United States slide into a technical race against *itself* now there are no new generations of Soviet MIGs to mesmerise the Pentagon's planners

[30] Do you really feel bad about *yourself*? [W]

[31] Schumacher likened the ideal business structure to a series of balloons freely floating *by themselves* with a hand at the centre lightly holding the strings to keep them all together. [David Icke *It Doesn't Have To Be Like This*]

[32] Her father had commissioned it: that *in itself* was unusual. [Denise Robertson *Remember the Moment*]

[33] The very witnesses to the death of God at Auschwitz sometimes, *despite themselves*, write at moments of Providence and faith. [*Wall Street Journal*]

> **NOTE**
>
> In many prepositional phrases expressing concrete spatial relationship the personal pronouns are used even though there is co-reference with the subject:
>
> [N1] She only had a few pounds on her
>
> [N2] He took the children with him

6.9.3.3 Reflexive verbs

There are a number of **reflexive verbs**. These require a reflexive as direct object. Common reflexive verbs are *absent, avail, busy, content, pride*:

[34] Regarding Paternoster, the consortium...then sought to *avail itself* of the opportunity for intensive development by planning to build a million square feet of office space within the 4.3 acre site. [*British Journal of Aesthetics*]

[35] We like to *pride ourselves* on the care which we lavish on our children, so, why is child abuse not an issue of popular debate, other than around the times of extensive media coverage? [Paul Johnson *Child Abuse*]

Some verbs that may take reflexives as direct objects may omit them with little or no effect on the meaning. They include *adjust, behave, dress, hide, prepare, shave, undress, wash*:

[36] I shall try to *prepare myself* for you turning up on our shores six foot tall. [W]

[37] The seat belts automatically *adjust themselves* to your shoulder height

6.9.4 Optional primary reflexives

Reflexives optionally replace personal pronouns after some prepositions, including *as, but, except,* and *like*:

[38] After the Last Supper Jesus wrapped a towel *around himself* poured water into a basin and washed the feet of his disciples

[39] She has always dismissed chess as being too intellectual a game for someone *like herself*, but it is a chessplayer's mind which she is bringing to bear on these situations. [Anne Melville 'Portrait of a Woman' in *Snapshots*]

[40] The German Generalissimo in London might be no more civilized than Attila himself, but he would soon feel the difference *between himself* and Attila. [*Wall Street Journal*]

They also optionally replace first and second person pronouns in coordinated constructions. *Myself* is particularly common, since it is felt to be less assertive than *I* or *me*:

[41] And the dispute lay between both Indiana on one side of the Atlantic *and myself* on the other

[42] When you have identified these people please ask either Mrs Robinson *or myself* to come over and have a short session with them (approximately 1 hour) to discuss their role and responsibilities. [W]

[43] Hong Kong had obviously been very carefully planned with Peter *and myself* in mind [Graham Stark *Remembering Peter Sellars*]

In this use the coordinate construction may be the subject of its clause:

[44] You have there the front and the back ... of a letter from North Sakara on which Professor Smith and *myself* are working

6.9.5 Separation of *self*

The two parts of the reflexives can be separated by an intervening word, but then the possessive pronoun is used in the first part:

[45] He doesn't sound *his* normal *self*. [W]

The separation may also occur without any intervening word:

[46] He is most satisfying on the famous dead, whom he meets halfway—something he does not always do with his living subjects—revealing more of *his self*. [*Wall Street Journal*]

In headlines and other abbreviated styles of language, *self* alone may be used as the reflexive:

[47] Enfield Corp. President Improperly Put *Self* on Board, Judge Rules [*Wall Street Journal*]

6.9.6 Genitive of reflexives

Reflexives have no genitive form. The combination of dependent possessives with *own* effectively have this function. In [48] *his own* parallels *himself*:

[48] He taught *himself* to play on *his own* piano

6.10 Emphatic reflexive pronouns

Emphatic reflexives function as a kind of **appositive** (cf. 10.11) to a noun phrase, which they emphasize.

6.10.1 Emphatic reflexives with explicit subject

If that noun phrase is the subject, the reflexive may either immediately follow the subject [1] or occur at various later positions in the clause [2]–[5]:

[1]   *Mr. McGovern himself* had said repeatedly that he intended to stay on until he reached the conventional retirement age of 65, 'unless I get fired.' [*Wall Street Journal*]

[2]   The House and Senate are divided over whether the United Nations Population Fund will receive any portion of these appropriations, but *the size of the increase* is *itself* significant. [*Wall Street Journal*]

[3]   They also provided videotapes, which *they* selected *themselves*, of the high points of her interrogation. [*Wall Street Journal*]

[4]   Astrophysicist John N. Bahcall, who thinks a lot about how the sun shines (the 'solar neutrino problem'), says his kids are 'deeply opposed' to the deer hunt, but *he* has no opinion *himself*. [*Wall Street Journal*]

[5]   *The new structures* wouldn't *themselves* conceal policy differences

6.10.2 Emphatic reflexives with implied subject

As with the primary reflexives (cf. 6.9), the subject of a non-finite clause may be implied in a host clause [6]–[7] or from the context as a whole [8]:

[6]   To survive a squeeze *himself, Mr Spitalnick* has switched most of his operation into the private-label business, making garments that carry a store's brand. [*Wall Street Journal*]

[7]   And the Greeks looked down on *the Romans* as being upstart barbarians *themselves*

[8]   He said to us it's strange to get used to having to make the decisions *yourselves*

6.10.3 Emphatic reflexives with noun phrase other than subject

If the reflexive is appositive to a noun phrase other than the subject, it must follow that phrase immediately:

[9]   In 1989, as often as not, the principal fights in the major campaigns are prompted by *the ads themselves*. [*Wall Street Journal*]

[10] … whether the relevant indemnity should be signed or countersigned by the bank rather than by the charterers *themselves* without any countersignature.

[11] It is taken for granted that any letter addressed only to either Will or to *Cathy herself* will be passed across the breakfast table as soon as it is read …

6.11 Reciprocal pronouns

The **reciprocal pronouns** are *each other* and the less frequent *one another* and their respective genitives, *each other's* and *one another's*. Like the primary reflexives (cf. 6.9), the reciprocals co-refer with a noun phrase; but unlike the primary reflexives, they co-refer only with noun phrases that are plural in form or meaning.

6.11.1 **Reciprocals co-referring with explicit subject**

[1] Oh I suppose it's a question *lots of people* ask *each other*

[2] *Chris and I* ... suited *each other*

[3] It's caused by *two germs* that live together ... and scratch *each other's* back

[4] We *none of us* poach *each other's* business

[5] Anyhow *you and Harriet* know *one another*

[6] Nell's a very prim little thing, *they*'ll be good for *one another*. [E. V. Thompson *Lottie Trago*]

6.11.2 **Reciprocals co-referring with noun phrases other than subject**

As with the primary reflexives, the reciprocals usually co-refer with the subject, but they may co-refer with noun phrases in other functions, such as direct object:

[7] Now you should be able to stack *all of these columns* on top of *each other*

[8] In programming, getting the sound you want typically involves constantly moving to and fro between different parameters, fine-tuning *them* against *one another*. [*Music Technology*]

In [9] the noun phrase *the banks* is the complement of a preposition and the reciprocal pronoun is within the postmodifier (*to each other*) of that phrase:

[9] Second, there is a reduced risk because the gross exposure of *the banks* to *each other* has been cut. [*Financial Times*]

6.11.3 **Reciprocals co-referring with implied subject**

As with the primary reflexives, the co-referring subject *you* is implied in subjectless imperatives [10] and may be implied from a host clause [11]–[12]:

[10] Love *one another*

[11] And then the prophet comes in and says well even if *we* all have one father that's no excuse for betraying *each other* and in particular for men to betray their wives and to take foreign wives

[12] On Wall Street *men and women* walk with great purpose, noticing *one another* only when they jostle for cabs. [*Wall Street Journal*]

6.11.4 **Separation of the two elements of reciprocals**

Constructions with *each other* correspond to constructions in which the two parts of the pronoun are separated into *each... other*. The separation places greater emphasis on the reciprocity:

[13] They will *each* know when to involve *the other* in responding to the task in hand. [W]

[14] Fortunately, this doesn't lead to *each* program looking like every *other* ... [*Personal Computer World*]

The corresponding constructions with the reciprocals are:

[13a] They will know when to involve *each other* in responding to the task in hand.

[14a] Fortunately, this doesn't lead to the programs looking like *each other*.

6.12 *Wh*-pronouns and determiners

The **wh-pronouns** and **determiners** are so called because they are spelled with an initial *wh*, the exceptions being *how* and its compounds. They fall into five sets according to the type of sentence or clause in which they occur:

1. interrogative
2. exclamative
3. relative
4. nominal relative
5. *wh*-conditional

USE OF *WH*-WORDS IN DETAIL

Some *wh*-words are used both as pronouns and as determiners. The *wh*-words or phrases with the *wh*-word are initial in their sentence or clause. Hence, if they are not the subject, they are generally fronted:

> They gave me *an expensive gift* for my birthday.
> *What an expensive gift* they gave me for my birthday.

For *wh*-adverbs, see 8.6.

6.12.1 Interrogative *wh*-pronouns and *wh*-determiners

6.12.1.1 **Interrogative** *wh*-pronouns and *wh*-determiners introduce *wh*-**questions** (see 2.5.2). They represent a piece of missing information that the speaker wants the hearer to supply. The pronoun is illustrated in **[1]** and the determiner in **[2]**:

[1] A: *Who*'s that then
    B. Well she's called Lynn

[2] A: *whose* project is it
    B: Uhm ... I'm not sure

Citations **[3]** and **[4]** illustrate their uses in subordinate clauses:

[3] A: I want to ask you *what* you think about the role of the father today
    B: Thank you very much

[4] A: Do you know *what* word is used to mean that something is life-giving or supportive in its function
    B: Growth factor

6.12.1.2 There are five interrogative pronouns:

> *who   whom   whose   which   what*

Three of these are also determiners:

> *which   what   whose*

6.12.1.3 *Who* and *whom* differ in case: *who* is subjective and *whom* is objective (cf. 6.4). But in practice *who* is commonly also used for object functions **[5]**–**[6]** except in formal style, where it is replaced by *whom* **[7]**:

[5] *Who* didn't you like

[6] Anyway so ... *who* else can we nominate

[7]   When was it last serviced, by *whom*, and what service agreements or guarantees exist? [W]

6.12.1.4 There are some **gender** contrasts between personal (masculine or feminine) and non-personal (cf. 6.4). *Who* and *whom* are only personal. Both as pronoun **[8]** and as determiner **[9]**, *whose* also has only personal reference:

[8]   *Whose* is that book?

[9]   *Whose* standards are you...invoking

Which, on the other hand, can be personal or non-personal both as pronoun **[10]**–**[11]** and as determiner **[12]**–**[13]**:

[10]   I mean *which* is better to do this and clean clean the wax out of your ears or to go round with wax in your ears

[11]   *Which* of your friends are you closest to?

[12]   'In a credit crunch,' Citicorp Chairman John S. Reed warns, 'financial institutions would be faced with a choice: *Which* customers do you take care of?' [*Wall Street Journal*]

[13]   *Which* car did you take

The gender of *what* varies according to its function. As a pronoun, *what* is only non-personal:

[14]   *What* were the first symptoms

[15]   *What* are other people doing

As a determiner, *what* can introduce personal **[16]** as well as non-personal noun phrases **[17]**–**[18]**:

[16]   *What* politicians have you met?

[17]   By *what* right do we impose our values on the residents of Colombia? [*Wall Street Journal*]

[18]   Why *what* size feet have you got

6.12.1.5 The speaker uses *which* to indicate an assumption that the hearer has a restricted set from which to make a response. In using *what*, the speaker assumes an open-ended set.

6.12.1.6 The interrogative pronouns may be postmodified by *else* or *otherwise* (*who else*, *what otherwise*) and by *ever* (*who ever*, *what ever*) and various intensifying phrases (*who the hell*, *what the devil*).

6.12.2. Exclamative *wh*-determiner

What is used as an **exclamative determiner**. It may precede the indefinite article:

[19]   And he's just been acquired by the slavers and they are washing him in ... in a stream and they're finding out *what* a very beautiful young man he is

[20]   If it were me I would rather spend the money on something else given *what* a cramped flat we have. [W]

[21]   *What* a mess she was in, *what* a labyrinth of lies and half-truths was closing around her, her own and those of a generation gone. [Denise Robertson *Remember the Moment*]

If the noun is non-count or plural, *what* is the only determiner:

[22]   *What nonsense* I'm writing.

[23]   *What* strong words you use. [W]

The exclamative noun phrase is often used alone:

[24] *What* a ridiculous letter. [W]

[25] *What* an appropriate introduction to San Francisco! [W]

[26] Oh *what* a nightmare

[27] *What* fun

Exclamative *what* has intensifying force similar to that of intensifying *such* (cf. 6.14). But, unlike *such*-phrases, *what*-phrases are always initial in their clause, and they can introduce subordinate clauses, as in citations **[19]** and **[20]** above.

6.12.3 Relative *wh*-pronouns and *wh*-determiners

Relative pronouns and determiners are used in the construction of relative clauses, which postmodify nouns (cf. 10.9). They normally come at the beginning of relative clauses:

[28] Oh my God I went to have dinner with this girl called Kate *who*'s on my course

But if the relative item is a *wh*-pronoun and it is the complement of a preposition, the preposition may precede the pronoun:

[29] Again I'm not so much concerned with meaning but the ways *in which* the satire is … achieved

Similarly, a preposition may precede a noun phrase that has the relative determiner:

[30] Outside the Church's boundaries lay the truly independent congregations, *of whose* political importance, small numbers and doctrinal divisions something has already been said. [Ronald Hutton *The British Republic, 1649–1660*]

6.12.3.1 There are three *wh*-relative pronouns:

who,   whom,   which

There are two *wh*-relative determiners:

whose,   which

In addition, relative clauses may be introduced by the relative pronoun *that*, which is sometimes omitted. When *that* is omitted, the relative is said to be the zero relative pronoun.

6.12.3.2 Like the interrogative pronouns, *who* and *whom* differ in case: *who* is subjective and *whom* is objective. As with the interrogative pronouns, *who* is commonly also used for object functions **[31]**–**[32]** except in formal style, where it is replaced by *whom* **[33]**–**[34]**:

[31] There's a group called Coimbre Flamenco *who* I saw at Sadler's Wells

[32] I wouldn't want to live with someone *who* I didn't have any sex life with

[33] Aeneas suffers perpetual isolation as he wanders from place to place, having lost those *whom* he loved.

[34] Now … as for actually … how … or to *whom* you send the messages … there's a standard convention … used … for addresses for e-mail

6.12.3.3 As with the interrogative pronouns, there are some gender contrasts. *Who* and *whom* are personal, as illustrated in **[31]**–**[34]**. *Which* is non-personal **[35]**–**[36]**:

[35] They can't fit me in for a week so I'm going to do it for a day *which* is useless really but … I just heard today

[36] All these are the dates of the context in *which* the artefact was found not the date that they think the artefact belongs to

---
NOTE

The older use of the pronoun *which* for personal reference ('Our Father *which* art in Heaven') is preserved in archaic forms of religious language.

That and the **zero relative pronoun** (symbolized by '[Ø]') are used for both personal and non-personal reference:

[37] Maybe they are people *that* have just never thought about it

[38] Your father actually is up to just about every trick *that's* in the book

[39] The people [Ø] we were staying with they ... uh cooked us a traditional Normandy dinner

[40] What's happened to the door [Ø] we had out there

Neither *that* nor the zero relative may be the complement of a preceding preposition. Citation **[36]** illustrates this difference between them and the *wh*-relatives. In **[36]** *which* is the complement of the preceding preposition in *the context in which* ...; but the preposition *to* is **stranded** at the end of the relative clause introduced by *that*: *the date that they think the artefact belongs to*. The zero relative pronoun does not function as the subject of the relative clause.

The determiner *whose* is used for personal and non-personal reference:

[41] It is for example clear ... that pharaonic Egyptian society did not contain people *whose* status was so elevated that they felt writing to be beneath them

[42] So in the case of the sensory system ... the central neuron is the neuron that aligns itself in the dorsary ganglia and *whose* axons make up peripheral nerves and dorsal roots

The determiner *which* is normally used for non-personal reference:

[43] It may be that the potential obstacles are not insurmountable, in *which* case I look forward to hearing from you to discuss things further. [W]

6.12.3.4 Only the *wh*-relatives are normally used in **non-restrictive** relative clauses, including **sentential relative clauses** (cf. 10.9f.):

[44] They also provided videotapes, *which* they selected themselves, of the high points of her interrogation. [*Wall Street Journal*]

[45] There are charges that these culminated in the kidnapping and execution of former Premier Aldo Moro, *whose* insistence on defying an American veto on admitting Communists into the Cabinet infuriated Washington. [*The Observer*]

6.12.3.5 Non-standard dialects often use *what* or *as* as relative pronouns for personal or non-personal reference:

That's the woman *what* told me.
Here's the car *as* I bought yesterday.

In some dialects, genitive *what's* is sometimes used as the determiner:

They're the people *what's* children are causing all the noise.

The relative pronoun is commonly omitted in non-standard dialects when it is the subject of the relative clause:

I'm taking the bus [Ø] goes to Manchester.

Resumptive pronouns are sometimes introduced, echoing the relative pronoun:

> They're making a birthday party for their youngest, *which* I'm invited to *it*.

6.12.4 Nominal relative *wh*-pronouns and *wh*-determiners

Nominal relatives introduce nominal relative clauses (cf. 14.3), which function like noun phrases as subject, direct object, etc.

[46] Excuse me I've got to do *what I did last time* (' ... the thing that I did last time')

6.12.4.1 There are twelve nominal relative pronouns:

who	*which*
whom	*whichever*
whoever	*whichsoever*
whomever	*what*
whosoever	*whatever*
whomsoever	*whatsoever*

Which and *what* and their compounds can also be determiners. The difference between the two sets parallels that for the interrogative determiners *which* and *what*. Those ending in *-soever* are archaic, except for *whatsoever*.

Here are some further examples of the nominal relative pronouns:

[47] You saw *what* happened

[48] No ... but it pays *what* I would call a part-time wage

[49] And ... I mean ... he'll have to think about *who* will look after Nell when she gets home from school

[50] I can't remember *who* he was talking to

[51] I was just wondering if it was worth complaining to *whoever* was in charge or not bothering

[52] Because she's still wondering ... why you haven't acknowledged *whatever* it was she last sent you

[53] I want to see *what* happens next

6.12.4.2 Here, as elsewhere, the *who* pronouns (*who, whoever, whosoever*) are subjective and the *whom* pronouns are objective, but the *who* pronouns are generally used for object functions except in formal contexts.

Here are examples of nominal relative determiners:

[54] He has chosen from the scribe's pattern books *what* scenes he wishes in his tomb

[55] But it's really quite arbitrary *which* by-elections they are

[56] So you will only see a very little of *whatever* fabric you choose at the sides

[57] The reason by-elections are given this great significance is that *whichever* by-elections occur before a general election are always seen as having been the pointers

6.12.4.3 *Who, whom,* and *what* may also be used in nominal relative *to*-infinitive clauses:

[58] It outlines some of the opportunities that are available at our main branches and *who* to contact for more information

[59] They were called media response teams which I thought was an interesting new development in which journalists were really carried around and shown *what* to report and told *what* to report effectively

6.12.5 *Wh*-conditional pronouns and determiners

Wh-conditional pronouns and determiners are compounds ending in -*ever*. They introduce *wh*-conditional clauses (cf. 14.5.3), which denote a range of possible choices. The clauses function not as nominal clauses but as **adverbial clauses**:

[60]   *Whatever* you've been doing you've been doing the right thing

There are six *wh*-conditional pronouns. *Whosoever* and *whomsoever* are archaic. *Whatever* and *whichever* are also used as determiners; the difference between them parallels that for the interrogative and nominal relative determiners *what* and *which*. As elsewhere, the *who* pronouns (*whoever* and *whosoever*) are subjective and the *whom* pronouns are objective, but the *who* pronouns are used for objective functions except in formal contexts.

Here are some further examples of the pronouns:

[61]   *Whoever* you are I'm not going to bother wasting my time

[62]   I used to set so much a day either so many hours or so many words *whichever* came first

[63]   *Whatever* people say I've noticed they are distinctly different

[64]   Piracy and robbery and fraud could occur between individuals at any time *whatever* treaties said

Here are examples of the determiners:

[65]   *Whatever* problem comes up you always have this issue in experimental psychology of how we test it

[66]   You will be surprised how much knowing you are using the best quality bait will do for your confidence and success, *whichever* species you are after. [David Batten *An Introduction to River Fishing*]

The pronouns can be used in **verbless clauses**:

[67]   *Whatever* the reason, the result has been only too predictable. [*Daily Mail*]

They can also be used alone to indicate indeterminate additions or alternatives:

[68]   I couldn't say well I'm personnel manager here or I'm this or that or *whatever*

[69]   And she knew an ex-professor because she did some M.Sc. in shipping trade and finance *whatever* and she's saying she's going to get no problem ah

[70]   They will then be passed on to another company that will make them into some sort of product and finally go to an end customer … something like NASA or *whoever*

Whatsoever can function as an **intensifier**:

[71]   The referee had no doubts *whatsoever*

6.13 Indefinite pronouns and determiners

The **indefinite** pronouns and determiners are so called because they have a general reference. Many items function both as pronouns and determiners. Compounds in -*one*, -*body* or -*thing* function only as pronouns, and so does *none*. *No* is only a determiner.

The indefinites fall into two sets. The primary set consists of four interrelated subsets:

assertive
non-assertive
negative
universal

The second set consists of the quantifiers (or quantifying indefinites).

6.13.1 **Primary indefinites**

Table 6.13.1 Primary indefinite pronouns and determiners

Assertive		Non-assertive		Negative		Universal	
pronoun	determiner	pronoun	determiner	pronoun	determiner	pronoun	determiner
some	some	any	any	none	no	all	all
someone		anyone		no one		everyone	
somebody		anybody		nobody		everybody	
something		anything		nothing		everything	
		either	either	neither	neither	both	both
						each	each
							every

Table 6.13.1 displays the four subsets of the primary indefinites. All the compounds in -*one* and -*body* have genitives; for example: *someone's, anybody's, no one's.*

The compounds in -*one* and -*body* have personal reference, the compounds in -*thing* have non-personal reference. All the others (including *none*) can have either personal or non-personal reference. The primary indefinites vary in countability and number. For example, *some, any, none, no,* and *all* can be used as non-count as well as count; *some wine, any money, none (of the information), no butter, all (of the evidence).* Some primary indefinites are count only: they may be singular (e.g. *everyone*), plural (e.g. *both*), or dual (*either, neither, both*).

6.13.1.1 **Non-assertive indefinites**
The **non-assertives** have a negative force, and they tend to occur in non-assertive contexts, particularly in negative, interrogative, and conditional clauses. The question in [1] indicates that the speaker expects a negative answer:

[1]   No uhm were you using *any* form of contraception

Here are further examples of non-assertives:

[2]   I said I don't want to do *any* more essays

[3]   Uh … I might come in on Tuesday depending if I've got *anything* to do

[4]   *Anybody* else like a piece of *anything* that they can see on here that I haven't given them

[5]   But uh hardbacks I wouldn't lend to *anyone*

[6]   Did you see *either* of those two gentlemen on *any* occasion in 1987

The non-assertives can also be used emphatically (e.g. 'any at all', 'anybody no matter who') outside non-assertive contexts:

[7]   This is always a question in psychology for *any* area

[8]   And so it's ... totally accessible ... for *anybody*

[9]   The cat will attack *anyone*.

The negative force is in the implied contrast. For **[9]** the meaning conveyed is that the cat will attack not just certain people. Similarly, in **[10]** the implication is that nobody has more fault than the speaker:

[10]   It's my fault as much as *anybody* else's more than *anybody* else's

6.13.1.2 Assertive indefinites
The **assertives** have a positive force. This is most obvious in questions. In **[11]** *some* indicates an expected positive response:

[11]   Dad will you have *some* more juice

Here are some further examples of assertives:

[12]   Listen can't we do this at *some* other time

[13]   Oh well I've never been *something* like that

[14]   Oh please eat *something*

[15]   Oh that was *someone* else

[16]   So I think from today's session you've realised I hope that you shouldn't start *somebody* on life-long anti-hypertensive therapy based upon one single blood pressure measurement

6.13.1.3 Negative indefinites
Here are examples of **negative** indefinites:

[17]   *Nobody* ever makes it like she used to make it

[18]   At the same time *neither* party can afford to ignore the two main messages from the electorate

[19]   *Neither* of these two types of new religious movements is likely to permit much in the way of 'internal pluralism'. [W]

It has been argued that *none* is singular because of its etymology. In practice, it is treated as both singular **[20]**–**[21]** and plural **[22]**–**[23]**:

[20]   There have been six federal presidents since the birth of the federal state and *none* has been as popular as the present president

[21]   We all know in our own lives what changes the last ten years have brought but *none* of us knows the picture overall and that's what the census supplies

[22]   There are many origami yachts, boats and ships, but *none* are as simple or as full of movement as this wonderful design by Japan's First Lady of origami, Mrs Toshie Takahoma. [Paul Jackson *Classic Origami*]

[23]   What worries me about regional theatres at the moment is that almost *none* of them have permanent companies

6.13.1.4 Universal indefinites
Here are examples of **universal** indefinites:

[24]   He denied *all* knowledge of it

[25]   And she said *all* I want is a vase

[26]   The ocean currents carrying warm water could reach *both* polar regions entirely unobstructed. [John Gribbin *Hothouse Earth*]

[27]   So *each* party has its own different rules for election of its leader

[28]   Environment is *everything* that happens to you which you sense happening to you as you grow up through life

[29]   And the imposition of calendar age on *everybody* ... by social life and by bureaucracy is something which I think we're right strongly to resist

6.13.2 **The quantifiers**

6.13.2.1 **Primary quantifiers**

The **primary quantifiers** can function either as pronouns or as determiners:

1. *many, more, most, a few, fewer, fewest, several, enough*
2. *much, more, most, a little, less, least, enough*
3. *few, little*

Subset (1) quantifiers are count, and subset (2) quantifiers are non-count. However, *less* is often treated also as count ('*less* people'). Subset (3) quantifiers are negative; *few* is count and *little* is non-count.

Here are examples of the quantifiers in their three sets:

(1) Count **[30]–[33]**:

[30]   And *many* of these earthquakes are caused by a rupture along a single fault

[31]   So we switched on and off uh *several* times which is uh the best way of coping with temperamental printers

[32]   And I've got so *many* events to go to I mean I know that sounds a bit odd but I mean I've got *a few*

[33]   This is a false belief you've been having for *a* good *few* years now and I think it's time ... that you got rid of this

(2) Non-count **[34]–[35]**:

[34]   You may have *a little* trouble getting in

[35]   And such wilderness as we do have is actually wearing out because we have so *much* access

(3) Negative **[36]–[37]**:

[36]   There was *little* time for research and there were *few* research students

[37]   There are very *few* clubs now which're exclusively male

6.13.2.2 **Compound quantifiers**

In addition, there are a number of **compound quantifiers** used only as pronouns; for example: *a bit, a lot, a couple*. Like the primary quantifiers, they can combine with a following *of*-phrase to denote quantity.

6.13.3 **Modification of indefinites**

Indefinite pronouns may be postmodified mainly by relative clauses **[38]**, and **prepositional phrases [39]**:

[38]   And *anybody* who thinks that there is great glory in war as such uh is off his head

[39]   Michele on Sunday was sort of pronouncing *some* of the Latin names

The compounds in -*body*, -*one*, and -*thing* can also be postmodified by **reduced relative clauses**:

[40]   Well Karen reckons that she's kind of jealous of Karen and Ian because she's got *nothing* out there apart from Salvatore

[41] The parent turns out to be *somebody* quite murderous

[42] I can never think of *anything* to say when I'm being being under stress

Some of the primary quantifiers can be premodified by intensifiers, such as *very* and *so*.

6.14 Demonstratives

6.14.1 **Primary demonstratives**

There are four primary **demonstratives**:

> *this*   *that*   *these*   *those*

They can function either as pronouns **[1]** or as determiners **[2]**:

[1] Oh you have to pay for *these*

[2] Do you have one of *those* houses with a view

The primary demonstratives present two types of contrast. The first is a contrast in **number**: *this* and *that* are singular, *these* and *those* are plural. The second is a contrast in **proximity**: *this* and *these* indicate relative nearness, *that* and *those* indicate relative remoteness. The proximity may be in space **[3]**–**[4]** or in time **[5]**–**[6]**:

[3] But in the presence of a scattering material the light has travelled a very convoluted path perhaps three or four times the distance between *this* side of the bottle and *that* side

[4] *This* paper builds on *that* study to propose a mapping to allow Mascot 3 to be used with Occam. [*Software Engineering Journal*]

[5] Lewis with a kind of half smile playing around his lips … and just dropping off his work rate a bit in *this* second after *that* fast start to it

[6] They would set out what *these* policy areas would be and then the foreign ministers of the twelve would implement *those* policies on the basis of majority voting

This is also used in informal speech as an indefinite determiner, roughly corresponding to *a* or *some*:

[7] And there'd be *this* guy that always used to snore with his mouth wide open in the tree and they the others used to pop acorns in through his mouth

Similarly, *these* may be indefinite, introducing new information rather than referring to something in the situational or linguistic context:

[8] There's all *these* horror stories about it happening but I've never actually heard of it … actually happened to anybody

6.14.2 **Other demonstratives**

Such may have a demonstrative sense ('like that') as a pronoun **[9]** or (more frequently) as a determiner **[10]**–**[11]**:

[9] I'd like to do it every day … but you know *such* is life

[10] Do I understand you to be saying that in *such* an accident uh a passenger would be thrown uh first of all forwards and then backwards

[11] He is entitled to *such* payments subject only to the limited category of cross-claims which the law permits to be raised as defences by way of set-off in *such* circumstances

In **[10]** the determiner *such* precedes the indefinite article.

Some non-standard dialects have a three-term system for the demonstratives. Distance further off than *that/those* is indicated by *yon* and *thon*, among several variants.

Common non-standard alternatives to *those* as determiner are *they* and particularly *them*:

[12] What was Moses doing going off in *them* wild jeans

There are also non-standard compounds in which *here* is added to *this/these* ('*this here* house') and *there* to *that/those* ('*that there* tree') and their variants (e.g. '*them there* politicians').

6.14.3 Modification of demonstratives

The demonstratives may be preceded by determiners:

[13] I don't know what *all this* is about
[14] Oh well let me take *both those* points uh at once
[15] They must not lay the paper upon which they are writing on *any such* book, etc, open or closed. [W]

The demonstrative pronouns may also be postmodified, particularly *that* and *those*:

[16] Conditions within the sands of the embryo dunes are similar to *those at the top of the intertidal zone*. [Colin Little *The Terrestrial Invasion*]
[17] But to *those who knew the river in its heyday* it's dead
[18] Is this an indication that the social structure within the church mirrored *that in society*? [W]
[19] Perhaps the most promising view is *that which suggests that amnesia is the result of damage to a specific systemic component of episodic memory*. [W]

6.14.4 Gender and demonstratives

The singular demonstrative pronouns generally have only non-personal reference. The exceptions are when they are subject and the speaker is providing or seeking identification:

[20] *This* is my daughter Felicity
[21] Is *that* Jane Warren

6.15 Numerals

There are three types of numeral:

1. cardinal
2. ordinal
3. fraction

Numerals constitute a closed system in that they comprise a restricted set of items, but there is no limit on the combination of these items. They may function as pronouns or determiners. They may be written out as words or as digits.

6.15.1 **Cardinals**

Cardinals (or **cardinal numerals**) refer to quantity. They include *zero* and its synonyms: *nought* or *naught*, *cipher* or *cypher*, and the terms used in various games—*nil, nothing, love*, and (in American English) *zip*. They also include *dozen* and *score*.

6.15.1.1 Here are examples of cardinals as pronouns **[1]–[3]** and as determiners **[4]–[6]**:

[1]   She wakes me up at *six* every morning

[2]   That was a mistake by a factor of *ten*

[3]   Uhm ... the reason for doing that is the *five* of us spread out over a little distance in the wood and we each took a patch

[4]   Stay in and watch *two* videos

[5]   Oh we had a long discussion about it on *one* occasion

[6]   Well the book's about *two hundred and fifty* pages long

6.15.1.2 Cardinal pronouns can be plural:

[7]   It does affect *millions* of people

[8]   He took me to what he called a place round the corner, a kind of club where youngish men, all civilians, sat in *twos* and *threes* at little tables with drinks in front of them, talking in low voices. [Julian Symons *Death's Darkest Face*]

[9]   Further north I came across *dozens* of Iraqi soldiers wandering slowly towards their border

The plural may indicate a range:

[10]   He was in his late *forties* I would say

[11]   They are wishing him back to the form that he showed throughout the *nineteen-eighties*

[12]   In the *1990s*, who knows what may happen? [W]

6.15.1.3 A range is also indicated by numerals that are hyphenated or linked by slashes:

[13]   Similar situations apply in India, a country in the World Bank's lower middle-income group of *35–40* countries. [W]

[14]   This is a mixed age group party rather than the planned *17–35* but will hopefully still be a much needed enjoyable relaxing break. [W]

[15]   Sunday work is *2pm–6pm* but is paid as a full day. [W]

[16]   At some time in the near future we will have to decide as to whether to allocate the pension payments to *1991/92* or relate them back to *1990/91*. [W]

6.15.1.4 Cardinals can be premodified by intensifiers:

[17]   I had it in that garage for *nearly thirty* years

[18]   But I mean my only recollection of it is sleeping in a wood for *about four or five* hours

[19]   Most people's vocabulary is *over fifteen thousand* words

[20]   They arrived *some two* minutes ago

[21] If a satellite is placed in orbit *around 41,000* km away and its motion is parallel to that of the Earth's rotation, its velocity matches that of the Earth and it remains above a fixed point on the surface. [W]

[22] For example, on average Cambridge has something like a dozen days a year when the temperature will reach 25°C (77°F), whereas Lerwick in the Shetland Isles can sometimes go *a full twelve* months without registering as high as 18°C (64°F). [Bill Giles *The Story of Weather*]

[23] It's *a good two* weeks' time

6.15.1.5 Approximation is also indicated by the postmodifying *odd* and by *or so*:

[24] He's *forty odd* I would have thought

[25] And of those *forty or so* jobs you've applied for have they mainly been in response to vacancies that you've seen advertised

[26] You've been in high office now only *three* years *or so*

6.15.1.6 Cardinals functioning as pronouns can also be postmodified:

[27] In Mexico City motor vehicles *three million of them* produce eighty percent of the contamination in the air

[28] Gildas dates the Saxon revolt to *446 A.D.* (which was later amended to *449 A.D.* by Bede). [W]

[29] Of the countries creating a diverse manufacturing economic base there are *four which have surpassed many of the others in economic development.* [W]

[30] When you write at *12.35 at night* that's what happens. [W]

[31] *One of the four nuclear reactors at the plant* was badly damaged by a chemical explosion after it seriously over-heated and went out of control. [W]

6.15.1.7 It is conventional to write out a numeral in words at the beginning of a sentence. Numerals of ten or under are normally written out except in formulae or in tables, but some publishers extend the rule to all numerals under 100.

6.15.2 Ordinals

Ordinals (or **ordinal numerals**) refer to positions in a sequence.

6.15.2.1 Primary ordinals

The primary ordinals are items such as *first, second, fifteenth, twenty-third*.

Here are examples of the primary ordinals as pronouns [32]–[33] and as determiners [34]–[35]:

[32] I've only mentioned the *first* of the analyses

[33] Two scans are made; the *second* being closer to the position of the teats as indicated by the *first*. [*Robotica*]

[34] It was the *first* time I'd met anyone in a wheelchair.

[35] Well now let's move beyond Elgar into the early years of the *twentieth* century

6.15.2.2 Other items resembling primary ordinals

A number of other items have a grammatical function and a meaning similar to those of the primary ordinals, including:

additional	*further*	*other*	*same*
another	*last*	*others*	*subsequent*
following	*latter*	*preceding*	
former	*next*	*previous*	

All of these can function as determiners. Most can also function as pronouns; the exceptions are *additional, further,* and *subsequent.* Here are some examples:

[36] One and a half billion babies will be born over the *next* ten years

[37] Unemployment had increased by over 400,000 in the *last* four months alone. [Lord Young *The Enterprise Years*]

[38] And Andy Smith who won his *previous* race is currently struggling at the back

[39] But before we get on to those let's just consider one *other* aspect of the climate system

6.15.2.3 Number in ordinals
The ordinals may have either singular or plural reference, except that *another* is only singular and *others* is only plural.

6.15.2.4 Premodification of ordinals
First, next, last, and *same* may be premodified by *very:*

[40] Today's ... lecture ... the *very last* lecture before Christmas ... uh is The Ancient Celts Through Caesar's Eyes

[41] Strong rumours were around about a reshuffle the *very next* day ... [Lord Young *The Enterprise Years*]

[42] And what arouses one's suspicions is that that *very same* Hebrew form Malachi ... means my messenger

6.15.2.5 Postmodification of ordinals
The ordinals functioning as pronouns may be postmodified:

[43] Incorporated in the great wooden beams which descended deep into the mineshaft was a revolutionary 'man-engine', the *first of its kind in the country.* [E. V. Thompson *Lottie Trago*]

[44] The findings of Rothwell (1985, p.375) are not encouraging in this regard, showing decisions on technology to be usually 'top-down' in character, to the extent that supervisors and end-users are often the *last to know about the nature of the changes proposed.* [W]

6.15.3 Fractions

The **fractions** refer to quantities less than one. They include *(a) half, two halves, a quarter, three-quarters,* and compounds of a cardinal number with an ordinal, such as *two-thirds, three-fifths, one-eighth.*

The fractions can be pronouns **[45]–[47]** or determiners **[48]–[51]**:

[45] In some areas, it states, as many as *one third* of homes have already been sold. [*The Scotsman*]

[46] Each one of these is about ten milliseconds *ten thousandths* of a second

[47] And just under *half* get invited to staff meetings

[48] Uh I did it for about *half* a term

[49] It's probably *half* the population at best that are covered

[50] At an altitude of 60 miles (96 kilometres)—the maximum height the V-2 reached—the air has about *one-millionth* the density at sea level, so the V-2 can be considered to have been in space for a brief period. [W]

[51] Even now jets can only operate up to about *one-sixth* satellite speed. [W]

Cardinals may be coordinated with fractions:

[52] *One and a half billion* babies will be born over the next ten years

[53] And that was how I flew, with the rest of the unit, to Hong Kong for *three and a half* wonderful weeks. [Graham Stark *Remembering Peter Sellars*]

Fractions may be premodified by intensifiers:

[54] The society in which we live is one in which two percent of the society own *about half* the wealth and it's getting worse the gap between the rich and the poor

[55] *Nearly three-quarters* of the water used is for agricultural purposes, and the area of irrigated land is increasing steadily each year. [W]

[56] John Turner who ... is playing the organ today has been Cathedral Organist here for *over quarter* of a century

Further examples appear in the citations given above: *as many as one third* **[45]**, *under half* **[47]**, *up to about one-sixth* **[51]**.

Chapter 7
Verbs

Summary

Summary

Verbs (or main verbs) by themselves or preceded by auxiliaries (or auxiliary verbs) function as the verb of a sentence or clause. Verbs have five form-types: base (without inflections), -s form (for the present tense), -ing participle, past, and -ed participle. In regular verbs the past and the -ed participle are identical, but they are distinguished in some irregular verbs.

Auxiliaries fall into two major sets: primary auxiliaries (be, have, do) and modals (e.g. can, will, must). They precede verbs to express notions such as time, permission, possibility. As operators they play a role in sentence processes such as negation and interrogation.

7.1 Characteristics of verbs

Verbs (or **main verbs** or **lexical verbs** or **full verbs**) function as the head of a **verb phrase**, either alone or preceded by one or more auxiliaries (cf. 7.9, 11.1ff.). For example, the main verb *prepare* in its various forms:

[1] They *prepared* the meal.

[2] They *may prepare* the meal.

[3] They *should have prepared* the meal.

[4] They *may have been preparing* the meal.

In [1]–[4] the verb phrases function as the verb of the sentence.

> **NOTE**
>
> In this sense the verb is a constituent of a sentence or clause just as are the subject and direct object. See 2.1.1.2 Note and 3.1.2 Note.

> **SOME TYPICAL VERB ENDINGS**
>
> -ate: translate, incorporate, abbreviate, contaminate, assassinate, demonstrate
> -en: sicken, happen, madden, toughen, strengthen, listen
> -ify: magnify, clarify, beautify, objectify, typify, amplify
> -ise, -ize: baptise, agonise, popularise, legalize, summarize, computerize
>
> Some of these endings were present when the words were borrowed from other languages.

7.2 Form-types of verbs

Verbs have five form-types. In all regular verbs (such as *prepare*) and in many irregular verbs (such as *make*), two of the form-types have the same form. In some regular verbs (e.g. *put*) three form-types have the same form. The full set of five forms appears in the irregular verb *write*.

Form-types:

1. base	*prepare*	*make*	*put*	*write*
2. -s	*prepares*	*makes*	*puts*	*writes*
3. -*ing* participle	*preparing*	*making*	*putting*	*writing*
4. past	*prepared*	*made*	*put*	*wrote*
5. -*ed* participle	*prepared*	*made*	*put*	*written*

The highly irregular verb *be* has eight forms, three of which have informal contracted forms. There are also informal contracted negative forms ending in *n't*. Some of the forms have stressed and unstressed pronunciations. Both are given below; the stressed pronunciation first and then the unstressed (with reduced vowels).

be

1. base	*be* /biː/, /bɪ/
2. present—1st person singular	*am* /am/, /əm/
	'm /m/
—in questions	*aren't* /ɑːnt/ or /ɑːrnt/
—3rd person singular	*is* /ɪz/
	's /z/ or /s/
	isn't /ɪznt/
—others	*are* /ɑː/ or /ɑːr/
	're /ə/ or /ər/
	aren't /ɑːnt/ or /ɑːrnt/
3. -*ing* participle	*being* /biːɪŋ/
4. past—1st and 3rd person singular	*was* /wɒz/ or /wəz/
	wasn't /wɒznt/
—others	*were* /wəː/ or /wəːr/
	weren't /wəːnt/ or /wəːrnt/
5. -*ed* participle	*been* /biːn/, /bɪn/

Is corresponds to the -*s* form-type in all other words, but *am* and *are* correspond to the present tense uses of the base form-type. For *'s*, contracted from *is*, and also the contracted forms of *has* and *does* (see below), /z/ follows a voiced sound and /s/ a voiceless sound (cf. 7.3). The alternatives with or without /r/ depend on whether the accent is rhotic or non-rhotic.

The irregular verb *have* also has informal non-negative and negative contracted forms:

have

1. base	*have* /hav/, /həv/, or /əv/
—for present tense	*'ve* /v/
	haven't /havnt/
2. -*s* form	*has* /haz/, /həz/, or /əz/
	's /z/ or /s/
	hasn't /haznt/
3. -*ing* participle	*having* /havɪŋ/
4. past	*had* /had/, /həd/, or /əd/
	'd /d/
	hadn't /hadnt/
5. -*ed* participle	*had* /had/, /həd/, or /əd/

The alternative unstressed pronunciation without initial /h/ is quite common. It accounts for misspellings of *have* in combinations such as *could of* (instead of *could have*) or *should of* (instead of *should have*).

The paradigm for the irregular verb *do* is shown below with informal contracted forms and with stressed and unstressed pronunciations:

do

1. base	*do* /du:/, /dʊ/	
—for present tense	*don't* /dəʊnt/	
2. -*s* form	*does* /dʌz/, /dəz/	
	's /s/ or /z/	
	doesn't /dʌzn̩t/	
3. -*ing* participle	*doing* /du:ɪŋ/	
4. past	*did* /dɪd/	
	didn't /dɪdn̩t/	
5. -*ed* participle	*done* /dʌn/	

The contracted form *'s* is only occasionally found in writing: *Who's she take after?*, *What's he say?* It is more common in informal speech.

The contracted forms of *be*, *have*, and *do* are used also when they function as auxiliaries. For the contracted forms of the **modal auxiliaries**, see 7.9. Two of the contractions have more than one expansion: *'s* can represent *is*, *has* or *does* (as well as the genitive marker), and *'d* can represent *had* ('I'd paid last month') or *would* ('I'd like another portion').

Five form-types are distinguished even when there are only three or four distinctions in form, because the fivefold distinction is made in some verbs and it coincides with differences in grammatical relations. The additional distinctions made in the verb *be* are not incorporated, because they are unique to that verb and do not affect grammatical relationships for other verbs.

7.2.1 Base form-type

The base form-type has the following uses:

7.2.1.1 **Present tense**, except for the third person singular (cf. 11.5 f.):

[1]   Of course you ... you get better repeatability the more readings you *take*

7.2.1.2 **Imperative** (cf. 2.7):

[2]   *Tell* me about your life

7.2.1.3 **Present subjunctive** (cf. 11.9):

[3]   I urged in my previous letter that these research staff *be* treated as their present colleagues and *be* permitted to apply for a redundancy payment when their contracts expire. [W]

For verbs other than *be*, the present subjunctive can only be distinguished from the present tense indicative in the third person singular, which has the -*s* form. Hence, there is not a distinctive subjunctive form in:

We recommend that they *repay* the full amount.

The subjunctive form can appear in the third person singular:

We recommend that he *repay* the full amount.

The present tense form here would be *repays*. British English rarely uses the present subjunctive except for the verb *be*, as in [3]. It uses instead *should* (*he should repay*) or the present tense -*s* form (*he repays*). Here is an example from an American source of the present subjunctive with a verb other than *be*:

[4]   Israel insists that it *remain* in charge on the borders [*International Herald Tribune*]

7.2.1.4 **Infinitive** (cf. 11.3), which has two major uses:

(a) **bare infinitive** (without *to*), follows a **modal auxiliary** (cf. 7.9):

[5]   I must *write* that message

(b) **to-infinitive** is the main verb in infinitive clauses (cf. 14.1.2):

[6]   I'd like to *write* something on process theology

> **NOTE**
>
> Infinitival *to* is a separate word, and therefore adverbials (especially single adverbs) sometimes intervene between it and the infinitive. The interruption results in what is traditionally known as the **split infinitive**.
>
> **[N1]**   But it's the sense of freedom of being able *to* just *lie* down if you want to roll over
>
> **[N2]**   How could people be so insensitive as *to* not *know* they've got wax in their ears
>
> **[N3]**   But you'd need to think carefully about the number of support people required *to* actually *administer* ... a process like this
>
> **[N4]**   Certainly all the members of the panel here tonight are too young *to* really *remember* the Second World War
>
> **[N5]**   Boeing Co. said that it is discussing plans with three of its regular Japanese suppliers *to* possibly *help* build a larger version of its popular 767 twin-jet [*Wall Street Journal*]
>
> **[N6]**   Some associates suspect that the 40 year old Mr Trumka would like *to* someday *head* the nation's largest labor group. [*Wall Street Journal*]
>
> **[N7]**   When must states make retroactive refunds of collected taxes that are later found *to* unconstitutionally *interfere* with interstate commerce? [*Wall Street Journal*]
>
> **[N8]**   They want to plug into the EC power grid, get a piece of Europe's Eureka high-tech research program and set up as an export platform for South Korea *to* conveniently *manufacture* and ship its wares into the EC. [*Wall Street Journal*]
>
> The split infinitive has been objected to because infinitival *to* has been perceived as part of the infinitive. This perception was at one time influenced by a knowledge of Latin grammar, which does not have an infinitival *to*. In some contexts splitting the infinitive avoids ambiguity. For example, if in a written form of **[N4]**, *really* was placed before *to* it could be misunderstood as focusing on *too young*, though in speech the intended focus could be conveyed intonationally. In other contexts, the infinitive must be split, unless the sentence is rephrased. This applies to **[N5]** above and to the longer interruption in **[N9]** below:
>
> **[N9]**   Who would cherish them as friends, when we have new, clean, up-to-date people *to*, if you like, *look* up to—people such as Richard Branson, Gary Lineker, Paul McCartney? [*The Sunday Times*]

7.2.2 **-s form-type**

The -*s* form-type is restricted to the third person singular present tense:

[7]   It *comes* with a small remote control and all the usual features, including wired and optical outputs [*Hi-Fi News & Record Review*]

[8] It still *is* very very difficult for me to be monogamous … and to have a satisfying ongoing sexual relationship with anybody

7.2.3 *-ing* participle

The *-ing* participle is used in:

7.2.3.1 **Progressive aspect,** following the auxiliary *be* (cf. 11.15):

[9] I think somebody's been *leading* you up the garden path

7.2.3.2 *-ing* **participle clauses,** as the main verb (cf. 14.1.2):

[10] Those involved in the deal are keeping details secret to avoid *putting* the sale in jeopardy. [W]

7.2.4 Past

The past is used for the past tense (cf. 11.5 f.):

[11] You *mentioned* that any lump should be excised.

[12] The photograph I thought *was* absolutely terrible

The past subjunctive (cf. 11.10) is *were*, and it can only be distinguished from the past indicative when the subject is *I* or third person singular:

[13] If I *were* you, I'd apply for the York position just for the experience. [W]

[14] Of course, BS would squeal, but it could hardly complain if closure *were* its only aim. [W]

In these instances the past indicative is *was*, which often replaces subjunctive *were*, particularly in less formal use:

[15] I'd go to the Palmer one if I *was* you.

7.2.5 *-ed* participle

The *-ed* participle is used in:

7.2.5.1 **Perfect aspect,** following the auxiliary *have* (cf. 11.11 ff.):

[16] We have *been* waiting for Her Majesty the Queen to arrive and we've *discovered* that there has *been* a fault in her transport arrangements

7.2.5.2 **Passive voice,** following the auxiliary *be* (cf. 2.12):

[17] I feel sure that some day it will be *published*

7.2.5.3 *-ed* **participle clauses,** as the main verb (cf. 14.1.2):

[18] The applications will then be published to enable public consultation, with winners *announced* in October and any newcomers taking over from January 1993. [W]

7.3 The -s form

For both regular and irregular verbs the spelling and pronunciation of the -s form is virtually always predictable from the base form. The rules for deriving the -s form from the base form are similar to those for adding the plural inflection to singular nouns in regular plurals (cf. 5.6).

7.3.1 Spelling of the -s inflection

The regular spelling of the -s inflection is s:

> run/ runs put/ puts revere/ reveres

Here are additional spelling rules for particular cases:

7.3.1.1 If the base ends in a sibilant sound (see 7.3.2.1) that is not followed by -e, add -es:

> buzz/buzzes pass/passes catch/catches fax/faxes rush/rushes

For a few words ending in -s, there is a variant in which the -s is doubled before the inflection:

> bus/buses or busses bias/biases or biasses focus/focuses or focusses
> gas/gases or gasses

Where sibilants are followed by -e, only -s is added:

> force/forces grudge/grudges rise/rises

7.3.1.2 If the base ends in a consonant plus y, change the y to i and then add -es:

> worry/worries fly/flies bury/buries deny/denies

If a vowel precedes the final y, the spelling is regular:

> play/plays annoy/annoys

7.3.1.3 For some verbs ending in -o, add -es:

> go/goes do/does echo/echoes veto/vetoes

Derivatives with go and do also have -es:

> undergo/undergoes overdo/overdoes

7.3.1.4 There are two irregular forms:

> have/has be/is

7.3.2 Pronunciation of the -s inflection

The -s inflection is pronounced /ɪz/, /z/, or /s/ depending on the final sound of the base:

7.3.2.1 /ɪz/ if the singular ends in a sibilant:

/s/	pass/ passes fax/ faxes
/z/	buzz/ buzzes
/ʃ/	rush/ rushes
/tʃ/	catch/ catches
/ʒ/	camouflage/ camouflages
/dʒ/	judge/ judges

7.3.2.2 /z/ if the singular ends in a vowel or a voiced consonant other than a sibilant (/b/, /d/, /g/, /v/, /ð/, /m/, /n/, /ŋ/, /l/, or (American English) /r/):

> *pay/pays   pursue/pursues   hum/hums   drive/drives   rebuild/rebuilds*

7.3.2.3 /s/ if the singular ends in a voiceless consonant other than a sibilant:

> *cook/cooks   convert/converts   worship/worships*

7.3.2.4 There are irregular pronunciations:

> (a) *do* /duː/ → *does* /dʌz/; so also for the derivatives of *do*, such as *overdoes*
> (b) *say* /seɪ/ → *says* /sɛz/

7.4 The *-ing* participle

As with the *-s* form, the spelling and pronunciation of the *-ing* participle is virtually always predictable from the base form of both regular and irregular verbs.

7.4.1 **Spelling of the *-ing* participle**

The inflection is spelled *-ing*, which is added to the base:

> *pass/passing   carry/carrying   go/going   be/being*

Here are additional spelling rules for particular cases:

7.4.1.1 If the base ends in *-e*, drop the *-e* before the *-ing*:

> *drive/driving   make/making   deceive/deceiving   co-operate/co-operating*

But if the base ends in *-ee*, *-oe*, or *-ye*, keep the final *-e*:

> *see/seeing   disagree/disagreeing   hoe/hoeing   dye/dyeing*

Also, *singe* keeps the *-e* in *singeing*, distinguishing it from *singing*, the *-ing* participle of *sing*. *Binge* and *tinge* have the variants *binging* or *bingeing; tinging* or *tingeing*.

7.4.1.2 If the base ends in *-ie*, change the *i* to *y* and drop the *-e*:

> *die/dying   tie/tying   untie/untying   lie/lying*

Contrast *die/dying* with *dye/dyeing*.

7.4.1.3 In general, double the consonant letter before *-ing* if all these three conditions apply:

> (a) the base ends in a single consonant letter
> (b) a single vowel comes before that consonant letter
> (c) the final syllable of the base is stressed, as it must be if the base is monosyllabic.

All three conditions apply in these examples:

> *tip/tipping*   *permit/permitting*
> *rob/robbing*   *defer/deferring*
> *sag/sagging*   *forget/forgetting*
> *hum/humming*   *upset/upsetting*
> *bet/betting*   *forbid/forbidding*

There is no doubling if:

(a) the base ends in two or more consonant letters:

sing/singing   fight/fighting   kick/kicking   remind/reminding

(b) there are two vowel letters before the final consonant of the base:

read/reading   reveal/revealing   despair/despairing

(c) the final syllable of the base is not stressed:

limit/limiting   differ/differing   deliver/delivering

The letters *y* and *w* count as vowel letters when they come at the end of the base (and are pronounced as vowels), and they are therefore not doubled:

apply/applying   fly/flying   show/showing

There are some exceptions to the rules for doubling:

(a) A few words ending in *-s* have variants with or without the doubling:

bus/busing or *bussing   gas/gasing* or *gassing   bias/biasing* or *biassing*
focus/focusing or *focussing*

Busing and *gasing* are irregular, and so are *biassing* and *focussing*.

(b) British English generally doubles the consonant letter if the base ends in *-l* even though the final syllable of the base is not stressed:

marvel/ marvelling   model/ modelling   quarrel/ quarrelling   travel/ travelling

American English generally follows the regular rule and does not double the consonant:

marveling   modeling   quarreling   traveling

British and American English differ in the same direction for a few bases ending in *-m(e)* or *-p*:

| British | *programme/programming   diagram/diagramming*
kidnap/kidnapping   worship/worshipping |
| American | *program/programing   diagram/diagraming*
kidnap/kidnaping   worship/worshiping |

However, in both British and American English, *handicapping* and *humbugging* are usual, even though the final syllable of the base is not stressed.

(c) If the base ends in *-c*, the *c* is in effect generally doubled as *ck* even though the final syllable of the base is not stressed:

mimic/mimicking   panic/panicking   picnic/picnicking   traffic/trafficking

---

7.4.2 **Pronunciation of the *-ing* participle**

The pronunciation of the *-ing* inflection by speakers of standard English is generally /ɪŋ/, at least in their careful speech. A common non-standard pronunciation is /ɪn/, which is sometimes represented in writing as *-in'*, e.g. *singin'*. Some non-standard dialects prefix the *-ing* participle with *a-* before consonants: *a-huntin', a-comin', a-runnin'*. The *a*-prefix is usually explained as a reduced form of the preposition *on*, originally attached to verbal nouns ending in *-ing* and then generalized to *-ing* participles.

7.5 The -ed form in regular verbs

The -ed form in regular verbs and in many irregular verbs represents two form-types: the past and the -ed participle (cf. 7.2):

> past: We *saved* some money.
> -ed participle: We have *saved* some money.

The -ed form in regular verbs is virtually always predictable from the base form.

7.5.1 **Spelling of the -ed form**

The regular spelling of the -ed form in regular verbs is -ed:

> *play/played   talk/talked   disturb/disturbed   distinguish/distinguished*

Here are additional spelling rules for particular cases, which largely coincide with those for the -s form (cf. 7.3) or the -ing participle (cf. 7.4):

7.5.1.1 If the base ends in -e, drop the -e before adding -ed:

> *deceive/deceived   save/saved   co-operate/co-operated*

But if the base ends in -ee, -oe, -ie, or -ye, keep the final -e:

> *disagree/disagreed   hoe/hoed   die/died   dye/dyed*

7.5.1.2 If the base ends in a consonant plus *y*, change the *y* to *i* and then add -ed:

> *worry/worried   cry/cried   apply/applied   deny/denied*

If a vowel precedes the final *y*, the spelling is regular:

> *play/played   annoy/annoyed*

There are exceptions where the *y* changes to *i* even though a vowel precedes the *y*:

> *lay/laid   pay/paid*

Derivatives of *lay* and *pay* are also exceptions:

> *mislay/mislaid   underpay/underpaid*

The verb *say* is similar to these two verbs in spelling:

> *say/said*

But *said* is irregular in pronunciation /sɛd/.

7.5.1.3 The rules for doubling the final consonant letter of the base are identical with those required before the -ing inflection (cf. 7.4), and they may therefore be restated here briefly. In general, double the consonant letter before -ed if all these three conditions apply:

> (a) the base ends in a single consonant letter
> (b) a single vowel comes before that consonant letter
> (c) the final syllable of the base is stressed

All three conditions apply in these examples:

> *rob/robbed   permit/permitted   defer/deferred*

Exceptions:

(a) A few words ending in -s have variants with or without the doubling:

bus/bused or bussed bias/biased or biassed
focus/focused or focussed gas/gased or gassed

(b) If the base ends in -*l* or for a few words in -*m(e)* or -*p*, British English generally doubles the consonant letter whereas American English generally follows the regular rule:

British   *modelled quarrelled travelled programmed diagrammed*
             kidnapped worshipped

American   *marveled modeled quarreled traveled programed diagramed*
             kidnaped worshiped

However, in both American and British English, *handicapped* and *humbugged* are usual.

(c) If the base ends in *c*, the *c* is generally doubled as *ck* even though the final syllable of the base is not stressed:

mimic/mimicked panic/panicked picnic/picknicked traffic/trafficked

---

7.5.2 **Pronunciation of the -*ed* form**

The rules for the pronunciation of the -*ed* inflection are analogous to those for the -*s* inflection (cf. 7.3). The inflection is pronounced /ɪd/, /d/, or /t/ depending on the final sound of the base:

7.5.2.1 /ɪd/ if the base ends in /d/ or /t/:

/d/   *mend/mended fade/faded defend/defended*
/t/   *net/netted visit/visited hesitate/hesitated*

7.5.2.2 /d/ if the base ends in a vowel or a voiced consonant other than /d/ (/b/, /g/, /v/, /ð/, /z/, /ʒ/, > /dʒ/, /m/, /n/, /ŋ/, /l/, or (American English) /r/):

flow/flowed try/tried revise/revised save/saved

7.5.2.3 /t/ if the base ends in a voiceless consonant other than /t/:

walk/walked notice/noticed fix/fixed help/helped

7.6 Irregular verbs

There are five form-types (cf. 7.2). Apart from the highly irregular verb *be* (which has eight forms), **irregular verbs** may have three, four, or five forms, depending on whether one form is used for two or three form-types. The -*s* form and the -*ing* participle are always available and can be predicted from the base for all verbs except the verb *be* (which has the unpredictable -*s* form *is* as well as the unpredictable present tense forms *am* and *are*). Except for the verb *be*, we therefore need list only three forms to show irregularities in the verb: the base, the past, and the -*ed* participle. These three forms are known as the **principal parts** of the verb.

For example, the principal parts of the verb *see* are *see* (base), *saw* (past), and *seen* (-*ed* participle). We can additionally derive from the base the remaining forms *sees* (-*s* form) and *seeing* (*-ing* participle). The principal parts of the verb *make* are *make, made, made*; the five form-types are therefore *make* (base), *makes* (*-s* form), *making* (*-ing* participle), *made* (past), *made* (*-ed* participle). The principal parts of the verb *put*, which has only three forms, are *put, put, put*; the base, the past, and the *-ed* participle are identical, and the additional forms are *puts* and *putting*. Dictionaries list the principal parts of irregular verbs and of regular verbs that have spelling changes across the principal parts, such as doubling of the consonant before the inflection or the change of *y* to *i*.

We can establish seven classes of irregular verbs according to whether or not four features apply to their principal parts:

1. The past and *-ed* participles are identical, as in regular verbs.
2. The past has a *-d* or *-t* inflection, as in regular verbs, and the same inflection may also be found in the *-ed* participle.
3. The vowel in the base form is identical with the vowel in the other two principal parts, as in regular verbs.
4. The *-ed* participle has an *-(e)n* inflection, which is not found in regular verbs.

Table 7.6.1 sets out in columns the four features and indicates whether they apply (+) or not (–) to each of the seven classes of irregular verbs. The '±' for class II indicates that some verbs in the class do not have the specified feature.

Two irregular verbs do not fit into the seven classes. The present-day forms of the verb *be* derive historically from different verbs: the past tense *was* and *were*; the present tense *am, is, are*; and *be, being, been* (cf. 7.2). The verb *go* takes its past form *went* from a different verb; the principal parts are *go, went, gone*.

Table 7.6.1 Classes of irregular verbs

		past = participle	-t/-d inflection	all vowels identical	-n inflection
I.	*bend bent bent*	+	+	+	–
II.	*show showed shown*	–	+	±	+
III.	*buy bought bought*	+	+	–	–
IV.	*break broke broken*	–	–	–	+
V.	*hit hit hit*	+	–	+	–
VI.	*find found found*	+	–	–	–
VII.	*begin began begun*	–	–	–	–

Examples of verbs in the seven classes follow, together with some brief comments.

I.	*bend bent bent*	*burn burnt burnt*
	build built built	*learn learnt learnt*
	have had had	*smell smelt smelt*
	make made made	*spell spelt spelt*
		spoil spoilt spoilt

The inflections are irregularly attached. The *-t* inflections follow a voiced sound, contrary to the general rule (cf. 7.5). Those in the second column also have regular variants: *burn, burned, burned* and *spoil, spoiled, spoiled*. The regular variants are usual in American English.

II.	*show showed shown*	*shear sheared shorn*
	mow mowed mown	*swell swelled swollen*
	sew sewed sewn	
	saw sawed sawn	

The past is formed regularly, but the participle has the -*(e)n* inflection. Those in the second column have a different vowel in the participle, hence the '±' in the table. All the verbs also have regular variants for the participle: *show, showed, showed.*

III.   *buy bought bought*   *dream dreamt dreamt*
       hear heard heard   *kneel knelt knelt*
       lose lost lost   *lean leant leant*
       say said said   *leap leapt leapt*
       feel felt felt
       keep kept kept

Despite the identity of spellings in some instances, the vowel sounds of the past and participle always differ from that of the base. Those in the second column also have regular variants: *dream, dreamed, dreamed.*

IV.   *break broke broken*   *see saw seen*
       speak spoke spoken   *take took taken*
       blow blew blown   *tear tore torn*
       hide hid hidden   *write wrote written*
       lie lay lain   *bite bit bitten*

All three forms differ. The past lacks an inflection, but the participle has the -*(e)n* inflection. The verbs vary in their sameness of vowels. For example, *blow* has the same vowel in the base and the participle (*blown*), *tear* has the same vowel in the past and the participle (*tore, torn*), and the vowels are different in all three principal parts of *write.*

V.   *hit hit hit*   *fit fit fit*
       burst burst burst   *rid rid rid*
       hurt hurt hurt   *quit quit quit*
       let let let   *sweat sweat sweat*
       set set set   *wet wet wet*
       put put put   *wed wed wed*
       cut cut cut
       cast cast cast

All three parts are identical. Those in the second column also have regular variants: *fit, fitted, fitted. Cost* belongs to this class, but it is regular in the sense 'estimate the value or cost of'.

VI.   *find found found*   *get got got*
       feed fed fed   *hold held held*
       read read read   *strike struck struck*
       bleed bled bled   *stand stood stood*
       fight fought fought   *wind wound wound*
       dig dug dug   *light lit lit*
       win won won   *speed sped sped*
       sting stung stung   *hang hung hung*

The past and participle are identical, as in the regular verb, but there is a change in the vowel and there are no inflections. A few verbs in this class also have regular variants: *light, lighted, lighted; speed, speeded, speeded.* In American English, *get* has two participles: *got* and *gotten;* the tendency is for *have got* to denote possessing something and *have gotten* to denote obtaining something. *Hang* also has a regular variant—*hang, hanged, hanged*—which tends to be used to denote suspension by the neck, especially in an official execution.

VII. *begin began begun*   *come came come*
     drink drank drunk   *ran run run*
     sing sang sung
     ring rang rung
     shrink shrank shrunk
     swim swam swum

Those in the first column have three different forms for the principal parts and no inflections. Those in the second column have the same form for the base and the participle.

7.7 Non-standard verb-forms: present tense

7.7.1 Present tense inflections

Non-standard dialects vary in how they treat the present tense. Commonly, the paradigm has been regularized to extend the -*s* form to all persons in the singular and to the plural (*I knows, we knows*, etc.). Alternatively, the uninflected base form has been extended to the third person singular (*she know*). Old inflected forms have been retained to a limited extent in some non-standard dialects: the -*eth* inflection for the third person singular (*she knoweth*) and the -*en* inflection for the plural (*they knowen*). Some non-standard dialects that have kept a distinctive *thou/ thee* pronoun for the second person singular have also retained the -*st* inflection that accompanies it.

7.7.2 The present tense of *be*

Dialect variation is particularly acute with the verb *be*, whether as a main verb or an auxiliary verb. In some non-standard dialects, the paradigm has been regularized by using *be* throughout (*I be, you be*, etc.). In some, regularization is achieved through *is* (*I is, you is*, etc.). There are also non-standard dialects that have *bin* or *are* (*I bin, I are*, etc.). In others, the verb *be* may be omitted in the present tense whenever it can occur in a contracted form (*They my friends*, corresponding to *They're my friends*), though omission does not usually apply to *am*.

7.7.3 *Ain't*

Ain't is a much stigmatized negative present tense form for *be* (both main verb and auxiliary verb) and for auxiliary *have* (*She ain't angry, I ain't telling, They ain't done it*). In standard English there is no corresponding negative verb for *(I) am not* in the declarative, though *aren't (I)?* serves the purpose in the interrogative, especially in British English. Earlier spellings of *ain't* included *an't, a'n't, i'n't, e'n't* for *be*, and *ha'n't* for *have*; they represent earlier pronunciations that more closely represent the positive forms. *Ain't* is stigmatized in both British and American standard English, though it is used informally in speech in certain contexts, particularly by speakers of standard American English.

American politicians may use *ain't* in public speeches to convey a folksy tone. In **[1]** the casualness is enhanced by the use of the double negative:

> **[1]**   The state leaders of United We Stand America, meeting in Dallas to debate their future, faced serious questions about whether Mr. Perot's claim last week that the country '*ain't* seen nothing yet' was more than an idle boast. [*International Herald Tribune*]

In non-standard dialects *ain't* is common, but *in't* is preferred in some dialects for tag questions. Some non-standard dialects have *amn't* for *am not*, and others use *aren't* for *am not* in the declarative (*I aren't*). Some Black English dialects use *ain't* also to correspond to *didn't*.

NOTE

A historical perspective is helpful for understanding the variations in verb forms in non-standard dialects and their differences from standard English.

The present tense in Old English distinguished the three persons in the singular. The inflections for the present can be generalized as follows (where the parentheses indicate variant omissions):

1st person singular	*-e*
2nd person singular	*-(e)st*
3rd person singular	*-(e)th*
plural	*-ath*

The present subjunctive was *-e* for the singular and *-en* for the plural.

The Northumbrian dialect of Old English eventually developed a somewhat different system for the present tense:

1st person singular	*-o, -e*
2nd person singular	*-as*
3rd person singular	*-es, -as*
plural	*-es, -as*

Phonological changes led to the neutralization of the unstressed vowels in the inflections to *e* /ə/ and then to the loss of final *-e*. By about 1300, the verb paradigms for the present tense had developed separately in the Middle English dialects:

	North	Midland	South
1st person singular	*-(e)*	*-e*	*-e*
2nd person singular	*-es*	*-es(t)*	*-est*
3rd person singular	*-es*	*-eth/-es*	*-eth*
plural	*-es*	*-en/-es*	*-eth*

The Midland dialects had adopted the subjunctive plural inflection *-en* as an alternative for the indicative plural. The *-es* inflection for the third person singular infiltrated into the Midland dialects from the North.

By the late fourteenth century, the London standard (which drew on various dialects) had the following paradigm for the present tense:

1st person singular	*-(e)*
2nd person singular	*-(e)st*
3rd person singular	*-eth*
plural	*-e(n)*

At the same time, a variant *-(e)s* inflection (spread from the North) was used in London for the third person singular as well as the *-eth* inflection (*she giveth, she gives*).

During the next two centuries there were losses of final *-e* in the first person singular and of final *-n* and then final *-e* in the plural, so that these assumed the base form that they now have in standard English. By the end of the seventeenth century, the *-s* form was the dominant form for the third person singular in the increasingly standardized English, though *doth* and *hath* continued to be used until well into the eighteenth century as a spelling convention rendered by /s/ in speech, as was perhaps often the case with other verbs in the seventeenth century. Plurals in -s are also occasionally found in the seventeenth and eighteenth centuries. By the nineteenth century, the distinctive second person singular was abandoned for general use as a result of the supplanting of *thou* by *you*; *thou* and the -st form (*thou walkst, thou knowest*) have continued to appear in the restricted domains of poetry and prayer. They are occasionally used facetiously; and so is the -eth inflection, as in this epigram advertising a lager:

The Lord giveth. The Landlord taketh away. [*The Independent Magazine*]

Present-day standard English retains only two forms in the present tense: the -s form for the third person singular and the base form for the rest. Hence, the anomaly in standard English that -s signals the singular in the present tense of verbs but the plural in nouns:

The students listen.
The student listens.

7.8 Non-standard verb-forms: past tense and -ed participles

7.8.1 Past tense inflections

Non-standard dialects generally have a single form for the past. Some that retain the *thou/thee* pronoun also retain the -st inflection for the second person singular. Some non-standard dialects may use the base form in combination with past time adverbials ('I *like* the movie I saw yesterday').

NOTE

The past tense inflections in Old English can be generalized as follows, where the parentheses indicate variant omissions:

1st person singular	-(e)
2nd person singular	-e, -(e)st
3rd person singular	-(e)
plural	-on

The past subjunctive had -e or -en for the singular and -en for the plural.
As a result of phonological changes (reduction of unstressed vowels to e /ə/ and subsequent loss of final -e and also loss of final -n), the emerging London standard looked like this by the late fourteenth century:

1st person singular	-(e)
2nd person singular	-(est), -(e)st
3rd person singular	-(e)
plural	-e(n)

By the nineteenth century, continuation of the phonological processes and abandonment of a distinctive second person singular had resulted in the levelling of the whole past paradigm to one form.

7.8.2 The past tense of *be*

Most non-standard dialects have generalized the forms of the past tense of *be*, either using *was* (*we was, you was*) or *were* (*I were, it were*). Some have used *was* for the positive (*we was, she was*) and *were* for the negative (*we weren't, she weren't*).

VERBS 159

NOTE

The distinctions in the past tense of the verb *be* in present-day standard English can be traced back to Old English, if we take account of phonological changes:

1st person singular	*wæs*	*was*
2nd person singular	*wære*	*were*
3rd person singular	*wæs*	*was*
plural	*wæron*	*were*

Old English subjunctives were singular *wære* and plural *wæren*. They were distinctive only in the first and third person singular, as in present-day standard English.

7.8.3 Irregular verb patterns

Non-standard dialects have irregular verb patterns that vary among themselves and differ from standard English. On the whole, the tendency is to generalize or regularize further than in standard English. Occasionally older forms have been retained; for example: *crope* as past of *creep* and *croppen* as participle. Here are examples of different treatments of the principal parts of verbs in non-standard dialects (cf. 7.6):

1. past generalized to participle:
   go, went, went
   hide, hid, hid
   take, took, took
   write, wrote, wrote

2. participle generalized to past:
   see, seen, seen
   do, done, done
   swim, swum, swum

3. base generalized to past and participle:
   come, come, come
   give, give, give
   run, run, run

4. regularization:
   know, knowed, knowed
   creep, creeped, creeped
   see, seed, seed
   catch, catched, catched

5. new irregular form introduced:
   write, writ, writ
   bring, brang, brung
   ride, rid, rid

The generalization and regularization tendencies are also found in present-day standard English (cf. 7.6). Some irregular verbs have regular variants, and speakers of standard English are sometimes unsure whether verbs such as *sing* and *drink* have distinctive forms for the past and *-ed* participle.

NOTE

Old English had two major classes of verbs. Weak verbs formed their past and -ed participles by the addition of inflections, generally containing t or d. Strong verbs did so by changing the vowels and adding an -en inflection to the participle, as in present-day ride, rode, ridden. The weak verbs were by far the more numerous, but many of the strong verbs occurred very frequently. However, since it was easy to add inflections to weak verbs, it was usual to create new verbs on the model of the weak verbs and to adapt borrowed verbs to that model. Nowadays all newly formed or borrowed verbs follow regular processes of adding inflections for the past tense and the -ed participle. In the course of time the tendency to regularize the verb forms led to many strong verbs becoming weak. Among common verbs that have changed from strong to weak since the Old English period are climb, help, melt, step, walk, wash. There are relatively few changes in the opposite direction. Among common verbs that have changed from weak to strong by analogy with other verbs are dig, fling, hide, spit, and wear. In some instances, strong verbs adopted forms from another class of strong verbs; for example, spoke has replaced the earlier spake, which is found in the King James Bible. Some strong verbs also had alternative weak forms, such as knowed, that have not survived in standard English.

7.9 Auxiliaries

Auxiliaries (or auxiliary verbs) fall into two major sets:

1. the **primary auxiliaries**:
   be, have, do

2. the **modals** (or modal auxiliaries or secondary auxiliaries):
   can, could
   may, might
   shall, should
   will, would
   must

7.9.1 **Forms of the auxiliaries**

Be, have, and do are also main (or lexical or full) verbs. Their informal contracted forms are given in 7.2. The modals also have informal non-negative and negative contracted forms. Some of the modals have stressed and unstressed pronunciations. Both are given below, the stressed pronunciation first and then the unstressed (with reduced vowels).

can	/kan/, /kən/	can't	/kɑːnt/ or /kant/
could	/kʊd/, /kəd/	couldn't	/kʊdn̩t/
may	/meɪ/	mayn't	/meɪnt/ (British)
might	/mʌɪt/	mightn't	/mʌɪtn̩t/
shall	/ʃal/, /ʃəl/	shan't	/ʃɑːnt/ (British)
should	/ʃʊd/, /ʃəd/	shouldn't	/ʃʊdn̩t/, /ʃədn̩t/
will	/wɪl/	won't	/wəʊnt/
'll	/əl/ or /l/		
would	/wʊd/, /wəd/	wouldn't	/wʊdn̩t/
'd	/əd/ or /d/		
must	/mʌst/, /məst/	mustn't	/mʌsn̩t/

The alternative pronunciations of *can't* are British /kɑːnt/ and American /kant/. In British English, *shan't* is sometimes used as a negative contracted form of *shall*, and *mayn't* is very occasionally found as a negative contracted form of *may*.

7.9.2 Uses of the auxiliaries

7.9.2.1 *Be, have,* and *do*
Auxiliary *be* combines with a following -*ing* participle to form the **progressive aspect** (cf. 11.15f.); e.g. *was playing*. It also combines with a following -*ed* participle to form the **passive voice** (cf. 2.12); e.g. *was played*. Auxiliary *have* combines with a following -*ed* participle to form the **perfect aspect** (cf. 11.11ff.); e.g. *has played*. Auxiliary *do* is the **dummy operator**: in the absence of any other auxiliary, it functions as the operator to form (for example) interrogative and negative sentences; e.g. *Did they play? They didn't play*.

7.9.2.2 The modals
The modals are followed by an infinitive, e.g. *can play*. They convey notions of factuality, such as certainty (e.g. *She could be at the office*), or of control, such as permission (e.g. *You may play outside*).

The modals differ from the primary auxiliaries in several ways:

1. They do not have an -*s* form for the third person singular present:
    He *may* be there.
    She *can* drive.
2. They do not have non-finite forms and therefore must be the first verb in the verb phrase.
3. Their past forms are often used to refer to present or future time:
    He *might* be there now.
    She *could* drive my car tomorrow.

Must has only one form.

7.9.2.3 Auxiliaries as operators
All the auxiliaries are used as **operators** for negation, interrogation, emphasis, and abbreviation (cf. 11.2). For negation, *not* is placed after the auxiliary or the negative contracted form is used:

[1]   Uhm ... I think I remember being with a girl ... that I'd met ... uhm ... who I was just impressing and she wanted me to ... go all the way when I was about sixteen and I just ... *could not* just *couldn't*

[2]   He *doesn't* think he'll even be at the talk

For interrogation, the operator is placed before the subject in *yes–no* questions and in most *wh*-questions (cf. 2.5):

[3]   *Does* an artist have to live with an artist

[4]   So why *didn't* you do the exam

The operator may be used for emphasis. In speech the emphatic function is signalled by placing the **nuclear tone** (a distinctive movement of pitch) on the operator. *Do* is introduced as the dummy operator for emphasis:

[5]   It *does* sound good

The operator may be used as an abbreviatory device to avoid repetition:

    [6]   I'll try and show you if I *can*

    [7]   A: It looks a good vehicle yeah
              B: It *does*

7.9.2.4 *Do* and *let* with imperatives

Do and *do not* (or *don't*) are used in front of imperatives (cf. 2.7):

    [8]   *Do* hang your coat up if you'd like to

    [9]   *Do* not hesitate to call us. [W]

Let is used for first and second person imperatives (cf. 2.7):

    [10]   *Let*'s stop for the moment

7.9.2.5 Co-occurrence of modals

In standard English, two modals cannot co-occur. However, in non-standard dialects some double modals can co-occur; for example: *might could, might should, won't can't, would could, should can, may can, will can*. They are used also after the infinitival *to*; for example: *have to can, used to could, going to can, would like to could, have to can*. The second modal is usually *can* or *could*.

7.9.3 Marginal auxiliaries and auxiliary-like verbs

There are several **marginal auxiliaries**, marginal in that they are also used as main verbs. When used as main verbs they require the dummy operator *do*. The marginal auxiliaries are *used to, ought to, dare,* and *need*; the informal negative contracted forms are *usedn't to, oughtn't to, daren't,* and *needn't*.

7.9.3.1 *Used to*

Used to is used as an auxiliary mainly in British English:

    [11]   Yeah we *used to* buy Mum a vase every year for her birthday

In **[12]** *used to* (also spelled *use to*) is used as a main verb with *do* as dummy operator:

    [12]   *Didn't* there *used to* be deer in Richmond Park

    [13]   I mean I *did use to* go down to Bournemouth

7.9.3.2 *Ought to*

Like *used to* and unlike the other auxiliaries, *ought* is generally followed by infinitival *to*. It is used as an auxiliary in **[14]**–**[16]**:

    [14]   I don't know if I *ought to* say this

    [15]   There were of course other casualties of war as well it *ought not to* be forgotten

    [16]   *Ought not* the government *to* be planning to spend more? [*The Times*]

In non-standard dialects and sometimes in informal standard English, it is used as a main verb with *do* as dummy operator: *didn't ought to*.

7.9.3.3 *Dare* and *need*

Dare and *need* are used as auxiliaries mainly in interrogative and negative sentences:

    [17]   And *dare* I ask as to the presence of a man in your life

    [18]   We *dare not* let that happen again

    [19]   Or *daren't* you ask

    [20]   You *needn't* read every chapter

[21] Nor *need* I look further than my own city of Sheffield … where the percentage of termination of pregnancy continues to be considerably higher than the average for England and Wales

As main verbs, *dare* and *need* may take the *-s* and past forms and infinitival *to* as well as dummy operator *do*:

[22] I can't distinguish between my different daydreams because I don't have any. I *don't dare* to have! [W]

[23] D'you *need to* know anything else

[24] I think this is the first action that *needs to* be taken and we *need to* take it very soon

[25] Something obviously *needed to* be done

The main verb *dare* may also be without infinitival *to*:

[26] I wouldn't *dare* look

7.9.3.4 Auxiliary-like verbs

There are also a number of other **auxiliary-like** verbs that convey notions of time, aspect, or modality; for example: *be going to, have to, start, had better* (cf. 11.17).

7.9.3.5 Non-standard auxiliaries

Other auxiliaries are found in some non-standard dialects:

1. habitual *be* and (with verbs other than *be*) habitual *do*:
    They *be* out every night, but we don't *be* out.
    He *do* work for me.

2. completive *done* (to indicate completion):
    They *done* painted it.

Chapter 8
Adjectives, Adverbs, and Interjections

Summary

Adjectives by themselves or with modifiers typically function both attributively as premodifiers of nouns and predicatively as subject predicative. Nominal adjectives (e.g. *the poor*) serve as head of a noun phrase. Most adjectives are gradable: they can take intensifiers (e.g. *very*) and comparison (e.g. *taller, tallest; more difficult, most difficult*).

Adverbs by themselves or with modifiers typically function as premodifiers of adjectives and other adverbs, as adverbials, or as complements of verbs. Sentence adverbials are either conjuncts (logical connectors, e.g. *therefore* and *nevertheless*) or disjuncts (commenting on the stance of the speaker or the content of the sentence, e.g. *frankly, fortunately*). Adjuncts are adverbials (e.g. referring to space, time, or manner) that are more closely linked to the processes or circumstances described in the sentence.

Interjections are exclamatory emotive words that are loosely attached to the rest of the sentence, e.g. *ah, ouch, sh, wow*.

8.1 Characteristics of adjectives

Adjectives serve as the head of an **adjective phrase** (cf. 12.1ff.). Used alone or with one or more modifiers, they have two characteristic functions (cf. 8.2): **premodifier** of a noun **[1]** and **subject predicative [2]**:

> **[1]** In short, she was one of those *happy* natures who find life 'fun' and never take offence if they are asked out to dinner at six o'clock. [Anthony Lambton 'Pig' in *Pig and Other Stories*]
>
> **[2]** Weather's been great these last few days so I'm *happy!* [Mary Wesley *A Sensible Life*]

SOME TYPICAL ADJECTIVE ENDINGS	
-able, -ible	*acceptable, suitable, capable, credible*
-al	*accidental, seasonal, dictatorial, political*
-ed	*frenzied, crooked, wicked, kindhearted*
-ful	*careful, faithful, doubtful, lawful*
-ic	*romantic, dramatic, historic, dynamic*
-ish	*childish, foolish, smallish, feverish*
-ive	*active, comprehensive, defective, affirmative*
-less	*careless, reckless, hopeless, harmless*
-ous	*famous, glorious, ambitious, erroneous*
-y	*tasty, moody, heavy, hungry.*

Some of these endings were endings of the words when they were borrowed from other languages.

8.2 Attributive and predicative adjectives

Most adjectives can be used both **attributively** (as **premodifiers** of nouns) and **predicatively** (as **subject predicative**). Attributive adjectives attribute a quality or characteristic to what is denoted by the noun they modify: *pleasant company, pleasant dreams.* Predicative adjectives are part of the predicate, linked to the subject by a copular verb such as *be* or *seem*: *The company was pleasant, Your dreams seem pleasant.*

8.2.1 **Adjectives that are attributive only**

Some adjectives are attributive only:

[1]   I usually think that advertising and publicity is a complete and *utter* waste of money

[2]   At encounters like this the *sheer* power which the United States can exert is glaring

[3]   Harry hurled himself at the soldier, knocking him off his feet and right out of the vehicle, leaving Harry as the *sole* occupant and in the driving seat. [Michael Dobbs *Wall Games*]

[4]   He will continue to report to Donald Pardus, president and *chief* executive officer. [*Wall Street Journal*]

[5]   She's sitting there at this *very* moment saying why doesn't he ring me at this moment

[6]   A defense lawyer thought this testimony an '*atomic* bomb' in the face of the prosecution. [*Wall Street Journal*]

Many adjectives that are only attributive are so when they are used in a particular sense. For example, *real* is attributive only in the sense 'rightly so called' [7]–[8] but is a central adjective in the sense 'actually existing' [9]–[10]:

[7]   And it's a chance to bring back Alan Ball who's uhm a *real* exponent and expert on Greek football

[8]   Is Yiddish a *real* language

[9]   He said there was a *real* danger of massacres in the absence of civil authority

[10] The possibility that the conducting filament is a mixture of microcrystallites and dielectric is *real*. [*Electronic Engineering*]

Similarly, *criminal, late,* and *old* are only attributive in [11]–[13] but central adjectives in [14]–[16]:

[11] One of the ... main principles of *criminal* law is judge the act not the actor

[12] Under the *late* dictator Gen. Franco, many Basques supported the radical nationalist organization ETA; now, ETA finds itself isolated. [*Wall Street Journal*]

[13] I have defeated them, these two *old* enemies of lovers

[14] It is unfortunate that some people are not exposed to better opportunities than welfare or *criminal* activities. [*Wall Street Journal*]

[15] *Late* payment of bills is the latest problem to surface as a result of the desktop-computer maker's much publicized switch to a new system for providing its management with information. [*Wall Street Journal*]

[16] He's got a wrinkled *old* face

Adjectives that are only attributive tend to be intensifiers (e.g. *utter*), restrictives (e.g. *only*), related to adverbials (e.g. *old* **[13]** 'of old'), or related to nouns (e.g. *criminal* **[11]** 'dealing with crime').

8.2.2 Adjectives that are predicative only

Some adjectives are only predicative:

[17] Caroline is *afraid* of Nellie's attempts to get her to join in the nude dancing and runs off. [Jennifer Breen *In Her Own Write*]

[18] I was getting quite *fond* of him

[19] Her office personality is a positive one; but she is not *aware* of this, any more than she is *conscious* of her breakfast-time vagueness. [W]

Many of these predicative adjectives resemble verbs in their meanings: *afraid of* 'fear', *fond of* 'like', *aware that* 'know that'.

8.2.3 Central adjectives

Central adjectives can be attributive **[20]** or predicative **[21]**. They can also function as an **object predicative [22]** (cf. 3.7) and **postmodify** nouns **[23]** or indefinite pronouns **[24]**.

[20] I spent some time looking for a *suitable* menu package to use to do this, but could not find a wholly *suitable* system [W]

[21] Some were drafted into the army if they were *suitable* for that and some went into palace service

[22] Thus it can be seen that choropleth has its advantages—good visual impression, easy to construct (in some ways) easy interpretation (also restricted) which may make it *suitable* for certain purposes in statistical analysis. [W]

[23] Reliance acquired a 7% UAL stake earlier this year at an average cost of $110 a share, and reduced its stake to 4.7% after UAL accepted the bid at prices *higher* than $282 a share. [*Wall Street Journal*]

[24] The moral is, try and learn what everybody else is using and then try something *better* or at least different. [W]

8.3 Nominal adjectives

Adjectives can serve as the head of a **noun phrase** (cf. 10.3).

Adjectives as heads of noun phrases are **nominal adjectives**. They are generally introduced by a definite **determiner**, commonly the definite article *the*. Nominal adjectives do not take plural inflections, but they can be plural in meaning. We can distinguish nominal adjectives that have plural reference from those that have singular reference.

8.3.1 Plural nominal adjectives

Plural nominal adjectives refer to animate beings, generally human, and they have generic reference (cf. 10.16):

[1] The vital decisions we reach on human fertilisation and embryology and subsequently pregnancy termination must affect how we regard the status of each individual ... his or her human rights the treatment of *the handicapped* the fate of *the senile* and *the terminally ill*

[2] A recent estimate puts the proportion of *the literate in Egypt* at around ... half of a percent certainly no more than one percent

[3] For the first time the 1991 census will include a question about long-term illness to help plan services and facilities for *long-term sick* and *elderly*

[4] In South East Asia and in South America there's less of a tradition of democracy less articulation of the consequences of the birth rate among *the very poor* but there's also less evident inadequacy of natural resources

[5] It is the *'old old'* or those over 75 who are most likely to experience major health and mobility problems. [W]

[6] There was a professional pessimism about the ability to help *the so called 'chronic sick'* and so the neglect of their services seemed justified

[7] So I thought this is an interesting ... uhm idea of bringing *disabled* and *abled* together

[8] All three are located in the mythified undifferentiated home counties and feature a common cast of supporting characters choleric retired generals do-gooding vicars absent-minded professors domineering cooks and assorted spinsters with bees in their bonnets and bats in their belfries the *dog-loving* the *boy-hating* the busybody the scatterbrain *the short-sighted* the *long-winded*

[9] And what the Government should have done straightaway to ease our collection problems is introduced one hundred per cent rebates as of April the first this year for *the poorest of society*

In most of the above citations the determiner is *the*, but determiners are absent in the coordinated phrases of **[3]** and **[7]**. Nominal adjectives may be premodified by adverbs, as is usual for adjectives: *terminally ill* **[1]**, *very poor* **[4]**. But like nouns, they may be premodified by adjectives—*old old* **[5]**, *so-called 'chronic sick'* **[6]**—and by nouns or noun phrases—*the long-term sick* **[3]**. They may be postmodified by **prepositional phrases**: *the literate in Egypt* **[2]**, *the poorest of society* **[9]**. The superlative *poorest* **[9]** shows that, like other adjectives, nominal adjectives can be inflected for **comparison**. In their potential for inflection and modification, nominal adjectives share features that are characteristic of both nouns and adjectives.

Some plural nominal adjectives are nationality or ethnic adjectives. They all end in a sibilant sound: *-(i)sh*, (*British, Welsh*), *-ese* (*Portuguese*), *-ch* (*French*), *-s* (*Swiss*).

[10] The imperial family's remoteness from *ordinary Japanese* will be underlined by the absence of a coronation procession. [W]

[11] Seventy years on, *the Chinese* are suddenly objecting to the plans for the new airport. [W]

[12] There were Celts of course in the British Isles the ancient Britons and *the ancient Irish*

8.3.2 **Singular nominal adjectives**

Singular nominal adjectives generally refer to abstractions:

[13] It looks as though she's verging on *the dreamy*

[14] Somebody may be doing *the dirty* on me ... behind my back

[15] There is a hidden plane of meaning (*the unconscious* for Freud; the imagination, perhaps *the divine*, in Symbolism). [W]

[16] So now ... can he keep *his cool* and really ... make his mark here

[17] Tonight I hope you'll not mind if I eschew *the academic* and pursue a more earthy albeit reflective tack analyzing the soil within which citizenship can root and thrive

[18] In fact if anything *the opposite* is true

[19] Please let me have everything for the brochure by August 21 at *the very latest*, and information for the factsheets by September 30. [W]

[20] Besides which, there's distinct evidence to *the contrary*. [W]

[21] By contrast, the new technocratic internationalism is shrewd in fusing principles of US and Western self-interest with *the good* of the coming world order [*Wall Street Journal*]

The features applying to plural nominal adjectives apply to the singular too. Determiners are absent in some instances where the singular nominal adjective is the complement of a preposition **[22]–[25]**.

[22] The concrete and steel chicane was meant to slow vehicles down for the customs check, not to stop them completely like the tank traps of *old*. [Michael Dobbs *Wall Games*]

[23] Among other things, it included checking, safe deposit box and credit card—all for *free*—plus a good deal on instalment loans. [*Wall Street Journal*]

[24] These questions in turn raise others about those buildings which, at *best*, fail to engage our admiration, or, at *worst*, repel us. [*British Journal of Aesthetics*]

[25] But GMAC approved the Buick program, he says, because the American Express green card requires payment in *full* upon billing, and so doesn't carry any finance rates. [*Wall Street Journal*]

8.3.3 **Nominal adjectives with non-generic reference**

Some nominal adjectives that have the form of -*ed* participles do not convey generic reference. They may be either singular or plural with specific reference:

[26] We shouldn't be concerned with the character and disposition of *the accused*

[27] We trust *the enclosed* is satisfactory, but if you have any queries, please do not hesitate to contact *the undersigned*. [W]

[28] At the graveside the curate adhered to the bald form of the funeral service, without any diversionary extolling of *the deceased's* particular merits as a human being. [Ronald Frame *Bluette*]

[29] Mrs Mandela, whose husband Mr Nelson Mandela is deputy president of the African National Congress, and *her co-accused* deny the charges. [W]

This type of nominal adjective can take the genitive *the deceased's* **[28]**. *Her co-accused* **[29]** could be singular, but the wider context shows that there were three co-accused. *The enclosed* **[27]** has concrete non-human reference.

8.4 Gradability and comparison

8.4.1 **Gradability**

Most adjectives are **gradable**. We can use intensifiers to indicate their point on a scale: *somewhat long, quite long, very long, incredibly long*. We can also compare things and say that something is longer than, or as long as, something else.

There are three directions of comparison:

1. higher
   (a) Frank is *taller* than Paul. (comparative)
   (b) Frank is the *tallest* of the boys. (superlative)

2. same
   Frank is *as tall* as Paul.

3. lower
   (a) Frank is *less tall* than Paul.
   (b) Frank is the *least tall* of the boys.

8.4.2 Degrees of comparison

There is a three-term contrast in **degrees of comparison**:

1. absolute   *tall*
2. comparative   *taller*
3. superlative   *tallest*

The **comparative** (*taller*) is used for a comparison in which one member (or more) of a set is contrasted with one or more other members and the **superlative** (*tallest*) where one member (or subset of members) is contrasted with the set to which it belongs. *Less* is a comparative adverb in *less tall* and *least* is a superlative adverb in *least tall*.

8.4.2.1 Expression of degrees of comparison
Degrees of comparison are expressed either through the inflections *-er* and *-est* or periphrastically through the premodifiers *more* and *most*:

	absolute	comparative	superlative
inflection	*calm*	*calmer*	*calmest*
premodifier	*difficult*	*more difficult*	*most difficult*

Monosyllabic words (e.g. *calm, tall, great*) generally form their degrees of comparison through inflections. Many disyllabic words (e.g. *polite, noisy, friendly*) can have either inflections or premodifiers. Words of three or more syllables (e.g. *difficult, beautiful, impolite*) require premodifiers, except that some words of three syllables with the negative prefix *un-* (e.g. *uncommon, unhappy, unhealthy*) can go either way. The inflectional option was available for adjectives of three or more syllables as late as the seventeenth century and is still found in some non-standard dialects.

8.4.2.2 Spelling of inflected comparatives and superlatives
1. If the base ends in *-e*, drop the *-e* before the inflection:
   polite/politer-politest   close/closer-closest

2. If the base ends in a consonant plus *y*, change the *y* to *i* and then add the inflection:
   sexy/sexier-sexiest   healthy/healthier-healthiest

3. Double the consonant letter before the inflection if all three conditions apply:
   (a) the base ends in a single consonant letter
   (b) a single vowel letter comes before that consonant letter
   (c) the final syllable of the base is stressed
   fat/fatter-fattest   wet/wetter-wettest

A final syllabic /l̩/ in the base, as in *subtle* and *gentle*, is not pronounced as syllabic when inflections are added. The final /r/ of the base is pronounced when inflections are added even by speakers who do not pronounce final /r/, as in *cleverer, cleverest*.

8.4.2.3 Irregular comparatives and superlatives
A few very frequent adjectives have irregular forms for their comparatives and superlatives:

good	better	best
well ('healthy')	better	best
bad	worse	worst
far	farther	farthest
	further	furthest

As late as the seventeenth century periphrastic *more* and *most* were commonly combined with the inflectional forms for emphasis: *more lovelier, most unkindest*. These combinations—double comparatives and double superlatives—persist in non-standard dialects.

The irregular comparison forms of *bad* are treated variously in non-standard dialects. In place of comparative *worse* we find *badder* (a regularized form), *worser* (double comparative form), and *worserer* (treble comparative form). In place of superlative *worst* we find the double superlative forms *worsest* and *worstest*.

8.5 Adjectives as unmarked term

Gradable adjectives can be used as the **unmarked** (or **neutral**) **term** in *how*-questions. The unmarked term is used for a question relating to the whole scale and not just to the particular adjective. For example, *old* in **[1]** does not mean that the speaker assumes that Nell is old:

[1]   *How old* is Nell now

On the other hand, *How young is she?* would mean that the speaker assumes that she is young. The unmarked term is the adjective that refers to the top of the scale: the end that denotes the greater extent of the quantity or quality.

Here are other examples of adjectives as the unmarked term in independent and subordinate *how*-questions (cf. 14.3.2):

[2]   And *how competent* do you think that system is

[3]   And I don't know *how accurate* it is

[4]   *How legitimate* is it

[5]   Did you personally uhm take any steps to see *how reliable* a sort of man he was

[6]   They claimed authority over all Britanny but how *effective* was this claim? [W]

In contrast *disinflationary* is a marked term in **[7]**:

[7]   If his forecasts this year go even slightly astray just *how disinflationary* will two hundred billion pounds of spending be

Some gradable adjectives are also used in measure expressions as the unmarked term: *deep, high, long, old, tall, thick, wide*. Here are some examples:

[8]   They're standing *nine ten deep*

[9]   It's *sixteen feet long six feet high six feet wide*

[10] Anna *seven years old* clings to any adult she meets

[11] When finished, shape into rolls, *about 4–5 inches long* and *1 inch thick* and put these, if there is time, in the fridge to chill for ¼ hour. [Michael Barry *The Crafty Food Processor Cook Book*]

8.6 Characteristics of adverbs

Adverbs are a heterogeneous class, varying greatly in their functional and positional ranges. They constitute a series of overlapping subclasses, and some of them belong to more than one subclass. For example, the adverb *very* is an intensifier that functions only as a premodifier (*very large, very carefully*), whereas *too* is an intensifier when it functions as a premodifier (*too small, too quickly*), but it has a different meaning ('in addition') when it functions as an adverbial ('The food was good, *too*'). We may regard as complex adverbs certain fixed expressions that have the form of prepositional phrases, such as *of course* and *as a result*.

The terms *adverb* and *adverbial* are distinct. **Adverb** is the name of a word class (or part of speech), so adverbs can be contrasted with adjectives. An **adverb phrase** is a phrase headed by an adverb; for example, *very carefully*, headed by the adverb *carefully*. **Adverbial** is the name of a constituent of a sentence or clause, so adverbials can be contrasted with complements of the verb such as subject predicatives and direct objects. An adverb phrase may function as an adverbial:

[1] I met my husband *here*.

But so can other linguistic units, such as a prepositional phrase or a clause:

[1a] I met my husband *in San Francisco*.

[1b] I met my husband *where he was working*.

8.6.1 Functions of adverbs

Used alone or with one or more modifiers, adverbs have two characteristic functions.

8.6.1.1 Adverbs as premodifiers

One function is as premodifier of an adjective **[2]**–**[3]** or of another adverb **[4]**–**[5]**:

[2] One foot's *slightly* bigger than the other though

[3] The truly disturbing aspect is that the CIA itself was also *laughably* amateurish in not challenging his obvious breaches of accepted procedure. [*The Sunday Times*] ('to a degree that was laughable')

[4] This really takes things *too* far doesn't it

[5] Well I used to get it *very* badly at night but if I take one of those tablets it's they help

As premodifiers or postmodifiers, adverbs are generally intensifiers, indicating degree or extent above or below an assumed norm: *slightly* (*bigger*) **[2]**, *laughably* (*amateurish*) **[3]**, *too* (*far*) **[4]**, *very* (*badly*) **[5]**.

8.6.1.2 Adverbs as adverbials

The other characteristic function is as adverbial in sentence or clause structure (cf. 3.8). There is often more than one adverb functioning as adverbial in the same sentence:

[6]   *Actually* you *probably* wouldn't have enjoyed it *here*

[7]   *Funnily enough*, many patients who show such learning *consequently* deny *ever* having done the task *before*! [W]

Though important informationally, adverbials are optional constituents of the sentence or clause, in the sense that if they are omitted the sentence remains well-formed:

[6a]   You wouldn't have enjoyed it.

[7a]   Many patients who show such learning deny having done the task.

Adverbs are obligatory constituents when they function as complements **[8]–[9]**:

[8]   I thought he was *here*

[9]   If the place grabbed me then I recreated it and put a story *there*

Adverbs functioning as adverbials and as complements are discussed in 8.7f. The full range of functions of adverb phrases is listed in 12.6. Modification of adverbs is illustrated in 12.7f.

8.6.2 **Types of adverb**

As with the other word classes, many adverbs do not have suffixes: *now, here, often, therefore, however.*

8.6.2.1 **Adverb endings**

The most common adverb ending is *-ly*, which is added to adjectives to form adverbs:

openly, madly, carefully, notably, frequently

If the adjective ends in *-ic*, the suffix is generally *-ically*:

romantically, heroically, electrically, sceptically, axiomatically

The exception is *publicly.*

Less common are adverb endings in *-ward* or *-wards* and *-wise*. The ending *-wards* usually has a directional meaning. The ending *-wise* generally has either a manner meaning or a viewpoint meaning:

-wards   *forward(s), upward(s), skywards, northward(s), inward(s), straightforward(s), afterward(s)*

-wise   *likewise, otherwise, lengthwise, snakewise; marketing-wise, stomachwise, pricewise*

NOTE

An Old English genitive inflection in *-es* is preserved in some adverbs ending in *-s*, e.g. *homewards, besides, needs* (as in *needs be*), *sideways; days* ('by day') and *nights* ('by night') in *They work nights*. The genitive inflection is obscured in *since, else, once, twice*.

Likewise and *otherwise* also have other meanings. *Clockwise* and *anticlockwise* combine manner with direction.

8.6.2.2 *Wh*-adverbs

A grammatically important class of adverbs are the **wh-adverbs**, so called because most of them are written with an initial *wh-*, the exceptions being *how* and its compounds (such as *however*). Several of them introduce **relative clauses** (cf. 10.9): *when, where, why* and (less commonly) *whereby, whereupon*, and the archaic *whence, wherein*. Here are examples of their use with relative clauses:

[10] Her father was in the oil business in Pennsylvania at a time *when* it was expanding very rapidly

[11] Uhm … the best cheese was probably the brie at the farmhouse *where* we were staying because uhm it was the local one

[12] The reason *why* a revived Halloween is approved is because it is a massive new advertising opportunity, in particular in the children's market. [W]

[13] If organisations operated according to classical free-market theory, *whereby* firms are guided by 'market forces' to make appropriate decisions, there would be no organisation problem. [W]

The *wh*-adverbs *how, when, where,* and *why* introduce **interrogative** sentences and clauses (cf. 2.5, 14.3.2):

[14] *How* does that suit you

[15] *Why* are you looking at me Bobby … I've never borrowed a hardback

[16] *How* long did you stay there

[17] I don't even know *where* Jesus College is

[18] Do you know *when* his office hours are

[19] Work is going well; I really enjoy it, though there is still so much that I don't know *how* to do yet! [W]

The adverbs may be postmodified by *else* and *otherwise* and by intensifiers; for example: *how else, when otherwise, why on earth, where in the hell, why ever.* The adverb *how* also introduces **exclamative** sentences and clauses (cf. 2.9):

[20] *How* true that is

[21] I was just saying outside … *how* these six months go round so rapidly

[22] I can remember going there and being amazed *how* pimply … the conscripts were

The *wh*-adverbs *how, when, why,* and *where* are used with **nominal relative clauses** (cf. 14.3.4):

[23] So that depends on *how* you want to do it

[24] I mean that's *why* I like faxes

[25] The most important thing you will ever learn is *how* to use your brakes effectively

Finally, *however* is used with **wh-conditional clauses** (cf. 14.5.6):

[26] You really are relatively speaking in comparison with the other two very inexperienced *however* talented you may be

In all these constructions *how* and *however* may modify adjectives or adverbs: *how long* **[16]**, *how true* **[20]**, *how pimply* **[22]**, *however talented* **[26]**.

8.6.2.3 **Adverbs without -ly**

In Old English, adverbs were derived from adjectives chiefly by adding *-e* or *-lice*. As a result of phonological processes, the suffix *-e* was dropped so that the adverb and adjective came to have the same form, and *-lice* developed into present-day *-ly*. Some adverbs still have the same form as corresponding adjectives; for example: *hard, long, fast, early, daily, kindly.* In other instances, adverbs have forms both with and without the *-ly* suffix, though sometimes differing in meaning:

[27] It's a bit *late* now

[28] Have you seen any of the others *lately*? [W]

[29] Incorporated in the great wooden beams which descended *deep* into the mine-shaft was a revolutionary 'man-engine', the first of its kind in the country. [E. V. Thompson *Lottie Trago*]

[30] Thought of Jeff and how *deeply* he cares about the political situation in this country. [W]

[31] I think you're doing *fine*

[32] Put the onions into the bowl and chop *finely* [Michael Barry *The Crafty Food Processor Cook Book*]

[33] Don't be intimidated by vehicles following too *close* behind

[34] One item *closely* matches your theme

[35] God that came out *quick* didn't it eh

[36] I'll just *quickly* show you one or two more

Only the *-ly* form can precede the verb.

Adjective forms of adverbs are more common in informal English:

[37] Dobrovolski getting away on the left hand side gets in the cross and Kalivanov gets in the first *real* good effort of the evening

In informal American English, *real* and *sure* are commonly used as intensifiers and *good* and *bad* as manner adverbs:

[38] I *sure* like them.

[39] He plays *real good*.

Non-standard dialects extend the use of adverbs (particularly manner adverbs) without the *-ly* suffix:

[40] They sing *terrible*.

[41] You don't talk *proper*.

8.6.3 Gradability and comparison of adverbs

Many adverbs are gradable, but most require the comparative to be expressed periphrastically through the premodifiers *more* and *most* (cf. 8.4). Those adverbs that take comparative inflections are generally identical with adjectives. Here are adverbs with irregular forms for their comparatives and superlatives:

badly	*worse*	*worst*
well	*better*	*best*
little	*less*	*least*
much	*more*	*most*
far	*farther*	*farthest*
	further	*furthest*

Here are some examples with regular inflections:

fast	*faster*	*fastest*
hard	*harder*	*hardest*
often	*oftener*	*oftenest*
soon	*sooner*	*soonest*

Like gradable adjectives (cf. 8.5), gradable adverbs can be used as the unmarked (or neutral) term in *how*-questions:

[42] I'm just wondering *how quickly* I can read this book

[43] And we can do that with female speakers and male speakers and children ... to see *how well* they can perceive pitch differences

[44] The first decision to be made is *how frequently* recordings should be made. [W]

Badly is the marked term in **[45]**:

[45]   *How badly* do the children have to behave before they are hit? [Paul Johnson *Child Abuse*]

8.7 Adverbs as adverbials

Grammatically, we can distinguish three major functions of adverbs (alone or with modification) as adverbials:

> conjuncts
> disjuncts
> adjuncts

Because conjuncts and disjuncts may relate to the sentence as a whole, they have been called **sentence adverbials**.

8.7.1 **Conjuncts**

Adverbs that are **conjuncts** (**conjunctive adverbs**) are logical connectors that generally provide a link to a preceding sentence **[1]** or clause **[2]**. They involve a great deal of compression of meaning, as paraphrases can show. For example, *therefore* in **[1]** is to be interpreted as 'because the more demanding the work the sooner fatigue sets in'.

[1]   The more demanding the work the sooner the fatigue sets in. It is *therefore* necessary to encourage the operators to take short breaks to keep them properly alert. [W]

[2]   If he was not taken in procession to the prison gates, as happens both to Samuel Pickwick and to William Dorrit, the relief and celebration must *nevertheless* have been much the same. [Peter Ackroyd *Dickens*]

The unit in which the conjunct is positioned may be part of a clause:

[3]   It'll mean traders will be able to offer a discount for cash … or *alternatively* charge extra to customers using credit cards

[4]   Could a tumour not cause obstruction and *hence* swelling

Here are examples of conjuncts, listed semantically:

> *first, second …; firstly, secondly …; next, then, finally, last(ly); in the first place …; first of all, last of all; to begin with, to start with, to end with*
> *equally, likewise, similarly, in the same way*
> *again, also, further, furthermore, moreover; what is more; in addition; above all*
> *in conclusion, to conclude, to summarize*
> *namely, for example, for instance, that is (to say)*
> *so, therefore, thus; hence, consequently; as a result, as a consequence, in consequence*
> *otherwise, else*
> *rather, alternatively, in other words*
> *on the contrary, in contrast, in comparison, on the other hand*
> *anyhow, anyway, besides, however, nevertheless, nonetheless, still, though, yet; in any case, at any rate, after all, at the same time, all the same*
> *incidentally, by the way*

8.7.2 **Disjuncts**

Disjuncts provide comments on the unit in which they stand. Two major types of disjunct are distinguished: style disjuncts and content disjuncts.

8.7.2.1 **Style disjuncts**
Style disjuncts can be paraphrased by a clause with a verb of speaking; for example, the style disjunct *frankly* by the paraphrase 'I say to you frankly', in which *frankly* functions as a manner adverb 'in a frank manner':

[5] Americans may say they'd like the idea of a simple President leading a simple life without all the trappings and paraphernalia of a world leader but *frankly* that's nonsense

[6] And the second uh purpose is in fact involved in sex or *more strictly* I suppose the exchange of DNA

[7] *Briefly* then the Sigma makes sensible use of its technology … it cruises very well and it comes with a three-year warranty

[8] But *simply* if I took a starting point as 1880 and the end-point as 1980 what would be the difference between the temperatures in those two dates

[9] *Personally* I agree with H G Wells that it is a great mistake to regard the head of state as a sales promoter

Here are examples of style disjuncts, listed semantically:

approximately, briefly, broadly, crudely, generally, roughly, simply
bluntly, candidly, confidentially, flatly, frankly, honestly, privately, strictly, truly,
    truthfully
literally, metaphorically, personally

There are a number of fixed prepositional phrases that function as style disjuncts. For example:

in brief, in all fairness, in general, in all honesty, in short

Style disjuncts are also expressed by fixed clauses of various types. For example:

to be candid, to be fair
to put it bluntly, to speak frankly
strictly speaking, crudely speaking
put simply, put briefly
if I may be candid, if I can speak confidentially, if I can put it bluntly

Most of the adverbs and prepositional phrases that function as style disjuncts can also function as manner adverbs within their sentence:

[10] I am going to speak *very honestly*

Honestly and *frankly* can also shade into a predominantly emphatic function:

[11] I don't *honestly* know

8.7.2.2 **Content disjuncts**
Content disjuncts may be modal (commenting on the truth-value) [12]–[13]:

[12] This is *probably* a woman's size

[13] He *obviously* felt he was being tested in some way

or evaluative (making a value judgement) [14]–[18]:

[14] Opposition candidates boycotted the vote. *Unmysteriously*, President Gnassingbe Eyadema won, with 96.5% of the vote. [*The Economist*]

[15] *Not surprisingly*, the socially depriving conditions had an adverse effect on children. [W]

[16] Progress has *naturally* been patchy … for confidence in the police is a fragile growth

[17] *Touchingly*, the prime minister seems to believe that the Italian public understands him, and that direct appeals will head off plummeting polls. [*The Sunday Times*]

[18] Moreover, Irish voters have *wisely* never given him an overall parliamentary majority. [W]

Wisely [18] makes a value judgement on the subject of the sentence as well as on the content of the sentence as a whole: 'Irish voters were wise never to have given …' and 'That Irish voters have never given … was wise'.

Here are examples of content disjuncts that are (a) modal, (b) evaluative, (c) evaluative and subject-related:

(a) *admittedly, certainly, clearly, evidently, indeed, obviously, plainly, surely, undoubtedly; apparently, arguably, (very, etc.) likely, maybe, perhaps, possibly, presumably, probably, supposedly; actually, basically, essentially, ideally, nominally, officially, ostensibly, really, superficially, technically, theoretically*

(b) *fortunately, happily, luckily, regrettably, sadly, tragically, unhappily, unfortunately; amazingly, curiously, funnily, incredibly, ironically, oddly, remarkably, strangely, unusually; appropriately, inevitably, naturally, predictably, understandably; amusingly, hopefully, interestingly, significantly, thankfully*

(c) *cleverly, foolishly, prudently, reasonably, sensibly, shrewdly, unwisely, wisely; rightly, justly, unjustly, wrongly*

8.7.3 Adjuncts

Adjuncts are more integrated into sentence or clause structure. Four major subclasses of adverbs as adjuncts are distinguished:

space
time
process
focus

The first two subclasses relate to the circumstances of the situation described in the sentence or clause; the third involves the process denoted by the verb and its complements; the fourth consists of adverbs that focus on a particular unit.

8.7.3.1 Space adjuncts
Space adjuncts include position [19]–[20] and direction [21]–[23]:

[19] Why have I got such a terrible collection of letters *here*

[20] There are cockroaches crawling around *inside* even if you have grates

[21] Well we could go *there* for about five minutes but then I have to leave again

[22] So I said don't worry about this and we ran *back* to my car

[23] Shall I move these *away*

8.7.3.2 Time adjuncts
Time adjuncts include position in time [24]–[26]:

[24] And have you *recently* had antibiotics for anything

[25] Ring her *tomorrow* and invite her out

duration **[27]–[28]**:

[26] You mean you haven't shaved it off *since*

[27] *How long* has he lived in this country

[28] Some fields remain grass *permanently*, others stay in grass for only a few years at a time before being ploughed up. [W]

and frequency **[29]–[32]**:

[29] None the less, it constitutes a sanctuary that *occasionally* helps more than 1,000 refugees. [W]

[30] The craving for more freedom of expression was *all too often* reduced to a need to call oneself by the name of one's nationality. [Keith Sword *The Times Guide to Eastern Europe*]

[31] After all the party that controls the White House *invariably* loses ground in the mid-term elections for Congress and *usually* much more ground than has been lost this year

[32] We were in telephone contact *daily*

8.7.3.3 **Process adjuncts**

Process adjuncts relate to the process conveyed by the verb and its complements. Adverbs functioning as process adjuncts are mainly manner adverbs, which convey the manner in which the action is performed:

[33] And I thought the overall impression in the hall was a bad speech *badly* delivered

[34] Apply the brake *very smoothly* and put it back on its side stand

[35] Cassie crouched forward, holding her arms *tightly* around her as if suffering from stomach pain. [Ian Enters *Up to Scratch*]

[36] The pup looked up and wriggled *happily* at the sound of his name. [Marion Babson *Past Regret*]

[37] Firstly, he suggests that the diagnostic process is non-comparable, in that, physical illnesses are assessed *objectively* and mental illnesses are assessed *subjectively*. [W]

Wh-adverbs often function as adjuncts. They have the special function of introducing certain types of clauses: interrogative, exclamative, relative, nominal relative, and *wh*-conditional (cf. 8.6.2.2). *How* and *however* can also function as premodifiers:

[38] *How* many classes are there that disabled people can go to

[39] And so *however* conservative their intention the ultimate effect of these philosophies was to weaken the idea of any moral authority beyond the self

8.7.3.4 **Focusing adjuncts**

Focusing adjuncts focus on a particular unit in a sentence or clause. The major semantic types are:

> additive
> particularizer
> exclusive
> intensifier

Additive adverbs emphasize that what is said applies also to the focused part. They include:

also	*neither*	*as well*
both	*too*	*in addition*
either	*yet*	
even		

[40] Besides being an academic sociologist ... Mike Grierson is *also* the warden of a small block of flats for people diagnosed as suffering from schizophrenia

[41] It's part of the complication of the countryside that it's *both* an ideal and a hard economic fact

[42] Did you intend then *even* then to become a writer

[43] I think he worked in a bank *too* at one stage

[44] The photon travels through without being *either* absorbed or reflected

Particularizer adverbs emphasize that what is said is restricted chiefly to the focused part. They include:

chiefly	*particularly*	*at least*
especially	*predominantly*	*in particular*
largely	*primarily*	
mainly	*principally*	
mostly	*specifically*	
notably		

[45] And those forty or so jobs you've applied for have they *mainly* been in response to vacancies that you've seen advertised

[46] They speak of continuing racial harassment *especially* of young black men

Exclusive adverbs emphasize that what is said is restricted entirely to the focused part. They include:

alone	*precisely*
exactly	*purely*
just	*simply*
merely	*solely*
only	

[47] You know there are *only* three vegetarian dinners here

[48] Well you should *just* stay till Sunday night

[49] Is that *simply* a question of money and cost

Intensifiers denote a place on a scale of intensity, either upward or downward. Intensifier adverbs are particularly numerous. They include:

almost	*fully*	*quite*	*a bit*
badly	*greatly*	*rather*	*a little*
barely	*hardly*	*slightly*	*a little bit*
completely	*highly*	*somewhat*	*a lot*
considerably	*immensely*	*strongly*	*at all*
deeply	*incredibly*	*thoroughly*	
enough	*less/least*	*totally*	
entirely	*much/more/most*	*utterly*	
extremely	*nearly*	*well*	

[50] She says there's now a change to re-allocate money to areas that *badly* need it

[51] The police have *greatly* improved their training and equipment ... for handling public disorder

[52] I've got another number and I don't like it *very much*

[53] But this *hardly* worries the recording industry, who want to deter multi-generation copying. [*Hi-Fi News & Record Review*]

8.8 Adverbs as complements

8.8.1 **Adverb as complement of** *be*

Adverbs often function as complements of the verb *be*, in which case they are **subject predicatives** (cf. 3.6). Generally, the adverbs have a spatial meaning, though the meaning may be extended metaphorically:

[1]   My friend who gets these seats is *away* she's ill

[2]   But the potential is *there* certainly

[3]   The flag is *up* for an offside decision

[4]   If you are *abroad* for more than six months in any tax year you will not be given automatic credits for any week in that tax year. [W]

[5]   I was *up* before her though ... yesterday

[6]   A: Is it flashing
     B: No But it is *on*

[7]   I wish it was *over* now

The complements of *be* may also have a temporal meaning:

[8]   Well, that was *then*, this is *now*. [W]

8.8.2 **Adverb as complement of phrasal(-prepositional) verbs**

The adverbs of **phrasal verbs** and **phrasal-prepositional verbs** (cf. 11.18f., 11.21) are complements of the verbs and have spatial meaning, literal or metaphorical:

[9]   How did that come *about*

[10] But it went *off* okay last night did it

[11] I would hold my breath if your arrival could be speeded *up* by doing so. [W]

[12] Drop *in* on the way in

[13] In which case we'd better get you to fill *in* one of these forms

[14] I think you'd know if you'd put *on* a lot of weight

[15] And I thought well now where shall I poke him to wake him *up*

[16] But when the two leaders emerged from their meeting they played *down* their differences

[17] Turn the heat *down* to low [Michael Barry *The Crafty Food Processor Cook Book*]

[18] Never do anything you can get *away* with not doing

[19] Is this the guy that was breaking *out* into a sweat

[20] And he thinks his wife is having it *off* with someone else

For some phrasal verbs the effect of the adverb is completive, indicating that the action has concluded and the result has been achieved: 'put *on* a lot of weight' **[14]**, 'wake him *up*' **[15]**. In **[11]** *up* is intensifying: 'could be speeded *up*'.

8.8.3 **Adverb as required complement of other verbs**

A few verbs other than phrasal verbs require a complement, usually one with spatial meaning. Here are some examples with adverbs:

[21] Seven successive popes lived *here* before the papacy returned to Rome

[22] By the time I got *home* they'd already phoned my agent

Here is an instance where the adverb has a manner meaning:

[23] So I don't think they have behaved *well* at any stage frankly

---

8.8.4 **Adverb as complement of complex-transitive verbs**

Complex-transitive verbs take adverbs as object predicative (cf. 3.7), again usually with spatial meaning:

[24] Yes but obviously by the fact that she wanted him *back* as I said to you she obviously wasn't leaving him

[25] Just as they were about to become corrupted or softened by a posting, orders moved them *somewhere else*. [Christopher Priest *The Quiet Woman*]

[26] Larry O'Connell calls them *together*

[27] It's to Dubrolsky in the end who plays it *through*

Here is an example where the adverb has a manner meaning:

[28] So how come you've been treated *differently*

8.9 Interjections

Interjections are exclamatory emotive words that are loosely attached to the rest of the sentence. They are common in the spoken language and in representations of conversation. Here is a list of common interjections:

ah	*ho-ho*	*sh*
aha	*hooray*	*shooh*
ahem	*humph*	*tsk*
boo	*oh*	*tut-tut*
eh	*oho*	*ugh*
gee	*ooh*	*uh-huh*
ha	*oops*	*uh-uh*
ha-ha	*ouch*	*whew*
hello	*ow*	*whoops*
hey	*phoo*	*wow*
hi	*pooh*	*yippee*
ho	*psst*	*yuk*

A few have been converted into nouns or verbs; for example: *boo* (noun or verb), *pooh-pooh* (verb), *shooh* (verb), *tut-tut* (noun and verb), *wow* (verb). *Cor* /kɔ:(r)/ is British.

There are also a number of hesitation noises, which may be represented by these spellings:

hm	*uh*
mhm	*uhm*
mm	*um*

In addition, there are many exclamatory words and phrases that have been considered interjections, though they are related to other words in the language. Here are some examples:

blimey (British)	*gosh*
bottoms up (British)	*hear, hear*
cheerio (British)	*heck* (American)
cheers (British)	*right on* (American)
crikey	*so long*
damn	*sure*
doggone it (American)	*well done*
drat	*well, well*

Some exclamatory words or phrases are borrowed from foreign languages; for example: *ciao, skol.*

Chapter 9
Conjunctions and Prepositions

Summary

Conjunctions are either coordinators or subordinators. Co-ordinators (*and, or, but*) link units of equal status. Subordinators (e.g. *if, although*) link subordinate clauses to their host clauses.

Prepositions (e.g. *of, in*) function as the first constituent of prepositional phrases and are typically followed by noun phrases as their complements. They may be simple (consisting of one word, e.g. *of, to*) or complex (e.g. *according to, as well as*).

9.1 Conjunctions

There are two classes of conjunctions: coordinators (or coordinating conjunctions) and subordinators (or subordinating conjunctions).

9.1.1 **Coordinators**

Coordinators link units of equal status. The central coordinators are *and, or*, and *but*:

[1] Well he'd better not get drunk *and* tell Jo what happened in the week-end … in the hope that she'll finish with me

[2] He married a girl from the Soviet Union *and* she followed him

[3] This was calibrated before flight using Freon 12, Freon 22 *and* filtered air [*Quarterly Journal of the Royal Meteorological Society*]

[4] All right then I'll see you later *or* I'll speak to you on the phone

[5] Intuitively the first mechanisms to account for mass movement in the situation of the device structure would be electromigration, *or* diffusion *or* a combination of both

[6] She would be drenched with a bucket of water, fall through a trap door, get blown up, *or* find herself shot from a cannon. [Nigel Rees *Dictionary of Popular Phrases*]

[7] I like mineral water *but* I don't like fizzy water

[8] I wear this occasionally *but* very rarely now

The **conjoins** (coordinated units) may be clauses [2], [4], [7]; the main verb (finite or non-finite) with its complements [1], [6]; or various kinds of phrases (including those consisting of just one word) [3], [5], [8]. Only *and* and *or* can link more than two conjoins [3], [5], [6]; the coordinator can be repeated between each conjoin [5], or it can be inserted only between the last pair of conjoins [3], [6]. See also 10.12f.

9.1.1.1 **Forms of *and* and *but***
The conjunctions *and* and *but* have both stressed and unstressed pronunciations. They are shown below, the stressed pronunciation coming first:

> *and* /and/, /ən/ or /n̩/
> *but* /bʌt/, /bət/

And is occasionally abbreviated in writing to '*n* or '*n*', generally in fixed expressions:

> *bed 'n breakfast*
> *rock 'n' roll*

It is also abbreviated as the ampersand **&**, a representation of Latin *et*, 'and'.

9.1.1.2 Initial correlative expressions

The coordination can be emphasized by **initial correlative expressions**: *both . . . and*; *either . . . or*, *not (only) . . . but (also)*:

[9]   But unfortunately *both* Saturday *and* Sunday it was really foggy

[10] Well nobody in their right mind wants war *either* in the Middle East *or* anywhere else

[11] It means that somehow or other religion in the modern world has been marginalised and that other agencies have taken over *not only* the bodies *but* souls of human beings

The marginal coordinator *nor* may be emphasized by the preceding correlative *neither*:

[12] We have also seen in the last few days that there was *neither* time *nor* reason to delay the land battle any longer

9.1.1.3 *For* and *nor*

Conjunctions that in certain respects are closer to coordinators than subordinators include *for* and *nor*. Unlike the other coordinators, however, *for* can only link clauses. For many speakers of English *nor* can be preceded by a coordinator, which in effect performs the linking of the conjoins in such instances:

[13] So you didn't have a lot of religious pressure *but nor* did you have a lot of religious thought

[14] I would simply say to them ... we won't forget those young men ... *and nor* in my judgement will we forget what they were out there to achieve ... what they accomplished

---

9.1.2 Subordinators

There are a large number of **subordinators**. Some of them consist of more than one orthographic word: *in order that, in that, rather than*. Some are historically composed of more than one word, but are now written as one word: *although, because, until, whereas*. Some are also used as prepositions (cf. 9.2.1.4): *after, as, before, like, since, than, till, until*. Some combine with other words to form **complex prepositions**: *because of, in case of*. *After, before, once, since*, and *though* are also used as adverbs.

9.1.2.1 Subordinators generally appear at the beginning of a **subordinate clause**:

[15] We can get that out *if* you want

[16] Well Toni's put an order in ... today *as* I said

[17] But I have such a thin skin I'm always terribly easily hurt and I find it very hard to forgive *although* I do ... eventually

[18] He does seem to be a good laugh *once* he's here in the house

[19] Laura likes tea bags you see *after* they've had taken some of the strength out

[20] *As* you say it's right at the heart of the process isn't it

[21] *Before* he was Prime Minister he was a great one for offering other people jobs that weren't at his disposal

[22] *Although* fungi are routinely observed in ponds in small numbers, little is known of their role and ecology. [N. J. Horan *Biological Wastewater Treatment Systems*]

[23] It looks *as though* it might have been open for quite a long time

[24] Would I be right in thinking *that* you're quite possibly marginally bored by what you're doing for work this week

[25] But I'll see *if* I can sort out some guest list

The subordinate clauses in [15]–[22] are adverbial clauses. They typically follow their host clauses [15]–[19], but they may also precede them [20]–[22]. The subordinate clauses in [23]–[25] are complements of the preceding verb. Complements virtually always follow the verb.

9.1.2.2 Some of the subordinators are used to introduce **non-finite** or **verbless clauses**:

[26] Add the meatballs to the tomato sauce, partially cover the pan, and simmer for another 15 minutes *while cooking the spaghetti*. [Michael Barry *The Crafty Food Processor Cook Book*]

[27] Cassie crouched forward, holding her arms tightly around her *as if suffering from stomach pain*. [Ian Enters *Up to Scratch*]

[28] Can you describe to me *if possible* a typical day in your home when you were a boy of less than fourteen

[29] We never spoke much, though that doesn't really matter as words are often inappropriate *when in the presence of feeling*. [W]

9.1.2.3 Some subordinators are restricted to certain types of non-finite or verbless clause: *for, in order to, in order for, so as, with, without*. *For, in order for, with*, and *without* introduce the subject of the clause.

[30] I shall try to prepare myself *for you turning up on our shores six foot tall*. [W]

[31] It will be impracticable *for them to be available as often as the media will now demand*. [W]

[32] I sometimes wonder whether Stephen actually went to prison... deliberately *in order to have something to talk about when he came on this show*

[33] *In order for the disc to be extruded* what type of force has to be applied to it

[34] So far as Muslims are concerned, the normal method of slaughtering is known as dhabh and it involves cutting the throat of the animal or fowl while it is still conscious *so as to allow the blood to start flowing out while it is still alive*. [Sebastian Poulter *Asian Traditions and English Law*]

[35] I put it on *with the zip done up*

[36] You'll never get a word in *with me talking*

[37] But they said because you've got to tell someone in advance you can't just put it on *without them knowing*

[38] I didn't mention this, however, for Mary Jane would have insisted on turning back and *with the sun out in full force* I was already too hot to be bothered. [Agnes Owens 'Patience' in Alison Fell *The Seven Cardinal Virtues*]

[39] Less than fifty feet away a US military jeep was flying through the air, headed straight for him, *with a demented Harry Benjamin as its pilot*. [Michael Dobbs *Wall Games*]

What with also introduces the subject of non-finite or verbless clauses:

[40] *What with his gambling debts and a son away at some expensive school near London*, he's hard-pressed for money to live on. [E. V. Thompson *Lottie Trago*]

9.2 Prepositions

Typically, prepositions function as the first constituent of a **prepositional phrase**. The second constituent is the **complement** (or **object**) of the prepositional phrase. Thus, *in a hurry* is a prepositional phrase, in which *in* is the preposition and *a hurry* is its complement. Prepositions chiefly take as their complements **noun phrases [1]**, nominal *-ing* **participle clauses [2]** (cf. 14.3), and nominal *wh*-clauses **[3]** (cf. 14.3).

[1]   And every single person *without a computer background* failed

[2]   That's a good way *of trying to get to know each other*

[3]   It's just a question *of which is the more efficient approach*

On the possible complements of prepositions and on constructions where the complement is either fronted or absent, see 12.9. On premodifiers of prepositions and prepositional phrases, see 12.11. On prepositional verbs and phrasal-prepositional verbs, see 11.18, 11.20f.

9.2.1 Simple prepositions

9.2.1.1 **Simple prepositions** consist of just one word.

SIMPLE PREPOSITIONS

aboard	concerning	out	versus (also 'v.'
about	considering	outside	and 'vs.')
above	between	like	since
across	beyond	minus (also '-')	than
after	but	near	through
against	by	nearby	throughout
along	circa (also 'c.')	next	till
amid	cum	notwithstanding	times (also 'x')
amidst	despite	of	to
among	down	off	toward
amongst	during	on	towards
anti	except	onto	under
apropos	excepting	over	unlike
around	excluding	past	until
as	failing	pending	unto
at	following	per	upon
atop	for	plus (also '+')	via
bar	from	post	vis-à-vis
before	given	pro	with
behind	in	qua	within
below	including	re	without
beneath	inside	regarding	worth
beside	into	round	
besides	less	save	

9.2.1.2 The most frequent simple prepositions are *about, after, as, at, before, between, by, during, for, from, in, into, like, of, on, over, than, through, to, under, with, within, without.* Some have both stressed and unstressed forms. They include the following, where the stressed form is given first:

as	/az/, /əz/
at	/at/, /ət/
for	/fɔ:/ or /fɔ:r/, /fə/ or /fər/
into	/ɪntʊ/, /ɪntə/
of	/ɒv/, /əv/ or /ə/
than	/ðan/, /ðən/
to	/tu:/, /tʊ/ or /tə/

The alternatives for *for* with /r/ are for those with a rhotic accent.

9.2.1.3 Here are examples of the use of some infrequent simple prepositions:

[4]   Well I'm a bit *anti* it

[5]   I conclude with the inescapable fact that, *bar* the Tantric tradition, it is the sexuality of the Goddess, and consequently the real women, that has suffered most in the transition that the Aryan heroes brought into the world's symbolic art forms so variously enshrined in each religious tradition. [W]

[6]   In particular, the varied pattern of incident, interval and allusion is of interest and compares well with the unimaginative and depressing grid plans offered by Foster Associates and by Richard Rogers Partnership, and with the animal-maze *cum* rural open-prison *cum* Japanese factory exercise-yard sketched out by MacCormack, Jamieson, Prichard & Wright. [*British Journal of Aesthetics*]

[7]   Access by sea is straightforward *given* the recognised hazards of the time such as storm wreck and piracy

[8]   These make up the normal weekly income, which (*less* any disregards) will be taken into account in calculating your Family Credit. [W]

[9]   We ourselves are having problems again at the moment because something else has threatened to be built *next* us

[10] We'll get that *out* the way tomorrow

[11] Uhm the esterase *plus* the water gives you the acid and the alcohol

[12] *Post* 1945, there was a general agreement by the western world to an obligation to help the development of the Third World and also to arrest the spread of communism. [W]

[13] I just feel sorry for them now: they're *pro* Boris Yeltsin. [W]

[14] Nothing remains of the chapels *save* the curved outer wall and window, producing the maximum enlargement of the window surface. [Paul Johnson *Cathedrals of England, Scotland and Wales*]

[15] It's mass *times* the distance from the centre if one's being pedantic about it

9.2.1.4 Many simple prepositions are also used in other word classes. They are functioning as conjunctions when they introduce clauses other than nominal *wh-* clauses and nominal -*ing* participle clauses; conjunctions include *after, as, before, but, except, since, than, till, until.* Some simple prepositions are used as -*ing* or -*ed* participles; e.g. *concerning, failing, following, given, granted. Given* and *granted* are used also as conjunctions. Many of the simple prepositions are used also as adverbs; e.g. *around, before, down, inside, off, out, over, under.*

9.2.2 Complex prepositions

Complex prepositions consist of more than one word.

COMPLEX PREPOSITIONS: A SELECTED LIST		
according to	*in comparison with*	*on account of*
along with	*in conjunction with*	*on behalf of*
apart from	*in connection with*	*on grounds of*
as a result of	*in contact with*	*on pain of*
as for	*in contrast to*	*on the part of*
as opposed to	*in favour of*	*on top of*
as to	*in front of*	*out of*
as well as	*in keeping with*	*outside of*
away from	*in lieu of*	*owing to*
because of	*in line with*	*prior to*
by means of	*in regard to*	*rather than*
by way of	*in respect of*	*regardless of*
care of (also *c/o*)	*in response to*	*relative to*
close to	*in return for*	*save for*
contrary to	*in spite of*	*short of*
down to	*in terms of*	*so far as*
due to	*in the case of*	*subject to*
except for	*in the course of*	*subsequent to*
for the sake of	*in the face of*	*such as*
further to	*in the light of*	*thanks to*
in accordance with	*in the wake of*	*together with*
in addition to	*in view of*	*up to*
in case of	*instead of*	*with reference to*
in charge of	*irrespective of*	*with regard to*
in common with	*next to*	*with respect to*

9.2.3 Other features of prepositions

The prepositions *close to, like, near, unlike,* and *worth* share a feature typical of adjectives: they can be premodified by *very. Close to* and *near* can also be inflected for comparison: *closer to/ closest to, nearer/ nearest,* while *like, unlike,* and *worth* can take the periphrastic comparison forms: *more/ most (un)like, more/ most worth.*

The variants *amongst, towards, round* (in place of *around*) are more common in British English than in American English. *Atop* ('on top of') is mainly American English. *Outwith* ('outside', 'beyond') is a common Scottish preposition that is beginning to be found in other varieties of British English.

In many non-standard dialects, *off of* is frequently used in place of simple *off* ('He took it *off of* me'), and a prepositional *while* is found in some non-standard dialects with the meaning 'till'.

There is not a sharp boundary between complex prepositions, which act as a unit, and sequences of (for example) preposition plus noun plus preposition. Some complex prepositions are fixed expressions that allow no variation, such as *because of* and *so far as.* Others allow some variation, such as *as a result of* (cf. *as a direct result of*), *in front of* (cf. *in the front of*), *in comparison with* (cf. *in comparison to*).

One indication of the degree of cohesiveness of complex prepositions is whether other words can be inserted within them. Those that permit insertions are less cohesive:

[16] I think probably what he meant is that the Jewish community in this country *in common* I should say *with* the United States community and maybe that in Israel ... is becoming religiously quite polarised

The same applies to those that allow ellipsis of part of the complex preposition. *Even to* in [17] is to be interpreted as *even up to*:

[17] But I don't think it should be *up to* us even *to* the alliance that fought Saddam Hussein in this case to make the decision about war crimes or whether there should be a prosecution

The prepositional complement generally takes the **objective** form, where this is available in pronouns: *about me, for her, to him, from us, with them*. However, subjective *who* and *whoever* are commonly used except in formal style. Objective *whom* is more usual when the preposition precedes its complement:

[18] Do you have long-term plans, such as where (—and *with whom*?—if anyone) you eventually want to settle? [W]

Part 4
Phrases

Chapter 10
Noun Phrases

Summary

Five types of phrase are distinguished, each named after the word class of the head of the phrase: noun phrase, verb phrase, adjective phrase, adverb phrase, and prepositional phrase.

The head of a noun phrase is a noun, a pronoun, a nominal adjective, or a numeral. It may be introduced by one or more determiners, and it may be modified by one or more premodifiers and by one or more postmodifiers.

Noun phrases commonly have one of the following functions; subject, direct object, indirect object, subject predicative, object predicative, complement of a preposition, premodifier of a noun, vocative. The most common premodifiers of nouns are adjectives, nouns, genitive noun phrases, participles, and numerals. The most common postmodifiers of nouns are prepositional phrases and relative clauses (finite or non-finite).

Modification of nouns may be restrictive or non-restrictive, a distinction depending on the meaning intended by the speaker/writer. Restrictive modification restricts the scope of the reference of the noun phrase, whereas non-restrictive modification does not do so but instead contributes further information. Sentential relative clauses, which are non-restrictive, have as their antecedent not a noun head but the whole or part of what precedes them in the sentence.

Appositives are typically non-restrictive noun phrases that have the same reference as the preceding noun phrases.

Noun phrases may be coordinated syndetically (with coordinators) or asyndetically (without coordinators). In polysyndetic coordination, coordinators are inserted between each pair of noun phrases. Coordination is segregatory if a paraphrase shows that each noun phrase could function independently. Coordination is combinatory when the noun phrases function as a unit that cannot be separated in that way.

The verb agrees with the subject in number and person wherever such distinctions are featured in the verb. Agreement is expected to be with the head of the noun phrase, but the number of the verb is sometimes attracted to that of another noun in the phrase, usually one that is nearer. Singular collective nouns may be treated as plural (especially in British English) when the focus is on the group as individuals.

Vocatives are predominantly noun phrases. They are optional additions to the basic sentence structures, and are used to address (usually) people, either to single them out from others or to maintain some personal connection with them.

Three types of contrast can be established for the reference of noun phrases: definite/non-definite, specific/non-specific, generic/non-generic.

10.1 The five types of phrase

The five types of **phrase** are named after the class of the word that is the head of the phrase. The phrase types are exemplified below in the order that they are discussed in this book.

1. noun phrase   *recent deluges of reports* (head: *deluges*)
2. verb phrase   *might have been accepted* (head: *accepted*)
3. adjective phrase   *surprisingly normal* (head: *normal*)
4. adverb phrase   *more closely* (head: *closely*)
5. prepositional phrase   *for a moment* (head: *for*)

Prepositional phrases always consist of two constituents: a preposition and the complement of the preposition. In the prepositional phrase *for a moment*, the constituents are the preposition *for* and its complement *a moment*, a noun phrase with two constituents—the indefinite article *a* and the noun *moment*. Other phrase types may consist of just one word as head (cf. 2.1); for example, in **[1]**–**[4]**, the noun phrase *lectures*, the verb phrase *brought*, the adjective phrase *cold*, and the adverb phrase *badly*.

- **[1]**   *Lectures* begin at nine.
- **[2]**   They *brought* me a box of chocolates.
- **[3]**   I'm feeling *cold*.
- **[4]**   They are behaving *badly*.

10.2 The structure of the noun phrase

A **noun phrase** has as its head a noun, a pronoun, a nominal adjective, or a numeral. See 5.3ff. for nouns, 6.1ff. for pronouns, 8.3 for nominal adjectives, and 6.15 for numerals.

NOUN PHRASES IN DETAIL

The noun phrases in **[1]** are indicated by italics:

- **[1]**   *Female spotted hyenas* are so much like *males* that *it*'s hard to tell *them* apart. Now, *scientists* believe *they* know why.
      Solving *a centuries-old puzzle*, *California researchers* have reported in *the journal Science* that *high levels of male hormone absorbed before birth* turn *female spotted hyenas* into *large aggressive animals* and make *the male hyena* *a second-class citizen of his own clan*. [*International Herald Tribune*].

The noun phrases at the end of **[1]**—*the male hyena* and *a second-class citizen of his own clan*—are two separate noun phrases ('make *the male hyena* into *a second-class citizen of his own clan*').

Some of the noun phrases in **[1]** consist of a single word; for example, in the first paragraph the nouns *males* and *scientists*, and the pronouns *it*, *them*, and *they*. Most of the noun phrases in **[1]**, however, have more than one word.

Noun phrases that have a noun as their head are often introduced by the **definite article** *the* or the **indefinite article** *a* or *an*. *The* and *a* are the most frequently used members of the class of **determiners**, which includes also *some*, *both*, and *this* (cf. 6.1, 6.13, 10.4). The second paragraph in **[1]** has several noun phrases introduced by the indefinite or definite article; for example *a centuries-old puzzle* and *the male hyena*.

Noun phrases may have **modifiers**. These may add information that characterizes more specifically what the head refers to. In **[1]** *California* modifies *researchers*: the researchers in question are restricted to those from California. Because it precedes the head noun *researchers*, *California* is a **premodifier**. In the noun phrase *high levels of male hormone*, there is both **premodification** and **postmodification**: the noun head is *levels*, which is premodified by *high* and postmodified by *of male hormone*. Modifiers are dependent on the head and can be omitted without disturbing the structure of the sentence, but like adverbials (cf. 3.8) they are usually important informationally and in that sense they cannot be omitted without damaging the communication.

We can now represent the structure of the typical noun phrase (**NP**) that has a noun as its head **(Fig. 10.2.1)**. The parentheses indicate the elements of the structure that may be absent.

Fig. 10.2.1 Structure of a noun phrase

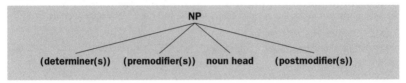

These four constituents are exemplified in the noun phrase *a second-class citizen of his own clan*:

determiner:	*a*
premodifier:	*second-class*
noun head:	*citizen*
postmodifier:	*of his own clan*

10.2.1 **Multiple determiners in the noun phrase**

More than one determiner can introduce a noun phrase (cf. 10.4); for example, *all* and *our* in **[2]**:

[2]   In the initial sorties *all our aircraft* have returned safely

10.2.2 **Multiple premodifiers in the noun phrase**

A noun head may have more than one **premodifier**. There are two sets of premodifiers in **[1]**, which differ in their relationship to the noun head: *female spotted hyenas* and *large aggressive animals*. *Spotted* modifies *hyenas*, and *female* modifies the unit *spotted hyenas*. On the other hand, *large* and *aggressive* separately modify the head *females*, since we can reverse their order (*aggressive large females*) and we can coordinate them (*large and aggressive females*). The structural difference is displayed in **Figure 10.2.2**.

Fig. 10.2.2 Premodifiers and NP heads

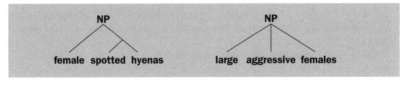

10.2.3 **Multiple postmodifiers in the noun phrase**

A noun head may also have more than one **postmodifier**. Two postmodifiers are exhibited in **[3]**:

[3]   I think it is a pity that LB is *the only major corporation I have worked for where this has been a problem*. [W]

The noun head is *corporation* and the two postmodifiers are *I have worked for* and *where this has been a problem*. The second postmodifier modifies the whole of the preceding noun phrase, including the first postmodifier, since clearly the writer does not want to generalize by extending the reference to major corporations where he has not worked. On the other hand, the two postmodifiers in **[4]** modify the head separately:

[4]   We could not trace *the invoice dated 22nd March 1990 for £43.13.* [W]

We could reverse the order of the postmodifiers without changing the meaning:

[4a]   We could not trace *the invoice for £43.13 dated 22nd March 1990.*

If we ignore the internal structure of the postmodifiers by using the convention of triangles, we can show the difference in the relation of the postmodifiers to the head in **Figure 10.2.3** and **Figure 10.2.4.**

Fig. 10.2.3 Postmodifiers and NP head: Sentence [3]

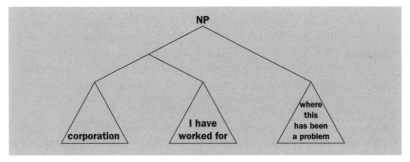

Fig. 10.2.4 Postmodifiers and NP head: Sentence [4]

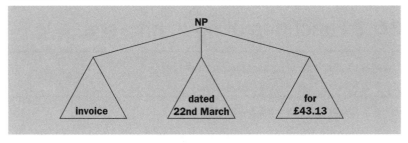

10.2.4 **Complex modification in the noun phrase**

Modification of nouns can be very complex. Here is an example of the heaping up of premodifiers in the headline in a local London weekly paper:

[5]   *Dog row sword death jury* told trial man 'didn't intend any harm' [*Hackney Gazette*]

As commonly in headlines, grammatical words such as *the* and *was* are omitted, so that a full version of the headline sentence might read as in **[5a]**:

[5a]   The dog row sword death jury was told that the trial man 'didn't intend any harm'.

The noun phrase subject is virtually unintelligible without the information supplied in the first paragraph of the news item:

[5b] An alleged murderer has denied deliberately plunging a sword into an unarmed man after a row over a dog fight.

Complex noun phrases usually have heavy postmodification. Here is an example, where everything after *What is* constitutes one noun phrase:

[6] What is *the single mechanism or dual mechanisms that allows a conducting filament to grow in the vertical direction immediately after breakdown and then at a later time and with the reapplication of a higher current to undergo radial growth to a lower resistance state?* [*Electronic Engineering*]

10.2.5 **Coordination and apposition in the noun phrase**

The structure of a noun phrase may be extended through coordination or apposition. In **coordination** (cf. 10.12), two or more noun phrases are joined by a coordinator to form one compound noun phrase, as in **[7]**:

[7] If you have left *school, college or an approved training course* you may be credited with contributions in one of the relevant tax years to help you to get benefit. [W]

In **apposition** (cf. 10.11), two noun phrases are typically juxtaposed. The appositive—the second noun phrase—typically refers to the same entity as the first noun phrase:

[8] Another tropism that may be of widespread occurrence, and which is also particularly evident in roots is *a directional response to injury, traumatropism.* [J.W. Hart *Plant Tropisms and Other Growth Movements*]

In **[8]**, *traumatropism* is in apposition to (or an appositive of) *a directional response to injury*. The appositive here (*traumatropism*) is the technical term for what is described in the first noun phrase.

10.3 Functions of noun phrases

The possible functions of noun phrases are listed below:

10.3.1 **Noun phrase as subject**

[1] And *my earliest memory of the theatre* is going to the Hippodrome in Ipswich

10.3.2 **Noun phrase as direct object**

[2] Sign *your name* there

10.3.3 **Noun phrase as indirect object**

[3] I always tell *people* I am not a musical person

10.3.4 **Noun phrase as subject predicative**

[4]   Uh faith has been *a gift* for me

10.3.5 **Noun phrase as object predicative**

[5]   I called this little talk *a survey of global bifurcations*

10.3.6 **Noun phrase as complement of a preposition**

[6]   Uhm but why isn't it in *French*

10.3.7 **Noun phrase as premodifier of a noun or noun phrase**

[7]   Simon's on this *revision* course
[8]   So a lot of my friends were in *one parent* families as well

> **NOTE**
>
> Genitive noun phrases generally have a determiner function: *the girls' parents* parallels *their parents*. They can also be premodifiers, as in *a girl's school* (cf. 5.12)

10.3.8 **Noun phrase as vocative**

[9]   You're a snob *Dad*

There are a number of other functions performed by restricted ranges of noun phrases.

10.3.9 **Noun phrase as adverbial**

Noun phrases function as adverbials in expressions of time, location, direction, manner, and intensification:

[10]   But you have to wait *a long time*
[11]   The flag goes up *far side*
[12]   Some of it's coming out this *way*
[13]   And would certainly not have been designed *that way* today
[14]   The loss in nineteen seventy hit him *a great deal*

10.3.10 **Noun phrase as premodifier of adjective**

[15]   The plane was *4 hours* late. [W]
[16]   It's *sixteen feet* long *six feet* high *six feet* wide

10.3.11 **Noun phrase as premodifer of preposition**

> **[17]** He revealed that Washington had informed the Kremlin *an hour* before the start of the assault
>
> **[18]** Two sleek, grey bodies were effortlessly riding our bow wave *just a foot or so* beneath the surface. [*BBC Wildlife*]

10.3.12 **Noun phrase as premodifier of adverb**

> **[19]** Now Mercedes have always been good at insulating their car but they've gone *a stage* further with this

10.3.13 **Noun phrase as postmodifier of noun**

> **[20]** Women may suffer from lack of 'acceptable partners' because too many of the men *their age* are dead [Betty Friedan 'Intimacy's Greatest Challenge', in *The Times*]

10.3.14 **Noun phrase as postmodifier of adjective**

> **[21]** We're short *fifteen dollars*.

Pronouns and nominal adjectives can perform the first six of the functions listed above for noun phrases. Clauses that serve the functions performed by noun phrases are termed **nominal clauses** (or noun clauses) (cf. 14.3).

10.4 Determiners

Determiners come at the beginning of a noun phrase. They convey various **pragmatic** and **semantic** contrasts relating to the type of reference of the noun phrase and to notions such as number and quantity (cf. 6.2, 6.12–15, 10.16). Determiners are distinguished according to the positions they can occupy relative to other determiners. They are also distinguished according to their co-occurrence with types of nouns.

10.4.1 **Predeterminers, central determiners, postdeterminers**

A noun phrase can be introduced by more than one determiner. It is usual to distinguish three sets of determiners that may co-occur in this sequence: (1) predeterminers, (2) central determiners, (3) postdeterminers. Here are examples with all three kinds of determiners:

all(1) *my*(2) *many*(3) friends
twice(1) *every*(2) *other*(3) day

Just one or two of these kinds of determiners may be present:

all(1) casualties	*all*(1) those(2) friends
my(2) friends	*my*(2) many(3) friends
every(3) day	*every*(1) *other*(3) day

Many determiners can also be premodified by **intensifiers**:

hardly any (money)	*no fewer than* twenty (claims)
virtually no (trees)	*just about* every (viewpoint)
almost all (instances)	*far too* much (time)
more than half (my efforts)	*so very* little (milk)
less than ten (per cent)	

10.4.1.1 Predeterminers

The predeterminers fall into four subsets;

(a) the subset *all, both, half* (cf. 6.13, 6.15)

> *all* ⎫
> *both* ⎬ the children
> *half* ⎭

(b) **multipliers** (cf. 6.15) consisting of:

(i) the subset *once, twice*, and (archaic or literary) *thrice*

> *once* ⎫ ⎧ a day
> *twice* ⎬ ⎨
> *thrice* ⎭ ⎩ every few weeks

(ii) the subset *double, treble, quadruple*

> ⎧ *double* ⎫
> (They now earn) ⎨ *treble* ⎬ their previous salary
> ⎩ *quadruple* ⎭

(iii) multiplying expressions headed by *times*:

> *ten times* the fatalities
> *three times* a day
> *four times* each month

(c) fractions other than *half*:

> *one-tenth* the speed
> *one-millionth* the density
> *two-thirds* the time

(d) exclamative *what* (cf. 6.12.2), which can precede the indefinite article:

> *what* ⎧ a day
> ⎨
> ⎩ a happy occasion

Such and *many* can also precede the indefinite article:

> *such* ⎫ ⎧ a friend
> *many* ⎭ ⎩ a good time

But *such* and *many* are not predeterminers, since they straddle the sets of determiners. Both *such* and *many* can be preceded by determiners from other sets. For example, *such* can follow the predeterminer *all*, central determiners such as *any*, and postdeterminers such as *several*:

> all ⎫
> any ⎬ *such* parties
> several ⎭

Many can follow central determiners:

$$\left.\begin{array}{l} \text{my} \\ \text{the} \\ \text{whose} \end{array}\right\} \textit{many} \text{ ideas}$$

Many and *such* can also co-occur:

    many such crises

The predeterminers do not co-occur. Those in subsets (a) and (b) also function as **pronouns** and can take **partitive** *of*-phrases:

    all of my children
    two-thirds of the time

Such and *many* can be similarly used:

    such of your people
    many of the cars

NOTE

The intensifiers *so*, *that*, and *too* followed by an adjective can precede a noun phrase:

    [N1] Certainly it was *so prominent a* punctuation in the landscape that one was positively drawn towards it. [James Lees-Milne *The Fool of Love*]

    [N2] I'd had a … reasonable lunch but not *that good a* lunch

    [N3] I think you're putting that in *too simplistic a* form

So may correlate with a *that*-clause after the head noun, as in **[N1]**, or with a *to*-infinitive clause introduced by the subordinator *as*. *Too* may correlate with a *to*-infinitive clause.

10.4.1.2 Central determiners

Like the predeterminers, the central determiners do not co-occur. The central determiners are all closed sets:

(a) **articles**, comprising the definite article *the* and the indefinite article *a* or *an*, and the zero article (cf. 6.2, 10.16)
(b) **demonstratives**: *this, these; that, those* (cf. 6.14)
(c) **possessive** determiners: *my, our, your, his, her, its, their* (cf. 6.3f.)
(d) **interrogative** determiners: *which, what, whose* (cf. 6.12.1)
(e) **relative** determiners: *whose, which* (cf. 6.12.3)
(f) **nominal relative** determiners: *which, whichever, whichsoever* (archaic); *what, whatever, whatsoever; whosoever* (cf. 6.12.4)
(g) ***wh*-conditional** determiners: *whatever, whatsoever; whichever* (cf. 6.12.5)
(h) **indefinite** determiners: *some, any, either, no, neither* (cf. 6.13)

    Enough can be a central determiner, but it can sometimes follow the head noun:
    enough food
    food *enough*

10.4.1.3 Postdeterminers

The postdeterminers fall into four subsets:

(a) **cardinals** (cf. 6.15.1)
    all my *six* children
(b) **primary ordinals** (cf. 6.15.2.1)
    her *twenty-first* birthday
(c) **general ordinals**; e.g. *another, last, next, other* (cf. 6.15.2.2)
    both her *other* daughters

(d) **primary quantifiers**: e.g. *many, several, few, little, much* (cf. 6.13.2.1)
the *several* poems by Blake in our anthology
your *few* suggestions
the *little* information you gave me

10.4.2 Singular count, plural count, non-count

Nouns may be **count** or **non-count** (cf. 5.5), and count nouns may be singular or plural. Determiners can be distinguished according to which nouns they co-occur with.

10.4.2.1 Determiners with singular count only
central determiners: *a* or *an, each, every, either, neither*
postdeterminer: cardinal *one*

$$\left.\begin{array}{l} a \\ every \\ neither \\ one \end{array}\right\} \text{suggestion}$$

10.4.2.2 Determiners with plural count only
predeterminer: *both*
central determiners: *these, those*
postdeterminers: cardinals from *two* up; primary quantifiers *many, a few, few, several*

$$\left.\begin{array}{l} both \\ five \\ these \\ several \end{array}\right\} \text{books}$$

10.4.2.3 Determiners with non-count only
postdeterminers: *much, a little, little*

$$\left.\begin{array}{l} much \\ a\ little \end{array}\right\} \text{luck}$$

10.4.2.4 Determiners with singular count, plural count, and non-count
predeterminers: *all*, multipliers, fraction, exclamative *what*
central determiners: *the, no*, possessives, interrogatives, relatives, nominal relatives, conditional-concessives
postdeterminers: ordinals

$$\left.\begin{array}{l} all\ their \\ half\ the \\ which(ever) \end{array}\right\} \left\{\begin{array}{l} house \\ houses \\ furniture \end{array}\right.$$

10.4.2.5 Determiners with singular count and non-count
central determiners: *this, that*

$$\left.\begin{array}{l} this \\ that \end{array}\right\} \begin{array}{l} car \\ information \end{array}$$

10.4.2.6 **Determiners with plural count and non-count**
central determiners: zero article, *some* (stressed /sʌm/, unstressed /səm/), *any*, *enough*

$$\left.\begin{array}{l} some \\ enough \end{array}\right\} \quad \left\{\begin{array}{l} \text{dollars} \\ \text{money} \end{array}\right.$$

Stressed *some* and *any* can also co-occur with singular nouns:

[1]   He was obviously afraid of mentioning *some girlfriend* and offending the wife

[2]   And also in *any area* of teaching you look for uhm *any* experience you've had with the relevant age range

10.5 Premodifiers of nouns

Adjectives are typical premodifiers of nouns, but other word classes are also used in this function. Nouns, participles, genitive noun phrases, and numerals are particularly common. Below are the types of premodifier.

10.5.1 **Adjective or adjective phrase as premodifier**

[1]   So I think from today's session you've realised I hope that you shouldn't start somebody on *life-long anti-hypertensive* therapy based upon one *single* blood-pressure measurement

10.5.2 **Noun or noun phrase as premodifier**

[2]   One of the *consortium* members uh … uh has all the files

[3]   And then I had the vegetarian option which was a wonderful *spinach cheese* thing with good uhm veggies

[4]   It's *a hundred and fifty pound* job to replace a door

[5]   My father had a *Church of Scotland* background

10.5.3 ***-ing* participle as premodifier**

[6]   But I hope to throw the net further in the *coming* weeks and get to know other nationalities. [W]

10.5.4 ***-ed* participle as premodifier**

[7]   The results of that in pollution and *wasted* natural resources every year is shameful. [David Icke *It Doesn't Have To Be Like This*]

10.5.5 **Genitive noun phrase as premodifier** Cf. 10.3.7 Note.

[8]   That's *the old soldier's* way isn't it

10.5.6 **Numeral as premodifier**

[9] Only do *six* essays not twelve

[10] Unfortunately, at the time the *first* launchers were required, jets could operate only up to about *one-tenth* satellite speed, so they could not be used to solve the problem. [David Ashford and Patrick Collins *Your Spaceflight Manual*]

10.5.7 **Adverb as premodifier**

[11] In the first week of May 1988 William Millinship, the *then* managing editor of the Observer, took me aside … and spoke to me with unaccustomed force, even severity. [Alan Watkins *A Slight Case of Libel*]

Apart from *then*, a few place adverbs and (before some pronouns and determiners) intensifying adverbs are used as premodifiers (cf. the adverbs as postmodifiers in 10.6.1.8). For example:

an *overhead* projector	*quite* a crowd
the *downstream* current	*quite* some time
offshore deposits	*rather* a good mathematician
the *inside* doors	*just about* everybody
overseas broadcasts	*nearly* everything
the *above* diagram	*almost* nothing
our *downstairs* tenants	*virtually* all the immigrants

10.5.8 **Prepositional phrase as premodifier**

[12] Both accords follow months of *behind-the-scenes* negotiations between PLO and Israeli officials, with Norway acting as a go-between. [*International Herald Tribune*]

Premodifying prepositional phrases tend to be *ad hoc*, and are generally hyphenated.

10.5.9 **Clause as premodifier**

[13] It is required to allow updating and track entries by data from several sensors using a **read and lock** procedure call (prior to writing) and a **write and unlock** procedure call (to complete writing). [*Software Engineering Journal*; bold in original]

[14] Had the *what-can-you-do*—? *Carry-a-card*—? problem again! [W]

Premodifying clauses also tend to be *ad hoc* and generally hyphenated. A few premodifying clauses, such as *keep-fit* in *keep-fit class*, are established expressions. Here are two other examples:

pay-as-you-earn tax   *do-it-yourself* store

10.6 Postmodifiers of nouns

The typical postmodifiers of nouns are prepositional phrases and relative clauses.

10.6.1 Types of postmodifier

10.6.1.1 Prepositional phrase as postmodifier Cf. 12.9ff.

[1]   It's just a question *of ... which is the more efficient approach*

10.6.1.2 Finite relative clause as postmodifier Cf. 10.9.

[2]   We don't have a constitution *which stops ... government from legislating certain things*

10.6.1.3 Relative *-ing* participle clause as postmodifier Cf. 10.9.

[3]   The air mass *bringing the coldest temperatures* is the polar continental mass which comes in from the Soviet Union. [Bill Giles *The Story of Weather*]

10.6.1.4 Relative *-ed* participle clause as postmodifier Cf. 10.9.

[4]   An intake shaft would provide higher ventilation efficiency for the more extensive layout *planned for the mine*. [*The Mining Engineer*]

10.6.1.5 Relative infinitive clause as postmodifier Cf. 10.9.

[5]   And again Fred when is the best time *to do it*

10.6.1.6 Appositive finite clause as postmodifier Cf. 10.11.

[6]   It's really shorthand for the view *that well-being depends on more than the absence of disease*

10.6.1.7 Appositive infinitive clause as postmodifier Cf. 10.11.

[7]   And finally today marks the beginning of a week of Christian unity ... so it's an opportunity *for Christians everywhere to at least unite in prayer for a speedy end to the war in the Gulf*

10.6.1.8 Adverb as postmodifier

[8]   The matter is to be considered when the new budget has been obtained, which should be some time *soon*. [W]

10.6.1.9 Adjective as postmodifier

[9]   Uhm let me find you something *ethnic*

[10] As well as the bonfire *proper* there was a second, more seriously built fire, where men were turning a sheep on a spit. [Mary Wesley *A Sensible Life*]

10.6.1.10 Noun phrase as postmodifier

[11] And yet in his address *this morning* President Bush referred to destroying his nuclear capability and destroying his chemical warfare capability

10.6.1.11 Comparative construction as postmodifier

[12] After five years of decline, weddings in France showed a 2.2% upturn last year, with *6,000 more* couples exchanging rings in 1988 *than in the previous year*, the national statistics office said. [*Wall Street Journal*]

A noun may be modified by a combination of a determiner *more, less,* or *as* before the noun and a comparative construction after the noun. In [12] the determiner is itself modified (*6,000 more*) and the comparative construction is *than in the previous year,* the two parts forming a discontinuous unit: *6,000 more than in the previous year.* Here are other examples:

[13] Moreover, the Japanese government, now the world's largest aid donor, is pumping *far more* assistance into the region *than the U.S. is.* [*Wall Street Journal*]

[14] He also claims the carrier costs less and takes up *less* space *than most paper carriers.* [*Wall Street Journal*]

[15] The cells are broken off … so I wasn't able to do *as* good an operation *as I would have wished* … on that lady

The combination may also involve a premodifying adjective:

[16] In part, this may reflect the fact that 'she speaks a *more progressive* language' *than her husband*, as Columbia's Prof. Klein puts it. [*Wall Street Journal*] ('a language more progressive than her husband speaks')

An inflected form of an adjective may be used:

[17] In particular, Mr. Coxon says, businesses are paying out a *smaller* percentage of their profits and cash flow in the form of dividends *than they have historically.* [*Wall Street Journal*]

Four of the primary **quantifier pronouns** may also be postmodified by **comparative** constructions: *much/ more, few/fewer, little/ less.* The absolute forms of the pronouns are used in constructions introduced by *as*:

[18] I was surprised to see more of them here than in NY, maybe *as* many *as in London* [W]

The comparatives are used in constructions introduced by *than*:

[19] Now you've been in *more* of this building *than I have*

10.6.2 Use of adverbs, adjectives, and noun phrases as postmodifiers

Adverbs, adjectives, and noun phrases are more restricted in their use as postmodifiers of nouns.

10.6.2.1 Use of adverbs and noun phrases as postmodifiers

Most adverbs and noun phrases in this function refer to time or place.
Time reference:

a month *ahead*	a day *later*
a year *ago*	the meal *last night*
some time *afterwards*	my appointment *the following day*

Place reference:

the weather *outside*	your way *home*
our journey *overseas*	the park *nearby*
the rooms *upstairs*	the road *that way*
the point *here*	the houses *this side*

NOTE

The adverb *else* is only a postmodifier. It follows indefinite pronouns and adverbs compounded with *some, any,* or *no*, interrogative pronouns (cf. 6.12.1), and interrogative adverbs (cf. 8.6.2.2):

[N1] I don't know what *else* I'll go to though

[N2] Well do it somewhere *else*

[N3] I don't know anyone *else* who could do it

[N4] Where *else* do you look John

> The genitive inflection is on *else* rather than on the pronoun:
>
> **[N5]** Is it part of your responsibility or someone *else's* responsibility to check whether the people who're running the hotel appear on the face of it to be competent and up to the job

10.6.2.2 Use of adjective phrases as postmodifiers

Postmodifying adjective phrases can usually be treated as reduced **relative clauses**: *something ethnic*—'something that is ethnic'; *the best way possible*—'the best way that is possible'. Compound **indefinite pronouns** and compound indefinite adverbs (which behave in some respects like pronouns) can only be postmodified:

somebody *taller*	somewhere *quiet*
nothing *interesting*	nowhere *better*
anyone *knowledgeable*	anywhere *cheap*

If the adjective itself has a postmodifier (cf. 12.4), then the adjective phrase generally postmodifies the noun or pronoun:

students *good at athletics*	the books *easiest to read*
those *sure of themselves*	a computer *powerful enough to cater*
candidates *confident that they will*	*for your needs*
be interviewed	an income *greater than mine*

But if the postmodifier of the adjective is a **to-infinitive clause** or a comparative construction, we can put the adjective before the noun and its postmodifier after the noun:

the *easiest* books *to read*
a *greater* income *than mine*

In a small set of noun phrases, the adjective always follows the noun. These derive from French or are based on the French word order; for example:

heir *apparent*
attorney *general*
president *elect*
court *martial*

(For the plurals of these compounds, see 5.7.9.) *Proper* in the sense 'in a strict designation' also always follows the noun, as in *the bonfire proper* in **[10]**. Similarly, *present* and *absent* follow the noun when they are equivalent to relative clauses: *the members present* —'the members who were present'; *the people absent*—'the people who were absent'.

10.7 Extraposed postmodifiers

Postmodifiers of noun phrases need not be attached directly to the noun that is head of the phrase. This is trivially so when two postmodifiers relate to the same noun, since the second postmodifier is distanced by the first:

[1] The Foreign Office has rejected a call *by families of British hostages in Lebanon* ... *for the restoration of diplomatic ties with Syria*

Both the *by*-phrase and the *for*-phrase postmodify *call*. In **[2]** there is only one postmodifier, of *concerns*: the *on*-phrase, which stretches to the end of the sentence. However, the postmodifier is separated from *concerns* by the parenthetic remark that is enclosed in dashes:

[2] We do have *concerns*—and believe staff should too—*on the more extreme agreements which sometimes get drafted by companies who are relatively unfamiliar with CASE contract norms.* [W]

Postmodifiers may be **extraposed** (moved outside their normal position) to the end of a sentence or clause, leapfrogging over other constituents:

[3] However, *new sets* soon appeared *that were able to receive all the TV channels.* [*Practical Electronics*]

Citation **[3]** contains a typical example of extraposition. The noun phrase (all of which is italicized here and in subsequent examples) is the subject of the sentence and the predicate (*soon appeared*) is considerably shorter than the subject. If the postmodifier were not extraposed, the sentence would be clumsy:

[3a] However, *new sets that were able to receive all the TV channels* soon appeared.

The stylistic principle of sentence (or clause) balance requires that the part before the verb should be much longer than the part after the verb (cf. 3.10). Another principle is also involved. The principle of **end focus** encourages the placement of the most important information at the climax of the sentence. *Appeared* is a verb that expresses the notion of coming into existence, which is relatively light informationally.

10.7.1 Extraposition of the postmodifier in the subject

Extraposition of the postmodifier in the subject tends to occur in contexts where the extraposed postmodifier cannot be misanalysed as modifying another noun. Favourable contexts for extraposition of the postmodifier in the subject are where there is no competing noun. Such contexts occur where the verb is **intransitive [3]** or **passive [4]**, or where the verb is **copular** and followed by an adjective phrase **[5]**:

[4] *A tape recording* was then published *in which Mr Lenihan freely admitted he had rung the president.* [*The Independent*]

[5] The format has a slight drawback in that *few VCRs* are available *that accept its tapes*; there are also few prerecorded Video 8 tapes available. [David Cheshire *The Complete Book of Video*]

As in **[3]**, the verb *was published* in **[4]** expresses the notion of coming into existence, while the predicate *are available* in **[5]** expresses the notion of being in existence. Here are some other examples of extraposition from a noun phrase that is the subject of a sentence or of a clause within a sentence:

[6] *A hunt's* begun *for two gunmen who burst into a pub in South London and opened fire on drinkers killing two*

[7] *Repeated attempts* were therefore rightly made *to fulfil the purposes of the United Nations without conflict*

[8] *The real nation* he contended already existed in Eastern Europe *possessed of an authentic Jewish culture passed down through the medium of the Yiddish language*

[9] The cause of ice ages is still a controversial subject, and *debates* continue *about the precise climatic effects of individual cycles.* [W]

> **NOTE**
>
> Extraposition of the postmodifying *of*-phrase would have forestalled the embarrassing suggestion reported without comment in this news item:
>
> A press release informs us that he hopes to raise the issue of 'street children and those sold into sex slavery *with Foreign Office ministers*'. [*The Independent*]
>
> Whereas the *of*-phrase is a postmodifier of the head noun *issue*, the *with*-phrase is an adverbial.

10.7.2 **Extraposition of the postmodifier other than in the subject**

Less frequently, extraposition takes place from noun phrases that are the direct object **[10]**–**[11]**, the subject predicative **[12]**, or the complement of a preposition **[13]**:

[10] They call *anything* a burger *that you slap into a roll*

[11] The invoice shows no deposit as having been paid; but in fact I paid *a deposit of £903.87* to Mr Swan on 11 December *in the form of a cheque which has since been cleared through my bank.* [W]

[12] I once had a fan letter from Neil Kinnock saying *what a good way* it was *to start Monday morning* and asking me how I got away with it. [Glyn Worsnip *Up the Down Escalator*]

[13] If she ever found herself in *a position*, by raising her little finger, *to save him from a painful and lingering death*, she hoped (she said) that she would still have the common humanity to raise it; but to be candid, she felt some doubt on the matter. [Sarah Caudwell 'An Acquaintance with Mr Collins' in *A Suit of Diamonds*]

10.8 Restrictive and non-restrictive modification

Modification of nouns may be restrictive or non-restrictive. The distinction is essentially a distinction of the meaning intended by the speaker or writer, though it may correlate with differences in intonation or punctuation.

Modification is **restrictive** when the modifier is intended to restrict the reference of the noun phrase. Modification is **non-restrictive** when the modifier does not restrict the reference, but instead contributes information about what is referred to in the rest of the noun phrase. The distinction between the two types of modification is illustrated in **[1]** and **[2]**:

[1] The *poor* areas of Mexico City are awash with polluted water

[2] He was obviously afraid of mentioning some girlfriend and offending the wife so eventually I had to help the *poor* guy out

Poor in **[1]** is restrictive, since it is used to distinguish one set of areas of Mexico City from other areas. On the other hand, *poor* in **[2]** is non-restrictive, since it is used to make an evaluative comment on the person in question and is not intended to distinguish him from other persons. In speech, restrictive premodifiers tend to be stressed; in writing, there is no difference in punctuation between the two types of premodification.

10.8.1 **Restrictive and non-restrictive premodifiers**

Whether a premodifier is restrictive or non-restrictive usually depends on the context beyond the noun phrase itself, sometimes the situational context as well as the linguistic context. In **[2]**, *light blue* is a non-restrictive premodifier of *carpet* if we assume—as seems likely—that there is only one carpet in the room:

> **[3]**   The room is hot and my feet are hot even though they are barely touching the *light blue* carpet. [W]

On that assumption we can paraphrase *the light blue carpet* by a non-restrictive relative *which*-clause separated by punctuation marks (cf. 10.9.1): 'the carpet, which is light blue'. In **[3a]**, on the other hand, *light blue* is a restrictive premodifier of *carpet*, since its function is to distinguish the carpet from other carpets:

> **[3a]**   I've decided to buy the *light blue* carpet, though my husband prefers the dark blue one.

10.8.2 **Restrictive modification and proper nouns**

Proper nouns are generally not modified restrictively, since they are generally identified uniquely. However, they may be modified restrictively when some kind of specification is needed. For example, in **[4]** one person named John is specified by the modification, in **[5]** one part of July is singled out, in **[6]** two types of Greek are contrasted, in **[7]** post-war Japan is implicitly contrasted with pre-war Japan, and in **[8]** the implicit contrast is with the present condition of the United Nations.

> **[4]**   That's the *only* John *I know*
>
> **[5]**   They come out *late* July August
>
> **[6]**   One of the ... synoptic gospels is written in *more or less colloquial* Greek ... sort of as it would be spoken rather than *literary* Greek
>
> **[7]**   *Postwar* Japan, pacific, industrious and in its own way democratic, belongs in the best, not the worst, traditions of the 20th century. [*The Times*]
>
> **[8]**   They will continue to work for a *stronger more effective* United Nations.

10.8.3 **Non-restrictive modification and punctuation**

Non-restrictive postmodifiers are often marked by punctuation or intonation separation from the rest of the sentence as a kind of parenthesis, as in **[9]** and **[10]**:

> **[9]**   I will begin with a look at the weather of our own country, *which is part of a temperate climate*, before moving on to the different very varied climates of the world. [Bill Giles *The Story of Weather*]
>
> **[10]**   The eagerly awaited gala première of the Pink Panther Strikes Again, *at the end of 1976*, made the front pages twice. [Graham Stark *Remembering Peter Sellars*]

In **[10]** the writer chose to insert the commas, thereby treating *at the end of 1976* as a separate piece of information, but he could equally have omitted them without affecting the non-restrictive sense of the phrase. For example, *of Russia* and *of Japan* in **[11]** are non-restrictive despite not being separated by punctuation, since the two named leaders are uniquely identified without the prepositional phrases:

[11]   Moving to thaw long-frosty relations, President Boris N. Yeltsin *of Russia* and Prime Minister Kiichi Miyazawa *of Japan* agreed Thursday to discuss the two nations' territorial dispute in a summit meeting here in October, raising the prospect of stepped-up Japanese aid. [*International Herald Tribune*]

If **[11]** had read *the President of Russia* and *the Prime Minister of Japan*, the two *of*-phrases would have been restrictive, since they would have been required to identify which President and which Prime Minister were being referred to. Although *of Russia* and *of Japan* are non-restrictive in **[11]**, they are not separated from the rest of the sentence by punctuation. The absence of punctuation is usual if the non-restrictive post-modifiers are brief prepositional phrases.

10.9 Restrictive and non-restrictive relative clauses

10.9.1 **Non-restrictive relative clauses**

Wh-relatives, such as *which* and *who*, are normally the only relatives used with non-restrictive clauses. Intonation or punctuation separation is a signal that the clause is non-restrictive:

[1]   There will be a break from 12.30 pm till 1.30 pm for lunch, *which will not be provided.* [W]

[2]   The other six include Diana Turbay, daughter of a former Columbian president, *who edits a leading news magazine.* [*The Independent*]

Punctuation separation is sometimes absent from what are obviously non-restrictive clauses, as in **[3]** (where Dr Funk of Tahiti is the name of a baby tortoise) and the two clauses in **[4]**:

[3]   Finally, into the garage to inspect Dr Funk of Tahiti *who was hibernating in a box of straw.* [Graham Stark *Remembering Peter Sellars*]

[4]   If you get a certificate AG3 *which shows you can contribute less than £11.20*, you should ask the optician for form ST(V) *on which you can apply for help with the cost of a private sight test.* [W]

Sometimes, however, punctuation makes a difference. The insertion of a comma after *prisoners* in **[5]** would indicate that the *who*-clause is non-restrictive and therefore that all prisoners breach rules:

[5]   The department is also likely to look at ending the dual role of the Prison Board of Visitors, who act as prison watchdogs as well as fulfilling a disciplinary role against prisoners *who breach rules.* [W]

10.9.2 **Restrictive relative clauses**

Restrictive relative clauses may also be introduced by *wh*-relatives. There are two restrictive relative clauses in **[6]**, one beginning with *who* and the other (embedded within it) beginning with *under which*:

[6]   In the meantime, I can give you the following list of commentators *who are on contracts under which they retain copyright.* [W]

That is commonly used in restrictive relative clauses instead of the *wh*-pronouns:

[7]   I enjoyed the time *that I was given to study and to explore*

The two types of relatives may co-occur in the same sentence:

[8]   Tumours *which grow slowly* are less radio-sensitive than tumours *that grow rapidly*

Indeed, *that* and the *wh*-pronoun may modify the same noun:

[9]   There are two directories *that I can direct you to* uhm *which will give you the first lead on that*

But there are stylistic objections to the use of both *that* and a *wh*-pronoun when the relative clauses are coordinated:

[10]   it was part of the anomalous froth now being blow off a boom *that* had run for 10 years *and which* had thrown up the usual number of excesses. [*Sunday Times*]

10.9.3 **Prepositions with relative clauses**

Relative *wh*-words may be preceded by a preposition. The preposition may be **fronted** with the *wh*-word, which is the complement of the preposition:

[11]   Now ... as for actually ... how ... or *to whom you send the messages* ... there's a standard convention ... used ... for addresses for e-mail

Compare with [11]: 'You send the messages *to them*.' *That*, however, cannot be preceded by a preposition. Instead, the preposition is **stranded**, i.e. left at the end in its usual place (cf. 12.9.2):

[12]   I knew my Wagner and my Beethoven and my Brahms very well but uh I saw that there were a great number of British composers *that I hadn't heard of*

(Cf. '*I hadn't heard of* a great number of British composers.')

[13]   Your instructor will also point out many things *that you haven't even thought about* (Cf. '*You haven't even thought about* those things.')

If the relative is a *wh*-word, the preposition can either be fronted or left stranded. Compare [13a] and [13b]:

[13a] Your instructor will also point out many things *about which you haven't even thought.*

[13b] Your instructor will also point out many things *which you haven't even thought about.*

Fronting of the preposition, as in [11], tends to occur more frequently in formal style.

The prepositional phrase may itself be the postmodifier of a noun in the relative clause:

[14]   Other people will have to pay for their sight test, *the cost of which may vary from one optician to another*, so it may pay you to shop around. [W]

The antecedent of *which* in [14] is *sight test*, so *the cost of which* corresponds to 'the cost of the sight test'. In a somewhat clumsy variant of [14], the prepositional phrase is fronted:

[14a] Other people will have to pay for their sight test, *of which the cost may vary from one optician to another*, so it may pay you to shop around.

A construction similar to that in [14] appears in [15]:

[15] This assumption is supported by the nature of the Latin used in the Llandaff Charters, *some of which have been shown to date from the second quarter of the sixth century* [W]

10.9.4 Zero relative

Relative *that* may be readily omitted from restrictive clauses if it is not the subject of the clause. In such cases it is usual to speak of a **zero relative**. In **[16]** the noun *tie* is modified by two restrictive relative clauses. The first clause has a zero relative pronoun and the second has the relative pronoun *that*:

[16] And she'd actually described the tie he was wearing that I'd given him for his Christmas before

In **[16]** *that* is required to mark the beginning of the second clause. It could be omitted (since it is not the subject) if the second clause was the only one:

[16a] And she actually described the tie *I'd given him for his Christmas before*.

Relative *that* cannot be omitted from the second clause in **[17]** because it is the subject:

[17] The worst *I've done* is like … why I can't think of anything *that's like approaching that really*

10.9.5 Other relative words

Relative words other than pronouns are also used to introduce relative clauses. The **relative determiner** *whose* is exemplified in **[18]** and **[19]**. In **[18]** *whose* is personal ('his face') and in **[18]** it is non-personal ('its achievement'). Although there are brief pauses before both relative clauses, the clause in **[18]** is non-restrictive and the clause in **[19]** is restrictive:

[18] Above him is the Byzantine emperor … *whose face has been somewhat rubbed* but one sees a little bit of the under drawing with a big black moustache and a baggy turban

[19] Our successor as Chancellor of the Exchequer … has during the last year … had to devote a good deal of his considerable talent … to demonstrating exactly how those Madrid conditions have been attained … so as to make it possible to fulfil a commitment … *whose achievement has long been in the national interest*

The **relative adverbs** *where*, *when* and *why* are exemplified in **[20]**–**[22]**. Of these citations, **[20]** is non-restrictive and **[21]**–**[22]** are restrictive:

[20] A similar scenario occurs around the margins of the Amazon basin, *where farmers are forced to encroach onto the forest margins in order to subsist.* [W]

[21] We hear little of the day-to-day successes but only of the odd occasion *when conflict arises*

[22] But that was one reason *why I never wanted to do that again* actually

The relative adverbs can be replaced by relative pronouns or by prepositional phrases with relative pronouns as complements. For example, *where* in **[20]** can be replaced by *in which*; *when* in **[21]** by *on which*; and *why* in **[22]** by *that* or zero.

10.9.6 **Restrictive and non-restrictive non-finite relative clauses**

The non-restrictive/restrictive distinction applies equally to non-finite relative clauses: -*ing* participle clauses **[23]** and **[24]**, -*ed* participle clauses **[25]** and **[26]**, and infinitive clauses **[27]** and **[28]**. The first in each of these pairs is non-restrictive and the second restrictive:

[23] Sometimes it carries red Saharan dust which falls with rain, *leaving a reddish film over buildings and parked vehicles in Southern England.* [Bill Giles *The Story of Weather*] ('which leave …')

[24] We are, of course, fully aware of the very difficult financial situation *facing your College* … [W] ('that faces …')

[25] The Prison Department's stance is likely to encourage Lord Justice Woolf to include proposals for minimum standards when he finally produces his report, *expected early next year.* [*The Independent*] ('which is expected …')

[26] An intake shaft would provide higher ventilation efficiency for the more extensive layout *planned for the mine.* [*Mining Engineer*] ('that is planned …')

[27] Please see attached notes, *to give you an idea of what we require.* [W] ('which will give you …')

[28] Indeed if some of my former colleagues are to be believed I must be the first minister in history *to have resigned because he was in full agreement with government policy* ('that has resigned …')

For postmodifying adjective phrases as reduced relative clauses, see 10.6.2.2. For non-standard relative pronouns, see 6.12.3.5.

10.10 Sentential relative clauses

Sentential relative clauses do not postmodify nouns, but it is convenient to deal with them at this point because in their form they resemble other non-restrictive relative clauses. In a **sentential relative clause**, the antecedent of the relative is the whole or part of what comes before it in the sentence. In **[1]**, for example, the antecedent of *which* is everything that precedes *which*:

[1] None of the three cities mentioned by the Anglo-Saxon Chronicle demonstrates any signs of habitation after the late fifth century (*which throws serious doubt on the usefulness of the Chronicle at this stage*). [W]

In **[2]**, the antecedent includes everything except the first word *certainly*:

[2] Certainly he was soon reapplying for retirement, *which suggests that he was no longer happy with the work upon which he had been engaged for some nineteen years.* [Peter Ackroyd *Dickens*]

The sentential relative clause is non-restrictive, and therefore it is generally separated from what precedes it by an intonation break or pause in speech and by a punctuation mark in writing.

Here are some further examples with sentential relative *which*:

[3] But the big tune at the centre of the Rhapsody and the blues melody in An American in Paris (given an upbeat reading) are lacking in sensuous warmth, *which means that a dimension is missing in both works.* [*Penguin Guide to Compact Discs*]

[4] He feels at ease with such people, *which is not true of all Indian politicians*, and that may explain why he decides to retain the external affairs portfolio for himself in his first government after the elections. [Nicholas Nugent *Rajiv Gandhi*]

[5] He left BSC shortly after I did to tackle the problems of the redirection of the Ocean Shipping Group, *which he did with no little success*. [Peter Thompson *Sharing the Success*]

[6] Chimps can grow as big as you or me, *which is something that most people do not realise*. [John Nichols *The Mighty Rainforest*]

In all these instances **[1]–[6]** it would be possible to transform the sentential relative clause into an independent sentence in which the demonstrative pronoun *that* has the same reference back to the preceding part of the sentence. For example:

[6a] Chimps can grow as big as you or me. *That is something that most people do not realise.*

NOTE

The quasi-independent status of the sentential relative clause is indicated by its ability to be punctuated as an independent sentence in writing **[N1]** and even to head a new paragraph **[N2]**;

[N1] You'll get a letter from me tomorrow and no doubt be embarassed [*sic*] when the lady gives it to you. *Which* reminds me, do you want me to post your toothbrushes? [W]

[N2] The news is not all bad. The Bank judges that six countries got the macroeconomic fundamentals right ... *All of which* is quite some achievement. [*The Economist*]

The relative may be the complement of a preposition **[7]** or the determiner of a noun phrase **[8]–[9]**:

[7] You may find the above questions obvious, *for which I apologise*, but I feel they are sufficiently critical to be worth emphasising. [W]

[8] It may be that the potential obstacles are not insurmountable problems, *in which case* I look forward to hearing from you to discuss things further. [W]

[9] What you should do is order one first and then eat it and then carry on from there ... *by which time* you wouldn't want a second anyway

Relatives other than *which* can introduce relative clauses. They include *whereupon*, *whence* (formal style), and *when* in combination with a preceding preposition.

[10] The Social Democrats did not have the sense to call off the visit, but they swore to confront the East Germans with 'reform' demands—*whereupon* they suffered the supreme humiliation: the communists withdrew their invitation. [*Wall Street Journal*] ('as a result of which')

[11] I finally got the parcel at the end of August, *since when* several factors have all delayed my writing to Edinburgh University Press. [W]

10.11 Appositives

Appositives may be either restrictive or non-restrictive.

10.11.1 **Non-restrictive appositives**

Typically, **appositives** are non-restrictive noun phrases, separated by an intonation break in speech and by punctuation in writing:

[1] Hong Kong has not forcibly deported any Vietnamese since the international outcry over an operation of December, 1989 when 51 protesting boatpeople were put on a plane to the Vietnamese capital, *Hanoi*, under armed police guard. [*Yorkshire Post*]

[2] David, *an apprentice mechanic*, was a natural athlete, played for Cheltenham Rugby Club's under-16 team and was also a keen cricketer. [*Yorkshire Post*]

[3] Your sight can be tested only by a registered ophthalmic optician (*optometrist*) or an ophthalmic medical practitioner. [W]

[4] This pipe is usually a 25mm (*1 in*) diameter steel pipe, wrapped with special tape to protect it from rusting, and buried to protect from frost. [George Collard *Do-it-Yourself Home Surveying*]

[5] Jordan, too, which maintains close military and political links with Iraq, might have used her strong army to take Hijaz, *the Saudi region in which the holy cities of Medina and Mecca stand*. [*Evening Standard*]

[6] Inside was the engine—*his engine*. [E. V. Thompson *Lottie Trago*]

The appositive may consist of a set of coordinated noun phrases:

[7] He wanted to break up their home, the fragile and wholly superfluous objects of their shared life—*mirrors, tables, the chiming clock, her idiotic, hated thimbles*—suddenly taking on a sinister appeal. [Paul Sayer *Howling at the Moon*]

Left and right dislocation (cf. 3.10.4, 3.10.5), found mainly in informal speech, can be viewed as special kinds of apposition. In **left dislocation**, an anticipatory noun phrase is followed by a pronoun in the normal position for the noun phrase:

[8] '*Your mother*, she was just misunderstood. *Time and patience*, it wouldn't have taken any more than that—' [Ronald Frame *Bluette*]

[9] *The Household Division* they wear these … Tudor coats in the presence of Her Majesty the Queen

[10] The hideous exterior looks might lead you to think that it's a tractor but *the innards* … well they suggest otherwise

In **right dislocation**, an anticipatory pronoun is in the normal position and an explanatory noun phrase appears later in the sentence:

[11] And there were still hundreds of people on it but *it* was so big *this boat* that you didn't meet them

[12] *They*'re not great social animals *computer scientists*

[13] It looks like *him* you know *the father*

The postponed noun phrase may itself be a pronoun—for example, the demonstrative pronoun *that* in **[14]**:

[14] *It*'s a tremendous amount of money *that*

The appositive may be separated from its antecedent apart from the special instances of left and right dislocation illustrated in **[8]**–**[14]**.

[15] A tremble spread outward from her spine until *the earth itself* seemed to shake, *an earth where the same sun rose as yesterday, the same scents drifted on the wind*; only she was so different that she didn't belong there any more. [Mary Napier *Powers of Darkness*]

The separation may be due to the presence of apposition markers—such as *for example*, *that is to say*, *namely*, and *such as*—which introduce appositives:

[16] I mean for instance when Trevor and I did the whole of the Roman plays *that's to say Titus Andronicus Coriolanus Anthony and Cleopatra Julius Caesar* I used curved Roman trumpets which I've specially made

[17] I then find that there is an impossible situation in the family … *say an unfaithful husband or something like that*

[18] Some satellites *for example the satellite known by its acronym as SPOT* … can view the same place from two directions

For coordinative apposition, see 10.12.7

10.11.2 Restrictive appositives

In restrictive apposition, the appositive is not separated by punctuation or intonation. Three types of restrictive apposition occur with noun phrases.

10.11.2.1 In the first type, the first noun phrase starts with a determiner and the second noun phrase, which is more specific, is usually a name:

[19] The unsuccessful intervention of Magnus Maximus into continental politics between 383–88 A.D., along with a considerable portion of the British army, set a dangerous precedent, which the usurper *Constantine III* followed in 407 A.D. with disastrous consequences. [W]

[20] In some cases, as with my agent *Dennis Selinger*, they are also obliged to play the part of best man, godfather to the children and lifelong friend. [Graham Stark *Remembering Peter Sellars*]

[21] Steffi Graf's three-year winning reign at the Australian Open ended when the Czech *Jana Novotna* beat her 5–7, 6–4, 8–6 in a gripping quarter final at Flinders Park. [*Evening Standard*]

The first type is also used with words that are cited and with the titles of works:

[22] Mary Jane tells me I shouldn't use the word *half-caste*

[23] Now in the present case the phrase *interim award* has been used or may have been understood to be used uh in another sense

[24] Kevin Kostner's epic film *Dance with Wolves* has been nominated for twelve Oscars

[25] It's actually the second play I've written for them uhm … which is kind of based on the uhm the Browning poem *The Pied Piper*

The first noun phrase is often ellipted in this type of apposition. For cited words (e.g.: *half-caste* [22] and *interim award* [23] above), the ellipted noun phrase would be expressions such as *the word, the phrase, the sentence, the expression, the slogan*, whereas for works it would be *the play, the film, the novel*, etc.

[26] Well I don't think you can negotiate if by *negotiations* you mean can we allow Saddam Hussein to hold on to part of Kuwait

[27] *Disraeli*'s a proper noun

[28] '*That was laid on with a trowel*' appears in Shakespeare's As You Like It (I, ii, 98) which the Arden edition glosses as '*slapped on thick and without nicety, like mortar*'. [Nigel Rees *Dictionary of Popular Phrases*]

[29] It's a short step from these to Ronald Reagan's '*Let's make America great again*' in 1980. [Nigel Rees *Dictionary of Popular Phrases*]

[30] *Twins* is definitely a film to watch

[31] In *Babes in Arms* (1939)—the only one in the genre I have looked at—Rooney and Garland play the teenage children of retired vaudeville players who decide to put on a big show of their own. [Nigel Rees *Dictionary of Popular Phrases*]

[32] But to say this is from the *New York Times* therefore it's American English is not very helpful lexicographically cos sort of ninety percent of the matter is common English of the world

The assumed ellipsis of *the film* explains why in **[30]** the verb is singular though *Twins* is plural.

10.11.2.2 The second type of restrictive apposition is the same as the first, except that the determiner is missing in the first noun phrase. This type commonly occurs in news reports:

[33] 'Italy has never questioned the need for unity of command in the United Nations Operation in Somalia,' Foreign Minister *Andreatta* said Thursday. [*International Herald Tribune*]

[34] Financial adviser *David Innes*, who is now the centre's general manager, explained that staff were 'very mindful' that the lifeline was being viewed as their last chance. [*Wembley Observer*]

[35] Art Student *Mulvey* and his tutor at Kingsway College in central London decided he would make the graffiti study as a project for his diploma, a court heard. [*Daily Mail*]

[36] Forest's equaliser in the 75th minute had an element of good fortune, Terry Wilson's drive spinning off defender *Richard Shaw* and looping over goalkeeper *Nigel Martyn* into the net. [*Evening Standard*]

Family designations are often found in this second type:

[37] This is Cousin *Renee* who is not to be confused with Auntie *Renee*

The second type resembles titles, except that titles are well-established whereas many of these appositives are *ad hoc* and outside news reports they follow the first or third types. Titles generally precede the name:

Senator Richard G. Lugar	*Prince* Charles
Chairman Mao	*Dr* Kissinger
Mr Clinton	*Emperor* Akihito
President Boris Yeltsin	*Chief* Buthelesi
Admiral Crowe	*The Reverend* Martin Luther King, Jr

> **NOTE**
>
> Exceptional titles that follow names include the (chiefly) American designations *Senior* (*Sr.*) and *Junior* (*Jr.*) to distinguish between fathers and sons with the same first names, as in *Martin Luther King, Jr.*; subsequent generations are given Roman numerals, as in *Sen. John D. Rockefeller IV* (read as 'the fourth'). *Major* and *minor* are sometimes used in British schools after family names of brothers in the same school (e.g. *Smith minor*). The courtesy title *Esq.* (abbreviation of *Esquire*) is occasionally used in addresses on letters with the full name when no other title is used with the name (e.g. *John Black, Esq.*)

When the titles are modified, they may follow the name, but in that case they are appositives rather than titles:

[38] Mikhail Gorbachev's meeting yesterday with Boris Yeltsin, *president of the Russian Federation*, came none too soon. [*The Times*]

NOTE

Descriptive phrases consisting of the definite article *the* and an adjective or numeral may follow the names of monarchs; *Elizabeth I* ('the first'), *William the Conqueror*. Those of the type *Ivan the Terrible* and *Elizabeth I* are postmodifiers (compare: *the terrible Ivan, the first Elizabeth*), whereas in *William the Conqueror, the Conqueror* is an appositive (compare *the poet Longfellow*).

Two titles may be combined:

> *His Royal Highness Prince* Charles
> *Her Majesty Queen* Elizabeth
> *Mr Chief Justice*

10.11.2.3 The third type of restrictive apposition is the reverse of the first: the name comes first and is followed by a noun phrase that is less specific and is introduced by a determiner:

[39]   Dad slowly rolled the belt round his wrist and pulled at the other end as if it were the old razor strop used in Perkins *the barber's* down the road. [Ian Enters *Up to Scratch*]

[40]   Simon doesn't pay but Laura *the student* does

The non-restrictive/restrictive distinction applies to appositive clauses as well as relative clauses. The finite clause in **[40]** is non-restrictive, the finite clauses in **[41]** and the infinitive clause in **[42]** are restrictive:

[41]   It will not be long before he asks his regular question: *'What would you like for your birthday?'* [Anne Melville 'Portrait of a Woman' in *Snapshots*]

[42]   Well is there very much that you can't do under DOS I mean given the fact *that machines get much faster*

[43]   Most of the time though the tendency of the blood *to clot* must be resisted ... but not so firmly that it won't clot at all ...

NOTE

Appositive clauses are to be distinguished from relative clauses (cf. 10.9). Appositive clauses are self-contained, whereas in relative clauses the relative item functions within the clause. For example in the appositive clause **[N1]** *that* is a subordinator and does not function (say as subject or direct object) in the clause;

[N1]   Police say they can't confirm a TV report *that the building had been hit by automatic fire*

We can extract the appositive clause without its subordinator and make it an independent sentence:

[N1a] The building had been hit by automatic fire.

We can show that it is an appositive by demonstrating its copular link with the preceding noun phrase:

[N1b] The TV report is that the building had been hit by automatic fire.

We can insert an appropriate apposition marker, in this case *namely*. On the other hand, the *that*-clause in **[N1c]** is a relative clause:

[N1c] Police say that they can't confirm a TV report *that we all saw last night*.

Here *that* is a relative pronoun functioning as direct object in the relative clause. We can replace it by the relative pronoun *which*, which refers back to the antecedent *a TV report* ('We all saw the TV report last night')

Appositive clauses are treated as complements of the noun head in 14.7.

10.12 The coordination of noun phrases

Coordinated noun phrases are at the same level of structure and constitute a unit, a **compound noun phrase**. Typically, noun phrases are coordinated explicitly by means of a **coordinator**. The usual coordinators for noun phrases are *and* and *or*, less frequently *nor* and *but*.

10.12.1 **Syndetic coordination**

If coordinators are present, the coordination is **syndetic**:

[1]   What is it like to be back home studying again in the company of *close friends and family*? [W]

The two noun phrases may be separated by an intonation break in speech or by a comma in writing to emphasize a separate unit of information:

[2]   His only answer to *his errors, and those of others*, is to isolate them. [W]

[3]   It was *attacks by their neighbours, or the fear of such attacks*, that gave early Rome the pretexts or motives for reducing them to submission; in addition, by confiscating some of their lands, the Romans were able to satisfy the land-hunger of their own peasantry. [P. A. Brunt *Roman Imperial Themes*]

More than two noun phrases may be coordinated in syndetic coordination. In that case, it is normal for the coordinator to appear only between the last two phrases:

[4]   Mr. Mandela has in turn been *activist, prisoner, martyr, statesman and conciliator*. [*International Herald Tribune*]

Punctuation usage varies as to whether a comma is inserted between the penultimate noun phrase and the coordinator. The comma is often omitted on the assumption that it is not necessary, since the coordinator is sufficient to signal the coordination. American usage omits the comma in journalistic writing, as in [4], but otherwise retains it:

[5]   For someone bound by classical concepts of *motion, inertia, and gravity*, it is hard to appreciate the self-consistent world view that went with Aristotle's understanding of a pendulum. [James Gleick *Chaos: Making a New Science*]

British usage tends to omit the comma [6], but sometimes retains it [7]:

[6]   Ideas that come to mind are *workload, allocation of the 1% flexibility element from the last salary settlement and the new College admissions procedure*. [W]

[7]   When I think of children I think of *imagination, generosity, and tantrums that are basically harmless*. [Graham Stark *Remembering Peter Sellars*]

10.12.2 **Polysyndetic coordination**

Coordination is **polysyndetic** when coordinators are repeated redundantly between each pair of noun phrases when there are more than two:

[8]   The mixture of warm air and moisture creates thunderstorms at altitude—maybe 3,000 metres (10,000 feet)—bringing *thunder and sheet lightning and heavy downpours* from France, often at night. [Bill Giles *The Story of Weather*]

[9]   It was agreeable, he thought, to have no ties, not to have to rush back to wife and family as did, for instance, Herbert, always in a hurry to fit in *the children's holidays or Venice or Paris* because Victoria must go between the children's half-terms, and still constantly travel for his own work. [Mary Wesley *A Sensible Life*]

The redundancy emphasizes that each item is a separate entity.

10.12.3 Asyndetic coordination

Coordination is **asyndetic** when the phrases are not linked by coordinators but co-ordinators could have been inserted, as in this example of left dislocation (cf. 10.11.1):

[10]   *Defence, international relations, economic management, honours, appointments, law enforcement*—all are excluded. [*The Economist*]

10.12.4 Hierarchical coordination

Coordination may be hierarchical, with one level of coordination embedded in another level:

[11]   So this is showing you this interesting balance in this classical Ottoman painting ... between *naturalism or pretend naturalism ... and stylisation*

In [11] the compound noun phrase *naturalism or pretend naturalism* is coordinated with the simple noun phrase *stylisation*.

10.12.5 Types of coordinated noun phrase

The coordinated noun phrases may include or consist of pronouns [12], nominal adjectives [13], and numerals [14]:

[12]   The optician cannot say that *he or she* will only test your sight if you buy glasses from *him or her*. [W]

[13]   We're at the moment when there's about to be a struggle between *the earthly and the divine* and that's why this episode illuminates a world that we know

[14]   It was easterly winds which brought the severe cold of the winters of *1947 and 1962/3*—two of the coldest winters this century in the British Isles. [Bill Giles *The Story of Weather*]

10.12.6 Other coordinators

Coordinators other than *and* and *or* are exemplified below:

[15]   The risk is not imposition ... *but* isolation

[16]   When I was a young and inexperienced gardener a thing that really whetted my appetite is a is a very dumpy thick tome or a series of tomes that you can't get your hands on for love *nor* money now which was sold in four and sixpenny weekly instalments called the Marshall Cavendish Encyclopedia of Gardening

[17] But, as has already been suggested, the pluralism of modern society also embraces options that are internally monolithic in belief *and/or* practice. [W]

And/or is an abbreviatory device ('*and* or *or*').

10.12.7 **Coordinative apposition**

In **coordinative apposition**, the two noun phrases linked by *and* or *or* are co-referential. The coordinators can be regarded as markers of apposition:

[18] Deng Rong, 43, *the book's author and Mr. Deng's youngest daughter*, makes clear that her aim is not to write a tell-all unauthorised biography but rather something closer to a Communist hagiography. [*International Herald Tribune*]

[19] The impulses that occur in the brain produce certain recognized patterns on an electroencephalogram (*eeg, or brain wave trace*). [Ruth Lever *A Guide to Common Illnesses*]

[20] With V-2 engines such a vehicle would have a maximum speed of only *about 6,000 miles per hour (9,600 kilometres per hour) or about one-third of satellite speed.* [David Ashford and Patrick Collins *Your Spaceflight Manual*]

10.13 Segregatory and combinatory coordination

Coordination of noun phrases may be segregatory or combinatory.

10.13.1 **Segregatory coordination**

The coordination is **segregatory** when each noun phrase could function independently in the clause, perhaps with some changes, such as in the number of the verbs. For example, **[1]** is roughly equivalent to **[1a]**:

[1] *Bomb warnings and drugs courier baggage* were mentioned. [*The Independent*]

[1a] *Bomb warnings* were mentioned and *drugs courier baggage* was mentioned.

10.13.2 **Combinatory coordination**

The coordination is **combinatory** when the noun phrases function semantically as a unit and could not be paraphrased in a coordination of clauses:

[2] This unscheduled stop provoked some consternation in the United States, coming so soon after *Rajiv and President Reagan* had met at the United Nations in New York, and just a month before the first Reagan–Gorbachev summit in Geneva. [Nicholas Nugent *Rajiv Gandhi*]

[3] The remark certainly didn't seem to bother Pete, as a week later, in Paris, *he and Lynne* were married. [Graham Stark *Remembering Peter Sellars*]

[4] Anyhow *you and Harriet* know one another

[5] They have their own companions, Frankenstein has a very caring family and the opportunity to make friends at University, *Adam and Eve* have each other, whilst the inhabitants of the Wasteland miss the chance to form meaningful relationships amongst themselves. [W]

10.13.3 Indicators of combinatory and segregatory coordination

One another [4] and *each other* [5] are explicit indicators of combinatory coordination. They can be inserted in [2] ('had met each other') and [3] ('were married to one another'). On the other hand, *both* and *neither* are common indicators of segregatory coordination of noun phrases:

[6] *Both Wales and the North* had never progressed beyond being military zones, so that there was no structure of government to be destroyed and consequently they were much harder to subdue. [W]

[7] We have also seen in the last few days that there was *neither time nor reason* to delay the land battle any longer ('there was not time and there was not reason')

10.13.4 Combinatory and segregatory coordination of modifiers

Coordinated modifiers of noun phrases are also open to the distinction between segregatory and combinatory coordination. In [8], *the beech and oak woods* is shown to be segregatory because of the previous mention of *your beech woods and your oak woods*:

[8] So uhm so then that means like you get your get *your beech woods and your oak woods* but within *the beech and oak woods* there are different kinds

Out of context, *the beech and oak woods* could have a combinatory interpretation: 'the woods containing both beeches and oaks'. In [8], however, the context makes it clear that the phrase is elliptical for 'the beech woods and the oak woods'.

10.13.5 Segregatory coordination with ellipsis

Segregatory coordination may involve ellipsis of some part or parts of the noun phrase.

[9] Poplar, as one of the most poverty-stricken boroughs in London, attracted the attention of *Beatrice and Sydney Webb* in 1914. [Bob Holman *Good Old George*] ('Beatrice Webb and Sydney Webb')

[10] Tape is the recording medium used by *both audio and video recorders*. [D. Cheshire *The Complete Book of Video*] ('both audio recorders and video recorders')

[11] Nor, to turn to *Marxist or quasi-Marxist interpretations*, is there any evidence that slavery was a decisive factor. [P. A. Brunt *Roman Imperial Themes*] ('Marxist interpretation or quasi-Marxist interpretations')

In combinatory coordination, there is no ellipsis:

[12] Add *the tomato and onion mixture* then bring to the boil before adding the contents of the tin of beans. [Michael Barry *The Crafty Food Processor Cook Book*] ('the mixture containing tomatoes and onions')

[13] For example, *the diagnostic and statistics manual* (DSM) has been updated twice, once in 1968, and again in 1980, with a revised version in 1986. [W]

[14] She had *egg and bacon breakfast* and it seemed enough, but she wants some milk. [D. Robertson *Remember the Moment*]

[15] Ultimate power would lie with the jury of 12 randomly selected *good men and true*. [Terry Jones 'Credit for Mrs Thatcher' in Ben Pimlott et al. *The Alternative*]

10.14 Subject–verb agreement

The verb agrees with the subject in number and person wherever such distinctions are featured in the verb. Subject–verb agreement applies to the first verb in the verb phrase, whether it is a main verb or an auxiliary. Except for the verb *be*, the distinctions appear only in the present tense, which has two forms: the **-s form** (ending in *-s*) and the **base** (or uninflected) **form**. The *-s* form is used for the third person singular, and the base form is used otherwise. Subject–verb agreement varies in non-standard dialects, where some verb forms are merged (cf. 7.7.1f.).

10.14.1 Relevant distinctions

10.14.1.1 Noun phrases
If the noun phrase has a noun as its head, the relevant distinction is only in number, since all such noun phrases are in the third person. The general rule then is that singular noun phrases require the *-s* form and plural noun phrases require the base form:

[1] His account *contains* many historical solecisms. [P. A. Brunt *Roman Imperial Themes*]

[2] Many terrestrial soils, in contrast, *contain* large proportions of very small particles made up of clay minerals. [Colin Little *The Terrestrial Invasion*]

Agreement is expected to be with the head of the noun phrase, the plural *schools* in **[3]**:

[3] In recent years several schools of thought *have* emerged, each championed by leading exponents of the period. [W]

10.14.1.2 Modal auxiliaries
Modal auxiliaries (cf. 7.9, 11.8) do not have an *-s* form, so the agreement rule does not apply to them. For example, modal *will* is used with a singular subject in **[4]** and with a plural subject in **[5]**:

[4] My door *will* always be open to you. [W]

[5] Our relationship is just beginning—growing pains *will* be part of its growth. [W]

10.14.1.3 Personal pronouns
Personal pronouns have distinctions in person as well as number. The third person singular pronouns *he, she*, and *it* take the *-s* form and the other personal pronouns—*I, we, you*, and *they*—take the base form:

[6] Well he *has* this stupid girl he *falls* in love with doesn't he or something

[7] And she *wants* to know when to move it uh before or after the budding

[8] So … I don't really want to go anyway so … I don't see it *makes* a difference … really

[9] I *hate* this

[10] Life goes on Matthew doesn't it regardless of the turmoil we *find* ourselves embroiled in. [W]

[11] Uhm ... and really you *need* it all through your life

[12] And as you can see they *look* ... quite different

10.14.1.4 **The verb** *be*

Whether used as a main verb or as an auxiliary, the verb *be* has further distinctions, which extend to the past tense. In the present tense, it has three forms, adding a distinctive form *am* for the first person singular in agreement with the pronoun *I*.

[13] At the moment I *am* at home doing some work on a word processor. [W] (1st person singular)

[14] Well you *are* going to be a doctor (2nd person singular)

[15] The other thing *is* uhm ... do you confide in her (3rd person singular)

[16] Like fallen leaves that the wind sweeps to and fro, we *are* indiscriminately swayed by our unsubstantial and frivolous emotions. [W] (1st person plural)

[17] Regards to your family—I hope you *are* all well. [W] (2nd person plural)

[18] More and more people *are* being arrested (3rd person plural)

The verb *be* is the only verb to display distinctions in number and person for the past tense. *Was* is used for the first and third persons singular, and *were* is used otherwise:

[19] Also, on reflection, I *was* baffled by the logic. [Graham Stark *Remembering Peter Sellars*] (1st person singular)

[20] However, one had to make allowances for youth, as Lynne *was* actually younger than one of the children she *was* talking about. [Graham Stark *Remembering Peter Sellars*] (3rd person singular)

[21] Well we *were* wondering about that (1st person plural)

[22] Robert Runcie it's it's wonderful meeting you just at this point after ten years is it when you *were* just leaving Saint Albans (2nd person singular)

[23] And within the dance field that you *were* both ... in before this ... uhm ... would you say the attitude is is fairly ... uhm ... rigid towards no not even thinking about including disabled people (2nd person plural)

[24] And they have a conventional cooker as well which they *were* using (3rd person plural)

10.14.2 **Singular or plural agreement**

10.14.2.1 **Nominal clauses**

Nominal clauses (cf. 14.3) functioning as subject generally take a singular verb:

[25] That his people believe that after last night *is* doubtful

[26] Once you've sent a message onto the e-mail system ... receiving them ... *is* as simple as sending them

[27] To say actors are childlike *is* to pay them a compliment. [Graham Stark *Remembering Peter Sellars*]

Nominal relative clauses (cf. 14.3.4), however, vary in number according to whether the nominal relative pronoun is interpreted as singular **[28]** or as plural **[29]**:

[28] One must do what *is* necessary given the circumstances. [W]

[29] And and also apt to take you know very completely irrational hates against people for what I think *were* probably sexual reasons

10.14.2.2 **Coordinated noun phrases**
The subject is plural if it consists of two or more noun phrases coordinated by *and*:

> [30] The truth the truth is Mister Speaker … that in many aspects of politics … *style and substance* … complement each other

If, however, the two noun phrases are viewed as referring to a single entity, they take a singular verb:

> [31] *The Stars and Stripes* was draped over Mr. Kempner's coffin last Tuesday at his funeral in Johannes Kirche in Berlin, the same Lutheran chapel where he was baptized and confirmed. [*International Herald Tribune*]

Similarly, if the coordinated noun phrases are in coordinative apposition (cf. end of 10.12.4), and therefore refer to the same single entity, they take a singular verb.

If two singular noun phrases are coordinated by *or* or by *nor*, they generally take a singular verb:

> [32] As far as Jordan is concerned will my honourable friend make Her Majesty's Government's position clear as follows that if either Iraq or Israel *invades* or *uses* Jordanian territory our attitude towards any such incursions would be the same as our attitude towards Iraq's incursion into Kuwait
>
> [33] Neither blanket television nor 24-hours-a-day radio news *is* well suited to reporting events that drag on, let alone a war with no clear time limit. [*The Observer*]

If the noun phrases differ in what verb form they would take separately, the plural is more usual:

> [34] Neither you nor your partner *have* to be a parent of the child or children provided they live with you as members of your family. [W]

10.14.2.3 **Singular collective nouns**
Singular **collective nouns**, which denote a group of people or things, are sometimes treated as plural in British English (less commonly in American English) when the focus is on the group as individuals rather than as a single entity:

> [35] The Argentine team *are* in possession now inside *their* own half
>
> [36] And his reaction to this uh mention of Mr Lampitt's company was that he was surprised that Mr Lampitt's company *were* on the acquisition trail *themselves*
>
> [37] Uhm so people are still confused because they keep telling me the Government *are* confused about what *they* want to do
>
> [38] Commenting on the timing of the two reports, Mr Kreindler said that they had surfaced just as his group *were* gathering critical evidence. [*The Independent*]
>
> [39] The public *have* been fair
>
> [40] The enemy *have* brought forward *their* elephant … to trample down the bridge but one of the Moguls has managed to shoot the elephant

10.14.2.4 **Titles and citations**
Titles of works and citations (cf. 10.11.2.1), even if plural in form, take a singular verb:

> [41] Larry Niven's 'The Integral Trees' *is* not set in the same universe as his delightful Big-Dumb-Object Novel 'Ringworld'. [*The Economist*]
>
> [42] Thus *sandshoes is* the word found in our Northeast area, while *gollies is* found in our Merseyside area. [Peter Trudgill *The Dialects of England*]

10.14.2.5 *None*

The pronoun *none* is treated as either singular or plural:

[43] We all know in our own lives what changes the last ten years have brought but none of us *knows* the picture overall and that's what the census supplies

[44] Anomalous innervation may suggest motor recovery where none *has* actually occurred. [P. J. Smith 'Nerve Injury and Repair' in F. D. Burke et al *Principles of Hand Surgery*]

[45] I wonder who supplies them at the moment because uh uh certainly none of the locals *do*

[46] There are many origami yachts, boats and ships, but none *are* as simple or as full of movement as this wonderful design by Japan's First Lady of origami, Mrs Tashie Takahama. [P. Jackson *Classic Origami*]

The variation exists irrespective of whether there is a postmodifier of *none* with a plural—*none of us* [43] and *none of the locals* [45]. The singular verb *has* is required in [44] because the antecedent of *none* (*motor recovery*) is a singular non-count noun.

10.14.2.6 Existential *there*

Existential *there* (cf. 6.8) is often followed by a singular verb, especially in informal speech, even when the noun phrase that follows the verb is plural:

[47] There's books as presents books for the children and so on

[48] There *is* £2 left which will be deducted from your spectacle voucher. [W]

10.14.3 Lack of number agreement

Lack of number agreement between subject and verb sometimes occurs, especially in speech and in unedited writing, because of the influence of another noun or pronoun that intervenes between the head of the noun phrase and the verb.

[49] *Depopulation* due to plague and migration in the fifth and sixth centuries *appear* to be responsible for the demise of the lowland British kingdoms. [W]

[50] You are, no doubt, aware of the Smith & Jones cases, in which an age *limit* of 27 years and of 35 years (37 years for clinical staff) *were* found to be indirectly discriminatory against women, in the civil service and UGC New Blood Scheme, respectively. [W]

[51] The *results* of that in pollution and wasted natural resources every year *is* shameful. [David Icke *It Doesn't Have To Be Like This*]

In [49] the head of the noun phrase is the non-count noun *depopulation*, but plural *centuries* immediately precedes the verb *appear*, which is therefore in the plural by attraction to the preceding plural noun. In [50] *were* is plural by attraction to the nearby plural *years* (and perhaps also the collective noun *staff*, which is often treated as plural in British English), though *limit*, the head of the relevant noun phrase, is singular. In [51], on the other hand, singular *year* has probably led to the use of singular *is* by attraction, in disregard of plural *results*, the head of the noun phrase.

10.15 Vocatives

Vocatives are predominately noun phrases. They are optional additions to the basic sentence structures, and are used to address the person or persons spoken to, either to single them out from others **[1]** or to maintain some personal connection with them **[2]**:

[1]   *Robin* what do you think

[2]   You're a snob *Dad*

In its function of singling out a person, the vocative may constitute the whole utterance, as in broadcast panel discussions where the presenter singles out one of the speakers **[3]** or a member of the audience **[4]**:

[3]   Kenneth Clarke

[4]   Gentleman with the beard ... sir

The utterance in **[4]** combines two vocatives.

Vocatives may appear initially **[1]**, finally **[2]**, or medially **[5]**:

[5]   It may well be an outcome *Peter* devoutly to be desired

In writing they are normally separated from the rest of the sentence by punctuation:

[6]   'You've done well too, *boy*. Your ma and me are proud of you.' [E. V. Thompson *Lottie Trago*]

In speech, vocatives are generally marked by distinctive intonation, varying according to their position in the sentence.

Vocatives are commonly names (as in **[1]**, **[3]**, and **[5]** above), family terms **[2]** and **[7]**, epithets **[7]**–**[10]**, titles **[11]**–**[13]**, and designations of respect **[14]**–**[16]**:

[7]   A: Will you have another cup of tea *grandpa*
         B: No thank you *sweetheart*

[8]   Well you can't ask for it back *dear*

[9]   Right okay then *love* so I'll hear from you at the beginning of next week

[10]   How are you *darling*? [W]

[11]   *My Lord* ... the first passage is at page 229

[12]   *Officer* I think that uh you examined that uh Ford Cortina make of car which you found present at the scene of the accident

[13]   *Mr Speaker* my right honourable friend is right

[14]   A: Did you not know it
         B: I didn't know that at the time *sir*

[15]   'That will do, Pritchard.'
         'Thank you, *m'm*.' [James Lees-Milne *The Fool of Love*]

[16]   'Can I help you, *miss*?' he said. [Christopher Priest *The Quiet Woman*]

Some noun phrases that do not belong to the above types are commonly used as vocatives:

[17]   Well good afternoon *ladies and gentlemen*

[18]   I asked what he was doing.
         'Just attached here and there, *old boy*. It's hush-hush, I can't really explain.' [Julian Symons *Death's Darkest Face*]

[19]   'You'll bend over that table, *lad*,' he said. [Ian Enters *Up to Scratch*]

[20]   Stick to your guns stick to your gun *girl*

[21]   Cor blimey I haven't spoken to you for a week *woman*

[22] Uhm I'm sorry *everybody* then it looks like that was a that was a definite pick-up then

Examples **[23]** and **[24]** are restricted to particular situations:

[23] Now *members of the jury* ... you and I tried this case ... as a ... team

[24] *Students or staff who feel that a situation has not been satisfactorily resolved* please contact ...

Finally, it is conventional for the salutation that heads letters to be a vocative beginning with *Dear* followed by a name or names or by designations such as *Sir, Madam, Colleagues.*

Vocatives may also be addressed to non-humans (e.g. supernatural beings and pets) or to abstract entities (e.g. *Spring, Virtue, Beauty*).

Some of the noun phrases used as vocatives would otherwise require a determiner such as *the* when they are used in the singular. For example, contrast the use of *young man* as a complete noun phrase in **[25]** with *the young man* in **[25a]**:

[25] And Playatsky in fact took off his glasses looked at him and said *young man* ... on what basis pray do you venture to contradict me

[25a] *The young man* ventured to contradict me.

10.16 Reference of noun phrases

Noun phrases generally refer to entities in the world. We can establish three sets of contrasts for noun phrase reference:

1. definite versus non-definite
2. specific versus non-specific
3. generic versus non-generic

10.16.1 **Noun phrases with definite reference**

A speaker or writer uses a **definite** noun phrase on the assumption that the hearer or reader can identify its reference. For example, in **[1]** the first mention of *cigarette* is in an indefinite noun phrase, but since the second mention refers back to the previous mention, it is in a definite noun phrase:

[1] A: But you only had one hand because you'd got *a cigarette* in the other
     B: No I was holding on with both hands but *the cigarette* was in my two fingers

The indefinite article *a* signals that *a cigarette* has indefinite reference (one of a type of object with that designation), and the definite article *the* that *the cigarette* has definite reference. Other signals of indefinite reference are indefinite determiners such as *some* (cf. 6.13.1.2) and the zero article (cf. 6.2).

Identification of the reference comes from three major sources:

1. The phrase refers to something previously mentioned, as in **[1]** above and in **[2]** below:

> **[2]** As the administration meanders, the House has sent to the Senate *a spending bill that chops away at what is already a tight aid request*. *The bill*'s huge engines—aid to Russia, Israel and Egypt—almost guarantee that most of the administration's money requests will safely pass through Congress in spite of overall budget constraints. [*The International Herald Tribune*]

2. The identification comes from the modifiers in the noun phrase:

> **[3]** Now over the course of the season ... *the steps to the swimming pool* might be used a very substantial amount mightn't they

3. The phrase refers to something that the speaker or writer believes is uniquely identifiable to the hearer or reader, either from general knowledge or from knowledge of the particular situation:

> **[4]** Today is Sunday 14th April, it's mid-afternoon and *the sun* is shining. [W]
>
> **[5]** Far more than that number, I judge, now believe that they would have a better chance of holding their seats and keeping power under another leader. This includes the majority of *the Cabinet*. [*The Guardian*]
>
> **[6]** I shall probably look in at *the College* once or twice during the autumn, and hope to see you then. [W]
>
> **[7]** 'I've got to take out *the dog*,' he said as finally as he could. [Ian Enters *Up to Scratch*]
>
> **[8]** Tanya appeared quite relieved as *the telephone* rang. [Marian Babson *Past Regret*]
>
> **[9]** Every Tuesday I stood there waiting by *the door* expecting you to come

The definite article is not the only signal of definite reference. Proper names are intended to be uniquely identifiable, either because the reference is generally known (e.g. *Ronald Reagan, Paul McCartney*) or because the speaker/writer expects the particular hearer/reader to know who or what is referred to when there is more than one possibility (*Springfield, Mary*). The personal pronouns are also definite, and in most uses so are the demonstrative pronouns (cf. 6.14).

10.16.2 **Noun phrases with specific reference**

A noun phrase has **specific reference** when it refers to a specific person, thing, place, etc., even if the reference is not definite (i.e. the speaker/writer does not expect the hearer/reader to identify the reference). For example, the analysis in **[10]** is a specific analysis:

> **[10]** Although I publish quite a lot I discovered a couple of years ago that no mainstream publisher wanted to publish *a negative analysis of the British monarchy that I've written*

On the other hand, *a historical novel* in **[11]** is non-specific, since it does not refer to a particular instance of a historical novel:

> **[11]** I'd always been interested in ancient history and I'd always wanted to write *a historical novel*

A film in **[12]** is probably intended to be non-specific too, though it is possible that a particular film is intended:

> **[12]** I had intended to take them dancing and to hear Colin sing but they wanted to see *a film* so I was outnumbered. [W]

Here is another clear example of non-specific reference:

[13] Your sight can be tested only by *a registered optician* (optometrist) or *an ophthalmic medical practitioner.* [W]

Noun phrases with non-specific reference normally have an indefinite determiner such as *a*, but *the* is also possible:

[14] I intended to write the definitive study on the present British monarchy.

10.16.3 **Noun phrases with generic reference**

Noun phrases with **generic reference** are used in generalizations:

[15] *Fractals* are wiggly lines which look equally wiggly whatever scale you examine them at. [*The Economist*]

Fractals is generic in that it refers to all members of the class of fractals. Generic noun phrases are by definition non-specific. The distinctions of definite and indefinite and also of singular and plural are neutralized, so that approximating to **[15]** are **[15a]**, **[15b]**, and **[15c]**:

[15a] *The fractals* are wiggly lines which look equally wiggly whatever scale you examine them at.

[15b] *The fractal* is a wiggly line which looks equally wiggly whatever scale you examine it at.

[15c] *A fractal* is a wiggly line which looks equally wiggly whatever scale you examine it at.

The four versions are also available for the generic phrases in **[16]** and **[17]**:

[16] I don't see *a French writer* voluntarily writing in English

[17] Okay ... here's just a ... few of the areas where ... *collisions of electrons with molecules* play an important role

In **[17]** the whole noun phrase is generic, and the noun phases within it—*electrons* and *molecules*—are also generic.

The four versions of the generic noun phrase illustrated in **[15]**–**[15c]** are not always available. Non-count nouns (cf. 5.5.2) do not have a plural and they cannot be used in a generic interpretation with *the*. All the noun phrases in **[18]** are generic, and six of them—all except *soft drinks* and *sandwiches*—are non-count:

[18] *Coffee, tea, soft drinks, confectionery, sandwiches, fruit* and *other food and drink* do not mix well *with computing equipment.* [David Royall and Mike Hughes *Computerisation in Business*]

However, plural generic noun phrases usually do not take *the* as a determiner. Although we could replace *sandwiches* in **[18]**, for example, with generic *a sandwich* or (more plausibly, in a sentence where it alone is subject) with generic *the sandwich*, we could not have *the sandwiches*. But plural generic noun phrases with nominal adjectives as their head do have *the*:

[19] *The French* report signs of chemical emissions after their bombing missions against chemical weapons plants

[20] The vital decisions we reach on human fertilisation and embryology and subsequently pregnancy termination must affect how we regard the status of each individual ... his or her human rights the treatment of *the handicapped* the fate of *the senile* and *the terminally ill*

In **[21]** the generic *the Dutch* is coordinated with two plural generic nationality nouns:

[21]   But now *the Danes, the Germans* and *the Dutch* are also having second thoughts about setting up such a bank before the 12 economies in the EC have achieved greater 'convergence'. [*Yorkshire Post*]

The reference of generic nouns phrases is interpreted as extending to those that are relevant in the context. In **[19]** *the French* does not refer to all the French people. In **[21]** the reference is presumably to the Danish, German, and Dutch governments.

Chapter 11
Verb Phrases

Summary

Summary

The head of a verb phrase is a main verb, which may be preceded by up to four auxiliaries in a specific sequence.

Operators are used for negation, interrogation, emphasis, and abbreviation. The functions of the operator can be performed by the first auxiliary in the verb phrase or by the main verb *be* (in British English especially, also *have*) when it is the only verb in the verb phrase. In the absence of another potential operator, *do* is introduced as a dummy operator.

Verbs may be finite or non-finite. A verb is finite if it is marked for the distinction in tense between present and past. In a finite verb phrase the first or only verb is finite.

The two tenses (as shown by verb inflections) are present and past. The two aspects are perfect and progressive.

The simple past is primarily used when the situation was completed before the time of speaking or writing. The simple present is primarily used for situations that include the time of speaking or writing.

The most common ways of expressing future time in the verb phrase are with *will* (or its contraction *'ll*) and *be going to*.

The present subjunctive has the base form of the verb; it is mainly used in *that*-clauses. The past subjunctive is *were*, used in hypothetical constructions.

Each of the modals has two kinds of meaning: deontic (referring to some kind of human control) and epistemic (a judgement of truth-value).

The perfect (auxiliary *have* plus the -*ed* participle) is used to indicate that a situation occurs within a period preceding another period or point of time. For the present perfect, the period extends from the past to the present time. For the past perfect, the period precedes another situation in the past.

The progressive (auxiliary *be* plus the -*ing* participle) primarily focuses on the situation as being in progress.

There are a large number of idiomatic verb combinations. A phrasal verb combines a verb and an adverb. Phrasal verbs may be intransitive, transitive, or copular. A prepositional verb combines a verb and a preposition. Prepositional verbs may be monotransitive (with a prepositional object), doubly transitive (with a direct object and a prepositional object), or copular. A phrasal-prepositional verb combines a verb, an adverb, and a preposition. Phrasal-prepositional verbs may be monotransitive (with a prepositional object) or doubly transitive (with a direct object and a prepositional object).

11.1 The structure of the verb phrase

11.1.1 **Main and auxiliary verbs**

A verb phrase has as its head a **main** (or **lexical**) **verb**. The main verb may be preceded by up to four **auxiliaries** (or **auxiliary verbs**), but see 11.17 for semi-auxiliaries.

The auxiliaries fall into two major sets:

1. the primary auxiliaries:
2. the modals (or modal or secondary auxiliaries (cf. 7.9)):

In addition, there are several marginal auxiliaries (*dare, need, ought to, used to*; cf. 7.9) and a number of semi-auxiliaries such as *had better* and *had got to*.

11.1.2 **Primary auxiliaries**

The **primary auxiliaries** are *be*, *have*, and *do*.

11.1.2.1 Auxiliary *be* has two functions: (1) it forms the **progressive** in combination with a following *-ing* participle, e.g. *is playing*; (2) it forms the **passive** in combination with a following *-ed* participle, e.g. *is played*.

11.1.2.2 Auxiliary *have* forms the **perfect aspect** in combination with a following *-ed* participle, e.g. *has played*.

11.1.2.3 Auxiliary *do* is the **dummy operator**: it functions as the operator to form (for example) interrogative and negative sentences in the absence of any other operator, e.g. *Did they play? They didn't play* (cf. 11.2.1).

11.1.3 **Modal auxiliaries**

The **modal auxiliaries** are *can*, *could*, *may*, *might*, *shall*, *should*, *will*, *would*, *must*. The modals convey notions of factuality, such as certainty (e.g. *They must be there*), or of control, such as permission (e.g. *You may play outside*). They are followed by an infinitive (cf. 11.8).

11.1.4 **Sequence of auxiliaries**

The auxiliaries appear in a set sequence:

> modal—perfect *have*—progressive *be*—passive *be*—main verb

It is not usual for all to be present in one verb phrase, though it is certainly possible, as in **[1]**:

[1]   *should* (modal) *have* (perfect) *been* (progressive) *being* (passive) *played* (main verb)

In **[1]** each of the auxiliaries is followed by the required verb form:

> *should* (modal) *have* (infinitive)
> *have* (perfect) *been* (*-ed* participle)
> *been* (progressive) *being* (*-ing* participle)
> *being* (passive) *played* (*-ed* participle)

Here are examples of verb phrases with combinations of three auxiliaries:

[2]   Those who had parents who slapped their faces if they misbehaved *would have been making* judgements about my behaviour which were influenced by their own childhood memories. [Paul Johnson *Child Abuse*] (modal perfect progressive)

[3]   Well there's no doubt at all that we would have wanted to see sanctions run on for a longer period to see if Saddam *could have been removed* from Kuwait without war (modal perfect passive)

[4]   If he were still alive, he *would*, at the very least, now *be being questioned* very searchingly by Scotland Yard. [*Evening Standard*] (modal progressive passive)

11.1.5 **Separation of auxiliaries from the rest of the verb phrase**

As **[4]** illustrates, the sequence of verbs in the verb phrase may be interrupted by intervening **adverbials**. Here are further examples of such interventions:

[5]   Now *I've* just *been working* on this and the problem has been to a certain extent the printer

[6]   But uh if you had the choice would you prefer to have a meal which *has been* freshly *prepared* with uh fresh ingredients and so on

[7]   The agreement *could* not even *have been considered* further unless it had been signed by all the members back in May

In questions the operator precedes the subject and is therefore separated from the rest of the verb phrase:

[8]   '*Was* the Sharptor mine *being worked* the way it should have been, before it went out of business?' [E.V. Thompson *Lottie Trago*]

11.1.6 Marking for tense, person, and number

The first or only verb in the verb phrase is obligatorily marked for **tense**—a main verb in **[9]** and **[10]** and an auxiliary in **[11]** and **[12]**:

[9]   Doug *makes* quince jelly sometimes doesn't he

[10] There's one I was going to show you because it it *made* my hair stand on end

[11] But time *is* going slowly

[12] Officially I *was* doing a unit of English

The first or only verb in the verb phrase is also marked for **person** and **number** where relevant:

[13] I *am* a secretary (1st person singular)

[14] They *are* very very concerned (3rd person plural)

The first or only verb in the verb phrase can function as the operator, for example in forming questions:

[15] *Can* you remember that

11.1.7 The dummy operator *do*

The dummy operator *do* (cf. 11.2) is followed only (if at all) by the main verb in the infinitive:

> *do play   does go   did say*

11.1.8 Auxiliaries and the subjunctive

The only auxiliary that can be in the subjunctive (cf. 11.9f.) is auxiliary *be*, which may function as the progressive auxiliary or the passive auxiliary:

> if she *be acting* as lead   if I *were playing*
> if it *be known*   if he *were told*

Semi-auxiliaries that begin with *be* (cf. 11.17) can also be in the subjunctive:

> *were* I *to tell* you
> if he *were going to write*

See 2.11 for negatives and 2.12 for passives.

11.2 Operators

The major characteristic of an auxiliary is that it can function as an **operator** when it is the first auxiliary in the verb phrase. When a form of the main verb *be* is the only verb in the verb phrase it can also function as an operator (e.g. '*Are* they upstairs?'); the same applies, especially in British English, to the main verb *have* (e.g. '*Have* you any children?'), although it is also treated as a main verb ('*Do* you have any children?'). In the absence of another potential operator, *do* is introduced as a dummy operator.

The operator is used for negation, interrogation, emphasis, and abbreviation.

11.2.1 **The operator in negation**

To form a negative sentence or negative finite clause *not* is placed after the operator:

[1]   He says that there should be one national police force.

[1a] He says that there *should not* be one national police force

[2]   It was pasteurised milk.

[2a] It *was not* pasteurised milk

[3]   The countries around the world fit into neat and precise categories of climate and weather.

[3a] The countries around the world *do not* fit into neat and precise categories of climate and weather. [Bill Giles *The Story of Weather*]

Not can be contracted as *n't* and attached as an enclitic (cf. 7.9) to most operators:

[4]   But *wouldn't* she remember him

[5]   You *can't* see from there

[6]   Perhaps this suggestion *isn't* absurd

[7]   He *didn't* play against England on Tuesday evening

11.2.2 **The operator in interrogation**

To form an interrogative sentence or interrogative finite clause, the operator is placed before the subject (**subject–operator inversion**):

[8]   You can remember that.

[8a] *Can* you remember that

[9]   They will cope with the environmental problems that we have created.

[9a] How *will* they cope with the environmental problems that we have created

[10] The poison is in that one.

[10a] *Is* the poison in that one

[11] I told you.

[11a] *Did* I tell you

[12] They went off to their parents.

[12a] Where *did* they go off to

There is no subject–operator inversion in *wh*-questions if the *wh*-item is the subject (cf. 2.5).

Citation [13a] contains a negative question with subject–operator question. The operator *didn't* is negative:

[13]   You didn't have enough sleep on the bus.

[13a]   'Honest to God, Dorothy—*didn't* you have enough sleep on the bus?' [Agnes Owen 'Patience' in Alison Fell *The Seven Cardinal Virtues*]

A more formal variant has the uncontracted negative particle *not* placed after the subject.

[13b]   *Did* you *not* have enough sleep on the bus?

Another rarer formal variant has the uncontracted negative particle immediately after the operator, particularly if the subject is lengthy **[13c]**, but not only then **[14]**.

[13c]   *Did not* all those travelling with you have enough sleep on the bus?

[14]   For instance why did not the author(s) use this information to compare the relationship of social attributes and health? [W]

Subject–operator inversion also occurs with initial negative expressions:

[15]   *No longer can* any member of the tribe of Levi … act as priest

[16]   *At no time were* they prepared to do so

[17]   *Never were* slaves so numerous as in Italy during the first century B.C. [P. A. Brunt *Roman Imperial Themes*]

[18]   *Rarely* in human history *has* the idea of an obligation imposed on us by others seemed so constricting and suffocating

11.2.3 **The operator in emphasis**

The operator may be used to convey **emphasis**. In speech, the emphatic function is signalled by placing the **nuclear tone** (a distinct pitch movement) on the operator; in writing, emphasis is occasionally signalled by italics or (mostly in manuscripts) by underlining. (The same methods are used to signal emphasis for words other than operators.) The emphasis on operator is usually intended to deny something that has been mentioned previously or that may have been assumed, or to reject what has been said by somebody else; e.g. an offer, invitation, advice, order. (See also 3.10.)

The emphatic function of the operator is unequivocally conveyed even in writing by the positive forms *do*, *does*, *did* when they are used in positive declarative sentences or clauses that are not abbreviated (see 11.2.4):

[19]   I *do* apologise for that

[20]   it *does* actually face … south-west not west

[21]   Well I *did* think about it

The non-emphatic equivalents are 'I *apologise*' for **[19]**, 'it actually *faces*' for **[20]**, and 'I *thought*' for **[21]**. Apart from such contexts, the operator *do* is not necessarily emphatic. For example, in **[22]** it is required as a dummy operator to form the *wh*-question:

[22]   Why *did* you buy it

Did in **[22]** may also be emphatic, but the emphasis would be conveyed by the intonation. Similarly, the negative forms of *do* (*doesn't*, *don't*, *didn't*) need not be emphatic, since they are used as dummy operators for negation.

Here are two examples of operators other than *do* that are used for emphasis. The context shows that they are intended to be interpreted as emphatic:

[23]   I read that in the paper … so it *must* be true

[24]   'I think it will be all right,' said Mr Hurd in a crowning sentence of elliptical emollience in which every word can have a different stress which renders a different overall meaning. But it *won't* be all right: the question is whether he, or any of the other questors after unity, can now help to make it so. [*The Guardian*]

Here are some examples from writing where the operator is shown to be emphatic because it is in italics **[25]** or because it is underlined **[26]**–**[27]**:

[25] 'I want my d-daddy,' Tommy sobbed without looking up. 'He *is* alive. He *is!*' [Steve Harris *Adventureland*] [italics twice in original]

[26] Anyway, I really *must* go now. [W] [underline in original]

[27] You *can* be certain that I love you. [W] [underline in original]

11.2.4 The operator in abbreviation

The operator may be used as an abbreviating device to avoid repetition of the verb phrase with perhaps also other parts of the predicate:

[28] I've got to phone Liz because she said she was going to phone ... on uh Monday night but she *hasn't* ('she *hasn't phoned*')

[29] And W G Grace was coached by his mother and she didn't do a bad job and neither *did* he ('neither *did* he *do a bad job*')

[30] A: Oh I wouldn't touch those ...
B: No I *wouldn't* either ('I *wouldn't touch those* either')

In British English an intransitive main verb *do* can be added to the abbreviating operator. It serves as a substitute for the rest of the predicate:

[31] Yes please don't bother for a moment because merely I wanted to know whether you disagree as I think you *might do* from what you've been saying with that passage that I've quoted from Dr Kendall's evidence

[32] Thank goodness I didn't say anything awful ... because I *could've done*

Abbreviating operators are commonly used in **tag questions** (cf. 2.6):

[33] She's company though *isn't* she

[34] Well you've got income coming in from the property I suppose *haven't* you

[35] Apparently he dithers, hardly surprising being a politician *is* it? [W]

[36] But you can't just pick them up off the counter *can you*

11.3 Finite and non-finite verb phrases

Verb phrases may be either finite or non-finite.

11.3.1 Characteristics of the finite verb phrase

In a **finite verb phrase** the first or only verb is finite. A verb is **finite** if it displays tense; that is, the distinction between present and past:

[1] What *stops* a Prime Minister ... or government ... from ... passing discriminatory legislation

[2] He added that the car *stopped* almost immediately and the young man, who was in a 'terrible state,' told him he had hit two people. [*Western Mail*]

In **[1]** *stops* is a finite verb phrase consisting solely of a finite verb in the present tense, and in **[2]** *stopped* is likewise a finite verb phrase but this time the finite verb is in the past tense.

The finite verb phrases marked in **[3]**–**[8]** contain more than one verb, but only the first verb in the verb phrase is finite:

[3] British and Irish nurses at a Baghdad hospital *have stopped* work in protest at not being allowed to leave Iraq

[4] Everything else *has been stopped*

[5] The reason I have a new landlord is cos I*'m starting* work in Finchley today. [W]

[6] The new contractors *will be starting* the week of the 22nd. [W]

[7] Now before I *can start* the instrumentation we need to know a little bit from maths of how we go from absorption measurement into measurement of concentrations of haemoglobolin and cytochrome

[8] Silvie kept me there $1\frac{1}{2}$ hours today and *did start* complaining about the electricity board. [W]

11.3.2 Characteristics of the non-finite verb phrase

The three non-finite verb forms have been illustrated in **[3]**–**[8]** as functioning within a finite verb phrase:

1. **-*ed* participle** (*stopped*), functioning as perfect participle in *have stopped* **[3]** and as passive participle in *has been stopped* **[4]**

2. **-*ing* participle** (*starting*), functioning as progressive participle in *'m starting* **[5]** and *will be starting* **[6]**

3. **infinitive** (*start*), functioning after modal *can* in *can start* **[7]** and after dummy operator *did* in *did start* **[8]**

If a non-finite verb is the first or only verb in the verb phrase, the phrase is a **non-finite verb phrase**:

[9] Well will you tell her that you might save Rebecca from complete despair because *being exposed* twice within a month would be rather awful for her

[10] It's right ... it's on a sort of hill ... and you've got lovely views *looking* out the South Downs

[11] I wouldn't really be looking forward to *be getting dressed* up on Friday

[12] I broke my right wrist *riding* my bike in Germany

[13] And I've got so many events *to go* to I mean I know that sounds a bit odd but I mean I've got a few

[14] Yeah he said he seemed quite quite happy *to meet* you

11.3.3 Functions of the finite verb phrase

A finite verb phrase can function as the verb of a **simple sentence [15]**, the verb of a main clause within a **compound sentence [16]**, or the verb of a **subordinate clause [17]**–**[18]** (cf. 13.4):

[15] Tonight I*'m going* to my first cocktail party at the Commission, my dears! [W]

[16] Now I*'ve* just *been working* on this and and the problem *has been* to a certain extent the printer

[17] Hackney has become fashionable among artists, actors and writers who *want* to live some way into London but who *don't have* much money. [W]

[18] We would get more information if they *were asked* for a doctor's letter to the College Occupational Physician. [W]

In [16] there are two **coordinated** main clauses, each with its own verb, the finite verb phrases *'ve been working* and *has been*. In [17] the finite verb phrases *want* and *don't have* function as the verbs in finite relative clauses (cf. 10.9), a type of subordinate clause, the main verb of the sentence being *has become*. In [18] the finite verb phrase *were asked* functions as the verb in a finite subordinate clause introduced by the subordinator *if*, the main verb of the sentence being *would get*.

11.3.4 Functions of the non-finite verb phrase

A non-finite verb phrase normally cannot function as the verb of a simple sentence or as the verb of a main clause within a compound sentence.

> **NOTE**
>
> Certain types of clause that have a non-finite verb phrase as their verb can serve as independent complete utterances. They mainly occur in informal conversation. Here are some examples of questions whose verb is non-finite, an *-ing* participle **[N1]–[N2]** and an infinitive **[N3]**:
>
> **[N1]** *How about pouring* a pint of oil over their heads or something
>
> **[N2]** *What about putting* legs on it and making it into an enclosed table type of arrangement
>
> **[N3]** *Why change* things

A non-finite verb phrase can, however, function as the verb of a non-finite subordinate clause:

[19] I don't recall *actually giving the name*

In [19] *giving* is the verb of an *-ing* participle clause. It is a transitive verb, and its direct object is *the name*.

11.3.5 Imperative sentences and clauses and clauses with subjunctive verb

Imperative sentences and clauses are generally called finite, even though the verb does not display a distinction in tense:

[20] Just *feed* in some of your tapes and *say look* this is what you've got to do

They are associated with other finite clauses because the imperative verb can be the verb of a main clause. The same applies to clauses whose verb is a subjunctive (cf. 11.9 f.).

11.4 Tense and aspect

Tense is a grammatical category referring to the location of a situation in time. Strictly speaking, English has only two tenses of the verb—**present** and **past**—if tense is defined as being shown by a verb inflection. However, English has many ways of referring to past, present, and future time. We use a number of auxiliary verbs in combination with main verbs to refer to time. Time is also conveyed with the help of adverbs (e.g. *nowadays, tomorrow*), prepositional phrases (e.g. *in 1990, before the next meeting*), noun phrases (e.g. *last week, this evening*), and clauses (e.g. *when we saw them, after the conflict is over*).

The **aspect** of the verb refers primarily to the way that the time of the situation is regarded rather than its location in time in absolute terms. English has two aspects: the **perfect** aspect and the **progressive** (or **continuous**) aspect. The aspects are expressed by a combination of an auxiliary and a following verb. The perfect aspect (as in 'I *have written* many times before now') is primarily used to place the time of one situation relative to the time of another situation.

NOTE

Some grammarians have argued that the perfect is a tense rather than an aspect, since it refers to a period or point in time: the past of the speaker/writer or a preceding past time. Others have considered it an aspect because it is retrospective in at least some of its uses.

The progressive aspect (as in 'I *am writing* a letter to my parents') primarily focuses on the duration of the situation.

TENSE DISTINCTIONS AND ASPECT IN DETAIL

Distinctions in tense are signalled by the inflections of the first or only verb in the verb phrase. For all verbs except the modals, the present tense distinguishes between the -*s* form (e.g. *saves*) for the third person singular and the **base** (or uninflected) form (e.g. *save*) for the rest. For regular verbs and many irregular verbs, the past tense has the -*ed* inflection (e.g. *saved*, cf. 7.5f.).

Aspect is always combined with tense. So *has left* and *have left* are **present perfect** (because *has* and *have* are present tense), whereas *had left* is **past perfect** (because *had* is past). Similarly, *am leaving, is leaving*, and *are leaving* are **present progressive**, whereas *was leaving* and *were leaving* are **past progressive**. The two aspects are combined in *has been leaving*. Further complexity is introduced when the two aspects are combined with modals or passives (cf. 11.1).

11.5 Simple present and simple past

When there is only one verb in the verb phrase, the choice is between the simple present and the simple past:

simple present	(it) *computes*	(they) *compute*
simple past	(it/they) *computed*	

The simple present has the wider use. It has been called the **non-past tense**, signifying that it can be used whenever the past tense is inappropriate. The simple past is generally used to refer to past time, i.e. before the time of speaking or writing. Auxiliaries, such as *will*, and semi-auxiliaries, such as *be going to*, are used to refer to future time (cf. 11.7).

11.5.1 **The simple past**

The simple past is primarily used when the situation was completed before the time of speaking or writing.

> **THE SIMPLE PAST EXEMPLIFIED**
>
> This paragraph from the beginning of a novel follows one in which the narrator introduces himself:
>
> [1]   I *grew* up in Plano, a small silicon village in the north. No sisters, no brothers. My father *ran* a gas station and my mother *stayed* at home until I *got* older and times *got* tighter and she *went* to work, answering phones in the office of one of the big chip factories outside San Jose. [Donna Tartt *The Secret History*]
>
> The narrator has introduced himself as 28 years old and it is therefore clear that he has finished growing up. The paragraph describes the situation during the time in which he was growing up ('I *grew* up in Plano'). Contemporaneous with that past situation is the situation of his father's work ('*ran* a gas station') and within that past situation are two sequences of other situations relating to his mother ('*stayed* at home' and '*went* to work') that are divided by a change ('I *got* older and times *got* tighter'). All the situations are set in a period before the narration and all are described with the simple past.

11.5.2 **The simple present**

> **THE SIMPLE PRESENT EXEMPLIFIED**
>
> In this first paragraph of a news report [2], the present situation described with present tense (*is transfixed*, a combination of present *is* and passive participle *transfixed*) is set in a background of past events, for which the past tenses *came* and *proclaimed* are used:
>
> [2]   Four years after the Berlin Wall *came* down and leaders *proclaimed* a new era of freedom and prosperity, Western Europe *is* transfixed by gloom. [*The International Herald Tribune*]

11.5.2.1 **The state present**

The simple present is primarily used for situations that include the time of speaking or writing, as in these examples of the **state present**:

[3]   I *feel* like doing something exciting
[4]   Well this *is* very tasty
[5]   She *sounds* quite sensible actually
[6]   There *is* no asbestos in our products now. [*Wall Street Journal*]
[7]   It *employs* 2,700 people and *has* annual revenue of about $370 million. [*Wall Street Journal*]
[8]   All four seats *have* memory devices
[9]   You *know* nothing
[10] He said half plus half *equals* one

The situations in **[3]–[10]** refer to a state that remains unaltered throughout. The duration encompassed in those situations varies immensely from the very brief periods in **[3]–[4]** to the timelessness in the simple arithmetic calculation in **[10]**.

11.5.2.2 **The recurrent present**

In contrast to the state present in **[3]–[10]**, the **recurrent present** is used for events that happen repeatedly. The period includes the time of speaking or writing, but the events need not be happening at that time:

[11] Again there are eight over ninety this year four men and four women and the oldest is Robert Weston who's ninety-seven and still *walks* to church

[12] I *work* in the Physiology Department

[13] If you *appease* a bully you *pay* for it later ... and you often *pay* more dearly

[14] Just as the warm air rising up *pushes* other air out of the way and *sets* the atmospheric convection circulating, so the sinking cold water at high latitudes *pushes* other water out of the way, eventually ensuring that water *rises* to the surface in the tropics and *is warmed* by the Sun as it *begins* to move out towards the poles. [John Gribbin *Hothouse Earth*]

[15] Seagrass *grows* in sand, silt or mud and resembles an underwater meadow. [*BBC Wildlife*]

11.5.2.3 **The instantaneous present**

The **instantaneous present** is used with a single event that occurs simultaneously with the time of speaking or writing. **Performative verbs** (cf. 2.10), for example, describe the **speech act** that is being performed by the utterance itself:

[16] I *apologise* for the very short notice but I have only just received the final list of names myself. [W]

[17] After much consideration we *regret* that we are unable to offer you the post on this occasion. [W]

[18] Well I *thank* my honourable friend for that question

[19] Smoking *is forbidden* in all parts of the building. [W]

Other common uses of the instantaneous present are in descriptions of events taking place simultaneously with the act of speaking:

[20] Now then Barnes *comes* inside on his right foot *waits twists turns feigns* to play to the left *clips* it nicely nicely to Platt on the far side

[21] The field officer ... Brigadier Braithwaite ... *rides* ... to face Her Majesty *salutes* with his sword ... and *rides* away to take command of the parade again ... as the quick march is The Thin Red Line

[22] The processions *move* towards the first representatives of other Christian churches ... as the sounds of this much loved hymn Praise to the Holiest in the Height *rise* to the height of the magnificent gothic vaulting of the nave almost a hundred and two feet

[23] I *enclose* the correct record form, and would be grateful if you would complete it and send it back. [W]

11.6 Secondary uses of the simple tenses

11.6.1 **Secondary uses of the past tense**

Besides its primary use in reference to past time, the past tense has several secondary uses. They involve a distancing—a metaphorical use of pastness.

11.6.1.1 The **backshift past** is used in indirect speech or thought in a backshift from the present tense—the **sequence of tenses** (cf. 15.2):

> **[1]**   The US Defence Secretary Dick Cheney speaking to a conference in Washington said the war *was* going well for the allies

The reporting verb *said* is in the past tense. The Defence Secretary may have actually said something like 'The war *is* going well for the allies.' Here are two other examples of backshift into the past tense:

> **[2]**   You see he told somebody I *was* weak

> **[3]**   Television viewers in Manhattan earlier this month might have thought they *were* seeing double. [*Wall Street Journal*]

11.6.1.2 The **attitudinal past** is used as a more polite or more tentative alternative to the present with verbs of thinking or wishing:

> **[4]**   A: Hello Can I help you
> B: Yeah I just *wondered* if I can … if these are to take away

> **[5]**   'Can I help you, miss?' he said.
> 'I *wanted* to know. Is it true about Mrs Hamilton?' [Christopher Priest *The Quiet Woman*]

> **[6]**   A: And *did* you want third party fire and theft or …
> B: Do I want what

The distancing in time may be viewed as a metaphorical distancing in the relation of the speaker to the hearer.

11.6.1.3 The **hypothetical past** is used mainly in hypothetical conditions that relate to present or future time, those that convey belief in the non-fulfilment of the condition (cf. 14.5):

> **[7]**   I wish it *was* over now

> **[8]**   I feel that if only he *had* a home, secure and fulfilling job, close friends, he could bounce back easily. [W]

If the verb is *be*, the past subjunctive *were* (cf. 11.10) is used in formal contexts in place of hypothetical past *was*:

> **[7a]**   I wish it *were* over now.

11.6.2 **Secondary uses of the present tense**

The simple present is used for several purposes, apart from its reference to include present time:

11.6.2.1 It can have future reference in subordinate clauses:

> **[9]**   When there *is* a withdrawal when there's the acceptance of the United Nations resolutions and all they stand for then the hostilities will end

[10] Well they won't learn anything if they *mess* about will they

11.6.2.2 It can refer to the future for scheduled events.

[11] You know you're welcome and the last No.38 *leaves* Haverhill at 3 pm! [W]

[12] Mr Major who *flies* to Bonn on Monday said Britain was strongly committed to the European Community

11.6.2.3 The **historic present** refers to past time. It is occasionally used in narration, to give a sense of immediacy: **[13]** comes from a novel, **[14]** from an unscripted talk, and **[15]** from a conversation.

[13] 'No, it isn't necessary,' he *protests*, as, to the accompaniment of a tabret, she *begins* to imitate the pelican of the wilderness, reviving her young ones with her blood.

> He *holds* up a hand to stop her.
> She *reads* it.
> He *turns* his head.
> She *reads* that.
> 'No,' he *says*. [Howard Jacobson *The Very Model of a Man*]

[14] And then the prophet *comes* in and *says* well even if we all have one father that's no excuse for betraying each other and in particular for men to betray their wives and to take foreign wives

[15] So he *moans* about money … and the fact that the college haven't yet billed him for my services and if they don't do it before April they won't get the money anyway So this is nothing to do with me anyway so I just *sympathise* because I need the job and I sort of *try* to keep him happy

11.6.2.4 The simple present refers to events in the very recent past time in newspaper headlines:

[16] Taiwan and China *Reach* Accord on Return of Hijackers [*International Herald Tribune*]

[17] Bagwell *Hits* 39th, *Trumps* Williams' 42d [*International Herald Tribune*]

The reports below these two headlines were in the simple past.

11.6.2.5 The **simple present** can also be used—as an alternative to the simple past—with verbs of communication or reception of communication when the message is still valid:

[18] Mary Jane *tells* me I shouldn't use the word half-caste

[19] He *says* he'd feel less of a man if he didn't speak up for what he believes in. [E. V. Thompson *Lottie Trago*]

[20] I *hear* we're doing a gig together

[21] I *understand* from our recent telephone conversation that your last certificate dates from September 1988 and that you would like to renew this by taking the refresher course this September. [W]

[22] It was, you may think, very natural and proper that she should take her mother's side, but I *gather* it went a good deal further than that. [Sarah Caudwell 'An Acquaintance with Mr Collins' in *A Suit of Diamonds*]

In an extension of this use, simple present can be used with past reference to writers, artists, musicians, etc., and their works:

[23] It's in the Bible that Abraham *stands* up and *argues* with God over the fate of the cities of the plain

[24] Freud *wants* to avoid the suggestion, that Jensen, his contemporary, was

consciously using his ideas. [Peter Collier 'The Unconscious Image' in Peter Collier and Judith Davies *Modernism and the European Unconscious*]

[25] if you look at theorem minus three it *says* it is differentiable provided the derivative of that point is non-zero

[26] If Beckett *makes* few value judgements in his text, it is because his whole position *is* one of assertive though ungrounded evaluation. In refusing to play the detached observer, Beckett *identifies* himself in a brashly partisan way with the text he *is* reading. [Leslie Hill *Beckett's Fiction*]

[27] In his book, A Plea for Reflectors, John Browning *describes* just such a telescope. [*Journal of British Astronomical Association*]

11.7 Future time

11.7.1 Future time: modal *will*, *'ll*, semi-auxiliary *be going to*

The two most common ways of expressing future time in the verb phrase are with the modal *will* and its contraction *'ll* and with the semi-auxiliary *be going to*:

[1] A: *Is* the whole system *going to* grind to a halt over the next two years
    B: No I don't think it *will* because we know that there is a reasonable amount of collection of the present poll tax and I would be fairly confident that that *will continue*

[2] Please arrive at 8.45 am for registration as the first teaching session *will* start at 9.00 am promptly.

[3] I won't be a second Richard I'*m* just *going to* go berserk for a while and I'*ll* then start again

[4] I'm hoping I'*ll* be on the 'phone at home too in the very near future. [W]

11.7.2 Future time: modal *shall*

Some speakers (in the south of England, in particular) use *shall* instead of *will* for the future when the subject is *I* or *we*:

[5] Well if I get bored with the company I *shall* come and find you

[6] We *shall* be away on holiday from Wednesday 29 August to Tuesday 12 September (both dates inclusive). [W]

11.7.3 Future time: simple present, present progressive

The **simple present** and the **present progressive** are both used to refer to future scheduled events:

[7] California politicians *face* a formidable opponent in the November elections: O.J. Simpson. [*International Herald Tribune*] (The reference is to the trial of Simpson scheduled to start during the election campaign season.)

[8] So we have to decide who *is going*

11.7.4 **Future time: other auxiliaries and semi-auxiliaries**

A number of auxiliaries and semi-auxiliaries may have future reference when used in the present tense, generally in combination with other meanings:

[9] I keep thinking I *must* do something about it

[10] She said that she'd find out precisely whether I *should* get Book One or Book Two tomorrow so I'll ring her Wednesday morning.

[11] We're at the moment when there's *about to* be a struggle between the earthly and the divine and that's why this episode illuminates a world that we know

[12] The spillage *is certain to* cause immense environmental damage. [*Evening Standard*]

11.7.5 **Future within a past period**

The auxiliaries and semi-auxiliaries may refer to a future within a past period when they are in the past tense:

[13] He was watching her being destroyed right in front of him. He *would* never thereafter know precisely why he did what he did next. [Michael Dobbs *Wall Games*]

[14] I was just thinking about art because I *was going to* get back to painting after not doing any for a year and a half

[15] We *were due to* go back to collect our boat from Andraitx in Majorca where we had left it in May. [Lord Young *The Enterprise Years*]

[16] Uh as I understood the completion date *was to* be the third of February

[17] I *was going* on holiday to Slovenia but HF (the walking hols. co.) cancelled this last weekend. [W]

The semi-auxiliaries in **[14]**–**[16]** allow the inference that the situation did not occur. In **[17]** the context indicates that that inference must be drawn. *Will* plus the perfect may have that time reference too:

[18] Next to that there's a manuscript of about sixteen hundred uh which *will have been* made in Baghdad

[19] You *will have noticed* this isn't a synthesizer this is a human being

For the use of *will* plus the perfect to refer to a past time within a future period, see 11.13.

11.8 Modal auxiliaries

When they appear, the **modals** (or **modal auxiliaries**) must be the first in the sequence of auxiliaries in a verb phrase (cf. 11.1) and they may function as **operators** (cf. 11.2). In standard English they function only as finite verbs and therefore only one modal may be present in a verb phrase, but in some non-standard varieties modals can co-occur (cf. 7.9). Unless they are functioning as operators, the modals are followed by an infinitive: *can be, may see*. Most of the modals have present and past forms: e.g. *can/could*.

Each of the modals has two kinds of meanings: **deontic** (or **root** or **intrinsic**) meanings and **epistemic** (or **extrinsic**) meanings. **Deontic** meanings refer to some kind of human control over the situation, such as permission or obligation. **Epistemic** meanings refer to some kind of judgement of the truth-value of the proposition, such as its possibility or necessity. Sometimes there is a merger of meanings:

[1]   *Can* you tell us how you first got involved in this project

Can you might be paraphrased by 'are you able to' (ability) or by 'is it possible for you to' (possibility).

The major meanings of the modals are listed below with examples.

11.8.1 *Can/could*

11.8.1.1 **Ability**

[2]   I *can* just about carry it

[3]   *Can* you cook any rice this way

[4]   *Could* you be a bit more specific than that

11.8.1.2 **Permission**

[5]   *Can* I borrow yours

[6]   You *can* take these

[7]   *Could* I have the ... slides on please and the lights out

11.8.1.3 **Possibility**

[8]   *Can* this be sent

[9]   These forces *can* be known and expressed only indirectly, through the condensations and displacements of dream imagery. [Peter Collier 'The Unconscious Image' in Peter Collier and Judith Davies *Modernism and the European Unconscious*]

[10]   I have not forgotten you—how *could* I. [W]

11.8.2 *May/might*

11.8.2.1 **Permission**

[11]   If I'm that interested I'll ask you if I *may* have a piece

[12]   In the meanwhile, *may* I just confirm a few administrative details. [W]

[13]   Having given you a brief outline of the scope of our interests and the way we are structured I wonder if I *might* now turn in more detail to the traditional examples of land management

In the permission sense, *may* and *might* are more formal than *can* and *could* and are used less frequently than they are, but *may* is sometimes prescribed.

11.8.2.2 **Possibility**

[14]   I *may* be staying around to the end of the week or I *may* go back tomorrow

[15]   Uh ... it *may* be worth your while ...

[16]   You *might* be interested in it

11.8.3 *Will/would*

11.8.3.1 **Future prediction**

[17]   He'll be nineteen on Friday

[18] And as she grows up she'*ll* see that her dislike of Gavin is irrational even if she can't admit it

11.8.3.2 **Present prediction**

[19] The procedure is very simple and *will* be familiar by now

[20] The tourist season *will* be over by now. [Agnes Owens 'Patience' in Alison Fell *The Seven Cardinal Virtues*]

[21] You might still talk about a moral consensus but that hardly justified making illegal what a minority of the population sincerely believed was permissible That *would* be what John Stuart Mill called the tyranny of the majority

11.8.3.3 **Habitual prediction**

[22] Hence if you smile, you *will* feel happy. [W]

[23] My door *will* always be open to you. [W]

[24] she'*ll* answer yes to every question you ask her

[25] If an outcrop of a syncline/anticline occurs on a horizontal face then the outcrop pattern *will* be wider than the thickness of the fold strata [W]

11.8.3.4 **Volition**

[26] *Will* you have a cup of tea grandpa ('Do you want to have a cup of tea')

[27] I *will* answer you in a minute ('I intend to answer you')

[28] Right I'*ll* ask her

[29] *Would* you please sit back close your eyes and try and envisage the scene

The combination *would like* is commonly used with volitional meaning.

[30] I *would like* it done on Wednesday if possible ('I want it done …')

[31] Now … where *would* you *like* to have it

11.8.4 *Shall/should*

The use of *shall* for the prediction and volition meanings is rare outside Southern English. The regulative use, imposing an obligation, is largely confined to legal and administrative language.

11.8.4.1 **Prediction**
(With 1st person subjects.)

[32] I *shall* regret this for the rest of my life! [W]

[33] I *shall* have a fever by tonight, blood poisoning soon after. [Mary Napier *Powers of Darkness*]

[34] As we *shall* discover, the concept of child abuse is an extremely elusive one and means different things to different people. [Paul Johnson *Child Abuse*]

The more common alternative is *will* or its contraction '*ll*.

11.8.4.2 **Volition**
(With 1st person subjects.)

[35] It is a far from boring topic, but there are so many favourite ways of doing it that I *shall* not add my own. [Nick Branwell *How Does Your Garden Grow?*]

[36] *Shall* I go first

[37] And we *shall* I promise you … bring our own forces back home just as soon as it is safe to do so

The more common alternative is *will* or *'ll* in declarative sentences. Interrogative *shall I/we* can be replaced by *should I/we* or *do you want me/us to*.

Those who use *shall* with first person subjects in place of *will* may also use *should* in place of *would*:

[38] I *should* like to help you as much as I can [W]

11.8.4.3 Regulative

[39] The committee *shall* consider the case after hearing any representations which the teacher may make. [W]

[40] Congress learned during the Reagan administration that it could intimidate the executive branch by uttering again and again the same seven words: 'Provided, that no funds *shall* be spent . . .' [*Wall Street Journal*]

11.8.5 *Should/ought to*

11.8.5.1 Probability

[41] Lesions such as these *should* be capable of a good recovery in the long term. [P. J. Smith 'Nerve Injury and Repair' in F. D. Burke *Principles of Hand Surgery*]

[42] When you've won every major medal in the sport and held the world record nerves *shouldn't* be a problem

[43] With a new labor force, service at Eastern Airlines is likely to improve sharply, and with its strong route structure, the Texas Air Unit *ought to* make a 'spectacular turnaround,' he says. [*Wall Street Journal*]

11.8.5.2 Obligation

[44] I can remember when common sense said that for instance women were weaker than men women *shouldn't* wear trousers women *should* earn less than men

[45] So does anybody else uhm have any topics that they feel we *should* pursue

[46] Oh well I suppose I *ought* to go to bed, as it's work tomorrow. [W]

11.8.6 *Must, cannot/can't, have to, have got to, need*

11.8.6.1 Certainty

[47] I read that in the paper ... so it *must* be true ('It is certain to be true')

[48] They *must* have been his daughters, *mustn't* they

[49] A Salomon managing director once said to me, 'If you think a million dollars is good money, you *must not* have kids.' [*Wall Street Journal*] ('It is certain that you do not have kids')

[50] So ... in all biochemical systems there *has to* be an off switch as well because otherwise ... things would burn out

[51] Loose shirts over jeans *has got to* be a sort of ... temporary prejudice hasn't it

In this meaning, *must* is not usual in negative or interrogative clauses, especially in British English. Possible replacements are *can*, *have to*, and *have got to*.

[52] You see ... as I explained there on that diagram ... if you get ... a swelling of the whole gland ... it *can't* be a tumour

[53] For a start the patients *cannot* have been brain dead ... otherwise they *couldn't* have adapted so well when awakened

The past of *must* in this meaning is *must have*:

[54] I *must have* lent it to somebody

11.8.6.2 Obligation

[55] They *must* be fed and they *must* be fed with their stir fry or whatever it is

[56] You *must* keep them moist

[57] Oh we *mustn't* be too late then

[58] Sorry we *have to* stop

[59] Do we *have to* take a bottle of white wine

[60] People *have got to* double their efforts. [*Evening Standard*]

In this meaning, the equivalent past is *had to* or *had got to*:

[61] And she *had to* be back on duty that day

11.8.6.3 Necessity

As a modal, *need* is restricted to negative and interrogative clauses and to the present tense:

[62] You *needn't* read every chapter ('It's not necessary for you to read every chapter.')

[63] We do not want a conflict I *need* hardly tell you that

[62a] *Need* I *read* every chapter?

The necessity meaning is generally conveyed by the main verb *need to* and by the semi-auxiliaries *have to* and *have got to*:

[64] I just *need to* check your blood pressure

[65] *D'*you *need to* know anything else

[66] You *don't need to* bother

[67] *Do* they *have to* sign on the back

[68] Have the right change for your fare with you so that you *do not have to* fumble in your wallet or bag. [W]

The modal perfect *need have* is used for past time, but more commonly the main *need to* and the two semi-auxiliaries:

[69] You probably didn't expect me to say such things Francoise, but I *need to* say them. [W]

[70] All I *had to* do was heat it up

11.8.7 Past time reference of modals

The modal *must* and the marginal modals *need* and *ought to* do not have past tense forms, and the marginal modal *used to* does not have a present tense form. There are four pairs of modals with present and past forms: *can/could, may/might, shall/should,* and *will/would*. However, as we will soon see, the past forms often have special uses.

Could and *would* may be used with past time reference:

[71] Free subjects of Rome *could* not legally be made slaves. [P. A. Brunt *Roman Imperial Themes*]

[72] There were the usual witty remarks about 'one too many', but the sad fact was that even two was one too many, and perhaps even one. A glass of wine *would* make me incapable, but not drunk. [Glyn Worsnip *Up the Down Escalator*]

Used to occurs more frequently for this past habitual meaning of *would*:

[73] I *used to* say what I thought

[74] At the start I *used to* get two or three abusive letters a week

We have also noted earlier the past time reference of *had to, had got to,* and *needed to.*
Past time reference is normally conveyed by the **modal perfect**, a combination of a
modal and the perfect auxiliary *have* (cf. 11.13). The modal itself may be in the present
tense or in the past tense. The past tense in this combination is a special use of the past
(cf. 11.8.8). Notice that the pastness may relate to the auxiliary or to the main verb. Here
are some examples:

[75] It *may have* saved his life ('It's possible that it saved his life')

[76] So when he felt he *might have been* wrong, he didn't acknowledge it. [Ronald
Frame *Bluette*]

[77] Uh I *could have* retired earlier ('It was possible for me to retire earlier')

[78] From his window the young boy *would have* looked across the green fields to
Camden Town [Peter Ackroyd *Dickens*]

[79] The dreadful truth to come out of the Cullen enquiry is that the 167 *need not have*
died. [*The Times*]

[80] They *must have* been his daughters, mustn't they ('It's certain that they were his
daughters')

[81] There was a thick rubber lifebelt clamped around his chest, constricting his
breathing when it *ought to have* helped [Ian Enters *Up to Scratch*]

There is no modal perfect of *can,* and the modal perfect is generally not used for ability
and permission meanings, for the obligation meaning of *must have,* and for the volition
meanings of *shall* and *will.* On the modal perfect *will have,* see 11.7 and 11.13.

11.8.8 Special uses of past modals

The past tense of the modals is often used with present or future time reference, as a
more tentative or more polite alternative to the present tense (cf. 11.6.2.5). These have
been illustrated above in the list of meanings of modals: the present time reference of
could for ability **[4]**, permission **[7]**, and possibility **[10]**; *might* for permission **[13]** and
possibility **[16]**; *would* for volition **[29]**; *should* for probability **[37]** and volition **[38]**.
The past tense modals *could, might, should,* and *would* are used for the backshifting of
the present tense forms in indirect speech (cf. 15.3). For example:

[82] It said that hysteria *could* not be ... distinguished from malingering

[83] She wondered how he *would* get back to Ramsford without a car.

All the past tense modals are used in the hypothetical past, particularly in conditions
(cf. 11.6.1.3, 14.5.3). For example:

[84] It *would* help if we *could* just get some sleep

Would (for present and future time) and *would have* (for past time) are regularly used in
the host clauses of conditions, as in **[84]** above and in **[85]** below;

[85] A judge told him and three others: 'If you had been older you *would have* gone
straight to prison.' [*Daily Mail*]

Putative *should* is used (especially in British English) in contexts that suggest that
some situation may exist now or in the future:

[86] But they recommend that any work by the water, electricity and gas authorities
should be done before the scheme is started. [*Western Mail*]

[87] It is disappointing, therefore, that the submitted design *should* fall far short of its clearly stated goal [*British Journal of Aesthetics*]

Putative *should* is often used in British English instead of the **mandative subjunctive** (cf. 11.9.3).

11.9 Present subjunctive

There are two subjunctives: the present subjunctive and the past subjunctive.

The **present subjunctive** is identical with the base form of the main verb:

[1] Israel insists that it *remain* in charge on the borders [*International Herald Tribune*]

Be is also used as the subjunctive of the progressive auxiliary **[2]** or passive auxiliary **[3]**:

[2] The technology of hard disk systems requires that the disk *be spinning* at about 3,000 revolutions per minute [David Royall and Mike Hughes *Computerisation in Business*]

[3] He proposed last June that American Medical *be acquired* by a new employee-stock ownership plan. [*Wall Street Journal*]

Negation of the present subjunctive is achieved by placing *not* before it:

[4] Consider the effect of requiring that ice *not be sold* for more than $1 a bag. [*Wall Street Journal*]

> **NOTE**
>
> The absence of an operator for negation shows that the verb is subjunctive even though it has the same form as the indicative:
>
> **[N1]** And every last one of the six who had children said he would prefer they *not* smoke. [*International Herald Tribune*]
>
> The indicative requires the dummy operator *do*: 'they *do not smoke*' or 'they *did not smoke*'.

The present subjunctive is used in three structures:

A. main clauses
B. adverbial clauses
C. *that*-clauses

The present subjunctive of verbs other than *be* is only distinct from the present indicative in the third person singular, where the indicative has the *-s* form. So *remain* in **[1]** is subjunctive because the indicative would be '(*it*) *remains*'. Its main use in present-day English is in *that*-clauses.

11.9.1 **Present subjunctive in main clauses**

The **optative subjunctive** is used to express a wish. It is largely restricted to a few fixed expressions. There may be subject–verb inversion:

[5] Poll tax is dead, *long live* the council tax! [*Daily Mail*]

[6] If they decide that it's necessary then *so be it*

[7]   *Far be it from me to* suggest that every politician or indeed every whip has been uh pure and chaste over the last fifty years

So also *So help me God.*

Normal word order is found with other expressions:

[8]   *Woe betide* the incumbent who raises taxes

[9]   At last, after all these years, I've learnt the truth about *Blue Peter. God rot* the grown-up who told me it was the name of the galleon in the programme's logo. [Margot Norman 'Shep was not the only bitch' in *The Times*—*Blue Peter* in italics in original]

The following are probably subjunctives with an implied subject rather than imperatives:

[10]   Andy, *bless* him, fixed my porch light up today [W]

[11]   *Damn* the Belgian refugees! [James Lees-Milne *The Fool of Love*]

An alternative—and less restricted—formulaic way of expressing a wish is with *may* and subject–operator inversions: *May you never have reason to regret your decision.*

11.9.2 Present subjunctive in adverbial clauses

The **suppositional subjunctive** is occasionally used in adverbial clauses, particularly in conditional and concessive clauses (cf. 14.5.3, 14.5.7):

[12]   The students would keep a record of what it is that's going on whether it *be* routine mundane day by day things or something out of the ordinary

[13]   But on the other hand if we're advancing ... even though that *be* quite slow ... quite different attitudes uh prevail

If need be ('if need exists', 'if there is need') and *be it remembered* ('it should be remembered', with subject–verb inversion) are fixed expressions:

[14]   You can teach him *if need be*

[15]   The Labour Party's 1983 election manifesto, which committed it to a non-nuclear defence policy and, *be it remembered,* to withdrawal from the European Community, became known as the 'longest suicide note in history'. [*The Independent*]

The present subjunctive is accompanied by subject–verb inversion in the absence of a subordinator:

[16]   There is very little tax manœuvre uh for the Chancellor *come* the budget ('when the budget comes')

[17]   If you opt for using the local supply, *be* it dirty, moderate or first-class, there is one exercise which will improve them all. [David Batten *An Introduction to River Fishing*] ('whether it be dirty, moderate or first-class')

The present indicative is far more usual than the subjunctive in these contexts.

11.9.3 Present subjunctive in *that*-clauses

The **mandative subjunctive** is used (especially in American English) in *that*-clauses that complement verbs, adjectives, or nouns (cf. 14.7.1.1) when the clauses convey an order, request, or intention. Citations **[2]** and **[3]** above are examples of the mandative subjunctive. Here are some further examples:

[18]   Still, bankers expect packaging to flourish, primarily because more customers are *demanding* that financial services *be tailored* to their needs. [*Wall Street Journal*]

[19]   In November 1294, as war with Philip the Fair of France loomed, Edward was seeking the *prayers* of the Franciscan chapter-general assembled at Assisi that 'the present tempestuous time *be succeeded* by a more tranquil one'. [Malcolm Vale *The Angevin Legacy and the Hundred Years War 1250–1340*]

[20]   The lawyer, Thomas Ward, was arrested here last week by U.S. agents in response to a *request* from the British government that he *be extradited* for trial, according to U.S. officials. [*Wall Street Journal*]

[21]   The latest absurdity grows out of a *demand* by Mr. Fernandez's lawyers that for a fair trial they *be allowed* to use secret government data in his defense. [*Wall Street Journal*]

The usual—and more common—alternative to the mandative present subjunctive is *should* with the infinitive in British English. In British English the indicative is sometimes used.

WORDS FOLLOWED BY *THAT*-CLAUSES WITH THE MANDATIVE SUBJUNCTIVE

verbs: *ask* ('request'), *decide, demand, intend, insist, order, propose, recommend, request, require, suggest, urge*

nouns: *decision, demand, insistence, proposal, recommendation, request, requirement, suggestion*

adjective: *crucial, essential, imperative, important, necessary, vital*

11.10 Past subjunctive

The past subjunctive is the **hypothetical subjunctive**. It is restricted to *were*, and it is distinct from the past indicative of the main verb *be* only in the first and third personal singular, where the indicative is *was* (*I was, she was*):

[1]   If it *were* correct it would make much twentieth century social legislation for example rent acts confiscatory and it would deny our property

Were is a subjunctive auxiliary—progressive **[2]** or passive **[3]**—when used as the first or third person singular:

[2]   All this would be great news if oil *were selling* at $40 a barrel. [*Wall Street Journal*]

[3]   These options would look more attractive if the capital-gains tax *were* reduced. [*Wall Street Journal*]

The same applies if *were* is part of a semi-auxiliary as in *were to*:

[4]   He said Sony would not object even if Columbia *were to make* a movie critical of the late Emperor Hirohito, although he added that people in Japan might not want to see it. [*Wall Street Journal*]

The past subjunctive *were* is used in **hypothetical conditional clauses** (cf. 14.5.3.2) and in some other hypothetical constructions:

[5]   For example, suppose Congress *were to give* every woman whose family income is under $10,000 a year $100 a month for every child she is caring for under the age of 12. [*Wall Street Journal*]

[6]   If I *were* you, I'd apply for the York position just for the experience. [W]

[7]   If my tabby, Genghis Khan, *were serenaded* by Mignon Dunn, he would speed down the fire escape never to return. [*Wall Street Journal*]

[8]   I felt as if I *were standing* in the grim grocery store Mr. Gumbel describes with such meaningful detail. [*Wall Street Journal*]

[9]   It's as though there *were* … a garden round him

[10]   And this is a French Revolutionary satire which tells uh projects as it *were* the fate of the British government uh if the French were to invade … in seventeen ninety-three

[11]   In fact, I rather think you wish it *were* true. [Paul Sayer *Howling at the Moon*]

In **[12]**, the subjunctive is involved in subject–verb inversion:

[12]   *Were* this a Yoshizawa book, the designs would be yet more beautiful, but western writers are not usually permitted to publish the best of his work. [Paul Jackson *Classic Origami*]

The past indicative *was* is more usual than subjunctive *were* in contexts that are not formal. The exception is the fixed expression *as it were*. In subordinate clauses referring to present time that are introduced by *as if* or *as though*, the present indicative is an alternative to subjunctive *were*.

11.11 Present perfect

The **present perfect** is a combination of the present tense of the verb *have* (*has*, *have*, and the contractions *'s*, *'ve*) with the perfect participle. Essentially, it refers to a situation in past time that is viewed from the perspective of present time.

11.11.1 **State present perfect**

The **state present perfect** refers to a state that began before the present time of speaking or writing and continues until that time, perhaps including it:

[1]   And how long *have* you *had* a full licence

[2]   The last few days *haven't been* quite so hot and on Friday night it actually rained. [W]

[3]   Estonia *has* until now *been* the calmest of the three Baltic republics

[4]   Today *has been* slightly less of a nightmare though not much. [W]

[5]   The food *has been* interesting so far. [W]

[6]   These are major reasons why the cost of space transportation *has remained* extremely high. [David Ashford and Patrick Collins *Your Spaceflight Manual*]

[7]   I *have* never *felt* at home since Flora told me she had heard us discussing her. [Mary Wesley *A Sensible Life*]

All of the citations **[1]**–**[7]** contain an expression denoting a period of time extending from some time in the past to the present. Generally the time expressions are adverbials, but *The last few days* **[2]** and *Today* **[4]** are subjects and in **[6]** it is the verb *remain* (*has remained*) that conveys the notion of duration to the present. Several of the citations— **[1]**, **[6]**, and **[7]**—suggest that the situation will continue into the future, but *until now* **[3]** and *so far* **[5]** imply an expectation of a change.

11.11.2 Recurrent present perfect

The **recurrent present perfect** resembles the state present perfect in referring to a period that extends from the past to the present time of speaking or writing, but the reference is to recurrent events and not to an unbroken state:

[8] The utility *has been collecting* for the plant's construction cost from its 3.1 million customers subject to a refund since 1986. [*Wall Street Journal*]

[9] As individual investors *have turned* away from the stock market over the years, securities firms *have scrambled* to find new products that brokers find easy to sell. [*Wall Street Journal*]

[10] The monthly sales *have been setting* records every month since March. [*Wall Street Journal*]

[11] Attorneys *have argued* since 1985, when the law took effect, that they cannot provide information about clients who do not wish their identities to be known. [*Wall Street Journal*]

[12] The fact that the villagers *have* always (or at least for seventy years) *played* cricket on this site implies that they want (and are entitled) to continue to do so. [Bernard S. Jackson *Narrative in Culture*]

11.11.3 Event present perfect

The **event present perfect** refers to one or more events that have taken place in a period that precedes the present time of speaking or writing. The period within which the event or events took place is viewed as relevant to the present. It may be relevant because the event has just been revealed, as in news broadcasts [13] or reports in newspapers [14]:

[13] The Democrats *have gained* a handful of additional seats in the House of Representatives where they already hold a big majority

[14] A man who killed his girlfriend more than 20 years ago *has* finally *confessed* after his wife complained of a foul smell coming from a cupboard in their home, Japanese police said yesterday. [*Yorkshire Post*]

[15] The company said it *has offered* to withdraw its bids in Hiroshima and Nagano. [*Wall Street Journal*]

[16] The Life Insurance Co. of Georgia *has* officially *opened* an office in Taipei. [*Wall Street Journal*]

Or the event may have just happened:

[17] Now very gradually release the clutch lever and as the engine starts to move forward ... very very gently open up the throttle ... That's all right The bike *has stalled* ... We will start again

The past period may be relevant because it is viewed as still operative in the present:

[18] It means that somehow or other religion in the modern world *has been marginalised* and that other agencies *have taken* over not only the bodies but the souls of human beings

[19] In this age of the microchip all sorts of gadgets *have been invented*, such as microwaves, video recorders and fax machines which were supposed to make life easier. [*Daily Mail*]

[20] She *has written* several books, some of which *have* recently *been translated* into English. [Paul Jackson *Classic Origami*]

[21] A: *Have* you *seen* The Silence of the Lambs ...
B: Yes It's only just come out in the cinema

In [18] the period in which the events have occurred ('in the modern world') includes the present. The present is invoked in [19] by 'in this age of the microchip'. The present perfect in [20] leaves open the possibility that the author may write additional books, which may also be translated. In [21] the present perfect indicates that it is still possible to see the film.

11.11.4 Present perfect and simple past

The present perfect competes with the past, which occurs more frequently. The present perfect is generally excluded if there are expressions that refer to a specific time in the past. Contrast:

[22]   I *worked* in New York *in 1990*.

[22a] I *worked* (or *have worked*) in New York for many years.

On the other hand, the past is generally excluded in the presence of expressions that refer to a period of time extending to the time of speaking or hearing:

[22b] I *have worked* in New York *since 1990*.

The present perfect is used less often in American English than in British English.

THE SIMPLE PAST AND PRESENT PERFECT CONTRASTED

In citation [23], the simple past in the first paragraph (repeated several times) contrasts with the present perfect in the second paragraph:

[23]   In its two-month rampage, the great Midwest flood of 1993 *cut* an awesome destructive swath. It *took* 50 lives, *left* almost 70,000 people homeless, *inundated* an area twice the size of New Jersey, *caused* an estimated $12 billion in property and agricultural damage and *stirred* anew a debate over the nation's flood-control system and its policies.
   The crest of the mighty flood, probably the worst ever to wash over the United States, *has roiled* down the Mississippi River past Cairo, Illinois, and from there south the swollen waters will steadily lose their deadly potency because the river bottom widens drastically. [*International Herald Tribune*]

The past in the first paragraph refers to a set of events occurring over a period of two months that were completed when the news item was written. These events had been reported previously, and therefore the present perfect was not appropriate. In the second paragraph the most recent event is reported—appropriately with the present perfect—and is followed by a prediction of a further event ('the swollen waters *will* steadily lose their deadly potency').

The present perfect can be used in subordinate clauses to refer to a time in the future:

[24]   We shall make up our mind when the IMF *has reported*

[25]   But what if a massive build-up of armed strength occurs before a war *has started*?
   [*The Guardian*]

This use of the present perfect accords with the use of the simple present for future time reference in subordinate clauses (cf. 11.6):

[25a] But what if a massive build-up occurs before a war *starts*?

The corresponding forms in main clauses would be *will have started* in [25] and *will start* in [25a], forms which occasionally occur also in subordinate clauses.

11.12 Past perfect

The **past perfect** (or **pluperfect**) is a combination of the past tense of the verb *have* (*had* or the contracted form *'d*) with the perfect participle. It is used to refer to a situation in the past that came before another situation in the past. The past perfect represents either the past of the simple past or the past of the present perfect. The distinction appears in **[1]**, where *had realised* is the past of the simple past and *hadn't been* is the past of the present perfect:

> **[1]** Uh, *had* you *realised* before this meeting that uh the Scott Coopers' surveyor *hadn't* yet *been* to the premises

These two verbs can be seen as the past of the verbs in **[1a]**:

> **[1a]** *Did* you *realise* before this meeting that Scott Coopers' surveyor *hasn't* yet been to the premises?

Here are some clear examples of the past perfect as past of the past:

> **[2]** It now transpires that Mr Sigrani *had issued* a writ against Mr Daniel on the twenty-first of April 1989

> **[3]** Confronted, Mrs. Yeargin admitted she *had given* the questions and answers two days before the examination to two low-ability geography classes. [*Wall Street Journal*]

> **[4]** In September, the department *had said* it will require trucks and minivans to be equipped with the same front-seat headrests that have long been required on passenger cars. [*Wall Street Journal*]

When the past perfect is the past of the simple past, it can co-occur with specific expressions of time.

Here are some examples of the past perfect as past of the present perfect:

> **[5]** A USX spokesman said the company *had* not yet *received* any documents from OSHA regarding the penalty or fine. [*Wall Street Journal*]

> **[6]** Equitable of Iowa Cos., Des Moines, *had been seeking* a buyer for the 36-store Younkers chain since June, when it announced its intention to free up capital to expand its insurance business. [*Wall Street Journal*]

> **[7]** I knew my Wagner and my Beethoven and my Brahms very well but uh I saw that there were a great number of British composers that I *hadn't heard* of

The **backshift past perfect** is used in indirect speech or thought in a backshift from the simple past **[8]** or the present perfect **[9]** (cf. 15.2):

> **[8]** The company said local authorities held hearings on the allegations last spring and *had returned* the plant to 'routine inspection' in August. [*Wall Street Journal*]

> **[9]** In his return toast to Mr. Nixon, Mr. Yang said the relationship *had reached* a 'stalemate.' [*Wall Street Journal*]

The **hypothetical past perfect** is used in hypothetical conditions that relate to past time, indicating the knowledge or belief that the condition was not fulfilled (cf. 14.5.3):

> **[10]** If a business *had made* the same mistake as the Government has made in introducing the poll tax against all informed advice I don't think we would allow them to run a business again

11.13 Modal perfect

The **modal perfect** is a combination of a modal (cf. 7.9, 11.8) with the perfect auxiliary *have* in the infinitive, e.g. *may have, could have.*

The modal perfect commonly serves to express the past time reference of the verb phrase:

[1]   You *must have been* a very fast driver ('It is certain that you were …')

[2]   Uhm … have you considered until now the effects that having an absent father *may have had* on your childhood ('possibly had')

[3]   She *might have been* so damaged by her own experiences that she is unable to think about protecting other children—'No one protected me, so why should I care?' [Paul Johnson *Child Abuse*] ('possibly was')

[4]   From his window the young man *would have looked* across the green fields to Camden Town, and to the Hampstead Road along which the old stage coaches still travelled. [Peter Ackroyd *Dickens*] ('probably looked')

Will have completed in **[5]** and *will have stopped* in **[6]** are future perfect, referring to a past within a future period:

[5]   Applications for General Course registration will be considered from undergraduates who *will have completed* at least two years in a foreign university by the time of their enrolment at the School. [W]

[6]   However, about 75 per cent of those affected *will have stopped* having attacks by the time they are twenty. [Ruth Lever *A Guide to Common Illnesses*]

The past modal perfect is often hypothetical:

[7]   Protests about his policy or even complaints about its results *would have been punished* with death

[8]   Modern means of communication now make the manipulation of public opinion possible on a scale that even Goebbels *would have found* unimaginable. [Terry Jones 'Credit for Mrs Thatcher' in Ben Pimlott et al. *The Alternative*]

[9]   You *should have insisted* it went ahead

[10]   There are many people, on both sides of the Atlantic, who wish it *could have been* different. [*The Observer*]

Hypothetical *would have* is particularly common in the host clauses of **unfulfilled conditions** (cf. 14.5.3.2):

[11]   Had they shown up, barristers *would have heard* a stirring account of how their leaders had routed the opposing army of the Law Society on the battlefield of the Courts and Legal Services Bill (now Act). [*The Guardian*]

[12]   A judge told him and three other youths: 'If you had been older you *would have gone* straight to prison.' [*Daily Mail*]

11.14 Perfect in non-finite phrases

The perfect in a non-finite verb phrase refers to a preceding time. For example, in **[1]** the causing of inconvenience preceded the expression of regret and in **[2]** the running preceded the breathlessness:

[1]   I am sorry *to have caused* you some inconvenience by misreading the subscription information. [W]

[2] He was almost breathless from *having run* towards her uphill from, it could only be, the lake. [James Lees-Milne *The Fool of Love*]

Here are some further examples of the infinitive and *-ing* participle perfects in non-finite phrases:

[3] They were wearing ski-masks and dark clothing and are thought *to have escaped* in a red car

[4] I'd have like not *to have worried* about the trembling fingers, but I was suddenly overwhelmed with a terrible feeling of sadness. [Graham Stark *Remembering Peter Sellars*]

[5] But *having taken* the first bend well Smith was never really in trouble after that

[6] Her daughter Carol *having produced* coffee for the waiting reporters offered some thoughts on the matter

11.15 Progressive

The **progressive** (or **continuous**) **aspect** consists of a form of the auxiliary *be* followed by an *-ing* participle. In this function, the participle may be termed the **progressive participle**. Here are examples of finite verb phrases with the progressive:

am making	may *be flying*
is writing	has *been running*
was playing	*are being* taught
were deciding	should have *been studying*

Here are examples of non-finite verb phrases with the progressive:

singing	to *be singing*
being explained	to *be being* explained
having *been listening*	to have *been listening*

The initial *being* that would be expected before *singing* and *being explained* is omitted as we can see from the corresponding infinitive phrases *to be singing* and *to be being explained* and the corresponding finite phrases *is singing* and *is being explained*. Presumably the omission is to avoid the juxtaposition of two *-ing* participles: *being singing*.

The progressive is primarily used to focus on the situation as being in progress at a particular time. Accordingly, it is not used to refer to a situation that is represented as a state. Hence, it is odd to say 'I am knowing English' or 'He is liking your sister'. Some verbs, such as *be*, are normally used in the depiction of states, but may occur in the progressive when they in fact depict an event in progress:

[1] I'*m being* sarcastic

[2] By then she *was having* difficulty with her teeth

[3] Who *am* I *thinking* of

11.15.1 **Event progressive**

The **event progressive** indicates that an event is or was in progress:

[4] A: What *are* you *doing* Bert ...
     B: I'*m walking* into the dining-room so I can sit down

[5] *Are* you *going* grey

[6]   She *was spooling* the programme on to the tape machine when the phone rang. [Valery Kershaw *Rockabye*]

[7]   When we *were walking* over the bridge Mary Jane stopped to take a shot of a woman on the other side of the road who *was dragging* a child along by the hand. [Agnes Owens 'Patience' in Alison Fell *The Seven Cardinal Virtues*]

[8]   He had his notebook out and *was flicking* the pages over, like a stage policeman. [Christopher Priest *The Quiet Woman*]

[9]   *Was* uhm John *appearing* distinctly sort of uneasy when uhm Kate *was* uhm all round him

The progressive is often used to indicate that one event is in progress when another event occurs, as in **[6]**–**[7]**. For example, in **[6]** the ringing of the phone occurred at one point of time during the spooling. The progressive is also often used to indicate the simultaneity of an event with a state or another event depicted with the simple present or the simple past, as in **[8]** and **[9]**.

11.15.2 **Recurrent progressive**

The **recurrent progressive** refers to a set of recurrent events that are viewed as in progress over a limited period of time:

[10]   A: Where *are* you *working* now
          B: I *'m working* in a software house in Kilburn

[11]   She *is dressing* to suit her husband's taste and, as long as he continues to tell her how nice she looks, there is no reason to change style. [Anne Melville 'Portrait of a Woman' in *Snapshots*]

11.15.3 **Secondary uses of the progressive**

One secondary use of the present progressive is to refer to a future scheduled event:

[12]   *Are* you *coming* tonight to the meeting

[13]   Or perhaps you will speak to me shortly when you *are* either *opening* a bottle of champagne or a bottle of hemlock

Another secondary use is as a more polite or more tentative alternative to the simple present or the simple past:

[14]   I *'m hoping* to find out if there's a bus service (direct) from Haverhill to London and vice versa. [W]

[15]   I *'m wondering* well what on earth is going to happen next

[16]   Mary Jane suggested that after we'd had some lunch we could take a stroll along by the river, but all I wanted was to lie down. 'Actually I *was thinking* of having a rest afterwards,' I said. [Agnes Owens 'Patience' in Alison Fell *The Seven Cardinal Virtues*]

This use tends to be employed with verbs of thinking. Because of its association with duration, the progressive suggests a less conclusive process of thinking than do the simple tenses. The progressive can be combined with the attitudinal past (cf. 11.6.1.2) to reinforce the tentativeness or politeness, as in **[16]** (if it has present reference) and in **[17]**:

[17]   I was wondering … would you like to do some sight singing

11.16 Progressive in non-finite phrases

The progressive in a non-finite phrase usually expresses simultaneity when it is in a subordinate clause:

[1]   Today is Sunday 14th April, and the mid-afternoon sun is illuminating my room—where I sit *facing* a WP screen *writing* you this letter. [W]

[2]   Pete was always a Leica enthusiast and in the Leitz showroom he was having a marvellous time *trying* out all their latest equipment. [Graham Stark *Remembering Peter Sellars*]

[3]   *Commenting* on the time of the two reports, Mr Kreindler said that they had surfaced just as his group were gathering critical evidence. [*The Independent*]

[4]   'I wanted to go to the castle,' she said huffily, *shoving* the camera back into her bag as if she had no further use for it, 'but it seems I've no choice.' [Agnes Owens 'Patience' in Alison Fell *The Seven Cardinal Virtues*]

The time reference of the participle clause is inferred from the host clause—present in **[1]** and past in **[2]–[4]**.

A contrast is sometimes possible with the perfect. Contrast **[4]** with **[4a]** where the perfect *having shoved* points to an action that precedes her saying 'I wanted to go to the castle':

[4a]   'I wanted to go to the castle,' she said huffily, having shoved the camera back into her bag.

The progressive is the only verb form possible in a non-finite clause functioning as the complement of a preposition (cf. 12.9.2):

[5]   He was obviously afraid of *mentioning* some girlfriend and *offending* the wife

There are also some verbs that take the progressive, rather than the infinitive, as the verb in their complement (cf. 14.7.6):

[6]   I would consider *trying* that

In instances where both the progressive and the infinitive are possible, the progressive may indicate that the event is viewed as having some duration or as recurring:

[7]   I heard you *speaking* Welsh yesterday

Contrast **[7]** with **[7a]**:

[7a]   I heard you *speak* Welsh yesterday.

The progressive may be combined with the infinitive to indicate duration:

[8]   So you know just uhm that it would be healthier for me *to be doing* something

Contrast **[8]** with **[8a]**:

[8a]   It would be healthier for me *to do* something.

There may also be a contrast with the perfect:

[8b]   It would be healthier for me to *have done* something.

The perfect refers to a hypothetical previous action. The addition of the progressive adds a reference to duration:

[8c]   It would be healthier for me to *have been doing* something.

11.17 Auxiliary-like verbs

A large number of verbs or verb combinations are similar in meaning to the auxiliaries in expressing notions of time, aspect, or modality, though they do not share all the characteristics of auxiliaries (cf. 7.9). Some have been illustrated (for example, *be going to*, *be to*, *be about to*) in 11.7.

OTHER AUXILIARY-LIKE VERBS

Followed by an infinitive:

appear to	*had rather*
begin to	*happen to*
be supposed to	*have to*
get to	*seem to*
had better	*tend to*

Followed by an *-ing* participle:

begin	*keep*
continue	*start*
go on	*stop*

The following citations illustrate their use in combination with other verbs:

[1] The next thing I *have to do* is have a drink of beer

[2] Loose shirts over jeans *has got to be* a sort of … temporary prejudice hasn't it

[3] He *happens to shave* three times a day

[4] Worst affected *is likely to be* the yellow-bellied sea-snake, which feeds on the surface. [*BBC Wildlife*]

[5] Well when you said you've got one that *seemed to be* the implication

[6] Actually today I'm nursing a very bad hangover so I decided I *had better stay* at home rather than throw up on the metro!! [W]

[7] I *kept saying* she will ring she will ring

Unlike auxiliaries, most of these auxiliary-like verbs can be non-finite, so that they can form chains of verbs, sometimes in combination with auxiliaries:

[8] I *'m going to have to get* round to it

[9] Well … you can't earn a living if they*'re going to keep cancelling*

[10] I'*ll have to stop talking* about the place, it's bringing tears to my cheeks. [W]

[11] If so, Bush *had better stop talking* about Hitler and start explaining how containment would work. [*Sunday Times*]

11.18 Phrasal and prepositional verbs

Multi-word verbs are combinations of verbs with other words that form an idiomatic unit, inasmuch as the meaning of the combination cannot be predicted from the meaning of the parts.

IDIOMATICITY OF MULTI-WORD VERBS

There are degrees of idiomaticity in multi-word verbs. The contribution of both the verb and the particle may be opaque, as in *give in* ('surrender') and *carry on* ('continue'). Or the verb's contribution may be transparent but the particle is not predictable, as in *call on* and *accuse of*. Or only the particle's contribution is transparent, as in *turn off* (e.g. *the lights*). With some multi-word verbs there is a set of contrasting transparent particles: *turn* plus *on, off, up, down*. In some, the particle *up* has a completive meaning: *drink up, eat up, shut up, wake up*. In free combinations, the verbs and the particles are both transparent in meaning and they can be separately contrasted with other verbs and with other particles: *bring/send/take/ push/lead*, etc., plus *in/out/up/down/along*, etc.

The most frequent types of multi-word verbs consist of a verb in combination with one or more **particles**, a term used for words that do not take inflections. The particles in such multi-word combinations are either adverbs or prepositions.

Seven types of multi-word verbs with particles are distinguished, which are discussed in the sections that follow (cf. 11.19–21):

1. intransitive phrasal verbs, e.g. *give in* ('surrender')
2. transitive phrasal verbs, e.g. *find* (something) *out* ('discover')
3. monotransitive prepositional verbs, e.g. *look after* ('take care of')
4. doubly transitive prepositional verbs, e.g. *blame* (something) *on*
5. copular prepositional verbs, e.g. *serve as*
6. monotransitive phrasal-prepositional verbs, e.g. look up to ('respect')
7. doubly transitive phrasal-prepositional verbs, e.g. *put* (something) *down to* ('attribute to').

In addition, there are various other idiomatic combinations with verbs (cf. 11.22).

The particles in **phrasal verbs** are adverbs and those in **prepositional verbs** are prepositions. In **phrasal-prepositional verbs** the first particle is an adverb and the second is a preposition. As the above examples show, for some multi-word verbs there are single-word verbs with approximately the same meaning, but these are generally more formal.

Phrasal verbs in particular have become a fertile field for new coinages in the twentieth century.

11.19 Phrasal verbs

11.19.1 Intransitive phrasal verbs

Intransitive phrasal verbs consist of a verb and an adverb, and they do not have an object. Here are some examples of the wide variety of such verbs:

[1] Uhm and he said can I *pop over*

[2] I thought you were going to *shut up*

[3] Was it alive do you think when she *set out* for the country

[4] I hope everything has *turned out* well for you both, and I am sure you've had no trouble with passing your courses. [W]

[5] Much of that activity though *goes on* within the framework of competitive sport

[6]   See how you *get on*

[7]   You *end up* by feeling quite compromised

[8]   Well they won't learn anything if they *mess about* will they

---

11.19.2 **Transitive phrasal verbs**

Transitive phrasal verbs also consist of a verb and an adverb, but they take a direct object. The adverb is generally separable in that it can appear either before or after the direct object. However, if the object is a personal pronoun it is normal for the adverb to follow the pronoun. Contrast:

[9]   A: You *picked up* a girl on the train
        B: I did not pick *her* up

[10] It's difficult to imagine people picking ... *picking* women *up* ...

Here are some examples of the wide range of transitive phrasal verbs:

[11] She said she'd *find out* precisely whether I should get Book One or Book Two tomorrow so I'll ring her Wednesday morning

[12] Can we *put* this big light *off*

[13] And Tarbull said he looked as if he was a man who was always on the lookout for enemies as if somebody was always trying to *do* him *down*

[14] I mean the newspapers *make up* a story and then they obediently trot in and try and perform it

[15] No dummies, the drivers *pointed out* they still had space on their machines for another sponsor's name or two. [*Wall Street Journal*]

[16] Earlier this year, Japanese investors *snapped up* a similar, $570 million mortgage-backed securities mutual fund. [*Wall Street Journal*]

[17] 'What sector is stepping forward to *pick up* the slack?' he asked. [*Wall Street Journal*]

[18] You can't *hold back* technology. [*Wall Street Journal*]

The adverb particle comes before the object if the object is long, as in **[16]**, and particularly if it is a clause, as in **[11]** and **[15]**.

In some transitive phrasal verbs the position of the adverb particle is fixed. This occurs when the phrasal verb and its object constitute an idiomatic whole. Usually the adverb comes immediately after the verb. Here are some examples:

> *take up arms*
> *let off steam*
> *put on airs*
> *shut up shop*

Sometimes the adverb follows the object:

> *keep one's shirt on*
> *put one's foot down*
> *cry one's eyes out*
> *keep one's hand in*

There are also instances of fixed positions where various direct objects are possible:

> *let out a cry*
> *carry off the trophy*
> *put up some resistance*
> *get somebody off* ('get somebody released from punishment')

Like other transitive verbs, transitive phrasal verbs occur in the passive, in which case there is no direct object:

[19] As I understand it people in the City are still being *laid off*

[20] The Dance Umbrella one of the the great dance festivals has been heavily *cut back*

[21] It is being *put up* for sale without going on the market and without being advertised. [*Daily Mail*]

The object may be **fronted** in a relative clause, and so be separated from the verb. In **[22]** the relative pronoun *which* is the object of *flesh out*:

[22] Diagrams can only show the bare bones of a design, which the folder through dedicated practice must *flesh out* and bring to life. [Paul Johnson *Classic Origami*]

If the relative is a **zero** pronoun (cf. 10.9), no object is present:

[23] First of all I think … relying on lecture notes alone is not enough for for any work you're going to *hand in*

11.20 Prepositional verbs

11.20.1 Monotransitive prepositional verbs

Monotransitive prepositional verbs superficially resemble transitive phrasal verbs when the particle of the phrasal verb precedes the object, but only the particle of a phrasal verb can also follow the object:

[1] I *looked at* the words. [prepositional verb]

[1a] I *looked up* the words. [phrasal verb]

[1b] I *looked* the words *up*. [phrasal verb]

The reason for the difference is that the particle of a phrasal verb is an adverb, which can be moved more freely, whereas a preposition comes before its complement. On the other hand, the adverb particle normally cannot precede the object if it is a personal pronoun, so that *looked at* in **[1c]** is a prepositional verb:

[1c] I *looked at* them. [prepositional verb]

Monotransitive prepositional verbs have only one object. The prepositional complement serves as the object of the verb. It is a **prepositional object**, because it requires a preposition to introduce it.

> **NOTE**
>
> Prepositional objects are sometimes termed **oblique objects**. In some analyses, prepositional objects that correspond to indirect objects are also termed **indirect objects**: 'I gave a book *to her*' (cf. 'I gave *her* a book').

Here are some examples of monotransitive prepositional verbs:

[2] Did you *apply for* anything in the final year

[3] Laura never *gets off* the phone

[4] I can't possibly *account for* it

[5] Tonight they're back in their constituencies doing it all again to try to *decide on* her successor

[6] The creation of a new elite and Soviet-style industrialization has *led to* large-scale social mobility. [Keith Sword *The Times Guide to Eastern Europe*]

[7] Her husband could always *rely on* the trustees to support his decisions. [Sarah Caudwell 'An Acquaintance with Mr Collins' in *A Suit of Diamonds*]

[8] Pamela Sebastian in New York *contributed to* this article. [*Wall Street Journal*]

[9] They *worry about* their careers, drink too much and suffer through broken marriages and desultory affairs. [*Wall Street Journal*]

[10] While giving the Comprehensive Test of Basic Skills to ninth graders at Greenville High School last March 16, she spotted a student *looking at* crib sheets. [*Wall Street Journal*]

As with the objects of transitive phrasal verbs, the prepositional object may be absent or may be **fronted**, so that the preposition is left **stranded** (cf. 12.9):

[11] The declarative by Economy Minister Nestor Rapanelli is believed to be the first time such an action has been *called for* by an Argentine official of such stature. [*Wall Street Journal*]

[12] Well I couldn't care less what the hell we *talk about*

[13] What was she *waiting for* [Valerie Kershaw *Rockabye*]

[14] I think that perhaps I could give them the backing to go out and win the election so that they can go on doing the jobs that they are so obviously … *succeeding at*

In a more formal variant, the preposition is fronted with a relative *wh*-pronoun:

[14a] … the jobs *at which* they are so obviously *succeeding*.

11.20.2 **Doubly transitive prepositional verbs**

Doubly transitive prepositional verbs have two objects. The first object is a direct object and the second object is a prepositional object, introduced by a preposition:

[15] No-one will *blame* you *for* a genuine mistake. [W]

[16] According to Mr Pitkin, Isabel was a strikingly attractive woman who could have married anyone she wanted, but she *set* her heart *on* Albert Barnsley. [Sarah Caudwell 'An Acquaintance with Mr Collins' in *A Suit of Diamonds*]

[17] She must not *put* him *through* that agony again. [Anne Melville 'Portrait of a Woman' in *Snapshots*]

[18] All manifestations of life, she felt, had validity; but interpreting that which was unconscious in terms which were conscious, she thought, was trying to *turn* an orange *into* a lemon. [Valerie Kershaw *Rockabye*]

Some doubly transitive prepositional verbs combine with a direct object in an idiomatic combination:

[19] I think it's a great shame that the Tories have never actually said to the British people we're sorry… we *made a mess of* it… and now we're going to try and do better

[20] It sounds that you're wanting to *take care of* yourself physically as well

[21] One of the more consoling aspects of our present dark age is that we now *give much more attention to* the mentally and physically handicapped than we did even twenty-five or thirty years ago

[22] But in the last forty years, agriculture has *lost touch with* its roots. [David Mabey et al. *Thorson's Organic Consumer Guide*]

[23] However, it did have some disadvantages, the main one being that slight changes in the phase of the signal *gave rise to* colour changes. [*Practical Electronics*]

Most of the doubly transitive prepositional verbs allow a passive with the direct object as subject (cf. **[11]** above):

[24] He was at once *involved in* getting out tenders interviewing clients and sometimes doing the wiring and installation work himself

[25] In other words, he accuses Mr Heseltine of ambition—as if that motive could ever be wholly *excluded from* politics—and lack of clarity. [*The Independent*]

[26] They were *accused of* wasting public money and encouraging idlers. [Bob Holman *Good Old George*]

A few idiomatic doubly transitive prepositional verbs normally have passives with the direct object as subject, but may also allow the prepositional object as passive subject:

[27] *insufficient attention* was *paid to* uh dictionary compilation

[27a] Dictionary compilation was *paid insufficient attention to.*

In these prepositional verbs, the direct object is part of the idiom: *pay attention to, make a fuss of, make a mess of, keep an eye on, take offence at, make an attack on.* In a few others—such as *catch sight of, keep pace with, get hold of, give rise to*—the direct object is even more cohesive with the verb, and if these allow the passive it is normally only the prepositional object that can be passive subject:

[28] Currently, the small average net gain of 15 million tons worldwide in grain harvests is well below the 28 million tons required merely to *keep pace with* the population growth. [Andrew Haines 'The Implications for Health' in Jeremy Leggett *Global Warming*]

[28a] The population growth is being *kept pace with.*

The doubly transitive prepositional verbs are not completely fixed, since most of them have some variability in the direct object: *give much more attention to* **[21]**, *pay insufficient attention to* **[27]**. Other examples of additions of determiners or adjectives to the nouns are: *make a complete mess of, make a vicious attack on, take good care of, lose all touch with, give unexpected rise to.*

Stranding of the preposition belonging to doubly transitive prepositional verbs has been illustrated above in **[24]**, where *involved in* is passive. Here is an example where the preposition is stranded at the end of a relative clause (cf. 12.9):

[29] So for example when you've been looking at the design of your process are there any uhm … features of the equipment that you've had to *pay any particular attention to*

In a more formal variant, the preposition is fronted with the relative if it is a *wh*-word (cf. **[14]** and **[14a]** above):

[29a] features of the equipment *to which* you have had to *pay any particular attention.*

There are a few prepositional verbs that seem to express a **copular** relationship with their complement, which should be regarded as a subject predicative rather than a prepositional object and can therefore not be made a passive subject:

[30] But they failed to *act as* parents because they didn't actually see the child (cf. 'They *are* parents')

[31] Any of these matters may *serve as* 'mitigating circumstances' reducing the defendant's moral responsibility and thus calling for a degree of leniency in fixing the appropriate sentence. [Sebastian Poulter *Asian Tradition and English Law*] ('constitute')

[32] Economic dislocation has reached the point at which insubordination could *turn into* revolution as yesterday's extension of rationing in Moscow emphasised. [*The Times*] ('become')

[33] The uncompromising nature of Beckett's declared commitment to his subjects is such that he might with good reason *pass for* little more than an apologist. [Leslie Hill *Beckett's Fiction*] ('seem')

[34] His Tokyo summit *looked like* a waste of time and money ('seemed')

[35] I was woken first by another relation who *sounded like* Pam's Mum and just kept saying 'Can I speak to Pamela?' [W]

[36] Dad was right and his stomach *felt like* water. [Ian Enters *Up to Scratch*]

11.21 Phrasal-prepositional verbs

Phrasal-prepositional verbs consist of a verb and two particles, the first an adverb and the second a preposition.

11.21.1 **Monotransitive phrasal-prepositional verbs**

Monotransitive phrasal-prepositional verbs have just one object, a prepositional object:

[1] Have the police *come up with* anything yet? [Valerie Kershaw *Rockabye*]

[2] Further to that we *got on with* the basic organisational work which was purely organisational work

[3] And the Greeks *looked down on* the Romans as being upstart barbarians themselves

[4] Why be good if you can *get away with* being bad

[5] Germany *did away with* its monarchy in November 1918

[6] The Labour Party, among others, has not *faced up to* this reality. [*The Observer*]

If the verb in a monotransitive phrasal-prepositional verb can by itself take a direct object, then the phrasal-prepositional verb can generally be in the passive. *Come up with it* [1] cannot be made passive, but the verbs in the other citations can be. For example:

[3a] The Romans *were looked down on* as being upstart barbarians themselves.

[5a] Its monarchy *was done away with* in November 1918.

[6a] This reality *has not been faced up to* by the Labour Party, among others.

Like other prepositional verbs, the preposition in a monotransitive phrasal-prepositional verb can be **stranded** (cf. 12.9):

[7] I've got the French written paper on Thursday which I'm not *looking forward to* at all

[8] It seems wrong to me (a retired civil servant) that people employed within any public service should, as its customers, be granted exemption from the limitations and delays that other customers have to *put up with*. [W]

A more formal variant is occasionally possible, in which the preposition is fronted with a *wh*-relative:

[7a] I have the French written paper on Thursday *to which* I am not *looking forward*.

But in most instances, the verb is too closely linked with both particles to allow separation.

11.21.2 **Doubly transitive phrasal-prepositional verbs**

Doubly transitive phrasal-prepositional verbs have two objects. In one type, the direct object either precedes or follows the first particle (an adverb), and the prepositional object follows the second particle (a preposition):

[9]   They should be honest about it and *put* the plant *up for* sale. [*The Scotsman*]

[9a] They should be honest about it and *put up* the plant *for* sale.

[10] The issue I would like to *take up with* you (cf. 'I would like to *take up* that issue *with* you')

Other verbs of this type are *put* (something) *down to* ('ascribe to') and *let* (somebody) *in on* ('allow to share'), *get* (something) *across to* ('communicate'), *fill* (somebody) *in on* ('acquaint with up-to-date information').

In another type, the direct object precedes the first particle and does not follow it:

[11] So it seems that if his captor dies exile is the only alternative to *keep* a politically undesirable person *out of* affairs. [W]

Other verbs of this type include *bring* (somebody) *up against*, ('make (somebody) confront'), *put* (somebody) *up to* ('encourage to behave mischievously or illegally').

Doubly transitive phrasal verbs can be made passive. The direct object becomes the passive subject:

[12] The most influential writer on the English constitution Walter Bagehot warned that daylight should not be *let in on* the magic of the monarchy if its prestige is to be preserved

11.22 Other multi-word verbs

In addition to phrasal and prepositional verbs, there are a number of other types of idiomatic verb combinations.

A multi-word verb may consist of two verbs and a preposition. The combination may function as a transitive verb and then takes a prepositional object:

[1]   They offered it to someone else but he changed his mind so they had to *make do with* me

[2]   You can now *let go of* the front brake

[3]   *Get rid of* the infection and your symptoms will subside

So also *have done with*, *put paid to*. The combination may consist of just the two verbs and function intransitively:

[4]   But ... after all these years it's sort of slowly taking its course but ... I still can't *let go*

So also *make do, let be, get going, get started*.

A verb may enter into an idiomatic combination with an adjective functioning as subject predicative. Combinations include:

come true	*ring true*
fall ill/sick	*run wild*
go crazy/native	*turn cold/sour*

Examples:

[5] For some this so-called age of plunder is a dream *come true* ... instant access to that guitar lick or drum pattern it would take years to play

[6] But in the past manufacturers have also responded to requests for a return to dedicated knobs and sliders with claims that 'it would cost too much' and 'there are far too many parameters these days for it to be practical'—claims which never really *rang true*. [*Music Technology*]

There are many other types of idiomatic verb combinations that have relatively few members. One common idiomatic construction is *make sure* followed by a *that*-clause, though the subordinator *that* may be omitted:

[7] *Make sure* that you don't miss out on Sunday April the twenty-first

[8] *Make sure* you've got your flak jacket with you

Sure is an object predicative in this construction (cf. 3.7), but it precedes the direct object because the object is a clause.

Other types include *take* (something) *for granted, take place, steer clear of, fall in love with.*

Chapter 12
Adjective Phrases, Adverb Phrases, and Prepositional Phrases

Summary

Summary

The head of an adjective phrase is an adjective, which may be preceded by premodifiers and followed by postmodifiers. A sequence of adjectives may constitute a hierarchy of modification or the adjectives may be coordinated (asyndetically or syndetically). The two major functions of adjective phrases are as premodifier of a noun and as subject predicative. The most common premodifiers of adjectives are intensifying adverbs. The most common postmodifiers of adjectives are prepositional phrases and clauses.

The head of an adverb phrase is an adverb, which may be preceded by premodifiers and (less commonly) followed by postmodifiers. The major functions of adverb phrases are as premodifiers of adjectives and adverbs and as adverbials. Adverbs can be premodified by intensifying adverbs and they can be postmodified by adverbs, comparative clauses, and prepositional phrases.

A prepositional phrase consists of a preposition and its complement. Prepositional complements are chiefly noun phrases, -ing participle clauses, and wh-clauses. Prepositional phrases may have the following functions: postmodifier of noun or adjective, subject predicative, object predicative, adverbial, and complement of verb. Prepositions and prepositional phrases may be premodified by intensifying adverbs.

12.1 The structure of the adjective phrase

The adjective phrase has as its head an adjective, which may be preceded by **premodifiers** and followed by **postmodifiers**. The structure of the typical adjective phrase is shown at **Fig. 12.1.1.** The parentheses indicate the elements that may be absent:

Fig. 12.1.1 Structure of an adjective phrase

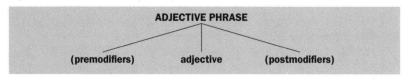

12.1.1 Hierarchy of modification

Adjectives may occur in sequence in a hierarchy of modification, where an adjective modifies the rest of the phrase that follows it:

[1] *Big brown* bears thunder through the deep woods, closing in on a remote site where campers wait, ready to squirt them. [*International Herald Tribune*]

[2] We had some *nice crisp white* wine to go with it

[3] I mean I don't mind *sillyish American* films if they're *goodish sillyish Americanish* films

In [1] *brown* modifies *bears* and *brown bears* is further modified by *big*. In [2] *wine* is first specified by *white* and then in turn by *crisp* and *nice*. Similarly, in [3] *American films* is first modified by *sillyish*, and then in the later phrase *sillyish Americanish films* is further modified by *goodish*.

12.1.2 Asyndetic coordination of adjectives

A sequence of adjectives may be **asyndetically coordinated**. That is to say, a **coordinator** is not present but could be inserted:

[4]   They only thrive in *dingy ... stagnant* areas where the oxygen levels are fairly low

[5]   Don Boswell at the Record has an opening for a *bright vital young* reporter, Army reject ideally suitable, must be *honourable, fearless, eager,* all the things young reporters are.

[6]   Has it gone to a different degree of development in different aspects of human life *physical economic social* etcetera

12.1.3 Syndetic coordination of adjectives

The adjectives may be **syndetically coordinated**, i.e. with a coordinator present:

[7]   She was expecting to see a commanding sort of mogul type of figure and Rockfeller kind of wandered in looking *very thin ascetic and nervous ...* and he sat with his back to the wall

[8]   We need to proceed with the greatest care therefore ... for embryo research is a complex issue which involves the whole spectrum of *medical scientific ethical ... and moral* issues

12.1.4 Modification of following adjective

In a sequence of adjectives, one adjective may modify the following adjective:

[9]   It's got a *bloody great* Sony sticker there

[10]   It's usually *dark brown ...* really

12.1.5 Repetition of absolute adjective

Repetition of the same absolute adjective has an intensifying effect:

[11]   He had been a monk at Kirkstall Abbey ... *long long* time ago

[12]   Just a hint of a swelling starting and if the eye closes he's in *big big* trouble

12.1.6 Repetition of comparative adjective

Repetition of the same **comparative** adjective, however, indicates incremental increase:

[13]   It makes him ... unhinges him and he just gets *weirder and weirder* and the film gets *weirder and weirder*

[14]   She hadn't returned since his birth, and she found it *harder and harder* to breathe as the afternoon wore on. [Ronald Frame *Bluette*]

The same applies if the comparison is expressed by *more and more*:

[15]   I think it's become *more and more difficult*

12.1.7 **Coordination of *nice*, *good*, and *lovely* with adjective**

Coordination of *nice* (in particular), *good*, or *lovely* with another adjective may express intensification:

[16] She rearranges her nightdress and falls asleep almost immediately, thinking about how *nice and safe* she is lying next to her husband. [Rosamund Clay *Only Angels Forget*]

[17] It's *nice and quiet*

[18] London is *good and warm*, though I've never spoken to her, just the impression I get. [W]

12.2 Functions of adjective phrases

The two major functions of adjective phrases are as premodifier of a noun and as **subject predicative**. They are listed first below, followed by other functions.

12.2.1 **Premodifier of a noun**

[1] Well it's a *much less popular* route

12.2.2 **Subject predicative** Cf. 3.6

[2] No I mean Auden was *extraordinarily ugly*

12.2.3 **Object predicative** Cf. 3.7

[3] He's opening his mouth *very wide* just now

12.2.4 **Postmodifier of a pronoun** Cf. 10.6

[4] There would still be eyes watching and wondering from a distance but, briefly, there was no one *close*. [Mary Napier *Powers of Darkness*]

12.2.5 **Postmodifier of a noun** Cf. 10.6

[5] To outsiders London seems one of the most vibrant cultural capitals of the world … a city *bright with theatres cinemas ballet opera art galleries and great museums*

12.2.6 **Nominal adjective** Cf. 8.3

[6] Tonight I hope you'll not mind if I eschew *the academic* and pursue a more earthy albeit reflective tack analyzing the soil within which citizenship can root and thrive

12.2.7 **Complement of a preposition** Cf. 12.9

[7] Kaye doesn't finish till *late*

12.3 Premodifiers of adjectives

Adjectives are premodified chiefly by adverbs.

12.3.1 **Premodification by intensifier**

Generally, the premodifier is an **intensifier** (cf. 12.7):

[1] This is a *perfectly* good conversation as far as I'm concerned

[2] I can remember going there and being amazed *how* pimply the … conscripts were

[3] She's *sort of* broad in the chest and she's *sort of* stocky

[4] That is *a bit* premature isn't it

[5] I found it *rather* tight

[6] Uhm … Dennis can we have your report which I trust won't be *too deeply* technical

[7] Grand mal epilepsy is a *surprisingly* common condition, affecting between four and eight people in every thousand. [Ruth Lever *A Guide to Common Illnesses*] ('common to a surprising degree')

[8] I'd be *quite* keen to try anything like that really

[9] What have you been doing then that's been *so* wild

[10] They're all young and *very* wet behind the ears

Very is the most common intensifier. Some of the intensifiers are combinations of words, such as *sort of* [3] and *a bit* [4]. The intensifier may itself be intensified; for example, *deeply* in [6] is intensified by *too*.

Intensifiers may also modify comparatives [11]–[14] and superlatives [15]–[18]:

[11] Actually Simon can't be *too much* older than us

[12] I feel *so much* better now I know he's in London and he's not going to come round

[13] So I think it's *slightly* lighter

[14] I think it is *far* better to increase the amount of democracy rather than to go ahead and reduce it which I believe would be wrong at this time

Very cannot intensify comparatives, though it can occur in intensifier combinations such as *very much*, where *very* is an intensifier of *much*. On the other hand, *very* is the most common intensifier of superlatives:

[15] My *very* best wishes to you both, take care. [W]

Other intensifiers of superlatives precede the determiner or follow the noun:

[16] And they are as I say *by far* the best side in Greece

[17] Firstly I am the youngest *by miles*. [W]

[18] *Much* the best pastry we've ever had

12.3.2 **Premodification by focusing adverb**

Focusing adverbs (cf. 8.7) are often used as premodifiers of adjectives. They include additive adverbs **[19]**–**[20]**, exclusive adverbs **[21]**–**[22]**, and particularizer adverbs **[23]**–**[24]**. The particularizer adverbs may also convey intensification.

[19] *Equally* important are the profoundly moral arguments over the origin of life ... the status of the embryo and the freedom to experiment on and then destroy human life in its first fourteen days

[20] The main problem confronting any study of the Picts is the complete lack of source material, or *even* archaeological evidence. [W]

[21] I'm *only* sorry that we aren't actually having a holiday in Provence

[22] How do you get it *just* right

[23] Is there anything *particularly* distinctive about that fermentor

[24] Belgravia as an estate is *predominantly* residential with offices and commercial property around the perimeter

12.3.3 **Premodification by viewpoint adverb**

Another type of premodifier of adjectives is the viewpoint adverb. For example, *morally* is a viewpoint adverb when it has the meaning 'from a moral point of view'. Here are some examples:

[25] In countries with *technically* advanced agriculture, milking is done by machine, rather than by hand. [*Robotica*]

[26] The orthodoxies of our time are that morality is a private affair a matter of personal choice ... and that the state must be *morally* neutral

[27] You mean it's *theoretically* possible

[28] It is *physically* impossible to force myself to work sometimes

[29] They often have to cope with negative public attitudes towards the stereotyped image of the *mentally* ill, borne of ignorance and fear. [W]

12.4 Postmodifiers of adjectives

Adjectives are typically postmodified by **prepositional phrases** and various kinds of clause.

12.4.1 **Types of postmodifier**

12.4.1.1 **Prepositional phrase**

[1] I was afraid *of him* ... didn't really know him and I was kind of glad when ... he left

12.4.1.2 *That*-clause

[2] I feel sure *that some day it will be published*

[3] I expect you're glad *you're not a vegetarian*

12.4.1.3 *Wh*-clause

[4] Yes you have to be careful *what's available in what colour*

[5] I think that Jim felt … slightly embarrassed taking over from the man who had actually facilitated his becoming Prime Minister and he was uncertain *what to do*

12.4.1.4 *To*-infinitive clause

[6] If you have any questions then I would be happy *to hear from you*, but would you please allow me until Tuesday 7 May to give me a little time to sort things at this end. [W]

12.4.1.5 *-ing* participle clause

[7] But police were busy *handing out letters about the operation to residents* and Supt Slater was happy with the result. [*Willesden and Brent Chronicle*]

12.4.1.6 Comparative clause

[8] No I'm sure it's easier *than they say*

12.4.1.7 Adverb

[9] It certainly tasted strong *enough*

12.4.2 Postmodifiers and complements

The relation between an adjective and its postmodifier in types [1]–[5] often resembles that between a verb and its **complement**, and indeed such postmodifiers are often termed complements (cf. 14.7), as are those of type [6]. Compare the following pairs;

[10] I am *afraid of him*.
[10a] I *fear him*.
[11] I'm *sure that it will be published*.
[11a] I *know that it will be published*.
[12] He was *uncertain what to do*.
[12a] He did not *know what to do*.
[13] I am *happy to hear from you*.
[13a] I *rejoice to hear from you*.

Some adjectives require a postmodifying prepositional phrase with the specified preposition, at least in the relevant sense. For example: *accustomed to, bad at, bent on, fond of, free from, good at, short of, subject to, tantamount to. Conscious* takes either a prepositional phrase with *of* or a *that*-clause.

12.4.3 *That*- and *wh*-clauses

As with objects of verbs, *that* may be omitted from the postmodifying *that*-clause, as in [3]. *Wh*-clauses may be finite [4] or non-finite with an infinitive verb [5].

12.4.4 Postmodifiers and analogous extraposed subject clauses

Types [2]–[5] may have analogous constructions with **anticipatory *it*** as subject and an **extraposed** subject clause (cf. 3.10.2). The subject clauses are not postmodifiers of the adjectives:

[14]   But after two days *it* was obvious *that it wouldn't work* because he didn't want me to even pick the child up (*that*-clause)

[14a]   *That it wouldn't work* was obvious.

[15]   Although a national park has been established at Morne Anglaise, *it* is doubtful *whether any of these large parrots live within its boundary.* [John Sparks *Parrots*] (*wh*-clause)

[15a]   *Whether any of these large parrots live within its boundary* is doubtful.

[16]   I detect in the United States' latest addition a realisation that *it* is important *to keep the United Nations Security Council consensus* and that I very much welcome (*to*-infinitive clause)

[16a]   *To keep the United Nations Security Council consensus* is important.

[17]   Oh I see I thought you said *it* was very frightening *being able to understand what they were saying* (*-ing* participle clause)

[17a]   *Being able to understand what they were saying* was very frightening.

12.4.5 *To*-infinitive clauses

12.4.5.1 Subject = superordinate clause subject
In most instances of *to*-infinitive clauses, the implied subject of the clause is the same as the subject of the superordinate clause, as in [6], simplified as [6a]:

[6a]   *I* would be happy *to hear from you.* ('I will hear from you')

12.4.5.2 Object = superordinate clause subject; with extraposition
But with some adjectives, the subject of the superordinate clause is identical with the implied object of the infinitive clause:

[18]   Generally motorbikes aren't as visible as cars and *their speed* is more difficult *to estimate*

[18a]   *To estimate their speed* is more difficult.

This construction in [18a] allows extraposition of the clause with an anticipatory *it* in subject position (cf. 6.7.2):

[18b]   *It* is more difficult *to estimate their speed.*

A number of adjectives belong to the set that functions like *difficult* in constructions like [18], [18a], and [18b]. They include *easy, hard, impossible, nice, pleasant, tough, unpleasant.* The superficial resemblance of constructions with these two different kinds of sets of adjectives in *to*-infinitive clauses has led to the linguistic puzzle on the differences between [19] and [19a]:

[19]   John is *eager to please.*

[19a]   John is *easy to please.*

12.4.5.3 Object = superordinate clause subject; no extraposition

Another set of adjectives resembles *difficult* when they are in infinitive clauses in that the superordinate subject is also the implied object of the infinitive clause but they do not admit extraposition of the clause:

> **[20]** Both Philips and Matsushita are now making DCC chip sets and the first batch of Philips chips were ready *to mount on a single board inside the stand-alone deck unit in time for CES at Las Vegas*. [*Hi-Fi News & Record Review*]

Other adjectives like *ready* in this respect include *available, free, hot, sufficient*. Since these can also function in constructions where the subjects are identical, there is potential ambiguity in isolation where both interpretations are possible:

> **[21]** *It* [i.e. the dog] is too hot *to eat*.
>
> **[22]** *It* [i.e. the food] is too hot *to eat*.

For **[21]** we can add an object to the infinitive clause:

> **[21a]** It is too hot *to eat any food*.

For **[22]** we can add a subject to the infinitive clause and optionally an object:

> **[22a]** *It* is too hot *for anyone to eat (it)*.

The addition of the object is only possible when the subject is present. Analogous to **[21]** and **[22]** is a third interpretation, since *it* can be used to refer to the weather:

> **[23]** *It* [i.e. the weather] is too hot *to eat*.

We can in this interpretation add a subject or an object or both.

12.4.6 Adverbs as postmodifiers

Only two adverbs are used as postmodifiers of adjectives, both of them intensifiers—*enough* and *indeed*:

> **[24]** Highway officials insist the ornamental railings on older bridges are not strong *enough* to prevent vehicles from crashing through. [*Wall Street Journal*]
>
> **[25]** And so we were very lucky *indeed* to have a statutory body agree for us to have five hundred hours of ethics and politics for our nursing course
>
> **[26]** Its a *very* good kick indeed.

The intensifier *indeed* commonly correlates with the premodifier *very*, as in **[25]**–**[26]**. However, it need not do so:

> **[27]** While some but as yet pretty few women are at last achieving promotion to senior rank ... senior black officers are rare *indeed*

12.4.7 Comparative clauses and phrases

Comparative clauses and phrases correlate with a preceding *more* or the *-er* inflection, *less*, and *as*:

> **[28]** Both agree that improvement is needed and should be *more* rapid *than is now the case*
>
> **[29]** The total of 18 deaths from malignant mesothelioma, lung cancer and asbestosis was far higher *than expected*, the researchers said. [*Wall Street Journal*]

[30] Yet our efforts are somehow *less* noble *than those of an investment expert studiously devouring press clippings on each company he follows.* [*Wall Street Journal*]

[31] You can be *as* personal *as you like*

12.4.8 Combinations of premodifier and postmodifier

Combinations of premodifier and postmodifier are often possible, since an intensifier can usually be used with the adjective. Here is an example with *no* ('not at all'):

[32] The nature of the work that we do is *no* different ... *from* ... *any other creative arts group*

12.5 The structure of the adverb phrase

The adverb phrase has as its head an adverb, which may be preceded by premodifiers and (less commonly) followed by postmodifiers. The structure of the adverb phrase is shown at **Fig. 12.5.1.** The parentheses indicate the optional elements.

Fig 12.5.1. Structure of an adverb phrase

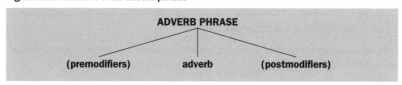

12.5.1 Coordination of adverbs expressing repetition

Adverbs may be coordinated to express repetition:

[1] Books that you come back to ... *over and over and over and over* again

[2] It goes *on and on* like this

[3] And there used to be islands and they used to go *round and round* and then one would stop at the top of the tree and they'd get on and experience whatever that land had to offer

Repetition may also be conveyed by the coordination of contrasting directional adverbs:

[4] Of course I assumed that as Mr Sainsbury was popping *in and out* from time to time that the scheme was proceeding anyway

[5] The side of the bed was weighed down with his father's bulk and his shoulder was being pumped *up and down.* [Ian Enters *Up to Scratch*]

[6] Tommy had fallen asleep by the time Anne had calmed down and she rocked him gently *back and forth* in her arms. [Steve Harris *Adventureland*]

12.5.2 Coordination of adverb phrases, syndetic and asyndetic

Adverb phrases may be coordinated with a coordinator:

[7] We had to do something *structurally and radically* different. [*Wall Street Journal*]

[8] I have a right to print those scripts if I go there and *laboriously—but no longer surreptitiously*—copy them out in long hand. [*Wall Street Journal*]

[9] *Rightly or wrongly, but not necessarily rationally*, currency traders use the monthly figures as an excuse to buy or sell if the deficit is more or less than predictions, notes a Commerce Department official. [*Wall Street Journal*]

Adverbs may also be coordinated asyndetically, without a coordinator (cf. 12.1.2):

[10] 'I think life is the exercise that can be a yogic practice, if you do it *lovingly, authentically, honestly,*' he says. Or: 'In ten years time, I hope I'm healthy—*physically, emotionally, psychologically, spiritually.*' [Sabine Durant 'Jeff Goldblum, you've got to hand it to him' in *The Independent*]

12.5.3 Coordination of comparative adverbs

Coordination of comparative adverbs or of *more and more* with adverbs indicates incremental increase (cf. 12.1.6):

[11] These become key issues in which the two groups become *further and further* divided

[12] That is happening and it's happening *more and more slowly* under John Major than it did under Mrs Thatcher

12.5.4 Repetition of an adverb expressing intensification

Repetition of an adverb expresses intensification, and if the adverb itself is an intensifier the repetition reinforces the intensifying effect:

[13] He's *desperately desperately* in love

[14] It escaped on the underground and it got out this poor wasp so *far … far* from home

[15] I was talking to this this guy at college and uhm he's *really really really* boring and he *always always* says the same thing

[16] I'm going to rehearse it *very very* slowly

[17] And I've been applying *quite quite* regularly since

12.6 Functions of adverb phrases

The major functions of adverb phrases are as premodifiers of adjectives and adverbs and as adverbials and complements of a verb. They are listed first below, followed by other functions.

12.6.1 Premodifier of an adjective

Cf. 12.3

[1] We're *far too* close to it

12.6.2 Premodifier of an adverb

Cf. 12.7

[2] I'm going to give you a prescription to clear up the infection ... then you need to have your teeth *extremely* thoroughly cleaned ... as soon as possible

12.6.3 Adverbial

Cf. 3.8, 8.7

[3] Refunds of fees are not *normally* available. [W]

12.6.4 Subject predicative

Cf. 3.6

[4] At least we're *outside*. [Agnes Owens 'Patience' in Alison Fell *The Seven Cardinal Virtues*]

12.6.5 Object predicative

Cf. 3.7

[5] Shall I move these *away*

12.6.6 Premodifier of a preposition

Cf. 12.11

[6] But I have a feeling they might be *right* by the door but if they're not then it's not worth it

12.6.7 Premodifier of a pronoun

Cf. 10.5

[7] When I look around at my friends, *virtually* all of them seem to have got careers. [W]

12.6.8 Premodifier of a determiner

Cf. 5.4

[8] Everybody knows that the results in fact have *absolutely* no meaning and can be interpreted any way you like

12.6.9 **Premodifier of a numeral**

Cf. 6.15.1.4

[9]   The chaps *around* forty to forty-five are all called John

12.6.10 **Premodifier of a noun phrase**

Cf. 10.5

[10]   This is really *quite* a problem I imagine

12.6.11 **Postmodifier of a noun phrase**

Cf. 10.6

[11]   Your friend *here* does she doodle a lot

12.6.12 **Postmodifier of an adjective or adverb**

Cf. 12.4, 12.8

[12]   Well right that's fair *enough* then
[13]   And oddly *enough* it's not only outsiders who ask it

12.6.13 **Complement of a preposition**

Cf. 12.9

[14]   Oh I should have thought he'd've had one before *now*

These functions are discussed elsewhere, as indicated.

12.7 Premodifiers of adverbs

Adverbs are premodified only by intensifying adverbs.

> **NOTE**
>
> The difference between the adjective and the adverb as premodifiers is starkly posed in a report of a printing mistake:
>
> > Foul-up corner, part two. From this week's *Fashion Weekly*, on an earlier article about the Hackett chain: 'In paragraph eight we referred to the company as "a *terrible* British company", this should of course have read "a *terribly* British company . . ." ' [*The Independent*] (italics in original)
>
> The adverb *terribly* has become an intensifier, having lost its pejorative connotation. The adjective modifies the unit *British company* ('a British company that is terrible'), whereas the adverb modifies only the adjective *British* ('a company that is terribly British').

The most common premodifying intensifier is *very*.

[1]   I wear this occasionally but *very* rarely now

Here are examples of other intensifiers:

[2]   And it's not *that* far away

[3]   I'm trying *so* hard to concentrate on this

[4]   But I did it *really* badly

[5]   I mean it worked *perfectly* well

[6]   We might die and then find ourselves going *straight* down

[7]   I think they did *pretty* well to get to ... end up like that

[8]   Let's go through them *fairly* systematically

[9]   I could not myself have expressed it *as* well

[10] You're sort of jumping *a bit* ahead

There may be a sequence of intensifiers premodifying an adverb, each modifying the following intensifier:

[11] Don't know if it fits me *all that* well now

[12] It takes *far too* long for us to get rid of the poll tax

[13] The prophet responds to this by saying that God will show to them *all too* clearly how just he is by coming against them in judgement

12.8 Postmodifiers of adverbs

12.8.1 *Enough* and *indeed*

Two adverb **intensifiers**—*enough* and *indeed*—commonly postmodify adverbs, as they do adjectives (cf. 12.4.6):

[1]   It was quoted often *enough* in the recent debate in the other place

[2]   On that occasion he used the original scoring; on Telarc he is accompanied by a full symphony orchestra and is recorded very sumptuously *indeed*. [*The Penguin Guide to Compact Discs*]

Very normally premodifies the adverb when it is postmodified by *indeed*. *Ever* is an intensifying postmodifier of *never*.

[3]   Never lecture with ... animals or children and *never ever* try to do chemistry experiments live

12.8.2 **Non-intensifiers**

A few postmodifying adverbs are not intensifiers:

[4]   Well do it somewhere *else*

[5]   Well it's not that far *away*

12.8.3 **Comparative clauses and phrases**

As with adjectives (cf. 12.4.7), comparative clauses and phrases postmodify adverbs and they may correlate with a preceding *more* or comparative inflection, *less* or *as*:

[6]   I think he's feeling the time going *more* slowly *than I am* since he's the one left behind. [W]

[7]   But you'd probably know that music scene *much* better *than I would*

[8]   Not everyone at the training sessions will be a complete novice so don't be discouraged if you don't pick things up *quite as* quickly *as everyone else*

[9]   Uhm ... also another factor which I think is not often taken into account is they have very low population densities so epidemics go through the population *much less* regularly *than they do through an urban population or uhm a rural village-based population*

[10] Indeed this dying month of March she has visited the Abbey on no less *than three occasions*

12.8.4 **Prepositional phrase**

Some attitudinal adverbs (cf. 8.7) can be postmodified by a prepositional phrase introduced by the preposition *for*:

[11] Unhappily *for Tanya*, the telephone was in a corner of the living-room. [Marion Babson *Past Regret*]

[12] And ... very luckily *for us* this also this enzyme has an absorption spectrum that changes depending upon whether the enzyme is oxygenated or de-oxygenated

[13] He didn't quite gather it cleanly the first time but uh thankfully *for Spurs* he got hold of it in the end and Adams was uh denied the chance

Viewpoint prepositional phrases are also possible, such as *in my view, from their point of view, in my belief, in my opinion*:

[14] But literature actually interestingly *in my belief* ... uh rather neglects it

Independently is unique in that it can be postmodified by a prepositional phrase introduced by *of*:

[15] They then determined whether audience judgments varied independently *of the true status of the story*, by comparing audience guesses to each storyteller's claim about his or her story. [Bernard S. Jackson 'Narrative Theories and Legal Discourse' in Christopher Nash *Narrative in Culture*]

12.9 The structure of the prepositional phrase

The prepositional phrase consists of two constituents: a preposition and the complement of the preposition. Optionally, the preposition may be premodified by an intensifying adverb (cf. 12.11). The structure of the prepositional phrase is shown in **Fig. 12.9.1**, with the optional intensifier in parentheses (see overleaf).

12.9.1 **The prepositional complement**

The prepositional complement is chiefly a noun phrase, an *-ing* participle clause, or a *wh*-clause. These are listed first below, followed by other linguistic units.

Fig. 12.9.1. Structure of a prepositional phrase

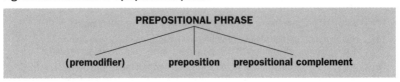

12.9.1.1 Noun phrase as complement

[1] But I mean my only recollection of *it* is sleeping in *a wood* for *about four or five hours*

12.9.1.2 *-ing* participle clause as complement

[2] I mean instead of *getting people up so early* she could stick around and have breakfast for an hour or two

For the use of the genitive case for the subject of the participle clause, see 14.7.6.1.

12.9.1.3 *Wh*-clause as complement

[3] It's just a question of *how we organise it and what the numbers should be*

12.9.1.4 Adverb as complement

[4] I have to wait till *then*! [W]

12.9.1.5 Adjective as complement

[5] When the public feuding ended, the insults continued in *private*. [*Wall Street Journal*]

ADJECTIVES AS COMPLEMENTS OF PREPOSITIONS IN DETAIL

Adjectives functioning as complements of prepositions are virtually confined to fixed expressions. They should all perhaps be regarded as nominal adjectives (cf. 8.3). Here is a list of such expressions, arranged according to the preposition:

at best	in brief
at large	in common
at worst	in full
	in general
for better or worse	in particular
for certain	in private
for free	in public
for good	in secret
for real	in short
for sure	
	of old
from bad to worse	on high

There are also a few expressions with determiners, e.g.: *all of a sudden, in the extreme, to the full.*

12.9.1.6 Prepositional phrase as complement

[6] That means he took one lamb burger out of there ... from *under the grill*

12.9.2 **Stranding resulting from absence of complement**

In certain constructions, the preposition is **stranded**—left by itself, without a following prepositional complement. Stranding may result from the absence of a complement or from the fronting of the complement.

> **NOTE**
>
> The preposition *but* ('except') is occasionally found with ellipsis of its complement, the ellipsis being recoverable from the preceding context:
>
> The campaign for the European election on Sunday was easy to ignore, but the new European Parliament will be anything *but*. [*International Herald Tribune*] ('anything *but* easy to ignore')

The complement is absent in three instances:

12.9.2.1 Where a prepositional verb or phrasal-prepositional verb is in the passive, the subject corresponds to what would be the prepositional complement in the active:

[7]   All she meant, I feel, is that McQueen popularized the term, for it is generally held to be a negro phrase and *was talked about* before the film star came on the scene. [Nigel Rees *Dictionary of Popular Phrases*] ('People talked *about that*')

[8]   A bill will be introduced to enable applications for asylum in the United Kingdom *to be dealt with* quickly and effectively ('They will deal *with applications for asylum*')

12.9.2.2 The subject of the superordinate clause is the same as the implied prepositional complement in an infinitive clause (cf. 12.4):

[9]   *Buses* are well lit, *easy to see into* from outside, and pick up and set down passengers at regular intervals, reducing the chances of violence or robbery. [W] ('It is easy to see *into buses*')

[10]   they're rather nice to look at as you'll see later ... I hope ('It's rather nice to look *at them*')

12.9.2.3 The subject of the superordinate clause is the same as the implied prepositional complement in an -*ing* participle clause (cf. 12.4.4):

[11]   Well *the swimming pool*'s not *worth talking about* ('It's not worth talking *about the swimming pool*')

12.9.3 **Stranding resulting from fronting of complement**

The complement of the preposition is **fronted** in three types of construction.

12.9.3.1 *Wh*-questions Cf. 2.5

[12]   *What* did you have it *on*

[13]   *Which part*'s he *from*

[14]   *Who* is it *by*

[15]   *How long* did you do English *for*

12.9.3.2 **Relative clauses** Cf. 10.9

[16]   Uhm ... had an exhibition *which* I forgot to invite you *to*

[17] So anyway ... then I found out he was going out with a woman *that* I was going out *with* you know

If the relative clause has a **zero relative** (cf. 10.9), the prepositional complement is of course absent:

[18] They may have to say that's the direction we were going *in* ('... the direction *that* we were going *in*')

The preposition must be stranded in relative clauses if the relative is *that* **[17]** or zero **[18]** since the preposition can only precede a *wh*-relative. In *wh*-questions and in relative clauses with a *wh*-relative there is usually a choice. Generally, the prepositional complement alone is fronted and the preposition is stranded, as in **[12]**–**[16]**. In a usually more formal alternative, the preposition is fronted with its complement in a *wh*-question **[19]** or relative clause **[20]**:

[19] First of all *to what companies* does that scheme apply

[20] There can't be many other countries for example where the retail price of a loaf of bread is lower than the wholesale cost of the ingredients *from which* it's made

If the *wh*-question or relative clause is long, the preposition is more likely to be fronted. Contrast **[21]** with **[21a]**:

[21] You find me preparing for a concert organized by friends *at which* for half an hour I will be reading one of my poems to an audience 1000% of the size of the normal audience for poetry. [W]

[21a] You find me preparing for a concert organized by my friends *which* I will be reading one of my poems *at*.

12.9.3.3 **Nominal relative clauses**

The relative in a **nominal relative clause** (cf. 14.3) must always come first in that clause. The relative may be the same as the implied prepositional complement:

[22] I think that's *what* everybody ... hopes for ... within a working situation ... uhm ('Everybody hopes *for that*')

[23] *Whatever* you want to look *at*'s there really ('You may want to look *at that*')

[24] I remember ... long long ago telling my publishers that that's *who* I would like to be *like* ('I would like to be *like that person*')

A preposition can precede a nominal relative clause, but then the whole clause is the complement of the preposition:

[25] I was just wondering if it was worth complaining *to whoever was in charge* or not bothering ('*She* was in charge')

[26] It's quite another for them to imagine that they can transfer or share the contract *with whoever they choose* (cf: 'They will choose *him*')

In **[25]** *whoever* is the subject of the clause, whereas in **[26]** it is the object and could be replaced by the more formal *whomever*.

12.10 Functions of prepositional phrases

12.10.1 **Postmodifier of a noun**

[1] Everybody questions the significance *of the results*

12.10.2 **Postmodifier of an adjective** Cf. 12.4

[2] And also it is alleged that uh he was ignorant *of the crucial lack of an extradition treaty*

12.10.3 **Subject predicative** Cf. 3.6

[3] Yesterday the sun was just as it is *in India*

12.10.4 **Object predicative** Cf. 3.7

[4] From the time I brought her *out of hospital* she never slept

12.10.5 **Adverbial** Cf. 3.8

[5] Every Tuesday I stood there waiting *by the door* expecting you to come

Prepositional verbs (cf. 11.20) and **phrasal-prepositional verbs** (cf. 11.21) can be analysed alternatively as verbs with prepositional phrases. In that case the prepositional phrase is also a complement of the verb:

12.10.6 **Complement of a verb** Cf. 3.8

[6] It was *in the process of going through*

Citations [7]–[9] contain **multi-word verbs** that have a preposition as a component (cf. 11.18, 11.20f.). These can also be analysed as single verbs with a prepositional phrase as their complement:

[7] Did you apply *for anything* in the final year

[8] No-one will blame you *for a genuine mistake* [W]

[9] Have the police *come up with* anything yet? [Valerie Kershaw *Rockabye*]

One argument in favour of this alternative analysis is that it is possible to separate the verb from the preposition by inserting an adverb or other linguistic unit between the two:

[10] But I look forward *tonight* to a thorough debate on the orders ... and on all aspects raised by the establishment of the new bank

[11] And the free world has reacted *quickly* to this momentous process and must continue to do so if it is to help and influence events

[12] We've been waiting *for so long* for it

Another argument in favour of the alternative analysis is that it is possible to coordinate the prepositional phrases:

[13] And and they were drawing inspiration *not from Palladio ... not from Lutyens ... not even always from le Corbusier ... but from car production hovercraft balloons robots*

[14] The path followed by such an oceanic current depends *partly on the difference in temperature between the equator and the poles, partly on the effect of the Earth's rotation, and partly on the shape of the ocean basin itself.* [John Gribbin *Hothouse Earth*]

The conjunction can also appear simply in front of a phrase that is not coordinated to another phrase:

[15] Fish could be seen feeding *but not on hook baits.* [David Batten *An Introduction to River Fishing*]

12.11 Premodifiers of prepositions and prepositional phrases

Prepositions may be premodified by intensifiers. Here are some examples:

[1] I don't think there's anything *quite* like Toblerone

[2] It's *so* near Christmas it's unbelievable

[3] The contribution of modern genetics has shown however that the genetic code is really a fundamental organising principle and there is a radical unity *long* before the fourteen-day stage

[4] The choir is placed *sharply* above the nave [Paul Johnson *Cathedrals of England, Scotland and Wales*]

[5] This stance was somewhat hypocritical, as for many years, indeed *ever* since the war, all the major investment decisions in the industry had been agreed by, and, in the main, financed by, government. [Peter Thompson *Sharing the Success*]

[6] A button labelled Layer/Active, handily located *just* below the Tone Buttons, allows you to switch between the two functions. [*Music Technology*]

In some instances the intensifiers modify the whole prepositional phrase rather than the preposition. In such instances the prepositional phrases are close in meaning to adjective phrases:

[7] I mean ... you were *very* on time

[8] Your heroines are *very much* of a type aren't they

[9] Of course he was *all* for that and so was his family

[10] What is happening is *perfectly* in order

[11] Notice how this section is *somewhat* at odds with the earlier part of the chapter

[12] I supposed they must be friends, because they were *so* at their ease, and always seemed to be involving themselves with my mother. [Ronald Frame *Bluette*]

Part 5
Sentences and Clauses

Chapter 13
Clause Relationships

Summary

The notional definition of a sentence as expressing a complete thought is too vague. Preference is given to a formal definition of a sentence as consisting of one or more grammatically complete clauses. Complete sentences are distinguished from elliptical sentences, unfinished sentences, and non-sentences.

Clauses may be linked through coordination or subordination. Coordinated clauses are at the same grammatical level. Subordinate clauses are dependent on other clauses, either embedded in them or loosely attached to them.

Traditionally, sentences are classified as simple (consisting of one main clause without subordination), compound (consisting of two or more main clauses that are coordinated), and complex (consisting of a main clause with one or more subordinate clauses). The classification is a simplification that does not take account of various patterns of coordination and subordination. The distinction between coordination and subordination can be subsumed under the broader distinction between parataxis and hypotaxis.

Orthographic sentences are not necessarily the same as grammatical sentences, which are identified with a cluster of clauses (minimally one) that are interrelated by coordination or subordination.

Coordination and subordination can sometimes express similar meaning relationships.

Coordination is signalled by the actual or potential presence of coordinators between clauses.

Subordination is generally signalled by subordinators and *wh*-words. Non-finite and verbless clauses are generally subordinate.

13.1 Complete and incomplete sentences

The traditional definition of a sentence states that a sentence expresses a complete thought. The trouble with this notional definition is that it requires us to know what a complete thought is. Does *God* or *our home* express complete thoughts? Is there just one complete thought in [1]?

[1]   Some 4,000 people (most of whom had heard about, but not actually read the book) wrote to Dr Robinson, telling him of their own faith, beliefs, convictions, feelings, or special knowledge concerning matters religious. [Eileen Barker 'New Lines in the Supra-Market: How Much Can We Buy?' in Ian Hamnett *Religious Pluralism and Unbelief*]

We can easily rewrite [1] as at least three separate sentences, each complete in itself:

[1a]   Some 4,000 people wrote to Dr Robinson. They told him of their own faith, beliefs, convictions, feelings, or special knowledge concerning matters religious. Most of them had heard about, but not actually read the book.

Similarly, [2] can be rewritten as two complete sentences:

[2]   An example of conforming individualism was recently provided for me by my daughter when I noticed that she was wearing only one ear-ring. [Eileen Barker 'New Lines in the Supra-Market: How Much Can We Buy?' in Ian Hamnett *Religious Pluralism and Unbelief*]

[2a]   An example of conforming individualism was recently provided for me by my daughter. It happened when I noticed that she was wearing one ear-ring.

We rightly feel that **[1]** and **[2]** have a unity and completeness, but we have the same feeling about the three sentences in **[1a]** and the two sentences in **[2a]**. What gives us that feeling is not that each sentence expresses one complete thought but that each sentence is grammatically complete.

We can distinguish the following four types of utterance:

1. complete sentences
2. elliptical sentences
3. unfinished sentences
4. non-clauses

13.1.1 The clause

The measure of grammatical completeness is the clause. The canonical sentence consists of one or more grammatically complete clauses. That is to say, each clause contains the constituents that must be present according to the general rules for constructing clauses—**subject, verb**, and **complements** of the verb (cf. 3.1)—except that the understood subject *you* is generally omitted in imperative sentences (cf. 2.7). Citation **[3]** is a simple sentence consisting of just one grammatically complete clause, and citation **[4]** is a sentence consisting of two grammatically complete clauses coordinated by *and*:

[3]   The conquest of Italy was certainly not a process of enslavement. [P. A. Brunt *Roman Imperial Themes*]

[4]   Some peoples were actually given Roman citizenship, *and* their chief men secured high office at Rome. [P. A. Brunt *Roman Imperial Themes*]

The writer of **[4]** could have punctuated the two clauses as separate orthographic sentences, the second sentence beginning with *and*, but they would remain grammatically linked by *and*. If the **coordinator** *and* is omitted, the two clauses constitute two independent sentences.

In **[5]**, by contrast, the subject *The Romans themselves* is shared by two predicates, one beginning *saw* and the other beginning *traced*:

[5]   *The Romans themselves* saw in this practice a major factor in their rise to world power *and* traced it back to the legendary origins of their city. [P. A. Brunt *Roman Imperial Themes*]

It is normal for the second subject to be omitted in such instances. We could say that **[5]** consists of two clauses: a complete clause (which could also be an independent sentence) and an incomplete clause—incomplete because the subject is omitted, though understood from the previous clause. Another way of analysing the sentence is to say that the sentence contains one subject and two coordinated predicates. This kind of analysis—stipulating coordination of parts of the sentence rather than ellipsis of parts—is adopted in this chapter wherever possible.

13.1.2 Ellipsis

There are incomplete sentences where it would be reasonable to posit ellipsis.

13.1.2.1 If the interpretation depends on the situational context, we have situational ellipsis. For example, **[6]** and **[7]** were uttered during a word game.

[6]   Haven't got one

[7]   Got an e

The interpretation of the ellipted subject as *I* in **[6]** and of the ellipted subject and auxiliary as *I've* in **[7]** depends on the situation, since the same incomplete sentences could have different ellipted words in a different situation: say, *we* in **[6]** or *she's* in **[7]**.

13.1.2.2 The other major type of ellipsis is **textual ellipsis**, which depends crucially on the linguistic context: we recover the ellipted words from what has been said or written before or after the ellipsis. In **[8]**, the elliptical sentence in B's utterance is interpreted by reference to the immediately preceding utterance by A:

[8]   A: You told me at the time ...
          B: Did I

Did I is incomplete since the main verb and its possible complements are missing. We readily understand *Did I* to mean roughly 'Did I tell you at that time?'

13.1.2.3 Elliptical sentences are incomplete sentences, but they are perfectly normal and acceptable. They are subject to rules. For example, while *Did I* is an acceptable response by speaker B in **[8]**, *Did* or *I* would be distinctly odd in that context. Elliptical sentences are particularly common in spoken dialogue and in written representations of dialogue.

13.1.3 **The unfinished sentence**

A different type of incomplete sentence, very common in speech, is the unfinished sentence. Speakers may fail to complete a sentence for a variety of reasons. For example, they may restart a sentence to correct themselves **[9]**, or they may become nervous, excited, or hesitant **[10]**, or they may lose the thread of what they are saying **[11]**, or they may be interrupted by another speaker **[12]**:

[9]   Right Friday morning *I will I am supposed to* go see Mrs Girlock

[10]   Well *you put it* uh yeah you put it here

[11]   A: I mean he's a bit odd
           B: Mm ...
           A: *But* uh ... What was I saying God I've lost me thread ... *I wanted*
           B: About you wanted to keep the fea uh feature geometry stuff
           A: Oh yeah

[12]   A: Do you want to go and see the film that evening or ... just have the ...
           B: No

Unfinished sentences are not rule-governed, since speakers may fail to finish their sentences at any point. Grammars, therefore, cannot account for them. There are equivalents of unfinished sentences in writing, but writers have the opportunity to complete them or to delete them in the process of writing or at the later stage of editing.

13.1.4 **Complete non-clauses**

Many utterances in speech are not analysable in terms of clause structures. They are complete in themselves, but they are non-clauses.

13.1.4.1 Particularly common are **backchannels**, items intended to encourage the other speaker to continue, often also expressing agreement. Most frequent among these are *yes* and its variants (such as *yeah*) and *uh* and its variants (such as *uhm*). They may constitute complete utterances, in that they are all that a speaker says at that point in the conversation:

[13] A: I mean she fell in love with him
B: *Yes*
A: the fifteen year old him
B: *Yes*
A: back in time
B: *Yes*

[14] A. … I'm afraid that I'm not going to hear him if he wakes up and I
B: *um*
A: don't want Jim to always be the one to get up and take care of him if he's up
B: *mm-hmm*
A: in the middle of the night

After a negative sentence *no* can also be used as a backchannel and to express agreement:

[15] A: I don't know what else I'll go to though …
B: *No* …
A: Because the thing is I'm going to be absolutely knackered

Numerous other items are used as backchannels. They include *exactly, fine, good, okay, really, right, sure,* and interjections such as *ah, oh, uhuh* (sometimes combined with other words, as in *oh dear*). Some backchannels take the form of clauses, for example: *that's right, that's true, I see, I know.* Combinations also occur, such as *yes I know, well that's true.* Most of the non-clausal items, as well as others, may be used primarily as reactions to previous utterances to convey sentiments such as agreement, disagreement, acceptance, refusal, reservation, surprise. They may be linked to a following clause by conjunctions: *yes, if …*; *sure, and …*; *oh, but …* Clauses such as *you know* and *you see* are intended to elicit support from listeners.

13.1.4.2 Other non-clausal utterances that commonly occur in conversation include greetings (e.g. *hello, good afternoon, happy birthday*) and expletives (e.g. *gosh, damn, good*). Some phrases, particularly noun phrases, stand alone as speech acts and the force they convey is clear in the situational context, though they cannot be analysed as elliptical clauses because we cannot be sure what has been elliptted. For example: *Taxi!, Fire!* (noun), *Your place or mine?, Next, Not a sound.* In print too, non-clausal language may appear in informal letters, notices, headlines, headings, titles of publications, and labels.

The types of non-clausal examples that have been outlined are perfectly normal and acceptable, and they can be analysed for their phrase structure: *Happy Birthday,* for example, is a noun phrase in which the noun *Birthday* is the head and the adjective *Happy* is its premodifier.

13.2 Coordination of clauses

Clauses may be related through coordination or subordination. **Coordinated** clauses are linked at the same grammatical level.

Two or more clauses may be coordinated to form a sentence. Such a sentence is traditionally termed a **compound sentence**, and the coordinated clauses are the **main clauses** of the sentence.

13.2.1 **Two coordinated clauses**

In **[1]** there are two main clauses coordinated by *and*:

[1]   The cause of ice ages is still a controversial subject, *and* debates continue about the precise climatic effects of individual cycles. [W]

The relationship of clauses is displayed in **Fig. 13.2.1**. The triangles represent the clauses, and M in the triangles stands for 'main clause'.

Fig. 13.2.1 Coordination of two main clauses: Sentence [1]

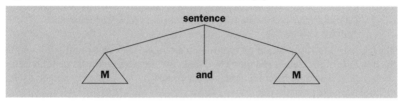

13.2.2 **Multiple coordinated clauses**

In **[2]** there are three coordinated main clauses:

[2]   Crime was awful, test scores were low, *and* there was no enrollment in honors programs. [*Wall Street Journal*]

The clause composition of **[2]** is represented in **Fig. 13.2.2**.

Figure 13.2.2 Coordination of three main clauses: Sentence [2]

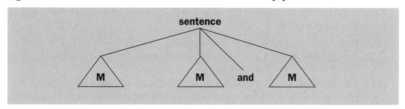

The three coordinated clauses are on the same level of coordination, but often two of the coordinated clauses are more closely linked and as a pair they are coordinated with the remaining clause. In **[3]**–**[4]**, the first two clauses form a pair that is coordinated with the third—clearly indicated in **[4]** by the reinforcing initial *Either*.

[3]   Money is not everything, *but* it is necessary, *and* business is not volunteer work. [*Wall Street Journal*]

[4]   *Either* defend the status quo *and* stop complaining about the resulting costs, *or* rethink the status quo. [*Wall Street Journal*]

In **[5]**–**[6]**, the first clause is coordinated with the pair that follows it—indicated in **[6]** by the comma at the end of the first clause and the absence of a comma between the last two clauses:

[5]　We have tried to train the youngsters, *but* they have their discos and their dances, *and* they just drift away. [*Wall Street Journal*]

[6]　Please read my enclosures carefully, *and* select the most appropriate option *and* return the papers to me. [W]

13.2.3 Syndetic and asyndetic coordination

Coordination may be either syndetic or asyndetic. It is **syndetic** when coordinators are present, as in **[1]**–**[6]**. It is **asyndetic** when coordinators are not present but can readily be inserted, for example, between the three units of **[7]** that are separated by semicolons. The sentence in **[7]** lists the results of damage to the ozone layer in the upper atmosphere.

[7]　Agricultural crops would be scorched, and yields would fall; marine plankton would be seriously affected; human health would suffer (there would be more eye cataracts, more problems arising from damage to people's body immune systems.) [*Geography*]

The first part of **[7]** consists of two coordinated clauses. They constitute a unit within the structure of the clause, and their closer links are signalled by the syndetic coordination by *and*. The final parenthetic clause elaborates on the damage to human health mentioned in the previous clause.

13.2.4 Coordination of predicates

Coordination of predicates is usual when the subject is shared:

[8]　Criminals prefer anonymity *and* are less likely to get to work where there is a chance of being recognised. [W]

[9]　Incorrect inflation pressures will cause abnormal tyre wear *and* may result in premature failure. [Ivor Carroll *Autodata Car Manual: Peugeot 309*]

In **[10]** the passive auxiliary *was* is shared and in **[11]** the modal auxiliary *will* is shared, in both cases together with the subject:

[10]　The Lorillard spokeswoman said asbestos was used in 'very modest amounts' in making paper for the filters in the early 1950s *and* replaced with a different type of filter in 1956. [*Wall Street Journal*]

[11]　A strong solution around their newly developing roots will upset their osmotic balance *and* stop them developing properly. [Nick Branwell *How Does Your Garden Grow?*]

13.2.5 Gapping

Gapping is a type of ellipsis that sometimes occurs in the middle of a coordinated clause. It affects the second clause and subsequent clauses. The main verb and/or an auxiliary is ellipted, possibly with any preceding auxiliaries and a following verb complement, such as a direct object, and an adverbial. The place of the gap is marked by a caret in the following examples. In **[12]** the main verb *is* is ellipted, in **[13]** the same main verb is ellipted in the second and third clauses, in **[14]** two auxiliaries—*will be*—are ellipted, and similarly in **[15]** two auxiliaries—*may be*—are ellipted.

[12]　But because individual amounts are relatively small *and* the occurrence ^ commonplace, not much fuss is made. [*BBC Wildlife*]

[13] The effect is of instability, in tone, literary register, genre, and idiom, the result ^ impermeability rather than clarity, *and* Beckett's language ^ a record of disruption rather than communication. [Leslie Hill *Beckett's Fiction*]

[14] The major criticism will then be presented, *and* counter arguments ^ considered. [W]

[15] Frequently this covering may comprise large filamentous algae such as Phormidium or Stigeoclonium, and under these conditions the distribution of flow may be impaired *and* the ventilation ^ decreased. [N. J. Horan *Biological Wastewater Treatment Systems*]

13.2.6 Final ellipsis

The first coordinated clause may have final ellipsis. In speech there is usually a distinct intonation break at the point of ellipsis and in the parallel point in the last of the co-ordinated clauses. In writing, these points are often marked by punctuation. In **[16]** the auxiliary *have* is at the point of ellipsis:

[16] We have ^, *and* I am sure others have, considered what our options are. [*Wall Street Journal*]

Final ellipsis with three coordinated clauses is exemplified in **[16a]**:

[16a] We have ^, you have ^, *and* I am sure others have, considered what our options are.

13.3 Subordination of clauses

13.3.1 **Subordinate clause as constituent of a clause**

Subordinate clauses can be constituents of other clauses. For example, they may function as subject **[1]**, or as complement of a verb **[2]**–**[5]**:

[1] *Whether he speaks or not* remains to be seen

[2] I've never wanted *to be a writer at all*

[3] No I've enjoyed *doing it*

[4] Do you think *that's possible*

[5] Guy the incredible thing is *that you've now written this year music for all Shakespeare's plays*

13.3.2 **Subordinate clause as constituent of a phrase**

Subordinate clauses can also be constituents of phrases. For example, they may function as **postmodifier** within a noun phrase **[6]**, as complement of a preposition **[7]**, or as complement of an adjective **[8]**:

[6] It's caused by two germs *that live together ... and scratch each other's back*

[7] You seem to have a capacity for *handling stress*

[8] By then I was sure *that he was not going to leave the Department* [Lord Young *The Enterprise Years*]

NOTE

If verb phrases include complements of the verbs, as in some analyses, then the subordinate clauses in **[2]**–**[5]** would also be constituents of phrases.

13.3.3 **Loosely attached subordinate clauses**

Subordinate clauses that function as subject, complement, or postmodifier are **embedded** within their **host** clause or host phrase. However, two types of subordinate clauses are attached to their clause in varying degrees of looseness: **adverbial clauses** and **non-restrictive relative clauses** (cf. 10.9f.). Both play a role in the semantics of interclausal relationships that is akin to the role played by coordinated clauses or juxtaposed clauses. Adverbial clauses are illustrated in **[9]**–**[10]** and non-restrictive relative clauses in **[11]**–**[12]**. The paraphrases below the examples demonstrate their resemblance to coordinated clauses or juxtaposed sentences:

[9]   *Although the lectures are called The Persistence of Faith* ... I did not speak about faith in the lectures

[9a]   The lectures are called The Persistence of Faith, *but* I did not speak about faith in the lectures.

[9b]   The lectures are called the Persistence of Faith. However, I did not speak about faith in the lectures.

[10]   Tears always come to my eyes *when I hear these notes*

[10a] I hear these notes *and* then tears always come to my eyes.

[11]   As anticipated, she queried your desire to stay in Sun City, *which has little to offer except gambling and 'dancing' girls.* [W]

[11a] As anticipated, she queried your desire to stay in Sun City. It has little to offer except gambling and 'dancing' girls.

[12]   The warnings, *issued to at least 100 criminal defense attorneys in several major cities in the last week,* have led to an outcry by members of the organized bar, *who claim the information is protected by attorney–client privilege.* [*Wall Street Journal*]

[12a] The warnings have led to an outcry by members of the organized bar. They were issued to at least 100 criminal defense attorneys in several major cities in the last week. The members of the organized bar claim the information is protected by attorney–client privilege.

The first of the relative clauses in **[12]** is a non-finite reduced relative clause (cf. 10.9).

13.4 The interplay of coordination and subordination

13.4.1 **Simple, compound, and complex sentences**

Traditionally, sentences are classified as simple, compound, or complex, depending on their clause composition.

13.4.1.1 A **simple sentence** consists of just one main clause:

[1]   The tears ran down my face. [Peter Akroyd *Dickens*]

A simple sentence need not be very short, since one or more of its phrases may be long; for example, the subject of the simple sentence in **[2]**:

[2] *A scattering of glass fragments beneath the streetlamp opposite it* confirmed her worst suspicions. [Marion Babson *Past Regret*]

> **NOTE**
>
> A subordinate clause may be embedded in a phrase (cf. 13.3). In one approach, the sentence is simple if the only subordinate clauses occurring in the sentence are in phrases. If complements of verbs are taken as constituents of phrases, this approach would extend the notion of simple sentence considerably.

13.4.1.2 A **compound sentence** consists of two or more main clauses, generally linked by a coordinator such as *and*:

[3] Somewhat to her surprise, the doorbell was working *and* she could hear the sharp peal on the other side of the door. [Marion Babson *Past Regret*]

13.4.1.3 A **complex sentence** contains one or more subordinate clauses:

[4] She looked towards the door, *as though Connie might materialize there at any second*. [Marion Babson *Past Regret*]

13.4.2 Clausal patterns in sentences

This triple classification is a simplification of the clausal patterns in sentences.

13.4.2.1 Subordination within coordination

There may be subordination within coordination. In **[5]**, for example, the second main clause (M) contains a subordinate (sub) *if*-clause at the end:

[5] I will be out of College for the next two weeks, *but* please contact me after this *if you have any queries*. [W]

Fig. 13.4.1. Subordinate clause within a main clause: Sentence [5]

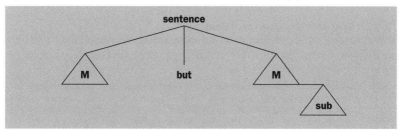

13.4.2.2 Coordination within subordination

Similarly, there may be coordination within subordination, as in **[6]** (where the subordinate clauses are final) and **[7]** (where they are initial):

[6] The military claim *that* all nuclear reactors have been destroyed *and that* fourteen chemical and biological factories and storage areas have been destroyed or heavily damaged

Fig. 13.4.2 Coordination of final subordinate clauses: Sentence [6]

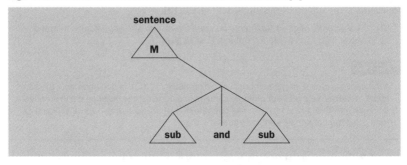

[7]   *Whether* this is necessary, *or whether* the prospect of being milked is sufficient inducement, is not yet known. [*Robotica*]

Fig. 13.4.3. Coordination of initial subordinate clauses: Sentence [7]

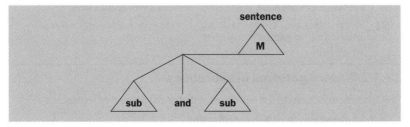

13.4.2.3 **Subordination within subordination**

There may be subordination within subordination. Sentence **[8]** contains a subordinate *if*-clause, which in turn contains a subordinate *because*-clause. The *if*-clause is host to the *because*-clause.

[8]   *If* you've been given a voucher *because* you have a low income, the value of your voucher may be reduced. [W]

13.4.2.4 **Coordination within coordination**

Similarly, there may be coordination within coordination. Sentence **[9]** consists of three main clauses. The last two clauses (coordinated by *and*) are more closely linked, and are at a lower level of coordination (cf. 6.2):

[9]   This variation on the meatball theme was originally made with veal, *but* in America and in this country veal can be hard to come by *and* turkey breast makes a surprisingly satisfactory substitute. [Michael Barry *The Crafty Food Processor Cook Book*]

Fig. 13.4.4. Subordination within subordination: Sentence [8]

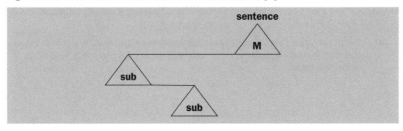

Fig. 13.4.5 Coordination within coordination: Sentence [9]

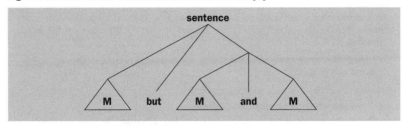

13.4.2.5 **Subordinate clause linked to two or more main clauses**

A subordinate clause may be linked jointly to two or more main clauses:

[10] *Whatever you decide on*, it must be convenient, acceptable and affordable, *or* you will not stick at it. [Rosemary Nicol *Everything You Need to Know About Osteoporosis*]

[11] *As Romanesque developed*, the roof of the structure was supported on piers *but* interior features were carried on the secondary support of columns. [Paul Johnson *Cathedrals of England, Scotland and Wales*]

[12] *Now that we have had advance warning*, I have put your information around the relative departments *and* we could build it in to next year's budget. [W]

[13] I'd go to that and I'd go to the Palmer one *if I was you*

We can represent [10] by **Fig. 13.4.6,**

Fig. 13.4.6 Initial subordinate clause linked by two main clauses: Sentence [10]

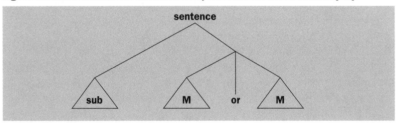

and [13] by **Fig. 13.4.7.**

Fig. 13.4.7. Final subordinate clause linked to two main clauses: Sentence [13]

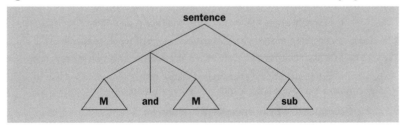

NOTE

An adverbial that is not a clause may also extend its scope to more than one main clause. Below, three coordinated main clauses are within the scope of the initial adverbial:

Here in wonderful London, the sun shines, the birds sing *and* the streets are still paved with gold. [W]

13.4.2.6 Parenthetic coordinated clause

A further complication is exhibited in sentence **[14]**. The *and*-clause is parenthetic, expressing an elaboration of the point made in the initial subordinate *when*-clause. The *and*-clause itself contains two subordinate *whether*-clauses that are linked by *or*.

[14]   When you tie a standard rose *and this applies to any standard rose whether you do it yourself or whether you buy it* you really need two ties on it

The structure of **[14]** can be represented by **Fig.13.4.8,** where the broken line indicates the parenthesis.

Fig. 13.4.8 Parenthetic *and*-clause containing coordination of subordinate clauses: Sentence [14]

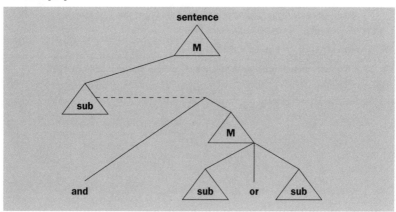

The second coordinated clause in **[15]** is similarly parenthetic. It expresses the stance that the writer is taking:

[15]   There is one thing that truly disturbs me, *and I speak as a Methodist clergyman.*

The clause can be paraphrased as a style disjunct, a type of sentence adverbial (cf. 8.7):

[15a] There is one thing that truly disturbs me, *speaking as a Methodist clergyman.*

By conveying the stance with a coordinated clause rather than an adverbial, it gains greater emphasis because it is more independent grammatically.

13.4.2.7 Subordinate clause embedded in a phrase

The subordinate clauses that we have considered so far have been embedded in, or attached to, a host clause, but subordinate clauses may also be embedded in a phrase. In

[16] the relative clause *she'd said this* is embedded as a postmodifier in the noun phrase *the first time she'd said this*:

> **[16]** This was absolutely the first time *she'd said this*. [W]

If we ignore details of its embedding, we can simply show it as a triangle linked by an arrow to the inside of the clause, as **Fig. 13.4.9**.

Fig. 13.4.9 Embedded relative clause: Sentence [16]

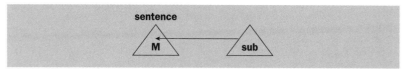

Here is a more complicated example of embedding in a phrase. In **[17]** there is one main clause. The verb of the sentence (*seek*) has an infinitive clause (beginning *to determine*) as its complement (more precisely, its direct object). That infinitive clause has as its direct object a noun phrase (beginning *the question*). The noun phrase has as its complement two coordinated clauses (both beginning *how far*) linked by *or*. The first of those clauses has an adverbial (beginning *as*).

> **[17]** I shall not seek to determine the question *how far aggression or fears of aggression by Carthage or by Hellenistic kingdoms or later by northern or eastern peoples provided Rome with motives, as they often provided pretexts, for expansion or how far the real cause of expansion must be sought in the mere desire for power and glory, or in greed for the profits of empire* [P. A. Brunt *Roman Imperial Themes*]

Fig. 13.4.10 Embedded coordinated clauses functioning as noun phrase complements: Sentence [17]

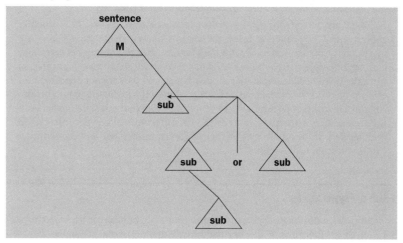

13.4.2.8 **Subordinate clauses in asyndetic coordination**

Finally, in **[18]** we see four *to*-infinitive clauses in asyndetic coordination (without a coordinator, cf. 13.2).

[18] Without compulsion, *though* sometimes encouraged by the Roman authorities, the natives began *to* adopt the Latin language, *to* build towns of the Italian type, *to* imitate Graeco-Roman architecture and sculpture, *to* copy the manners of the Romans. [P. A. Brunt *Roman Imperial Themes*]

Fig. 13.4.11. Four *to*-infinitive clauses in asyndetic coordination: Sentence [18]

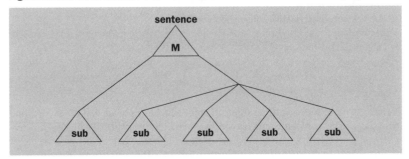

13.5 Parataxis and hypotaxis

The distinction between coordination and subordination can be encompassed under the broader distinction between parataxis and hypotaxis. **Parataxis** is the relation between two or more units of equal status, and **hypotaxis** is the relation between two units of unequal status, where one is dependent on the other.

PARATAXIS AND HYPOTAXIS BELOW CLAUSE LEVEL

Although here we are concerned with the relations between clauses, the distinction applies equally to structures below the level of clauses. Hence, *large houses* is a hypotactic structure, since *large* modifies *houses*. The relationship between *large* and *inexpensive* in *large inexpensive houses* or *large but inexpensive* is paratactic, since the two adjectives separately modify *houses* and they are not dependent on one another. On the other hand, *my first good meal* is a hypotactic construction, since *first* modifies *good meal* and not simply *meal*. Similarly, the relation between the premodifiers in the ambiguous *our French history teacher* is hypotactic; *French* is either dependent on *history* ('teacher of French history') or on *history teacher* ('history teacher who is French').

13.5.1 **Hypotaxis**

By definition a subordinate clause and its host clause or phrase are in a hypotactic relationship, since subordination implies that the two units are of unequal status.

13.5.2 **Parataxis**

Parataxis covers a variety of clause structures:

1. syndetically coordinated clauses
2. asyndetically coordinated clauses

3. juxtaposed clauses
4. a parenthetic clause and the clause to which it is attached
5. a tag question and the clause to which it is attached
6. a reported clause in direct speech and its reporting clause

13.5.2.1, 13.5.2.2 The coordination of clauses has been illustrated in 13.2 and 13.4. The coordination is overt in syndetic coordination, where a coordinator is present. The coordination is implicit in asyndetic coordination, since a coordinator can be inserted between the clauses.

13.5.2.3 **Juxtaposed clauses** are paratactically related clauses that do not imply coordination. In the written language the clauses may be set out as separate orthographic sentences, as in **[1]**:

[1] One wants as much information as it is possible to get. This is not the same as getting as much data as possible. The first decision to be made is how frequently recordings should be made. For example, one could record every minute of the operation and gain an enormous amount of data. [*International Journal of Project Management*]

However, the clauses may be linked by a comma or some other punctuation mark internal to an orthographic sentence so as to signal a close relationship between the clauses. In **[2]** a comma links the two juxtaposed clauses:

[2] I'll have to stop talking about the place, it's bringing tears to my cheeks. [W]

The second clause in **[2]** provides the reason for what is said in the first clause. We could therefore insert a subordinator such as *because* or *since* between the two clauses to make their relationship explicit. In **[3]** three punctuation marks link the four clauses in the orthographic sentence—a colon, a semicolon, and a dash:

[3] On organic farms, straw is used in a variety of ways: it can be fed to animals or used as bedding; it can also be used for roofing—thatchers claim that straw from organic farms is easier to work and lasts twice as long as the same stuff grown conventionally. [David Mabey et al. *Thorson's Organic Consumer Guide*]

The two clauses beginning *it* can be asyndetically coordinated. As a set, they are juxtaposed to the first clause, detailing the generalization made in that clause. The final clause is juxtaposed to the previous clause, explaining why organic straw is used for roofing. The two clauses in **[4]** provide a further example of juxtaposition:

[4] Things have been mad I haven't had a moment to myself

13.5.2.4 Independent **parenthetic clause**s (those not marked as coordinate or subordinate) enter into a paratactic relation with the host clause in which they are inserted:

[5] The ten per cent we pay our agent rewards him for settling the terms regarding billing, salary *(note the order in which an actor puts priorities)* and accommodation. [Graham Stark *Remembering Peter Sellars*]

[6] Barbara Hendricks is at her finest in the operatic numbers *(I loves you, Porgy is particularly eloquent)*, and the warm beauty of the voice gives much pleasure throughout the programme. [*The Penguin Guide to Compact Discs*]

[7] The first vehicle capable of reaching space—the V2 ballistic missile *(see right)*— demonstrates the essential simplicity of the principles behind the design of a rocket-propelled spacecraft. [David Ashford and Patrick Collins *Your Spaceflight Manual*]

Some expressions function in dialogue to convey various kinds of interaction with other speakers, such as a positive response or softening the impact of what is said. Some of these expressions are clauses that allow little or no variation in their form; for example: *I mean, I think, you know, you see*. They are loosely attached to their host clauses or inserted inside them:

[8]   But of course *you see I mean* if you say classical feature theory handles it then of course then you're back to all the old problems

13.5.2.5 Similar to the fixed parenthetical clause expressions in their interactive role are **tag questions** (cf. 2.6), which are generally intended to elicit confirmation or agreement from listeners:

[9]   It's up to Laura really *isn't it* ... in the end

[10]   I am a very strong swimmer but even the most confident swimmers can drown *can't they* my dear? [W]

13.5.2.6 **Reported clauses** function as syntactic units that are independent of the reporting clause (cf. 15.1). Reporting clauses may precede **[11]**, follow **[12]**, or interrupt **[13]** reported clauses:

[11]   He looked slowly round at the crew and said, 'Anyone know if it's raining in Rio?' [Graham Stark *Remembering Peter Sellars*]

[12]   'Blake Edwards is a sadist,' I said. [Graham Stark *Remembering Peter Sellars*]

[13]   'Why,' asked Blake, 'are you here?' [Graham Stark *Remembering Peter Sellars*]

Reported speech can consist of more than one sentence:

[14]   'Ah,' she said and looked at me with her huge dark eyes. 'Now if only Peter could give me a child like that I'd get pregnant tomorrow. The only trouble is . . .' her look now enveloped Peter as well, 'his children have turned out so badly.' [Graham Stark *Remembering Peter Sellars*]

13.6 Sentences and clause clusters

13.6.1 **In the written language**

The orthographic sentence is not necessarily identical with the grammatical sentence. For rhetorical reasons it may incorporate two or more grammatical sentences, which are perhaps separated by semicolons, colons, or dashes:

[1]   She was the widow of a curate from the south of France; with her daughter she kept a small day school and had a few paying guests. [W]

[2]   The problem is easily solved if they rotate their crops: wild oats, for instance, cannot survive in a field of grass. [David Mabey et al. *Thorson's Organic Consumer Guide*]

[3]   It all depends on the sun—a south-facing window will add more heat than it loses, winter or summer, though not always when you want it. [George Collard *Do-it-Yourself Home Surveying*]

Conversely, an orthographic sentence may be coterminous with a non-sentence or an incomplete sentence. Citation **[4]** is an extract from an informal personal letter, **[5]** from a newspaper editorial, **[6]** from a review in a newspaper:

[4]   Gill was also upset as they made no effort to speak to her new man. But enough of my news. What have you been doing this weekend? *Anything nice.* I'm trying to psyche myself up to do some computer theory revision. *BORING.* [W]

[5]   Resolve in the Gulf and determined leadership on the budget and the economy could still make Mr Bush the president nobody ever really thought he could be. The jury is still out, but not for long. *Your move, Mr President.* [*Sunday Times*]

[6]   The cigarettes she puffs on during the play are tobaccoless. *Herbal. Nonaddictive.*
[*International Herald Tribune*]

13.6.2 In the spoken language

The spoken language does not have oral sentences that correspond to the orthographic sentences of the written language. There are no equivalents in speech to the written signals of the beginnings and ends of orthographic sentences. Neither intonation nor pauses signal unequivocally the ends of speech units that might be thought to correspond to orthographic sentences. For that reason, some grammarians have preferred to abandon the term *sentence* for the grammatical structures of the spoken language. Instead, we might refer to clause clusters or clause complexes to denote the equivalents of the canonical grammatical sentence. A **clause cluster** is a set of clauses that are interrelated by coordination or subordination, or simply just one clause if it is not linked to other clauses.

> **NOTE**
>
> We could define a clause cluster as a set of clauses related by parataxis or hypotaxis, as Halliday does for clause complex. Certainly we would want to include within a clause cluster most of the paratactically related clauses listed in 13.5. There is, however, a problem with juxtaposed clauses. For example, should all the juxtaposed clauses in citation **[1]** in 13.5 be considered as belonging to one cluster, or just the two linked by *For example?* In the written language we might follow the clues provided by punctuation, so that citations **[2]** and **[3]** in 13.5 are regarded as having one cluster each because the clauses are linked by punctuation that is internal to an orthographic sentence. In the spoken language we may need to take account of intonation linkage that suggests that the cluster has not been completed. If we attempt to establish logical connections as the basis of a clause cluster, we may find ourselves designating a complete written text or speech as a cluster.

The following is taken from a broadcast discussion. The speaker has been called upon to contribute to the discussion:

[7] [a]   Yes I I think it's infinitely more entertaining

[b]   And I think the only real value of politics is that you should make people laugh …

[c]   And uh so therefore I think that it adds greatly to the gaiety of the nation

[d]   And what I think is is really funny about it is that these people are totally to follow the fiction that's written in the newspapers

[e]   I mean the newspapers make up a story

[f]   And then they obediently trot in and try and perform it

The extract consists of two clusters. The first cluster consists of four coordinated main clauses **[a]–[d]**, and the second of two coordinated main clauses **[e]–[f]**.

The next extract is more complicated. It is a private conversation between two speakers:

[8] [a]   A: We could come round with a bottle of something *and* I could bring the odd bottle of cider

[b]   B: We could do that *but* then I can't actually take you to the station …

[c]   A: Uhm oh that's true

[d]   *Or* Coke Coke will do …

[e]   B: Yes

[f]   I could probably manage to take you back to the station on some Coke

Each of the first two clusters **[a]** and **[b]** consists of two coordinated main clauses. The third cluster **[c]** is a simple clause preceded by interjections. The fourth cluster **[d]** begins with the coordinator *or*, but *or* does not link to the immediately preceding clause; it in fact presents an alternative to what is said in the second main clause of **[a]**: *I could bring the odd bottle of cider. Or* in **[d]** is equivalent to *alternatively* and might be regarded as a connective adverb rather than as a true coordinator. *Yes* **[e]** is a response item—a non-sentence, since it does not have clause structure. The fifth cluster **[f]** is one main clause with a subordinate *to*-infinitive clause.

We could generally refer to clause clusters instead of sentences, even for the written language, so as to avoid confusing grammatical sentences with orthographic sentences. But *sentence* is preferred in this book to *clause cluster* because it is familiar to readers.

13.7 Meaning relationships in coordination and subordination

Similar meaning relationships are sometimes expressed through coordination and subordination. In **[1]** the subordinate *while*-clause is concessive and contrastive in meaning:

[1]   *While* some politicians and communicators may identify themselves with some transnational culture, many of them are great patriots. [William Bloom *Personal Identity, National Identity and International Relations*]

A similar meaning can be conveyed through coordination with *but*:

[1a]   Some politicians and communicators may identify themselves with some transnational culture, *but* many of them are great patriots.

The second clause may be juxtaposed and may more explicitly show the relationship through a conjunct such as *however*:

[1b]   Some politicians and communicators may identify themselves with some transnational culture. *However*, many of them are great patriots.

In **[2]** the clauses are in a cause–effect relation. They are asyndetically coordinated, linked by the conjunct *so* ('therefore'):

[2]   The economies are too small to supply a large range of products now universally sought and desired, *so* these have to be imported, at great cost relative to the money earned by the primary sector. [Peter Calvert and Susan Calvert *Latin America in the Twentieth Century*]

The two clauses could be syndetically coordinated by *and*: '*and so* these have to be imported'. Alternatively, the first clause could be subordinated, introduced by (for example) *since*, and the redundant conjunct *so* would then be omitted.

The cause–effect relationship in **[2]** can be emphasized by making the second clause explicitly identify the relationship:

[2a]   The economies are too small to supply a large range of products now universally sought and desired. *That is why* these have to be imported, at great cost relative to the money earned by the primary sector.

Again, the two clauses can also be coordinated: *and that is why*.

Coordination, syndetic or asyndetic, is an option that is also available for the time relation exemplified in [3]:

[3]   *When* Monsieur Savlon came back to clear the table he asked me in perfectly good
      English, 'You do not like snails?' [Agnes Owens 'Patience' in Alison Fell *The Seven
      Cardinal Virtues*]

The subordinator *when* makes the time relation explicit. If the clauses are coordinated by *and*, the assumption is that the two events (his return to the table and his question) are in chronological order:

[3a] Monsieur Savlon came back to clear the table *and* he asked me in perfectly good
      English, 'You do not like snails?'

Since the two clauses share an identical subject, it would be possible to omit the second subject *he*, so that we would now have coordination of the predicates. Alternatively, the two clauses could be set out as two orthographic sentences, and optionally *then* could be inserted after the subject *he* to make explicit the time relation between the clauses.

Similar meaning relationships can be conveyed at the level below the clause through nominalizations—noun phrases that correspond to clauses. For example, corresponding roughly to [3] is [3b], where *return* is a noun converted from the verb *return*:

[3b] *On Monsieur Savlon's return to clear the table* he asked me in perfectly good
      English, 'You do not like snails?'

Coordination (syndetic or asyndetic) and juxtaposition put the clauses on the same grammatical level. Syndetic coordination emphasizes their connection. Subordination downgrades the subordinate clause grammatically in relation to the host clause or host phrase, and nominalization provides a further downgrading to the level of the phrase.

13.8 Signals of coordination

Coordination of clauses is signalled by the presence of a **coordinator** between the clauses (syndetic coordination) or by the potentiality for its presence (asyndetic coordination, cf. 13.2).

13.8.1 *And* and *or*

The central coordinators are *and* and *or*. They alone can link more than two clauses at the same level, and all but the final instance of the coordinator are then usually omitted. Thus in [1] *or* links four *to*-infinitive clauses:

[1]   On the other hand I long to travel, to get out of London, to go to America *or* just to
      see wide open unspoilt spaces. [W]

In **polysyndetic** coordination, the coordinator *and* or *or* is repeated, contrary to normal practice. The effect is to emphasize the individuality of each of the clauses:

[2]   Columba then prophesied that he would become a beggar *and* that his son would
      run from house to house with a half empty bag *and* that he would die in the trench
      of a threshing-floor. [W]

13.8.2 *But*

The other clear coordinator is *but*. Unlike the central coordinators, it can link only two clauses at the same level. Like them, it can also link subordinate clauses:

[3]   When my plate was clean I asked her if she would mind telling him when she got the chance *that* I couldn't stand snails or garlic, *but that* this was no reflection on his excellent cooking. [Agnes Owens 'Patience' in Alison Fell *The Seven Cardinal Virtues*]

[4]   Cut the meat into even-sized cubes, leaving on any fat *but* removing all gristle. [Michael Barry *The Crafty Food Processor Cook Book*]

13.8.3 *For* and *so that*

There are several other items that are sometimes considered to be coordinators. *For* and *so that* ('with the result that') resemble the coordinators in not allowing a coordinator to precede them. We cannot, for example, add a second *for*-clause in [5] linking it to the first by *and, or, but*:

[5]   'It doesn't matter,' I said, *for* I didn't want to admit that I sometimes feel shy with foreigners. [Agnes Owens 'Patience' in Alison Fell *The Seven Cardinal Virtues*]

By contrast, we can coordinate two *because*-clauses:

[6]   However, *because* in many cases the condition is well controlled by medication *and because* sufferers don't necessarily like to talk about their illness, most people are not aware of the extent of epilepsy in the population. [Ruth Lever *A Guide to Common Illnesses*]

For and *so that* can link only main clauses. Unlike the coordinators, they cannot link subordinate clauses or parts of clauses.

13.8.4 *Nor* and *yet*

Other putative coordinators are *nor* and *yet*. Both of these can be preceded by a co-ordinator:

[7]   So you didn't have a lot of religious pressure *but nor* did you have a lot of religious thought

[8]   But the fact is you're part of an alliance *and yet* you are acting unilaterally

Because they can themselves be preceded by coordinators, both *nor* and *yet* are better regarded as adverbs, more specifically **conjuncts** (conjunctive adverbs, cf. 8.7). In the absence of a coordinator, clauses linked by *nor*, *yet*, and other conjuncts are asyndetically coordinated:

[9]   It's been available now for two decades *yet* in that time a hundred million children have died from diarrhoea

> **NOTE**
>
> Many Americans cannot use *nor* with a coordinator. For them, *nor* itself is a coordinator. However, it differs from the other coordinators in that, like *neither*, it causes subject—operator inversion, as in [7] in 13.8.4.

13.8.5 *However, therefore,* and *nevertheless*

Conjuncts such as *however, therefore,* and *nevertheless* are more removed from the coordinator class because they need not be positioned at the beginning of their clause:

[10] None of France's wine regions can steal a march on Burgundy, *however.* [*Wall Street Journal*]

[11] But not all concerted action is *therefore* ineffectual. [*Wall Street Journal*]

Like *nor* and *yet*, their clauses can be linked by coordinators:

[12] The early evidence suggests the strategy has worked *but nevertheless* Iraq's surviving aircraft and huge quantities of guns and missiles will be more effective in daylight

13.9 Signals of subordination

There are two types of signals that a clause is subordinate: the identity of the initial item in the clause and the nature of the verb phrase or its absence.

13.9.1 **Initial item**

A clause is subordinate if it is introduced by a **subordinator** (or subordinating conjunction) such as *if, because,* and *although* (cf. 9.1). Certain subordinate clauses are introduced by **wh-words** (cf. 14.3). Some of these *wh*-words are used only with subordinate clauses; for example: *whoever, whatever, however.* Others may also be used with interrogative main clauses; for example: *who, which, when, where, why, how.*

The subordinators *as, that,* and *though* are exceptional in that they occasionally do not come at the beginning of their clauses (cf. concessive clauses in 14.5.7).

That may be either a subordinator like *whether* [1] or a **relative pronoun** like *which* [2]:

[1] We decided *that* we would work together

[2] I very much enjoyed the work *that* I was involved in

As a subordinator, *that* can usually be omitted ('**zero that**') when its clause is not functioning as subject:

[1a] We decided we would work together.

In [1a] there is no overt signal of subordination for the complement *we would work together,* but we could point to the option of inserting the subordinator *that.* As a relative pronoun, *that* is functioning in place of *wh*-relative pronouns:

[2a] I very much enjoyed the work *which* I was involved in.

Like the subordinator, relative *that* can often be omitted ('**zero relative**'):

[2b] I very much enjoyed the work I was involved in.

Again, the covert signal of subordination in [2b] is the optionality of inserting *that.*

13.9.2 **Verb phrase**

Subject–operator inversion may signal subordination without a subordinator, mainly in **conditional clauses** (cf. 14.5.3):

[3]   It acts as a metaphor representing his early awakening for literature which could have been channelled into something better *had he been taught how.* [W] ('if he had been taught how')

If the verb in a clause is non-finite [4] or if there is no verb [5], the clause is generally subordinate (cf. 14.1):

[4]   She paused, sighed winsomely, *looking aged.* [Paul Sayer *Howling at the Moon*]

[5]   He began running, feeling light and purposeful, scarcely seeming to touch the pavement with his feet, *his heart strong and amazingly compliant with his sudden awakening.* [Paul Sayer *Howling at the Moon*]

Chapter 14
Subordinate Clauses

Summary

Summary

Subordinate clauses are finite, non-finite, or verbless. The verb in a non-finite clause is an -*ing* participle, an -*ed* participle, an infinitive preceded by *to*, or a bare infinitive. Non-finite and verbless clauses may have their own subject or may be subjectless.

Subordinate clauses function as nominal clauses, relative clauses, adverbial clauses, or comparative clauses.

Nominal clauses are declarative, interrogative, exclamative, or nominal relative.

Adverbial clauses express a range of meanings: place, time, condition, circumstance, concession, reason or cause, purpose, result, manner, proportion, similarity, and comment.

Comparative clauses involve a standard of comparison and a basis of comparison. Comparatives are inflected forms or phrases constructed with *more*. They are used with a postmodifying *than*-clause to express higher degrees of comparison. Lower degrees are expressed by premodifying *less* with a postmodifying *than*-clause, and equivalent degrees by premodifying *as* with a postmodifying *as*-clause. Comparative clauses are often elliptical.

Nominal clauses can function as complements of verbs, adjectives, and nouns.

14.1 Forms of subordinate clause

14.1.1 **The three major forms**

There are three major forms of subordinate clause:

14.1.1.1 The **finite clause**, whose verb is a finite verb (cf. 11.3):

[1] *When we were walking over the bridge* Mary Jane stopped to take a shot of a woman on the other side of the road *who was dragging a child along by the hand.* [Agnes Owens 'Patience' in Alison Fell *The Seven Cardinal Virtues*]

14.1.1.2 The **non-finite clause**, whose verb is a non-finite verb (cf. 11.3):

[2] *To test the belt tension,* press the belt down at a point midway on the longest run between pulleys (Fig. A:25), *using firm thumb pressure.* [Ivor Carroll *Autodata Car Manual: Peugeot 309*]

14.1.1.3 The **verbless clause**, which does not have a verb:

[3] In accordance with the principles of direct play the ball should be thrown forward *where possible.* [Charles Hughes *The Winning Formula*]

14.1.2 **Forms of the non-finite and verbless clause**

The verb in a non-finite clause may take any of four non-finite forms and the clause may be with or without a subject:

14.1.2.1 -*ing* participle clause with subject:

[5] I don't see *a French writer voluntarily writing in English*

14.1.2.2 -*ing* participle clause without subject:

[6] Yes the thing is we we do notice very much that there's difficulty in *attracting younger members to the societies*

NON-FINITE AND VERBLESS CLAUSES IN DETAIL

Non-finite and verbless clauses are treated as clauses because we can analyse their structure in the same way as we analyse finite clauses. So in **[2]** the infinitive clause can be analysed as having a verb *to test* and a direct object *the belt tension*; similarly, the *-ing* participle clause has a verb *using* and a direct object *firm thumb pressure*. The analyses of the non-finite clauses can be compared with those for corresponding finite clauses (cf. 3.1ff.):

[2a]   You (S) test (V) the belt tension (O).

[2b]   You (S) use (V) firm thumb pressure (O).

The structure of the verbless clause *where possible* **[3]** can be analysed as having a conjunction *where* and a predicative *possible*. Compare the corresponding subordinate finite clause:

[3a]   Where [conj] that (S) is (V) possible (P)

A non-finite or verbless clause may be host to a finite clause:

[4]   'It doesn't matter,' I said, for I didn't want *to admit that I sometimes feel shy with foreigners.* [Agnes Owens 'Patience' in Alison Fell *The Seven Cardinal Virtues*]

The infinitive clause in **[4]** is host to the *that*-clause.

14.1.2.3 *-ed* participle clause with subject:

[7]   *This said,* the Isozaki scheme is not entirely without merit. [*British Journal of Aesthetics*]

14.1.2.4 *-ed* participle clause without subject:

[8]   *Unless otherwise stated* the tuition fees will be charged on a simple hourly rate.

14.1.2.5 *To*-infinitive clause with subject:

[9]   Uh well do you want *me to tell you the truth* ('that I should tell you the truth')

14.1.2.6 *To*-infinitive clause without subject:

[10]   And I just thought well now where shall I poke him *to wake him up*

14.1.2.7 Bare infinitive clause with subject:

[11]   But what made *him want to go to Disneyworld for the job*

14.1.2.8 Bare infinitive clause without subject:

[12]   I think it helps *support our style of policing structure*

14.1.2.9 Verbless clause with subject:

[13]   *No soldiers here*, although those waiting squads in trucks were only minutes away. [Mary Napier *Powers of Darkness*]

14.1.2.10 Verbless clause without subject:

[14]   Women, however, *although under subjection*, are not actually in a class of their own, but in an underrated grouping according to gender, which cuts across all classes. [Jennifer Breen *In Her Own Write*]

14.2 Functions of subordinate clauses

The functions of subordinate clauses can be consolidated into four major types:

1. Nominal clauses, which can have a range of functions similar to those of noun phrases (cf. 10.3)
2. Relative clauses, which postmodify noun phrases (cf. 10.9)
3. Adverbial clauses, which can have a range of functions similar to adverb phrases or prepositional phrases when these function as adverbials (cf. 12.6, 12.10)
4. Comparative clauses, which together with the comparative items *more, less,* or *as* or the comparative inflection *-er* function as intensifiers (cf. 12.3, 12.7).

14.2.1 **Functions of nominal clauses**

All **nominal clauses** (cf. 14.3) may have the following first two functions (subject and complement of the verb) in a host clause, and most nominal clauses may also have functions 14.2.1.3–14.2.1.5:

14.2.1.1 **Subject:**

[1] *That his people believe that after last night* is doubtful

[2] *Whether a stock offering is in the best interest of Mr. Wisner or his shareholders* is unanswerable. [*Wall Street Journal*]

[3] *To talk of it as a United States operation* simply misreads history or intentionally misinterprets history

[4] And *mastering this technique* can be a lot of fun

14.2.1.2 **Complement of a verb**, chiefly as direct object (cf. 3.4):

[5] Only nine per cent answered *that religious leaders played a significant part in their life*

[6] I don't know *what my mother would have done if we had not come out naturally bookish*

[7] I've never wanted *to be a writer* at all

[8] Depending on who comes, you'll possibly need to bring sleeping bags and I hope you don't mind *sleeping on the floor*. [W]

Most nominal clauses may also function as:

14.2.1.3 **Complement of an adjective** (cf. 12.4):

[9] It's strange, I don't look like my mother and everyone here presumes I'm Spanish and is surprised *that I don't speak a word*. [W]

[10] They are not sure *what did happen*

[11] I'm not quite sure *if that's right actually*

[12] And they say they're prepared *to take industrial action to back their demands for shorter hours*

> **NOTE**
>
> Unlike these nominal clauses, noun phrases functioning as complements of adjectives require linking prepositions: *surprised at that, sure of that, prepared for that.*

14.2.1.4 **Complement of a preposition** (cf. 12.9):

> **[13]** At the time of the original meeting nobody had any idea of *what would happen*
>
> **[14]** I'll come on to *when you went off to Germany* shortly
>
> **[15]** You seem to have a capacity for *handling stress*
>
> **[16]** You've talked in various articles over the years about *her making you feel utterly inadequate and and horrible*

14.2.1.5 **Complement of a noun** (cf. 14.7):

> **[17]** It had a lovely wood letter-rack and a sort of in-tray done in wood which I fancied despite the fact *that I haven't got anything to put in it*
>
> **[18]** Police say they can't confirm a TV report *that the building had been hit by automatic fire*
>
> **[19]** Many more people can look forward to a retirement in the knowledge *that in addition to the basic state retirement pension they will benefit from their employer or personal pension scheme*
>
> **[20]** And uh she then said well look uhm you because you're a national figure you've been in eight million homes tonight uh you really must get used to the idea *that people will come up to you*

14.2.2 Function of relative clauses

Relative clauses postmodify noun phrases. They can be **restrictive [21]** or **non-restrictive [22]**:

> **[21]** Individuals *who need professional help* are those *who cannot handle these problems themselves.* [W]
>
> **[22]** We can send two representatives and additional observers (*who can participate but not vote*). [W]

Reduced relative clauses have a non-finite verb:

> **[23]** It was a very contemporary version of the play ... although most people *responding to it* didn't feel that it had been updated to a specific period ('most people *who responded to it*')
>
> **[24]** Uh this is an action *authorised by the Security Council of the United Nations* ('an action *that is authorised by the Security Council of the United Nations*')
>
> **[25]** But according to the United Bible Societies these figures don't tell the whole story ... as some countries imported paper ... *on which to print their own Bibles* ('paper *on which they would print their own Bibles*')

Relative clauses are discussed in 10.10 and therefore need not be treated in this chapter.

14.2.3 Functions of adverbial clauses

Adverbial clauses have two main functions in relation to their host clause (cf. 8.7):

14.2.3.1 **Disjunct:**

> **[26]** Do you know where it might be *because uhm Bob and I were talking about it the other day* ('I'm asking the question for that reason')
>
> **[27]** *Broadly speaking*, there are three types of theories in scientific subjects. [W] ('I'm speaking broadly when I say this')

14.2.3.2 **Adjunct:**

[28]   But you said you're not familiar with it in practice ... *because you're not working as a counsellor*

[29]   Add the meatballs to the tomato sauce, partially cover the pan, and simmer for another 15 minutes *while cooking the spaghetti.* [Michael Barry *The Crafty Food Processor Cook Book*]

14.2.4 **Function of comparative clauses**

Comparative clauses (cf. 14.6) are introduced by the **subordinators** *than* or *as*. Together with a preceding **correlative**, the comparative clauses function as **intensifiers**. In **[30]** the preceding correlative of the *than*-clause is *more*:

[30]   Both agree that improvement is needed and should be *more* rapid *than is now the case*

The discontinuous intensifier *more* ... *than is now the case* modifies the adjective *rapid* ('How rapid?'—'More than is now the case'). In **[31]** the inflection *-er* on *lower* combines with the *than*-clause to intensify the adjective *low*:

[31]   In five out of the seven leading industrial nations industrial output is now low*er than it was a year ago*

In **[32]** the preceding correlative is the intensifier *less*, a comparative of the adverb *little*. The intensified item is the noun *harm*:

[32]   And the Ixtoc blow-out in the Gulf of Mexico—even though it gushed for months— did *less* harm *than it might have* because it was well out at sea and in deep, choppy, warm waters. [*BBC Wildlife*]

The correlative of *as*-clauses is the adverb *as*:

[33]   I'm perfectly happy for you to clap and sing and be *as* loud *as you want*

14.3 Nominal clauses

We can distinguish four types of nominal clause:

1. subordinate declarative clauses
2. subordinate interrogative clauses
3. subordinate exclamative clauses
4. nominal relative clauses

The four types are exemplified below.

14.3.1 **Subordinate declarative clauses**

14.3.1.1 **Finite subordinate declarative clauses**
Subordinate **declarative** clauses that are finite are introduced by the subordinator *that*. They may function as complement of a verb **[1]**, an adjective **[2]**, or a noun **[3]**:

[1]   And she told me *that my father who'd died many years before was standing by my side*

[2]   I was quite surprised *that that argument is still playing*

[3]   Unexpected help for the prosecution comes from a young Japanese officer a
Christian played by Noriyake Shioyi who had executed one of the airmen in the
belief *that the order to do so had been lawfully issued*

The conjunction *that* is generally omissible:

[4]   Tell me this however...your lectures were widely noticed and I imagine *you've had a
good deal of feedback since you delivered them*

However, *that* must be retained when the clause serves as subject, since otherwise the
subordinate clause may be misinterpreted as a main clause:

[5]   *That his people believe that after last night* is doubtful

Subject *that*-clauses are generally **extraposed**, and their subject position taken by **anticipatory *it*** (cf. 6.7). Since there is then little or no danger of misinterpretation, *that* can
usually be safely omitted:

[6]   We were advised to have our luggage ready as it was quite possible *we might be
flying on to Rio de Janeiro.* [Graham Stark *Remembering Peter Sellars*]

> **NOTE**
>
> *So* is frequently used as a **pro-clause** for a *that*-clause functioning as direct object, and
> similarly *not* as a negative pro-clause. The *that*-clause is generally a complement of a
> verb of saying, cognition, or perception:
>
> **[N1]**   He was happy to return to Manfield Terrace and to Norma, and often said *so*.
> [Julian Symons *Death's Darkest Face*] ('and often said that he was happy to
> return to Manfield Terrace and to Norma')
>
> **[N2]**   A: Oh I would imagine she would have left by now if she said twenty minutes
> B: You would have thought *so*
>
> **[N3]**   A: Uhm ... were your first ... sexual relationships anything like you'd
> expected them to be ...
> B: I guess *not*
>
> A similar range of verbs of cognition and perception (but not verbs of saying) are in-
> volved in **transferred negation**, the transfer of negation from the subordinate clause to
> the host clause. The negative in *I don't think they know you* can negate the host clause
> ('I'm not of that opinion')—and it clearly does so if *think* is stressed—or it can negate
> by transferred negation the subordinate clause ('I think they don't know you'), though
> the negative force is weaker in transferred negation than when the subordinate clause
> is directly negated. Compare also the direct negation in *They don't know you, I think.*
> Here are some examples of transferred negation:
>
> **[N4]**   I *don't suppose* anyone can guess what this is ('I suppose no one can
> guess what this is')
>
> **[N5]**   I *don't believe* that's correct
>
> **[N6]**   The vet *didn't think* she would live but she's nearly 7 months old now. [W]
>
> Transferred negation applies also with complements that are *to*-infinitive clauses and
> finite clauses or *-ing* participle clauses introduced by *as if*, *as though*, or *like*:
>
> **[N7]**   I *don't expect to* make a profit ('I expect not to make a profit')
>
> **[N8]**   Anne *didn't seem to* be listening [Steve Harris *Adventureland*]
>
> **[N9]**   You *don't look as if* you need it
>
> **[N10]**   They all of them *didn't feel like* doing their exams because he died like the
> night before a lot of uh the exams

Can't seem to and *couldn't seem to* transfer also the meaning of the modal:

[N11] I honestly feel great now, although my stomach *can't seem to* handle anything stronger than fruit at the moment! [W] ('my stomach seems not able to handle')

The pro-clause *so* is commonly used in transferred negation:

[N12] A: Are you going grey
B: I don't think *so*

It is less formal than direct negation with *not*:

[N12a] I think *not*.

14.3.1.2 Non-finite subordinate declarative clauses

Corresponding to the declarative *that*-clauses are **non-finite** clauses. Below are examples of -*ing* participle clauses **[7]**–**[8]**, *to*-infinitive clauses **[9]**–**[10]**, and bare infinitive clauses **[11]**–**[12]**:

[7] The one piece of real good that could come out of all this is *the United Nations acting with authority* ('that the United Nations is acting with authority')

[8] And I find *myself sympathising very much with … this* ('that I sympathise very much with this')

[9] Secondly people expect *this countryside to be conserved* ('that this countryside will be conserved')

[10] Uh well do you want *me to tell you the truth* ('that I should tell you the truth')

[11] And that's the sort of thing that makes *one say well uhm I shall show em* ('causes that one will say …')

[12] Uhm let *me bring you in Eric Groves a naval specialist on this* ('allow that I bring you in …')

14.3.2 Subordinate interrogative clauses

Three types of subordinate **interrogative** clauses can be distinguished, corresponding to the three types of main interrogative clauses (cf. 2.5): **yes–no clauses**, **alternative clauses**, and **wh-clauses**.

14.3.2.1 *Yes–no* and alternative clauses

Yes–no and alternative clauses are introduced by the subordinators *whether* and *if*. *Yes–no* clauses are exemplified in **[13]**–**[14]**:

[13] The whole purpose of meeting was to decide *whether it was worth going ahead at all*

[14] I don't know *if you ever tried running a business* but it's very difficult

The alternatives in alternative clauses are introduced by *or*:

[15] It doesn't matter *whether it's marsh or fen or heathland or bog or sand dunes or what*

[16] Well I didn't know for sure *if it was free or not*

14.3.2.2 *Wh-clauses*

Wh-interrogatives are introduced by *wh*-pronouns **[17]** (cf. 6.12), or *wh*-determiners (cf. 6.12), or *wh*-adverbs **[18]** (cf. 8.7):

[17]   At another point during the hearing, Rep. Markey asked Mr Phelan *what would be discussed at a New York exchange board meeting today*. [*Wall Street Journal*]

[18]   A spokesman said he could not speculate as to *when a new proposal would be presented* or *how long it would take to complete*, and Ramada officials declined to elaborate. [*Wall Street Journal*]

What would be a determiner in **[17]** if it were followed by (say) *issues*. As with main clauses (cf. 2.5), if the *wh*-element is the complement of a prepositional phrase, the preposition may be **stranded** at the end **[19]** or (in formal style) may be **fronted** with its complement **[20]**:

[19]   I'm not sure *who I should speak to*.

[20]   I am not sure *to whom I should speak*.

14.3.2.3 *To-*infinitive clauses within interrogatives

*To-*infinitive clauses may serve in all three types of interrogatives, as *yes–no* interrogatives **[21]–[22]**, alternative interrogatives **[23]–[24]**, and *wh*-interrogatives **[25]–[26]**.

[21]   The municipalities said they have not decided *whether to try to force the company to go through with the contracts*. [*Wall Street Journal*]

[22]   As a result, Fed officials may be divided over *whether to ease credit*. [*Wall Street Journal*]

[23]   It is hard to know *whether to laugh at or cry about the impoverished woman who raises rabbits to sell as pets or as meat*. [*Wall Street Journal*]

[24]   During the coming weeks, President Bush must decide *whether to veto the bills containing them—or, alternatively, to sign these bills into law with a statement declaring their intrusions on executive power to be in violation of Article II, and thus void and severable*. [*Wall Street Journal*]

[25]   It is hard to know *what to do about drugs*. [*Wall Street Journal*]

[26]   These issues weigh on Mr. Clausen as he considers *whom to anoint as his successor*. [*Wall Street Journal*]

14.3.2.4 **Restrictions on *if***

If is more restricted than *whether* (cf. 14.3.2.1). For example, only *whether* can be used to introduce *to-*infinitive clauses serving as *yes–no* and alternative interrogatives (**[21]–[24]** above). Only a *whether*-clause can be the complement of a preposition **[27]** and only *whether* can be followed immediately by *or not* **[28]**:

[27]   There's no indication as to *whether the shots were aimed at the Soviet leader*

[28]   No … she said she was coming tomorrow to tell me *whether or not she could do the following week*

14.3.2.5 **Word order in subordinate interrogative clauses**

In standard English, subordinate interrogative clauses differ from main interrogative clauses in word order. Main clauses require **subject–operator inversion** except when a *wh*-element is the subject (cf. 2.5):

[13a] *Was it* worth going ahead at all?

[16a] *Was it* free or not?

[18a] How long *would it* take to complete?

Subordinate clauses, on the other hand, place the subject first, as in declarative clauses. However, non-standard dialects commonly have subject–operator inversion in subordinate clauses:

[13b] You can decide *was it* worth going ahead at all.

[16b] I didn't know *was it* free or not.

[18b] He didn't know how long *would it* take to complete.

In consequence, non-standard dialects omit in such cases the subordinators *whether* and *if*, which are redundant when the interrogative is signalled by inversion.

14.3.2.6 *Whether* (and *if*): repetition and coordination

Whether or *if* can be repeated in alternative clauses if the alternative clauses are in full:

[29] The issue is whether fleet requirements can be met by remanufacturing previously built aircraft *or whether additional new production is required*. [*Wall Street Journal*]

If the alternative clause is infinitive, *whether* can be repeated when infinitival *to* is retained:

[23a] It is hard to know whether to laugh at *or whether to cry about* the impoverished woman who raises rabbits to sell as pets or as meat.

Or whether and *or if* introduce *yes–no* interrogative clauses when they are coordinated with a *wh*-interrogative:

[30] The indictment does not say how the alleged bid-rigging was to be done *or whether the two companies went through with the alleged scheme*. [*Wall Street Journal*]

[31] How soon Wang will stage a comeback, *or if it will at all*, are still matters of debate. [*Wall Street Journal*]

14.3.3 Subordinate exclamative clauses

As in main **exclamative** clauses (cf. 2.8), *what* introduces noun phrases **[32]** and *how* is used otherwise **[33]**. *What* and *how* are intensifiers in this use.

[32] And I know *what great joy he's brought not only to his family but to so many of his parents' friends* ('very great joy')

[33] My agent called me in this morning to tell me *how good he was*. [W]

14.3.4 Nominal relative clauses

Nominal relative clauses (or independent relative clauses or free relative clauses) closely resemble noun phrases. Like noun phrases and unlike other clauses, they can take a plural verb:

[34] '*What the market wants to see* are deals in non-recessionary businesses,' said Brian Doyle, a senior analyst at Salomon Brothers. [*Wall Street Journal*]

They can have concrete reference **[35]** and indeed personal reference **[36]**:

[35] In two years, I probably have eaten *what looked like 20 different types of fish*, only to be informed each time that I was eating 'snapper' or 'garoupa.' [*Wall Street Journal*]

[36] We bribe *whoever needs to be bribed to get on that plane* before anyone thinks we might try anything so crazy. [Mary Napier *Powers of Darkness*]

[37] So before the centralisation of the Temple … you had local officials where anybody could do *whatever they liked in them more or less* … ('anything that they liked …')

[38] And this is *where the eighty-nine earthquake occurred* ('the place at which the eighty-nine earthquake occurred')

[39] This enables you to get your weight evenly distributed, and to push off to *whichever side the ball comes*. [Sue Rich *Know about Tennis*] ('any side that the ball comes')

[40] This is *how she put it* ('the way that she put it')

To-infinitive clauses can also be nominal relative clauses:

[41] 'It is absurd that societies so stricken with crime should attempt to apply their standards to us and teach us *what to do*,' he said. [*International Herald Tribune*] ('that which we should do')

[42] It outlines some of the opportunities that are available at our main branches and *who to contact for more information* ('the person that you should contact ...')

[43] So ... he directed me *where to go* ('the place that I should go to')

[44] You don't just learn words and grammar you learn *how to* uh *behave more generally* ('the way that you should behave more generally')

Nominal clauses that are complements of verbs or adjectives may be **fronted**. The motivation for doing so is generally **end-focus**: to place at the climax the information that is new or at least relatively less familiar to the hearer. Here are two examples:

[45] Uh the record of Saddam Hussein does not lead us to believe that *what he says he says he'll do* he necessarily will do

[46] I hope to go to the States sometime soon but *whether it will materialise* I don't know. [W]

NOTE

Some grammarians have considered the nominal relative clause to be a noun phrase rather than a clause. They analyse the nominal relative item as consisting of a pronoun or general noun phrase that is fused with a relative item as in these examples drawn from citations in this section: '*the things that* the market wants to see' **[34]**, 'things that looked like 20 different types of fish' **[35]**, 'any person who needs to be bribed to get on that plane' **[36]**. In this alternative analysis, the nominal relative clause is regarded as a noun phrase whose head (*what* in **[34]**–**[35]** and *whoever* in **[36]**) is a fused relative with a built-in antecedent, and the head is followed by the rest of a postmodifying relative clause.

14.4 Forms of adverbial clauses

Adverbial clauses may be finite, non-finite, or verbless, and the verb of a non-finite clause may be an -*ing* participle, an -*ed* participle, a *to*-infinitive, or a bare infinitive (cf. 14.1).

14.4.1 **Use of subordinators**

Adverbial clauses that are finite generally have a subordinator, such as *if* or *although*; exceptionally, subject–operator inversion may be used instead of the conditional subordinator *if* (cf. 14.5). Non-finite and verbless clauses may have a subordinator **[1]**–**[2]**, but they are commonly used without a subordinator **[3]**–**[4]**:

[1] Embarrassingly, my seat broke. *When reclined* it was not long enough for my legs [*The Times*]

[2] Defend yourself physically only *if really necessary*. [W]

[3] And you condemn the series *having seen a bit of one of them*

[4] They met six years ago while both worked at a bank in Nazareth, *she a clerk and he a computer instructor*. [*International Herald Tribune*]

In the absence of a subordinator, the meaning of the adverbial clause in relation to its host clause may be vague when the sentence is viewed in isolation. For example, the *-ing* participle clause in **[3]** might be temporal ('after you have seen a bit of one of them') or causal ('because you have seen a bit of one of them'). In the wider context it is clear that the clause is concessive ('though you have seen (only) a bit of one of them').

14.4.2 **Subjectless clauses**

If the non-finite or verbless clause does not have a subject, its understood subject is normally interpreted as identical with the subject of the host clause. Thus, the subject of the *-ed* participle clause *When reclined* **[1]** is understood to be *it*: 'When it (i.e. my seat) was reclined'.

An adverbial participle or verbless clause is said to be **dangling** (or **unattached**) when its understood subject is not identical with the subject of the host clause. In **[5]** the subject of the verbless clause *If severe* is in the previous sentence—*these* (changes):

[5] Injury at any point along the length of the axon process produces biochemical and ultrastructural changes within the nerve cell body and *these* are more pronounced if proximal. *If severe*, nerve cell death may result. [P. J. Smith 'Nerve Injury and Repair' in F. D. Burke et al. *Principles of Hand Surgery*]

More commonly, the understood subject of a dangling clause can be deduced from some item in the host clause—*his* in **[6]**, yielding the interpretation 'When he was in the company of Bob Fagin and Paul Green':

[6] *When in the company of Bob Fagin and Paul Green,* no doubt *his* hurt was assuaged by routine duties and by companionship. [Peter Ackroyd *Dickens*]

Violation of the identical-subject rule is usually considered to be an error if it is noticed. But the rule is felt not to apply in certain cases. The main exceptions are:

14.4.2.1 If the dangling clause is a **style disjunct** that has the speaker's *I* as the understood subject (cf. 8.7.2.1):

[7] *Broadly speaking,* the process followed reflected the revised priorities. [*International Journal of Project Management*] ('I am speaking broadly')

[8] And our links as we all know uh elsewhere uh are uh *to put it mildly* uh inadequate

14.4.2.2 If the understood subject refers to the whole of the host clause:

[9] I would like it done on Wednesday *if possible* ('if it is possible')

[10] Firstly, the head may twist sharply, *tearing and twisting the connections and membranes of the brain.* [W] ('the sharp twisting of the head will tear ...')

14.4.2.3 In scientific usage, if the understood subject refers to the *I* or *we* of the speakers or writers:

[11] Concentrations of substances below ten to the seventh cannot be measured *using these radioactive-based methodologies*

[12] Each question will be considered in turn *before looking at an alternative approach.* [*International Journal of Project Management*]

14.4.2.4 If the understood subject is a generic *you*, *we*, or *one* (cf. 6.5):

[13] It's the same deal *when setting off on a slippery surface*

[14] *Bearing in mind that many retired people can still contribute usefully to society,* it seems probable that the burden of a dependent child is, overall, at least as high as

> **NOTE**
>
> Some participles—*assuming, judging, considering, supposing*—are commonly used in adverbial clauses with an understood generic subject:
>
> **[N1]** As usual, the second half is expected to be better, *assuming that the recession is shallow* [*The Guardian*]
>
> **[N2]** *Judging by the experimental evidence,* any reduction of lean body mass is likely to be mainly at the expense of slowly metabolizing tissues, particularly muscle. [W]
>
> **[N3]** The baby tortoise, so tiny when Pete christened him on the docks at Southampton, was now the size of a large soup plate which, *considering how many of our plants he'd devoured over the years,* was hardly surprising. [Graham Stark *Remembering Peter Sellars*]
>
> **[N4]** *Supposing we want to create a large commercial monopoly for some reason* we'll come back to why in a few moments how would we do it

that of a retired person. [Eric McGraw *Population*]

14.4.3 **Absolute clauses**

Absolute clauses are adverbial participle clauses or adverbial verbless clauses that are not introduced by a subordinator and that have their own subject:

[15] *Sanctions on Haiti having produced no useful results so far,* the United States is now considering whether to tighten them further. [*International Herald Tribune*]

[16] It may seem perverse to derogate AA, NA etc., *they being organisations which do fine and irreplaceable work in offering salvation to those afflicted by addiction.* [*The Independent Magazine*]

[17] There are populated areas all around the bay *the total population being in excess of ten million*

[18] While the government holds the towns, Unita controls much of the countryside, *its troops equipped with American-supplied ground-to-air missiles to deter air transport.* [*Sunday Times*]

[19] Lesley talked with animation, *the restraint of their first meeting all gone.* [Denise Robertson *Remember the Moment*]

[20] *College work aside,* I have just ended this strange relationship with the girl we spoke about in Paris. [W]

14.5 Meanings of adverbial clauses

Below are given, with examples, the major types of adverbial clause according to their meaning relation with the host clauses. Some subordinators can be used with more than

> **NOTE**
>
> Complements of verbs may have the same form as adverbial clauses and express the same kinds of meanings as they do. An example is **[5]** below. See the subsection on manner clauses (14.5.11).

one type of clause; for example, *since* can serve with time or reason clauses, *so that* with purpose or result clauses.

14.5.1 **Place clauses**

Place clauses may refer to position **[1]**–**[3]** or direction **[4]**–**[5]**:

[1]   They fired rockets and artillery last night but *where I was* they made no move to advance

[2]   *Where the mighty Rhone river meets the Mediterranean Sea* its silt has created a spreading triangle of wild marshes … the Camargue

[3]   DDT should still be used, with appropriate safeguards, *wherever pests can be well controlled,* and particularly when more expensive chemicals cannot be afforded. [*Wall Street Journal*]

[4]   And Mr. McPhee is the envy of other writers for his ability to follow *wherever his fancy leads.* [*Wall Street Journal*]

In **[5]**, the *where*-clause is the complement (object predicative) of the verb *put*:

[5]   With the footballing folk of Newcastle urged to put their money *where their mouths are* [*The Guardian*]

14.5.2 **Temporal clauses**

The situation in the host clause may occur before that of the temporal clause **[6]**–**[8]**, at the same time **[9]**–**[12]**, or at a later time **[13]**–**[15]**:

[6]   And she's advised them to get a good grounding *before they go*

[7]   I didn't realise they were wisdom teeth *until someone pointed them out*

[8]   What the chain does is sell even cheaper petrol to undercut this independent *till he's driven out of business or until he can be bought out by the main corporation*

[9]   Mrs Mandela sat impassively *while Mr Kgase gave evidence in the court,* which was half-empty for the first time since the case opened last month. [*Yorkshire Post*]

[10]   Uhm … and I think one of the things that I felt *when I was studying dance* … was I very much enjoyed the work that I was involved in

[11]   *Whenever Adam and I hug and say hello* he sits on my knee and he you know he puts one leg on either side and we hug and we're close physically

[12]   It was supposed that a king had the right to rule only *as long as he was acting in the interests of his people.* [Terry Jones 'Credit for Mrs Thatcher' in Ben Pimlott et al. *The Alternative*]

[13]   Laura likes tea bags you see *after they've had taken some of the strength out*

[14]   So *when this nerve is cut* not only will you be numb in the area not only will the relevant muscles not be able to move but muscle will be all floppy through lack of tone

[15]   *Once we're convinced that we have the right to determine when life becomes human and when it ceases to be so* … then we stand in danger of creating a society that is potentially self-destructive

When a *since*-clause and its host clause refer to a period leading up to the present (and perhaps including the present), the host clause generally takes the present perfect (cf. 11.11):

[16]   Well I *'ve read* about three books *since I finished my degree*

[17] The Pentagon *has called* up more than thirty thousand reservists *since the crisis began* but most of them have been support units doctors cargo handlers mechanics

14.5.3 **Conditional clauses**

> **NOTE**
>
> Conditional clauses exhibit a number of parallels with subordinate interrogative clauses (cf. 14.3):
>
> 1. Both indicate that information is missing. For conditional clauses, the missing information is about the fulfilment of the condition. In fact, we can often rephrase a conditional construction as a question with its response:
>
> > **[N1]** You're going to have huge trouble if you've infected me.
> >
> > **[N1a]** Have you infected me? If so, you're going to have huge trouble.
>
> 2. The semantic and formal distinctions between the three types of interrogative clauses (*yes–no*, alternative, *wh-*) are analogous to those between the three types of conditional clauses (direct, alternative, *wh-*).
>
> 3. *If* and *whether* are used as subordinators in both interrogative and conditional clauses.
>
> 4. Rhetorical questions (cf. 2.9) are paralleled by rhetorical conditions:
>
> > **[N2]** Is there anybody stronger than me?
> >
> > **[N2a]** If anybody is stronger than me, I'll eat my hat.

Conditional clauses generally express a **direct condition**, indicating that the truth of the host clause (or apodosis) is dependent on the fulfilment of the condition in the conditional clause (or protasis).

However, some conditional clauses may express an **indirect condition** that is related to the speech act:

[18] And *if I remember rightly* you had jaundice didn't you ('if I remember rightly it would be true to say')

[19] I mean *if I told you honestly* things can be really interesting

[20] I did need to have a need to say … that I was doing something because uhm … otherwise I wouldn't be anybody *if you see what I mean*

14.5.3.1 **Open conditions**
Direct conditions may be either **open** (or **real**) or **hypothetical** (or **closed** or **unreal**). **Open conditions** leave completely open whether the condition will be fulfilled:

[21] You're going to have huge trouble … *if you've infected me*

In **[21]** the speaker does not give any indication whether he or she believes that the condition—the infection by the person addressed—has been fulfilled.

14.5.3.2 **Hypothetical conditions**

> **HYPOTHETICAL CONDITIONS IN DETAIL**
>
> The hypothetical nature of the condition is conveyed through the verb forms, which are **backshifted** (cf. 15.2). Future and present hypothetical conditions take the past in the conditional clause and a past modal in the host clause. The future

hypothetical condition is exemplified in **[22]**, where the modal *'d* (= *would*) appears in the host clause and the past *scratched* in the conditional clause:

> **[22]** I'd be far more upset if somebody say scratched one of my records ... than tore one of my books

The present hypothetical condition is shown in **[23]**, where the modal *could* appears in the host clause and the past *had* in the conditional clause:

> **[23]** Now *if I had an S* ... I *could* do a really clever word

The past hypothetical condition takes the past perfect in the conditional clause and a modal past perfect in the host clause:

> **[24]** I mean do you think she *would have been* different *if there'd been* ... a supportive man in the home

The modal in all three types of conditions is generally *would* or its contraction *'d*. It is used in the host clause unless some additional modal meaning is required, as with *could* in **[23]**, which can be paraphrased by 'would be able to'.

Hypothetical conditions, on the other hand, express the speaker's belief that the condition has not been fulfilled (for past conditions) or is not fulfilled (for present conditions) or is unlikely to be fulfilled (for future conditions).

If the verb in the conditional clause of a present or future hypothetical condition is *be*, subjunctive *were* (cf. 11.10) is sometimes used instead of indicative *was* in the conditional clause, particularly in more formal contexts:

> **[25]** I would *if I were you*

> **[26]** It certainly provided a pretext, *if one were needed*, for the foreign tours he undertook to fifteen different countries during his first year after being elected to office. [Nicholas Nugent *Rajiv Gandhi*]

14.5.3.3 **Subject–operator inversion in conditional clauses**

Conditional clauses may also have subject–operator inversion without a subordinator. In such cases the auxiliaries are usually *had*, *were*, or *should*:

> **[27]** I think *had he won the 1970 election* he would have resigned in 1972 or 1973

> **[28]** I am confident that I can deal with the problems uh of Prime Minister *were I to be elected*

> **[29]** However, *should I briefly tire of cisatlantic life, and discover the means to journey to North America*—some conference might perhaps afford the opportunity—then perhaps, I trust, we might meet again. [W]

14.5.3.4 **Conditional subordinators**

The most frequent conditional subordinator is *if*, but there are others. Some are exemplified below.

> **[30]** He says the country faces paralysis *unless a solution is found quickly*

> **[31]** The Democratic leadership agrees to relent, *provided the president asks for a modest tax increase—modest in the present year, but increasing rapidly thereafter. [Wall Street Journal]*

> **[32]** So *given that a micrometre is a thousandth of a metre* this'll normally be about point two five of a micrometre

> **[33]** The magazine will reward with 'page bonuses' advertisers who in 1990 meet or

> **NOTE**
>
> *If* can be a subordinator in an abbreviated conditional clause with the pro-clause *so* or *not* (cf. 14.3.1.1 Note):
>
> **[N1]** Should you buy a separate transport unit and, *if so*, which one? [*Hi-Fi News & Record Review*]
>
> **[N2]** Seen anyone else I know? *If not*, then what the hell have you been doing?!! [W]

exceed their 1989 spending, *as long as they spent $325,000 in 1989 and $340,000 in 1990*. [*Wall Street Journal*]

[34] *Supposing she'd said that to a psychiatrist* what would they say

14.5.4 Circumstantial clauses

Some place, time, and conditional subordinators may be used to introduce clauses that express a more general meaning of circumstances. In such cases, the subordinators *where, wherever, when, whenever,* and *if* are interchangeable.

[35] So we believe in more investment better management some deregulation *where appropriate* to improve and expand those public services

[36] Finally, *when straw is combined with manure and composted*, it can be spread onto the land to return fertility to the farm. [David Mabey et al. *Thorson's Organic Consumer Guide*]

[37] Avoid vigorous evening exercise *if possible*, as the increased adrenaline it produces may cause sleep problems, so try to take exercise in the morning or up to late afternoon. [Rosemary Nicol *Everything You Need To Know About Osteoporosis*]

14.5.5 Alternative-conditional clauses

Alternative-conditional clauses express two or more stated possible conditions:

[38] When you tie a standard rose and this applies to any standard rose *whether you do it yourself or whether you buy it* you really need two ties on it ('if either condition applies')

[39] I hope you'll think it's sensible law ... but *whether you do or not* ... uh you'll have to accept it from me because I am the judge ... of the law

[40] *Whether or not we believe in God* we inhabit a culture in which religious teachings are marginal to many people's moral choices

[41] Furious, Peter assured all and sundry that, *Prince Charles or no Prince Charles*, he would boycott the premiere. [Graham Stark *Remembering Peter Sellars*]

[42] The steering is just too vague and I'm still not convinced that two hundred horsepower and front-wheel drive ... make desperately happy bedfellows ... *trace control or no*

[43] When the Gothic designer was faced with an aedicular feature in a blank wall, *whether window, doorway, blank arch or niche*, he immediately began to anchor it into the wall by a system of mouldings, which swept up one side and down the other. [Paul Johnson *Cathedrals of England, Scotland and Wales*]

14.5.6 *Wh-*conditional clauses

Wh-conditional clauses leave open the number of possible conditions:

[44] *Whatever you've been doing* you've been doing the right thing ('Whether you've been doing x, y, z ...')

[45] *Wherever I now travelled around the country* I would hear complaints about the quality of young people leaving our schools: undisciplined, illiterate or innumerate were the mildest criticisms of them. [Lord Young *The Enterprise Years*]

[46] You really are relatively speaking in comparison with the other two very inexperienced *however talented you may be*

However, *whichever* offers a limited number of conditions, implied from the context:

[47] The final film of the evening Fear is a cheerfully dopey thriller about this psychic Allie Sheedy ... who can see into the minds of serial killers and thus help the otherwise baffled cops to bring them to justice or blow them away *whichever seems more convenient*

14.5.7 **Concessive clauses**

Concessive clauses indicate that the situation in the host clause is unexpected in view of what is said in the concessive clause.

[48] It is quite clear that *although individual sheets of papyrus ... must have sat in piles in workshops* you could not go and buy them ('It is surprising that you could not go and buy them')

[49] The best parts of this building are seven hundred years old *though there has been worship here for a good deal longer*

[50] Good to see Willy Banks competing of course *even though he's no longer a challenger and won't of course be in the American Championships team for Tokyo*

[51] And *while some of the senior executives still remain from those early days* we now find it more effective to recruit locally

Whereas clauses usually combine concession with contrast:

[52] She now wears ... size ten in clothes ... *whereas formerly she wore size fourteen*

Even if clauses combine conditional with concessive meaning. We cannot therefore assume that what they describe is factual. In this respect they differ from *even though* clauses. The condition may be open **[53]** or hypothetical **[54]**:

NOTE

If may be used concessively (usually in abbreviated clauses) as well as conditionally. It may be synonymous either with *even if* **[N1]** or with *even though* **[N2]**:

[N1] Unfortunately there remain some strong *if not stronger* arguments in favour of the opposite view: that an excessive show of force inevitably leads to war. [*The Guardian*] ('even if they are not stronger')

[N2] But can't that fantastic technical ingenuity ... at last be applied to civilian production turning *if not swords into ploughshares* F Fifteens into kidney machines ('even though not turning swords into ploughshares')

---

[53] Nevertheless, *even if the tax cut is made permanent*, its effects on the economy may be far less than its proponents anticipate. [*Wall Street Journal*]

[54] And, experts say, *even if oil were discovered there tomorrow*, none of it would enter the market until the next century. [*Wall Street Journal*]

In concessive clauses introduced by the subordinators *as*, *though*, and *that*, the predicate is sometimes **fronted** except that auxiliaries and the verb *be* are stranded:

[55] 'Prisoners for the All Highest's personal attention', their sergeant bawled at the gate guard, and, *tense as she was,* Jean felt a quite different shiver in her spine. [Mary Napier *Powers of Darkness*]

[56] *Unbelievable as it seems,* we are inundated with Russians. [*Evening Standard*]

14.5.8 **Reason clauses**

Reason clauses express such notions as reason and cause for what is conveyed in the host clause. As with conditions, the reason may be indirect, related to the speech act or the belief of the speaker:

[57] Well wouldn't it be a granular texture *because pears are granular aren't they* ('I say that because of my belief that pears are granular')

Most reason clauses convey a direct reason or cause:

[58] *Since you're not having anything else* you can have two of everything

[59] We need to proceed with the greatest care therefore … *for embryo research is a complex issue which involves the whole spectrum of medical scientific ethical … and moral issues*

[60] I'm the patient and *as I don't know much about it* uhm he briefly explained what needed to be done

[61] But the cancer tests are unique *in that they can be used to identify who in a family must be frequently monitored and who is free of the danger and need not be checked for symptoms.* [*Wall Street Journal*]

14.5.9 **Purpose clauses**

14.5.9.1 **Finite purpose clauses** require a modal auxiliary (cf. 11.8), since they refer to an event that has yet to take place:

[62] Skilled ringers use their wrists to advance or retard the next swing, *so that one bell can swap places with another in the following change.* [*Wall Street Journal*] ('in order that one bell can …')

[63] You'll just have to take an overnight bag with all the possibilities in *so you can zip up to the bathroom and change*

[64] This problem is made all the more difficult with automated inspection because a large amount of data needs to be processed, preferably as quickly as possible, *in order that further, more detailed, inspection may be carried out on suspect regions if required.* [*British Journal of Non-Destructive Testing*]

14.5.9.2 **Infinitival purpose clauses** are more frequent than finite purpose clauses. The *to*-infinitive clauses are commonly used without a subordinator, but they may also be introduced by *in order to* and *so as to*:

[65] The other day she did it and disappeared *to use the phone*

[66] I sometimes wonder whether Stephen actually went to prison … deliberately *in order to have something to talk about when he came on this show*

[67] You'll learn assertiveness *so as not to be inhibited by other people's agendas*

14.5.10 **Result clauses**

In contrast to purpose clauses, **result clauses** refer to a situation that is or was in effect, the result of the situation described in the host clause.

[68] They actually said it was their fault you see *so that they paid all the costs and everything else* ('with the result that they paid ...')

[69] But the thing is you always have to write them in a slight code *so people don't know exactly what you are talking about* ...

So in **[69]** may be the conjunctive adverb, since the difference between the conjunction and the adverb is neutralized in asyndetic co-ordination (cf. 13.2.3). If the co-ordinator *and* is used, *so* is clearly an adverb:

[70] The final possibility is the electron can come in ... and actually knock off an electron ... which is bound to one of the atoms in the molecule ... *and so* you get two electrons ... coming away from the molecule

14.5.11 **Manner clauses**

Manner clauses refer to the manner of the action expressed by the verb. Though treated here for convenience, they are complements of the verb (cf. 14.7):

[71] And the lecturers do *as they're instructed*

[72] The dilemma was whether you carry on *as if he could take over* or you'd have to start all over again

[73] It is misleading to talk *as though ninety percent are covered*

14.5.12 **Proportion and similarity clauses**

Both **proportion** and **similarity clauses** involve kinds of comparison. A common type of proportion clause has comparatives in both clauses:

[74] *The simpler* the business, *the better off* you are. [*Wall Street Journal*]

[75] 'He used to say that *the faster* he could sell MiniScribe, *the better*,' recalls the former manager. [*Wall Street Journal*]

> **NOTE**
>
> *The* in proportion clauses is not the definite article. it derives from the use in Old English of the instrumental case *thy* of the demonstrative pronoun in expressions of comparison ('*by that* the faster, *by that* the better'). Somewhat similar is the verbless construction *so ... so ...*

[76] *The more sons* a man has *the more labour*, and so *the larger* he can make his herd. [W]

This type can be reduced to verbless clauses:

[75a] The faster, the better.

[77] I told her I was in a hurry, but I've transformed her house while she's taught Emily, *so far so good*. [W]

Another type of proportion clause is introduced by *as* or *just as*. The host clause begins with the correlative *so* and has subject–operator inversion:

[78] And *as lawsuits against directors and officers mushroomed in the mid-1980s*, so did the policy claims. [*Wall Street Journal*]

[79] But *as fears of a recession in the near future fade*, so does the Fed's incentive to ease. [*Wall Street Journal*]

Similarity clauses resemble the second type of proportion clause in form:

[80] *Just as the October 1987 'meltdown' in the stock market did not produce an economic recession (as we correctly predicted at the time), so* the present strength in the stock market does not necessarily mean that the economy will avoid recession. [*Wall Street Journal*]

[81] *Just as Newsday has had to acknowledge and cater to the differences between Long Island and New York, so* too must the Times appeal to the varying tastes of readers in far-flung communities. [*Wall Street Journal*]

14.5.13 **Comment clauses**

Various types of parenthetical **comment clause** are used, particularly in speech. The finite clauses are generally introduced by the subordinator *as*:

[82] Well now *as far as I know* I've never been raped or anything

[83] *As he said to me* well we didn't seem to be going anywhere fast

[84] Uhm so I think he may not have the confidence to go ahead *as it were*

[85] *As I remember* it used to be sort of like fairly common for a Tuesday ... that I'd pretend to be sick ... and so I didn't have to go to school

[86] Assuming that post at the age of 35, he managed by consensus, *as is the rule in universities*, says Warren H. Strother, a university official who is researching a book on Mr. Hahn. [*Wall Street Journal*]

Non-finite comment clauses are style disjuncts (cf. 4.27):

[87] *Broadly speaking*, there are three types of theories in scientific subjects. [W]

[88] *Put simply* ... the principles of policing as asserted at the top ... have not yet made in their view a sufficient penetration at all levels

[89] *To be fair* you used to come when your Mum and Dad were still living in Portland Road but you haven't been since

14.6 Comparative clauses

Comparative clauses involve a comparison with what is conveyed in the host clause. The **comparative element** signals the standard on which the comparison is made. In **[1]** the comparative element is *much more attention*:

[1] We now give *much more attention* to the mentally and physically handicapped *than we did even twenty-five or thirty years ago*

The standard of comparison is the amount of attention given to the mentally and physically handicapped. *Attention* is modified discontinuously: *much more ... than we did even twenty-five or thirty years ago*. In **[1]** *more* is an irregular comparative form of *much* and is itself intensified by *much*. The basis of comparison is the situation twenty-five or thirty years ago, which is compared with the present situation.

14.6.1 **Comparatives and comparative elements**

Comparatives are either inflected forms (*older*) or phrases constructed with *more* (*more convenient*); cf. 8.4. They are used to express a higher degree of comparison, as in **[1]** above and in **[2]** below:

[2]   And here am I actually working *longer* hours *than I've ever worked in my life*

A lower degree of comparison is expressed by premodifying *less* (itself a comparative of *little*) with a postmodifying *than*-clause:

[3]   Guidelines have been issued by the various health authorities which dictate that if patients suffer heart attacks over the age of seventy they should receive *less* priority treatment *than those who suffer similar conditions under the age of seventy*

An equivalent degree of comparison is expressed by premodifying *as* with a postmodifying *as*-clause:

[4]   Many felt Hearst kept the paper alive *as* long *as he did*, if marginally, because of its place in family history. [*Wall Street Journal*]

The comparative element may be a noun phrase **[5]**, an adjective phrase **[6]**, or an adverb phrase **[7]**:

[5]   Yet however much one might prefer the trilogy over earlier texts, the criteria of purity, continuity and authenticity create *more problems* than they solve. [Leslie Hill *Beckett's Fiction*]

[6]   I'm so glad—she was *more despondent and depressed* than I've ever seen her when I left her to come home last September. [W]

[7]   I think he's feeling the time going *more slowly* than I am since he's the one left behind. [W]

14.6.2 **Ellipsis in comparative clauses**

Comparative clauses are often elliptical, omitting elements that they share with their host clauses:

[8]   The implication is that physical illnesses can be diagnosed more reliably *than can mental illnesses*. [W]

On the other hand, we can restore the ellipted elements of **[8]**:

[8a]   The implication is that physical illnesses can be diagnosed more reliably *than mental illnesses can be diagnosed*.

We can also omit a further shared element in **[8]**, the auxiliary *can*:

[8b]   The implication is that physical illnesses can be diagnosed more reliably *than mental illnesses*.

In **[8b]** we are left with only the subject of the comparative clause. In **[9]** only the direct object remains and in **[10]** only an adverbial:

[9]   If you hate these photographs more *than the one that's on the back of the album* I think you should leave the one that's on the back of the album ('than you hate *the one that's on the back of the album*')

[10]   Pastoralism was much more widespread in the past than *at present* [W] ('than it is (widespread) *at present*')

When the only element left in the comparative clause is the subject and an auxiliary, the auxiliary functions as an **operator** (cf. 7.9). If the subject is not a pronoun, then subject–operator inversion is an option, as in **[8]** above and in **[11]**:

[11]   When the scientists dosed forest land in Harvard, Mass., with a common nitrogen fertilizer, ammonium nitrate, they found the soil absorbed about 33% less methane from the air *than did unfertilized ground*. [*Wall Street Journal*]

The subject alone may be ellipted in the comparative clause:

[12]   The effects on San Francisco were much less *than would've occurred with the same earthquake at a closer distance*

[13]   Not all sects are new religious movements, but many of the new religions exhibit the sectarian characteristic of proclaiming an exclusive truth, and even those that claim that they do not do so may, in practice, turn out to be far less internally tolerant of diversity than *might at first appear*. [Eileen Barker 'New Lines in the Supra-Market: How Much Can we Buy?' in Ian Hamnett *Religious Pluralism and Unbelief*]

[14]   But the increase cited in the API report was larger *than had been expected*. [*Wall Street Journal*]

[15]   The government sells timber on a sustained basis, never selling more *than is grown*. [*Wall Street Journal*]

However, in such instances the comparative clause seems to imply a relative clause:

[14a] … larger than (the increase that) had been expected.

[15a] … never selling more than (the timber that) is grown.

When the only element left is a pronoun that has both **subjective** and **objective** cases (cf. 6.3), the tendency is to use the objective case even when the pronoun would be the subject in a restored *than*-clause:

[16]   In fact she'd get somewhere quicker *than me* ('than I would (get)')

But some writers are uneasy at using the objective case, as shown in **[17]** by the parenthetic question mark after *me*:

[17]   There are about 50 other girls, most appear younger *than me (?)* and are very unfriendly. [W]

The alternative is to use the subjective pronoun with the operator (cf. 11.2.4):

[18]   Now you've been in more of this building *than I have*

14.6.3 **Metalinguistic use of *more … than***

More … than can also be used **metalinguistically**, to indicate a more accurate ascription:

[19]   He was content to think that nature was *more acting than acted upon*, that the mind was more easily conceived as a thing made than a thing making. [Graham Davidson *Coleridge's Career*] ('more accurately described as acting than acted upon')

[20]   I thought actually when he came on he was very blond but in fact he's *more ginger-haired than blond-haired* on this near side

[21]   'I think you'll find the administrator *more than happy* to talk to you about his work,' he said, firmly overriding me. [Andrew Puckett *Terminus*] ('happy to a degree that is not adequately described merely by the word *happy*')

[22]   The action however we should describe *more as painting than scribbling*

[23]   Now this car coming up behind me is getting closer … so I'm making my intentions *more than clear* … and acting early

Unlike the normal use of comparatives, this use can apply to verbs—for example, *acting* and *acted upon* in **[19]**. Metalinguistic *more* also occurs without the *than*-clause:

[24] As he looked he knew this was not a woman about to achieve happy release, *more a woman about to be cast into damnation.* [Michael Dobbs *Wall Games*]

More cannot be replaced by an inflected form:

[25] His account of the motif further disguises the village of Voisins in the middle distance, makes the landscape appear *more wild than cultivated*, and all but effaces the acqueduct. [W] (not: '*wilder* than cultivated')

NOTE

The concept of complementation has been extended to adjectives and nouns by analogy with its use with verbs. As with verbs, complements of adjectives and nouns need not be obligatory. Indeed, very few adjectives (e.g. *fond of*) or nouns (e.g. *lack of*) require a complement. But just as the same verb (e.g. *eat*) may be used as either intransitive (without any complement) or transitive (with a direct object as complement), so specific adjectives or nouns may occur with or without a complement.

With respect to complement clauses, clauses are considered to be complements if their form is determined by the subclass of adjective or noun; for example, whether the complement is finite, what subordinator is used, what forms of verbs are possible. Thus, the adjectives *aware* and *sure* are followed by *that*-clauses, though if the host clause is negative *sure* can also take interrogative clauses. Similarly, nouns such as *impression* belong to a subclass that can take appositive clauses. Another criterion for complementation is that when the complements are omitted the sentence, though grammatical, is felt to be semantically incomplete, as in *Are you sure?* Further evidence is provided by resemblances, in meaning and perhaps also in form, to verbs with the same complements. So, *you are aware that she is abroad* parallels *You know that she is abroad*, and *their decision to leave early* parallels *they decided to leave early*.

14.7 Complementation of verbs, adjectives, and nouns

Nominal clauses (cf. 14.3) can function as complements of verbs, adjectives, and nouns.

14.7.1 *That*-clause as complement

The complement clauses can be *that*-clauses, and the subordinator *that* can be omitted. Here are examples with verbs **[1]–[2]**, adjectives **[3]–[4]**, and nouns **[5]–[6]**:

[1] Only nine per cent answered *that religious leaders played a significant part in their life*

[2] I suppose *I was looking for something else* and just passed over it

[3] Were you aware *that there came a time when a deposit had to be paid by Ward for the property*

[4] You are sure *you informed us*

[5] And I got the impression *that people only knew if they'd got one themselves* uhm

[6] I get the impression *people are borrowing lots of money as well to fund them because supposedly at the other end there's this big pay-off*

14.7.1.1 Subjunctive in *that*-clause

In most complement *that*-clauses, the verb in the clause is indicative, but if the complement clause conveys the meaning of a directive, the **present subjunctive** is sometimes used instead, particularly in American English:

[7] I *urged* in my previous letter that these research staff *be* treated as their present colleagues and *be* permitted to apply for a redundancy payment when their contracts expire. [W]

[8] In the face of nuclear holocaust, not to mention the horrors of contemporary non-nuclear war, it is *imperative* that a new maturity *be* achieved in domestic and international communications. [William Bloom *Personal Identity, National Identity and International Relations*] (The *that*-clause is an extraposed subject. Compare 'That a new maturity be achieved is imperative'.)

[9] But *suggestions* that Saddam *be* given cash compensation, an oilfield or an island, would only encourage future extortion. [*Sunday Times*]

14.7.1.2 Alternatives to the subjunctive in *that*-clause

Alternatives to the present subjunctive in such contexts are the modal *should* (particularly in British English) **[10]** and the indicative **[11]**:

[10] Although Somalis are *determined* that he *should* never be allowed to stage a come-back

[11] It was *essential* that the Pope *appeared* to be the most important ruler in the world (Here too the *that*-clause is an extraposed subject.)

Another common alternative is to use a *to*-infinitive clause in place of a *that*-clause:

[12] Would you call into the station, or would you prefer *him to come to your house*? [Christopher Priest *The Quiet Woman*] (Compare the subjunctive in a finite clause: '... or would you prefer that he *come* to your house?')

14.7.2 *Wh*-clause as complement

Verbs, adjectives, and nouns may take as complements various types of *wh*-clause: interrogative, exclamative, and nominal relatives (cf. 14.3). These may be either finite clauses or *to*-infinitive clauses:

[13] I wonder *why he's holding a globe*

[14] Because she's still wondering ... why you haven't acknowledged *whatever it was she last sent you*

[15] I am not sure *if I want to become a Foster Corporate Parent*, but I am very interested. [*Wall Street Journal*]

[16] He was uncertain *what to do*

[17] Mr Rogers you asked the question *when should the allies according to you cease hostilities*

[18] On the basis of this already filtered and framed information the inspector takes a decision *whether to respond with an investigation*. [*British Journal of Criminology*]

The complement *wh*-clauses may also be linked to nouns by prepositions:

[19] It's just a question *of ... which is the more efficient approach*

[20] In other words the notion of worsening educational standards reflects the decision *about how to interpret the evidence ... rather than anything derived from the evidence itself*

[21] There is also growing doubt *as to whether further embryo research is the best way forward* ... and even increased recognition that assisting fertility does not depend on IVF alone

14.7.3 *To*-infinitive clause as complement

Complements for verbs, adjectives, and nouns may be *to*-infinitive clauses and these may be without their own subject. The understood subject is generally identical with that of the host clause:

[22] *I* want *to see what happens next*

[23] *I* certainly have no desire *to mislead anybody*

But with nouns the understood subject may also be generic (cf. 6.5):

[24] The first is the notion that freedom *to experiment on human embryo ... is* necessary *to help infertile couples* ('freedom for one to experiment')

Or it may just be left vague:

[25] As far as Watson was concerned ... you had his ... interviews when the decision *to seize the vessel* was taken on the twenty-second of August

When a noun phrase intervenes between the host verb and the *to*-infinitive, it is often unclear whether the phrase belongs to the host clause or the complement clause. In either case, if it is a pronoun it is in the objective case. Here are some examples:

[26] I don't want *her to catch your cold*

[27] I told *him to drive the forklift truck*

[28] Could I ask *you to look at certain passages of his interviews*

[29] The data entry controllers allow *you to edit the parameters.* [*Music Technology*]

In **[26]** *her* belongs to the complement clause as its subject, so that we can refer to the clause including *her* by *that* **[26a]** and we can make the clause passive **[26b]**:

[26a] I don't want *that.*

[26b] I don't want *your cold caught by her.*

Other common verbs that resemble *want* in this respect are *hate, like, love,* and *prefer.* On the other hand, in **[27]** and **[28]** the pronouns do not belong to the infinitive clause. We can refer to the clause separately from the pronoun **[27a]–[28a]** and we can make the pronoun the passive subject of the host clause **[27b]–[28b]**:

[27a] I told him *that.*

[28a] Could I ask you *this*?

[27b] *He was told* to drive the forklift truck.

[28b] Could *you be asked* to look at certain passages of his interviews?

Like *tell* and *ask* are some other verbs that can take indirect objects; for example: *order, persuade, recommend, teach.* Finally, **[29]** is an example of a construction that does not fit either the *want* type or the *tell* type.

If we apply the previous tests, we find that **[29]** yields:

[29a] The data entry controllers allow *that* (i.e. *you to edit the parameters*).

[29b] The data entry controllers allow *the parameters to be edited by you.*

[29c] The data entry controllers allow *you that.*

[29d] *You will be allowed* to edit the parameters.

Many verbs fall into this intermediate range but they vary and do not necessarily share the features of the infinitival complementation of *allow.* They include *consider, encourage, expect, help, permit.*

14.7.4 Bare infinitive clause as complement

Some verbs—but no adjectives or nouns—may take bare infinitive clauses (where the infinitive is without *to*) as complement. The verbs *help*, *let*, and *make* may take bare infinitive clauses that do not have their own subject:

[30] Japanese money will help turn Southeast Asia into a more cohesive economic region. [*Wall Street Journal*]

[31] You can now let *go of the front brake*

[32] They offered it to someone else but he changed his mind so they had to make *do with me*

Let and *make* are restricted to certain verbs in their complements, mainly *let go, let fly, let be, make do.*

A somewhat larger number of verbs may take as complement a bare infinitive clause with its own subject. They include *get, have, let, make, feel, hear, see, watch, help*:

[33] Theoreticians would have *us believe that if digital audio data are transmitted correctly, the resulting audio must also be correct.* [*Hi-Fi News & Record Review*]

[34] What would make *Guy de Maupassant decide to write through an Englishwoman*

[35] I let *them have ten minutes to get there at Union Council yesterday* and you shouted at me

[36] I had intended to take them dancing and to hear *Colin sing* but they wanted to see a film and so I was outnumbered. [W]

[37] Uhm ... I saw *Heidi get out* ... *go and get a drink* and I saw *her climb in miss the step* and then it was just ... lot of commotion after that getting her out

[38] Emma felt *her eyes prick suddenly*. [Denise Robertson *Remember the Moment*]

Help may be followed by either a bare infinitive clause or a *to*-infinitive clause:

[39] Well a few drops helped *you remember*

[40] He's a fifty-two-year-old business man and hotelier ... who helped *to finance the United Somali Congress when it was first established in Rome*

14.7.5 *-ed* participle clause as complement

Some verbs—but again no adjectives or nouns—may take *-ed* participle clauses as complement. They include *get, have, make, feel, hear, see, watch, like, need, want.*

[41] The person who booked me in had *his eyebrows shaved & replaced by straight black painted lines* [W]

[42] They will find great difficulty in making *their wants known to those in authority* [Peter Calvert and Susan Calvert *Latin America in the Twentieth Century*]

[43] We've seen *our great piles of bricks built up* while the homeless grow

[44] The council wants *the proposals 'abandoned' until a means is found to replace temporary accommodation with permanent housing.* [*Wembley Observer*]

Most of these verbs also take bare infinitive clauses, which can serve as the corresponding actives of the *-ed* participle clauses:

[42a] They will find great difficulty in making *those in authority know their wants.*

If the verbs cannot be complemented by bare infinitive clauses, *to*-infinitive clauses may serve the same purpose:

[44a] The council wants [people] to abandon the proposals.

14.7.6 *-ing* participle clause as complement

Some verbs may take *-ing* participle clauses as complements. With adjectives and nouns, the complement clause is typically introduced by a preposition. In this function the *-ing* participle is traditionally termed a **gerund**.

14.7.6.1 Verbs with *-ing* participle clause as complement

Common verbs with subjectless *-ing* participle clauses as complement include *avoid, (can't) bear, dislike, enjoy, hate, involve, like, love, mean, (not) mind, need, prefer, try*:

[45] Eleanor did not like *talking about herself,* and usually avoided personal questions. [Christopher Priest *The Quiet Woman*]

[46] The boys also enjoyed *seeing you* immensely. [W]

[47] Depending on who comes, you'll possibly need to bring sleeping bags and I hope you don't mind *sleeping on the floor* [W]

[48] This evidence involved *testing patients with spine severs.* [W]

[49] I'm sorry I missed *hearing your voice tonight.* [W]

[50] He increased the number of inspectors even though it meant *diverting manpower from inspections of domestically produced food.* [*Wall Street Journal*]

[51] Twelve people also described *going through a mock execution*

[52] I don't know if you ever tried *running a business* but it's very difficult

Many of the same verbs may be complemented by an *-ing* participle clause with its own subject.

[53] Law enforcement duty ... requires *a very real power over the citizen being entrusted to the policeman*

[54] But it doesn't stop *people surging forward into the sea*

[55] Yes it's easy to imagine *you doing all this.* [W]

[56] And I didn't in the least mind *you talking about Caroline.* [Valerie Kershaw *Rockabye*]

[57] That need not mean *allied tanks and troops going all the way to Baghdad* [*Sunday Times*]

If the subject is a pronoun or proper name it is often in the genitive case [58]–[59] (more precisely, a **possessive pronoun** in [58] and [59]), though the objective case for pronouns [55]–[56] and the **common case** for names are also often used:

[58] I hope you don't mind *my rubbing my hands*

[59] But most of the numbers are done in an upbeat style, which has the advantage of carrying the vocal introductions before the verse and preventing *their sounding superfluous out of stage context.* [*The Penguin Guide to Compact Discs*]

Nouns other than names generally take the common case, as in [54] and [57].

14.7.6.2 Adjectives with *-ing* participle clause as complement

Complementation of adjectives by *-ing* participle clauses is illustrated below. The clause may be without its own subject:

[60] I'm busy *eating* as a matter of fact

[61] And he will be happy *sticking to blue wallpaper* won't he

In [60]–[61] a preposition (here *with*) may be inserted between the adjective and the complement clause. For most adjectives the preposition is obligatory:

[62] He was afraid *of mentioning some girlfriend and offending the wife*

If the clause has its own subject, the preposition is always obligatory:

[63] Once the instructor is happy *with you riding quiet roads with minimal traffic* ... you'll both venture out onto busier roads

[64] Well I was wrong *about it being a show-place.*

[65] I could never get rid of the feeling that she was responsible *for his buying all the Prattertons,* and that through them she had somehow enticed him into marriage. [Julian Symons *Death's Darkest Face*]

The same options of case apply as with verb complementation. The possessive pronoun is used in **[65]** but the objective case of the personal pronoun in **[63]** and **[64]**.

14.7.6.3 **Nouns with *-ing* participle clause as complement**

Complementation of nouns by *-ing* participle clauses always requires a linking preposition, whether or not a subject is present. Examples are given below of complement clauses with their own subject:

[66] There is no question *of it being necessary or not.* [W]

[67] What are the chances *of it being* used? [*The Guardian*]

[68] Was there any realistic prospect ever *for it working*

[69] Now that we have adopted a system *of my paying all expenses and then claiming,* the problem should be solved. [W]

[70] And it is sometimes coupled to a charge *of Coleridge collapsing through a drug-induced fatigue into a snug intellectual cocoon.* [Graham Davidson *Coleridge's Career*]

The possessive pronoun is used in **[69]** but the objective case in **[66]–[68]**. The common case *Coleridge* is employed in **[70]** rather than the genitive *Coleridge's.*

14.7.7 **With noun phrase independent of complement clause**

The citations that follow resemble those in **[53]–[57]**. They differ in that the noun phrase that immediately follows the verb is independent of the complement clause. As a consequence it can be made the passive subject of the host clause, as in a construction that corresponds to **[71]**:

[71] I saw *him smiling and pointing up* as the ... fly-past came by

[71a] *He* was seen *smiling and pointing up* as the fly-past came by.

Furthermore, since the noun phrase is independent of the complement clause, it can be a personal pronoun—as in **[71]**—but not a possessive pronoun. Verbs commonly used in this type of construction include verbs of perception (e.g. *feel, hear, see*), *catch, discover, find, get, have, leave:*

[72] I can feel *you beginning to buckle under the weight of all this sincerity.* [W]

[73] The most notable was EMI who soon had *an all electronic scanning system running.* [*Practical Electronics*]

[74] We've got *Dim Dimitri Conichev just moving forward in our picture there*

[75] Not surprisingly we get uhm *the bulk of the heat coming in from the sun*

[76] You saw *the pool being cleaned* when you arrived

[77] I heard *the sound of a body hitting the car*—it's a very soft impact sound. [*Western Mail*]

[78] But for others it's a nightmare as they find *their work being used without*

permission

[79] I will leave *that question* uhm … *hanging for now*

[80] Keep *the indicator going*

[81] She could feel *the lie making her blush*. [Christopher Priest *The Quiet Woman*]

14.7.8 Choice of complement clause

For some verbs there is a choice of complement clause. The choice may be from two or three clause types: a finite clause, an *-ing* participle clause, or an infinitive clause. *Remember*, for example, may take all three:

[82] Most of the time I remember *I felt nothing at all* [W]

[83] I remember *learning French*

[84] We must remember *to get on that plane* you know

The finite and *-ing* participle clauses **[82]**–**[83]** are **factual**, referring to some situation that has existed, whereas the infinitive clause **[84]** is **non-factual**, referring to a situation that may come into existence. It is possible to replace the finite clause in **[82]** by a participle clause and to replace the participle clause in **[83]** by a finite clause, in both instances preserving roughly the same meaning:

[82a] Most of the time I remember *having felt nothing at all*.

[83a] I remember *that I learned French*.

The finite *that*-clause is more flexible than the non-finite clauses. We can obtain a rough equivalent of the infinitive clause of **[84]** by inserting an appropriate modal auxiliary (in this instance the semi-modal *be to*) in the *that*-clause:

[84a] We must remember *that we are to get on that plane*.

Furthermore, *that*-clauses allow a range of tense and modal possibilities not open to the non-finite clauses:

[85] Remember *that alcohol affects your judgement of both people and situations*. [W]

[86] And one must also remember *that uh the same Arnold Bax has written poetry and I think plays under the pseudonym of Dermot O'Brien*

[87] Remember *that other people may be just as apprehensive as you are* [W]

Apart from the factual/non-factual distinction, *-ing* participle and infinitive clauses sometimes differ aspectually. The participle clause may indicate duration or iteration:

[88] I hate *being rushed*. [W]

[88a] I hate *to be rushed*.

In contrast with the infinitive clause in **[88a]**, the participle clause adds an indication of duration.

Chapter 15
Reported Speech

Summary

The major categories of reported speech (including reported thought) are direct speech and indirect speech. Indirect speech involves an orientation to the deixis of the reporting situation, generally resulting in shifts of (particularly) pronouns and a backshift in tense. Minor intermediate categories of reporting are free direct speech and free indirect speech.

15.1 Direct speech and indirect speech

Reported speech conveys reports of acts of communication, including those of the reporters themselves. The reports may represent unspoken thoughts, either self-reports or deductions about the thoughts of others. In literature, the narrator is given the conventional licence (if the author so wishes) of knowing the thoughts and feelings of some or all the characters as well as what they say in private conversations from which the narrator is supposedly absent.

The two major categories of reported speech are direct speech and indirect speech. **Direct speech** purports to convey the exact words that were spoken or written. **Indirect speech** conveys the content rather than the form. Of course, in both types only a part of the total communication may be reported. Citation **[1]** contains two examples of direct speech extracted from a fictional dialogue that presents a question and a response:

> **[1]** One day the question that had dominated him all this time slipped from him, almost as if it had no meaning for him:
> *'Was the child mine?'*
> *'Yes,'* Susan said. *'Though I know I could never convince you of that.'* [Paul Sayer *Howling at the Moon*]

A possible indirect report of the exchange in **[1]** would be:

> **[1a]** He asked *whether the child was his*. She said *that it was, though she knew she could never convince him of that*.

The continuation of **[1]** provides an example of indirect speech, which represents the man's unspoken thought:

> **[2]** Quietly doomed, he felt *he must continue*. [Paul Sayer *Howling at the Moon*]

A possible direct report of his feeling would be:

> **[2a]** Quietly doomed, he felt, *'I must continue'*.

DIRECT SPEECH IN DETAIL

The reporter is held responsible for the accuracy of direct speech. By convention it is considered unnecessary to provide replications of pronunciation or the other speech features, though the manner of speaking is sometimes indicated (particularly in literature) by the choice of verb (e.g. *mumble, whisper, screech, sigh*) or by the addition of an adverbial (e.g. *hastily, placidly, sarcastically, indignantly, in trepidation*). In the written language, verbatim accuracy is generally expected (and may be legally required) in direct reporting. Omissions from quotations are supposed to be indicated by ellipsis periods and any changes by editorial comments.

15.1.1 **Direct speech accompanied by a reporting clause**

In writing, direct speech is typically enclosed in quotation marks. The **reporting clause**, with any accompanying description or comment, may precede the direct speech [3], follow it [4], or come in the middle [5]:

[3]   Cosmo said, '*Can I lend a hand?*', and, pushing, asked, '*What is the picnic in aid of?*' [Mary Wesley *A Sensible Life*]

[4]   '*Where's the sea?*' I asked. [Agnes Owens 'Patience' in Alison Fell *The Seven Cardinal Virtues*]

[5]   '*Something's wrong with Derek?*' Anne wailed, getting to her feet. '*I knew it. He's dead!*' She swayed back and forth on the spot, her shoulders shuddering. [Steve Harris *Adventureland*]

When the reporting clause is medial or final, its subject is not a pronoun, and its verb is in the simple present or simple past, then **subject–verb inversion** is sometimes used:

[6]   'It can't be far away,' *said Mary Jane*, swivelling her head. 'Isn't that a castle on the top of the cliff?' [Agnes Owens 'Patience' in Alison Fell *The Seven Cardinal Virtues*]

Reporting clauses are often omitted in fiction writing where there is a sequence of exchanges and it is clear who is speaking in each turn:

[7]   She was spooling the programme on to the tape machine when the phone rang.
      'Isobel? It's Bruno here.'
      'What's that frightful noise in the background?' [Valerie Kershaw *Rockabye*]

15.1.2 **Reported speech introduced by a noun of speaking**

The reported speech, whether direct or indirect, may be introduced by a **noun of speaking** rather than a verb:

[8]   A firm point of law can be seen in *the wife's statement* 'Take up the spike from the ground. If people, or if cattle should perish upon it, you yourself and I, with our children, will either be put to death, or be led into slavery'. [W]

[9]   The essence of religion ... is *the answer to everybody's question* ... what is the meaning of me and the other and the world

[10] This reinforces *the earlier statement*, that man is blind to what he cannot see. [W]

[11] When did we last hear in a television discussion or a newspaper editorial *the simple assertion* that something was wrong because God or religious doctrine said so

The reported speech may be connected to some nouns of speaking by a preposition:

[12] This is going to be *a question of* who you know not what you know

[13] I can't give *a satisfactory explanation as to* why that should have occurred

It may also be a **predicative** following the verb *be*:

[14] You've anticipated my next question again because *my next question was* how do you think you viewed women at that time and how does that compare with your views today

[15] *What I want to claim is* ... that communication now extends far beyond language ... because of technologies which have matured from infancy during the twentieth century

15.1.3 **Mixed indirect and direct speech**

A report may be partly in indirect speech and partly in direct speech. The mixture is clearer in writing, where the quotation marks can signal direct speech:

[16] The Motor-Cycle Crash Helmets (Religious Exemption) Act 1976 provides that any requirement imposed now or later by regulations under the 1972 Act shall not apply to any follower of the Sikh religion 'while he is wearing a turban'. [Sebastian Poulter *Asian Traditions and English Law*]

15.1.4 **Hypothetical and abstracted reported speech**

Both direct and indirect speech may be hypothetical rather than a report of what was actually spoken, or they may present an abstraction of what might be said:

[17] If I say *I haven't done anything*, then you think I'm being deceitful. [Paul Sayer *Howling at the Moon*]

[18] I was going to tell you *Ginny's got engaged* but you knew that anyway

[19] People would say *you've just got cold feet*

[20] They nearly said *they weren't going to op let me operate on her*

[21] And everybody said *oh after dinner we're looking forward to hearing this*

[22] I can remember when common sense said *that for instance women were weaker than men women shouldn't wear trousers women should earn less than men*

15.2 Forms of indirect speech

Indirect speech is used to report **declaratives**, **interrogatives**, **directives**, and **exclamatives** (cf. 2.4).

15.2.1 **Types of nominal clause reporting indirect speech**

The nominal clauses reporting indirect speech are commonly **complements** of verbs of speaking or thinking, though they may also be complements of nouns (cf. 15.1).

15.2.1.1 **Indirect declaratives**
Nominal *that*-clauses are used for indirect declaratives:

[1] General Schwarzkopf claims *that continuing the fighting a few days longer would have made no difference to the fate of the Kurds* [*Daily Mail*]

The subordinator *that* is often omitted after most of the verbs:

[2] You see he told somebody *I was weak*

Some verbs also allow **infinitive clauses** [3]–[4] or *-ing* **participle clauses** [5]–[6] for indirect declaratives:

[3] But first he'd had to find out who claimed *to be speaking on behalf of the company its executives or the shareholders*

[4] The communiqué warns that the reporters will be executed immediately if the police capture any of the traffickers' families to exchange for the hostages; it also promises *to murder relatives of police officers and politicians*. [*The Independent*]

[5] The patients were interviewed and tested in a laboratory and results consistently showed that the higher the spine sever the less patients reported *being able to 'feel' an emotion*. [W]

[6] He recalled *visiting both Yugoslavia and Indonesia as a boy with his grandfather and mother, the latter when he was only six years old*. [Nicholas Nugent *Rajiv Gandhi*]

15.2.1.2 Indirect interrogatives

Indirect interrogatives are reported by various finite interrogative clauses; *yes–no* questions **[7]**, alternative questions **[8]**, and *wh*-questions **[9]** (cf. 2.5):

[7] In a reference to the Hindu claim over a mosque in the northern holy town of Iodia he asked *whether religious faith could be placed above the constitution and whether India was heading towards becoming a theocratic state*

[8] Could you also inform me *whether individual members receive the journal or whether they need to be journal subscribers as well*. [W]

[9] I want to ask *what you think about the role of the father today*

15.2.1.3 Indirect directives

Indirect directives (orders, requests, and the like) may be reported by **nominal finite clauses**. The verb is then usually **subjunctive** (especially in American English) or it is used with a modal such as *should*:

[10] The project was first proposed four years ago and until recently the Quebec government had insisted *that the Canadian government help pay for the project*. [*Wall Street Journal*]

[11] But they recommend *that any work by the water, electricity and gas authorities should be done before the scheme is started*. [*Western Mail*]

Suggest also allows an **-*ing* participle clause** as an indirect request:

[12] Mr. Bennett has suggested *sending drug dealers to military-style camps designed to build self-esteem*. [*Wall Street Journal*]

Indirect directives are commonly **infinitive clauses**:

[13] The Louisiana attorney general and New Orleans district attorney have asked a federal district court *to allow them to revive laws making it a crime to perform abortions, punishable by as much as 10 years in prison*. [*Wall Street Journal*]

[14] A marijuana smuggler is told *to work with AIDS patients*. [*Wall Street Journal*]

[15] As a result, the FDA ordered importers *to detain most of China's canned-mushroom shipments for tests and began a nationwide recall of cans that had been linked to outbreaks*. [*Wall Street Journal*]

15.2.1.4 Indirect exclamatives

Indirect exclamatives are reported by exclamative clauses introduced by *what* or *how*:

[16] My agent called me in this morning to tell me *how good he was*. [W]

15.2.2 Referential shifts

Indirect speech is geared to the reporter's **deixis**: that is to say, it is geared to references to time, place, and participants from the point of view of the reporter and the person or persons being addressed by the reporter, and not to the original discourse that is being recorded. There are consequential referential shifts from the original discourse.

15.2.2.1 Pronoun shifting

Personal pronouns, possessive pronouns, and reflexives are **shifted** to take account of the reporting situation. Hence, in **[17]** the original *I* and *my* of the speaker are shifted from first person to third person, and a possible original utterance might have had only either *my husband* or *Mark*:

[17] Mrs Collier said *she*'d like to come down one day and uh get some knowledge of *her husband Mark*

Similarly, in [18] the original *I* has been shifted to *you*, the addressee in the reporting situation:

[18] And you said *you* were looking in the Guardian uhm on Monday obviously

In [19] *I* replaces *she* or the name in the original discourse:

[19] My mother said to my cousin apparently that *I* was getting fat

And in [20] the instances of *I* and *my* replace *you* and *your* in the original discourse:

[20] The last doctor said that it was quite a lot to do with breathing through *my* nose because *I* couldn't breathe through *my* nose during the night when *I*'m sleeping

15.2.2.2 **Tense shifting**
Another type of shift from the original discourse to the reported or indirect speech is **backshift**: a shift from the original present tense to past tense. The original simple past or present perfect may also be shifted to past perfect. The relationship between the tenses in the reporting clause and the reported clause as a result of backshift is the **sequence of tenses**.

[21] I felt a little consolation when a policewoman told me how lucky I *was* that the bullet fragments *were embedded* in my car door frame and dashboard rather than my head. [*Wall Street Journal*]

[22] And what he said was that alcohol *was* good for the memory

[23] Mr. Cohen, the new Drexel general counsel, says several attorneys have told him they *would* not *submit* detailed bills because of a concern the bills *would* later *be viewed* by the government. [*Wall Street Journal*]

[24] And he said that uh Mr Hook *had told* him that he *'d been* at a health farm for a fortnight worrying about what to do with his business and his uh private life

[25] Andreotti said that 139 secret arms dumps *had been gathered* in over the last decade—but 12 *were* seriously *missing*. [*The Observer*]

The past perfects in [24] and [25] could be replaced by simple pasts:

[24a] He said that Mr Hook *told* him that he *was* at a health farm for a fortnight.

[25a] Andreotti said that 139 secret arms dumps *were* gathered in over the last decade.

15.2.2.3 **Retention of present tense**
The original present may be retained if the content still applies at the time of the reporting situation:

[26] On Friday, Sen. Boren told a meeting of the Democratic committee members that he *intends* to offer an amendment to Sen. Bentsen's proposal that would reduce the capital gains rate. [*Wall Street Journal*]

The report in the newspaper [26] evidently precedes the actual offer of an amendment. Similarly, in [23] the refusal to submit applies at the time of reporting, so that the pasts could be replaced by presents (*will not submit*; *will later be viewed*). In [21] the luck of the interviewee and the embedded fragments were still in evidence in the reporting situation, and so presents could have been used in that sentence too (*how lucky I am*; *the bullet fragments are embedded*). The same principle can be applied to [22], where a generalization is stated (*alcohol is good for the memory*).

Further examples appear below of the retention of the original present tense forms:

[27] The organisation ARK has said that sea-level *will rise* by one meter ... if present pollution levels and conditions *continue*

[28] Rabbi Sacks said at one point faith *is* not *measured* by acts of worship alone

[29] Well you all know that Malthus said two hundred years ago ... population when unchecked *increases* in a geometrical ratio

[30] Zox said to me recently that he *doesn*'t *think* there *'s going to be* a rehearsal for the wedding. [W]

[31] Novell demonstrated NetWare and said that it *'s* a very fine network operating system. [*Personal Computer World*]

15.2.2.4 **Present tense in reporting clause**

The simple present may be used—as an alternative to the simple past—in the reporting clause (cf. 11.6), as in:

[32] But the referee *says* it wasn't straight

15.2.2.5 **Place and time reference adjustment**

Place and time references may also need to be adjusted to take account of their deixis in the reporting situation. For example, *there* in [33] may have been shifted from *here* in the original discourse:

[33] Like going in and being told one's never had an account *there* at all. [Sarah Caudwell 'An Acquaintance with Mr Collins' in *A Suit of Diamonds*]

15.3 Free direct speech and free indirect speech

The two minor modes of reporting are related to the two major modes.

15.3.1 **Free direct speech**

Free direct speech is essentially direct speech without reporting clauses. It is employed in fiction for interior monologue, to represent a character's stream of thought. Present tense is used where appropriate, as in direct speech.

The thoughts of Cathy in [1] are in the present tense, and there is no backshift. But, as is typical in free indirect speech, the third person is used instead of the first person. The reporting of Cathy's thoughts constitutes a mixture of free direct speech (in tense) and free indirect speech (in person shift):

[1] 'Would you have liked something like that for your fiftieth?'
'Heavens, no! You know me. Not a man for surprises. I must be off. See you this evening.'
'See you this evening.'
Not a man for surprises. Cathy smiles to herself with the truth of that remark as she washes up the breakfast dishes. *So much is Will not a man for surprises that he is no more capable of giving them than of receiving. Her own fiftieth is not far away. It will not be long before he asks his regular question: 'What would you like for your birthday?' However outrageous or impossible the answer, he will get her what she wants. Only on one occasion, earlier in their marriage, when she asked for 'A surprise, please', has she seen him completely thrown, searching miserably for ideas. She must not put him through that agony again.*

But instead of considering possible suggestions, Cathy finds her thoughts still concerned with the surprise party. [Anne Melville 'Portrait of a Woman' in *Snapshots*]

15.3.2 **Free indirect speech**

In general, free indirect speech has tense backshift verb forms as well as pronoun shift, but it retains some of the expressive features of direct discourse, such as vocatives, direct questions, and interjections. In **[2]–[4]** we see the free indirect speech merging with the narration:

[2] Before leaving the house, he had gone down into the kitchen, and cut one thick slice of bread and butter, and he ate that, now, with one of the cheese triangles. As soon as he had finished, he wanted a drink. *He had been stupid not to find some sort of bottle. Well, there was no drink, it would be better to try and not think about it.* Instead he got up and crossed to the other side of the clearing. [Susan Hill *I'm the King of the Castle*]

[3] My father refused to complete the financial aid papers; finally, in desperation, I stole the tax returns from the glove compartment of his Toyota and did them myself. More waiting. Then a note from the Dean of Admissions. *An interview was required, and when could I fly to Vermont?* I could not afford to fly to Vermont, and I wrote and told him so. Another wait, another letter. *The college would reimburse me for my travel expenses if their scholarship offer was accepted.* Meanwhile the financial aid packet had come in. [Donna Tartt *The Secret History*]

[4] On the rare occasions he thought of Joyce, it was to reproach himself for stupidity. *There's no surer way to lose a good friend than to marry her. High-spirited, bouncy, generous Joyce had in middle age and close proximity become a bore; and as for sex, so good in experimental and lusty youth, that had switched to something akin to aerobics. But now, after the Bodmin Assizes, he had a free weekend. He would dawdle back to London, bird-watch on the way. Should he head for Slapton Ley and the Exe Estuary for migratory birds, or chance the cliffs of North Devon?* He drove as far as Launceston enjoying his indecision. [Mary Wesley *A Sensible Life*]

Further Reading

Section 1 Among the numerous introductions to linguistics, mention may be made of *Language and Linguistics: An Introduction*, by John Lyons (Cambridge: Cambridge University Press, 1981) and *General Linguistics: An Introductory Survey*, by R. H. Robins (London: Longman, 4th edn., 1989). *Teach Yourself Linguistics*, by Jean Aitchison (London: Hodder & Stoughton, 4th edn., 1992) is a highly readable, wide-ranging, elementary introductory text.

Section 1.1 There are now a sizeable number of books dealing with English throughout the world. A useful reference work is *The Oxford Companion to the English Language* edited by Tom McArthur (Oxford: Oxford University Press, 1992). A range of statistics on the uses of English appears in *English: A World Commodity* by Brian McCallen (London: The Economist Intelligence Unit, 1989). A summary account of differences between national standard varieties of English can be found in *International English: A Guide to Varieties of Standard English*, by Peter Trudgill and Jean Hanna (London: Edward Arnold, 2nd edn., 1985). Among other general works on English internationally are *The Story of English*, by Robert McCrum, William Cran, and Robert MacNeil (London: Faber & Faber, 2nd edn., 1992), *The Other Tongue: English Across Cultures*, edited by Braj B. Kachru (Urbana: University of Illinois Press, 2nd edn., 1992), *The New Englishes*, by John Platt, Heidi Weber, and Ho Mian Liam (London: Routledge & Kegan Paul, 1984), *English as a World Language*, edited by Richard W. Bailey and Manfred Görlach (Ann Arbor: University of Michigan Press, 1982), *The English Language Today*, edited by Sidney Greenbaum (Oxford: Pergamon, 1985). Devoted to English internationally are the quarterly magazine *English Today* (Cambridge University Press) and the scholarly journals *World Englishes* and *English World-Wide*. On the history of English and other languages in the British Isles and their present status and uses, see *Language in the British Isles*, edited by Peter Trudgill (Cambridge: Cambridge University Press, 1984).

Section 1.3 *Webster's Dictionary of English Usage* (Springfield, Mass.: Merriam-Webster, 1989) is recommended for those who wish to know the historical background to usage controversies, the views of writers who have commented on disputed usages, and the evidence for present-day usage. A recent practical usage guide for quick reference is the *Longman Guide to English Usage*, by Sidney Greenbaum and Janet Whitcut (London: Longman, 1988). The best of the newspaper commentators on language is William Safire, who writes a weekly column in *The New York Times*, which is reprinted in *The International Herald Tribune*. He has published several books based on his column and has included in his books the letters generated by his observations. On issues concerned with the standard language, see *Authority in Language*, by James Milroy and Lesley Milroy (London: Routledge, 2nd edn., 1991). On grammars in relation to the standard language, see 'A Grammarian's Responsibility', in *Good English and the Grammarian*, by Sidney Greenbaum (London: Longman, 1988), ch. 3.

Section 1.4 On variation according to use, see *Investigating English Style*, by David Crystal and Derek Davy (London: Longman, 1969). A lively and enlightening discussion of jargons appears in *Jargon: Its Uses and Abuses*, by Walter Nash (Oxford: Blackwell, 1993).

Section 1.6 On correct English and good English, see *Bad Language*, by Lars Andersson and Peter Trudgill (Oxford: Blackwell, 1990) and 'Good English', in *Good English and the Grammarian*, by Sidney Greenbaum (London: Longman, 1988), ch. 1. Excellent analyses of abuses of language appear in *Language—The Loaded Weapon*, by Dwight Bolinger (London: Longman, 1980). On swearing, see *Swearing: A Social History of Foul Language, Oaths and Profanity in English*, by Geoffrey Hughes (Oxford: Blackwell, 1991). On political correctness, see *The Official Politically Correct Dictionary and Handbook*, by Henry Beard and Christopher Cerf (London: Grafton, 1992) and *The Politically Correct Phrasebook*, by Nigel Rees (London: Bloomsbury, 1993). A history of sexist bias in English and attempts to counter it appears in *Grammar and Gender*, by Dennis Baron (New Haven: Yale University Press, 1986).

Section 1.8 The grammars of non-standard varieties have not been researched to anywhere near the extent that standard varieties have been. Summary accounts of the grammars of British non-standard varieties can be found in *English Accents and Dialects*, by Arthur Hughes and Peter Trudgill (London: Edward Arnold, 1989), *The Dialects of England*, by Peter Trudgill (Oxford: Basil Blackwell, 1990), and *Real English: The Grammar of English Dialects in the British Isles*, edited by James Milroy and Lesley Milroy (London: Longman, 1993). Selective information on the grammars of American non-standard varieties appears in *Dialects and American English* by Walt Wolfram (Englewood Cliffs, NJ: Prentice Hall, 1991). Essays on aspects of non-standard dialects in the USA, Canada, Australia, and the British Isles appear, with summary introductions, in *Dialects of English: Studies in Grammatical Variation*, edited by Peter Trudgill and J. K. Chambers (London: Longman, 1991). Works that deal with these grammars focus on certain features that display differences from standard varieties. It is assumed that most of the grammar will be identical for all varieties.

Section 1.11.3 Accounts of English traditional grammars appear in *The English Reference Grammar: Language and Linguistics, Writers and Readers*, edited by Gerhard Leitner (Tübingen: Max Niemeyer, 1986); *Grammatical Theory in Western Europe 1500–1700: Trends in Vernacular Grammar*, by G. A. Padley (Cambridge: Cambridge University Press, 1985); *English Grammatical Categories and the Tradition to 1800*, by Ian Michael (Cambridge: Cambridge University Press, 1970). A comprehensive study of English teaching in earlier periods, including the teaching of English language, is to be found in *The Teaching of English: From the Sixteenth Century to 1870*, by Ian Michael (Cambridge: Cambridge University Press, 1987).

Section 2.1 The major reference grammar of present-day English is *A Comprehensive Grammar of the English Language*, by Randolph Quirk, Sidney Greenbaum, Geoffrey Leech, and Jan Svartvik (London: Longman, 1985). An abridgement of that work, with some revisions, is *A Student's Grammar of the English Language*, by Sidney Greenbaum and Randolph Quirk (London: Longman, 1990). Other recent general grammars that are worth consulting are *A New Approach to English Grammar, on Semantic Principles*, by R. M. W. Dixon (Oxford: Clarendon Press, 1991) and the 2-volume *English Grammar: A Function-Based Introduction*, by T. Givón (Amsterdam: John Benjamins, 1993).

Section 2.10 The classic works on speech act theory are by philosophers: *How To Do Things With Words*, by J. L. Austin (Oxford: Oxford University Press, 1962), *Speech Acts*, by John R. Searle (Cambridge: Cambridge University Press, 1969), *Expression and Meaning: Studies in the Theory of Speech Acts*, by John R. Searle, chs. 1 and 2 (Cambridge: Cambridge University Press, 1979). For a concise account by a linguist of various theories dealing with speech acts and a critique of them, see *Pragmatics* by Stephen C. Levinson (Cambridge: Cambridge University Press, 1983), ch. 5.

Section 11.18 For a readable and enlightening study of multi-word verbs, see *The Phrasal Verb in English* by Dwight Bolinger (Cambridge, Mass.: Harvard University Press, 1971).

Section 13.1 The concept of a sentence is discussed in *Syntax*, by P. H. Matthews (Cambridge: Cambridge University Press, 1981), ch. 2.

Section 13.2 For coordination and subordination, see *A Comprehensive Grammar of the English Language*, by Randolph Quirk, Sidney Greenbaum, Geoffrey Leech, and Jan Svartvik (London: Longman, 1985), chs. 13–15.

Section 13.6 On clause complexes, see *An Introduction to Functional Grammar*, 2nd edition, by M. A. K. Halliday (London: Edward Arnold, 1994), ch. 7.

Section 15.1 On reported speech, with particular reference to indirect and free indirect speech, see *The Fictions of Language and the Languages of Fiction*, by Monika Fludernik (London: Routledge, 1993).

Glossary of Grammatical Terms

This glossary contains only terms that occur in the main text, most of which are discussed there; a reference (by chapter, section, and subsection) to the place where this discussion occurs is given at the end of the glossary entry. Items in bold within entries are cross-references to other entries in the glossary where further information is given.

absolute describing the uninflected form of a gradable adjective or adverb. 4.4

absolute clause an adverbial participle clause or adverbial verbless clause that is not introduced by a subordinator and that has its own subject. 14.4.3

abstract noun a noun used to refer to an entity that is not perceptible and tangible, such as quality, state of mind, or an event. 5.5.3

active see **passive**. 4.2.5

additive adverb a type of focusing adjunct that emphasizes that what is said applies also to the focused part. 8.7.3.4

adjective. An adjective is a word such as *wise* that typically can premodify a noun such as *decision* (*a wise decision*) and function as **subject predicative** after a **copular verb** such as *be* or *seem* (*The decision is/seems wise*). When used as the premodifier of a noun, the adjective is attributive; when used as subject predicative, it is predicative. Adjectives that can be used both attributively and predicatively are central adjectives. Most adjectives can be intensified by adverbs such as *very* (*very wise/informative*) and permit **comparison** either inflectionally (*wiser/wisest*) or periphrastically (*more informative, most informative*). The inflectional forms are comparative (*wiser*) or superlative (*wisest*). Adjectives that accept intensification and comparison are gradable adjectives. See **gradability, nominal adjective**. 4.4

adjective phrase. An adjective phrase has an adjective such as *heavy* or *informative* as its head. Within the adjective phrase the adjective may be premodified (*too heavy*) or postmodified (*afraid of spiders*) or both premodified and postmodified (*too heavy to carry, extremely afraid of spiders*). 12.1

adjunct. An adjunct is an **adverbial** (an optional element) that is integrated to some extent in sentence or clause structure. The major semantic subclasses of adjunct are space, mainly referring to location (*in my city*) or direction (*to New York*); time, mainly referring to time location (*on Monday*), duration (*permanently*), or frequency (*every week*); process, mainly conveying the manner in which the action denoted by the verb is performed (*smoothly*); focus, adverbials that focus on a particular unit (*only, mainly, utterly*). Adverbials that are not adjuncts are sentence adverbials, either **conjuncts** or **disjuncts**. 8.7.3

adverb. An adverb is a word that typically functions as a premodifier of an adjective or another adverb or as an **adverbial**. *Very* is an adverb that can be a premodifier of an adjective (*very sharp*) or another adverb (*very carelessly*). *Often* is an adverb that functions as an adverbial (*They often complained about the noise*). Many adverbs can be either premodifiers (*too loud, too loudly*) or adverbials (*I too have complained*), though not necessarily with the same meaning. Adverbs that have the same form as adjectives can take **comparison** inflections: comparative ('work *harder*'), superlative ('work *hardest*'). 4.4

adverb phrase. An adverb phrase has an adverb such as *badly* or *luckily* as its head. The adverb may be premodified (*so quickly, very luckily*), or postmodified (*quickly enough, luckily for me*), or both premodified and postmodified (*very luckily for me*). 8.6, 12.5

adverbial. An adverbial is an optional element in sentence or clause structure. There may be more than one adverbial in a sentence or clause. Adverbials are either sentence adverbials or **adjuncts**. Sentence adverbials are loosely attached to the sentence or clause. They are either **conjuncts** or **disjuncts**. 3.8

adverbial clause. An adverbial clause is a clause that functions as an **adverbial** in sentence or clause structure. 14.2.3

affected role a semantic role which refers to the person or thing directly affected by the action. 3.9.1.4, 3.9.2.1

affix. An affix is a segment that is not itself a word but is attached to a word. If it is attached to the beginning of a word it is a prefix (*un-* in *undecided*), and if it is attached to the end of a word it is a suffix (*-ize* in *polarize*). Suffixes that represent grammatical categories, such as plural for nouns and past for verbs, are inflections (*-s* in *computers* and *-ed* in *revealed*). The process of adding affixes to form new words is affixation or derivation.

agent the doer of an action

agentive role a semantic role that refers to the doer of an action. 3.9.1.1

agreement see **subject–verb agreement**

alternative clause see **alternative question**

alternative condition. An alternative condition presents two or more conditions (*'Whether you buy the house or rent it,* you'll find the monthly payments too expensive').

alternative-conditional clause a clause which expresses two or more stated possible conditions. 14.5.5

alternative question. An alternative question offers two or more options for the response (*Do you want to stay a little longer or go home straightaway? Which would you prefer, coffee or tea?*). 2.5.3

anaphoric. Anaphoric reference is a reference to a preceding expression (*it* referring to a draft in *I'll write a draft and show it to you for your comments*). Cataphoric reference is a reference to a following expression (*she* referring to the doctor in *As soon as she had finished questioning the patient, the doctor phoned for an ambulance*). See also **deixis, ellipsis**.

anaphoric ellipsis ellipsis preceded by the antecedent. 3.11.2.1

antecedent. The antecedent of an expression is the expression that it refers to. The antecedent of *who* in *the official who spoke to us so rudely* is *the official*, and the antecedent of *she* is *the doctor* in *The doctor will see you as soon as she is ready*.

anticipatory *it*. Anticipatory *it* takes the position (usually a subject) that might have been occupied by a clause. Instead of the clausal subject in *That they refused to sign our petition is surprising*, anticipatory *it* is introduced as subject and the clause is extraposed (postponed to the end) in *It is surprising that they refused to sign our petition*. 6.7.2

apposition. Apposition is a relationship between two units that refer to the same entity or overlap in their reference. Typically the units are noun phrases and are juxtaposed (*George Washington, the first president of the United States*). Sometimes an apposition marker introduces the second unit (*namely, that is to say, for example*). In coordinative apposition the two units are linked by *or* or (less usually) *and* (*eeg, or brain wave trace*). 4.5.2, 10.11

appositive an item linked by apposition to another which is identical in its reference (refers to the same person or same thing) or overlaps in its reference (one appositive is included in the reference of the other). 4.5.2, 10.11

aspect. Aspect is a grammatical category referring primarily to the way that the time denoted by the verb is regarded. English has two aspects: the perfect aspect and the progressive (or continuous) aspect. The perfect aspect is expressed by a combination of the auxiliary *have* and the *-ed* participle (*has mentioned, have called, had seen*); it is used to locate the time of a situation as preceding that of another situation (*She has mentioned it several times since she arrived*). The progressive aspect is expressed by a combination of the auxiliary *be* and the *-ing* participle (*is mentioning, was calling, were seeing*); it is chiefly used to focus on the duration of a situation (*He was calling for help*). The two aspects may be combined, the perfect followed by the progressive (*He had been calling for help*). See also **participle**. 4.2.4, 11.4

assertive determiner, pronoun a determiner or pronoun with a positive force. 6.13.1.2

asyndetic coordination coordination when coordinators are not present but can readily be inserted. See **coordination**. 4.5.1, 13.2.3

attitudinal past the use of the past tense as a more polite or more tentative alternative to the present with verbs of thinking or wishing. 11.6.1.2

attributive describing an adjective used as the premodifier of a noun. 8.2

auxiliary. An auxiliary (or auxiliary verb or helping verb) is one of a small set of verbs that combine with a main verb to form the perfect or progressive aspect or the passive, or to convey distinctions of modality (such as possibility or permission), and to function as operator for forming negative sentences and questions. The three primary auxiliaries are *be*, *have*, and *do*. *Be* is used to form the progressive (*was making*) and the passive (*was made*) and *have* to form the perfect (*has made*). *Do* is used to perform the functions of an operator when no auxiliary is otherwise present (*Did they make it?*, *They didn't make it*). The modals (or modal auxiliaries) are *can, could, may, might, shall, should, will, would, must*. In addition, there are a number of marginal auxiliaries (*dare, need, ought to, used to*) that share some of the characteristics of the auxiliaries and a larger group of auxiliary-like verbs (or semi-auxiliaries) that convey similar notions of time, aspect, and modality (e.g.: *be going to, have to, had better*). 7.9, 11.1

auxiliary-like verb a verb that resembles an auxiliary in conveying notions of time, aspect, or modality. 7.9.3, 11.17

backchannel an item intended to encourage the other speaker to continue, often also expressing agreement. 13.1.4.1

backshift past the use of the past tense in indirect speech or thought in a backshift from the present tense (sequence of tenses). 11.6.1.1

backshift past perfect the use of the past perfect in indirect speech or thought in a backshift from the simple past or the present perfect. 11.12

backshifting. Backshifting is a shifting in the tense of a verb of a reported clause in indirect speech. *She said Pam was looking well* reports an utterance such as *Pam is looking well*, where the verb (*is*) is in the present tense. Similarly, the simple past and the present perfect may be backshifted to the past perfect: *Pam played well* and *Pam has played well* may both be reported as *She said Pam had played well*. The present tense may be retained if the situation (including an expressed opinion) holds at the time of reporting: *She said Pam writes well*. Backshifting also takes place in **conditional clauses**. 15.2.2.2

bare infinitive see **infinitive**. 7.2.1.4

base form. The base form of the verb is the uninflected form (*remain, take, write*), the form to which inflections are added (*remained, takes, writing*), except that for the highly irregular verb *be* the base form is *be*. The base form is used for: (1) the present tense except for the third person singular (*They remain in good spirits*), but *be* has the equivalents *am* and *are*; (2) the imperative (*Remain here*); (3) present subjunctive (*I recommended that he remain here*); (4) infinitive, which may be the bare infinitive (*You must remain here*) or the *to*-infinitive (*I want you to remain here*). 10.14

cardinal, cardinal numeral a numeral that refers to quantity. 6.15.1

case. Case is a grammatical category in which distinctions in the forms of words indicate grammatical relationships between words. In present-day English, case distinctions apply only to nouns and certain pronouns. For nouns, the only case form is the genitive (or possessive) case (as in *man's* and *men's*), all other forms having no inflection (common case). Certain pronouns, chiefly personal pronouns, distinguish between subjective case (*I, we*), objective case (*me, us*), and genitive case (*my, our*), though the genitives of personal pronouns are often separately designated as possessive pronouns. 4.3.1.2, 5.10

cataphoric see **anaphoric**

cataphoric ellipsis ellipsis which precedes the antecedent. 3.11.2.2

central describing a member of a word class which conforms to all the characteristics of that class. 5.1.3

characterized role a semantic role which refers to someone or something characterized by the subject predicative (which has the characterizing role). 3.9.1.2, 3.9.4.1

circumstantial clause a clause which expresses general circumstances. 14.5.4

clause. A clause is a construction that typically consists minimally of a subject and a verb (*I laughed*), though in an imperative clause the subject is generally absent but implied, so that minimally only the verb needs to be present (*Sit*). A clause may be within a larger construction: coordinated with another clause (the two clauses coordinated by *and* in *I paid this time and you can pay next time*), or subordinated within another clause (the subordinate *whether*-clause in *They asked whether I would pay*), or within a phrase (the *that*-clause in the noun phrase *the company that employed me*). In all the examples given so far, the clauses are **finite** in that their verb phrase is finite. But clauses may be non-finite (the infinitive clause in *I wanted to pay*, the *-ing* participle clause in *I enjoy paying*, and the *-ed* participle clause in *They wanted the house sold before the end of the year*) or verbless (the *when*-clause in *When in Rome, do as the Romans do*). A set of clauses interrelated by coordination or subordination (or minimally one clause that is independent of any such links) constitutes a sentence (or—a less misleading term for the spoken language—a clause cluster). 2.1.1, 13.1.2

clause cluster see **clause**. 13.6.1

cleft *it* the pronoun *it* serving as subject of a **cleft sentence** or cleft clause. 6.7.3

cleft sentence. A cleft sentence is a sentence that is cleft (split) so as to put the focus on one part of it. The cleft sentence is introduced by *it*, which is followed by a verb phrase whose main verb is generally *be*. The focused part comes next, and then the rest of the sentence is introduced by a **relative pronoun, relative determiner**, or **relative adverb**. If we take the sentence *Tom felt a sharp pain after lunch*, two possible cleft sentences formed from it are *It was Tom who felt a sharp pain after lunch* and *It was after lunch that Tom felt a sharp pain*. 3.10.1, 6.7.3

clitic. A clitic is a word that cannot occur independently but must be attached to another word. Clitics in English are contracted forms of words (*n't* for *not*, *'ll* for *will*). Generally they are attached at the end as enclitics (*wasn't, we're*), but they may also be attached at the beginning as proclitics (*d'you, 'tis*). A combination of proclitic and enclitic appears in *'tisn't*.

closed class. Closed classes are in contrast with open classes, and both denote classes of words (or parts of speech) that are required for grammatical description. A closed class is a set of words that is small enough to be listed fully and that does not readily admit new members. The closed classes that are generally recognized for English include **auxiliaries, conjunctions, prepositions, determiners**, and **pronouns**. The four open classes, which readily admit new members, are nouns, adjectives, verbs, and adverbs. Closed-class words are termed grammatical words or function words because of their importance in grammatical relations, whereas open-class words have been called lexical or content words. 4.1.2, 5.1.1

closed condition a hypothetical condition

collective noun. A collective noun denotes a group of people, animals, or institutions. A singular collective noun may be treated as plural (more commonly in British English than in American English) and therefore take a plural verb and (particularly) plural pronouns when the focus is on the group as individuals: *The enemy have brought in more of their paratroops.* 5.7.8, 10.14.2.3

combinatory coordination coordination of noun phrases where the noun phrases function semantically as a unit and could not be paraphrased in a coordination of clauses. See **coordination.**

comment clause a clause expressing a parenthetical comment. 14.5.13

common case the case of the noun that is normally used, whenever the genitive case is not required. 5.10.1

common noun see **proper noun.** 4.3.1.1

comparative see **adjective, adverb, comparison.** 4.4, 8.4

comparative clause. A comparative clause involves a comparison with what is conveyed in the host clause. Comparative clauses are introduced by the subordinators *as* or *than*. They correlate with a preceding comparative element: *more* or the *-er* comparative inflection, *less*, or *as* (*more tolerant than I thought; cleverer than his brothers are; less important than the other items on the agenda were; as tall as she is*). 14.6

comparative element the element in a comparative clause which signals the standard on which the comparison is made. 14.6

comparison. Comparison applies to adjectives or adverbs that are gradable. There are three directions of comparison: higher (*taller than Sue*), same (*as tall as Sue*), lower (*less tall than Sue*). There are three degrees of comparison: absolute (*tall*), comparative (*taller*), superlative (*tallest*). The superlative *least* is used to express the lowest direction, *least tall* contrasting with *tallest.* 4.4

complement. A complement is a phrase or clause whose form is determined by the word it complements. For example, the verb *asked* in *She asked me three questions* admits two complements: *me* (**indirect object**) and *three questions* (**direct object**), whereas the verb *answered* in *I answered her questions* admits just one complement: *her questions* (**direct object**). Apart from direct and indirect objects, complements of verbs may be **subject predicative** (*responsible* in *Jeremy is responsible*) or **object predicative** (*responsible* in *I consider Jeremy responsible*). Prepositions generally require complements (*my parents* in *from my parents*). Complements also occur with adjectives (*of tomato juice* in *fond of tomato juice*) and nouns (*whether it is hers* in *the question whether it is hers*). See also **preposition.** 3.1.3

complementation the addition of a complement to a linguistic unit such as a verb, adjective, or noun. 14.7

complex preposition a preposition consisting of more than one word. 9.2.2

complex sentence. A complex sentence consists of a main clause that has one or more subordinate clauses. The that-clause is a subordinate clause in the complex sentence 'Everybody thought *that he had won*'. 2.3.3, 13.4

complex-transitive verb. A complex-transitive verb has two complements: a **direct object** and an **object predicative**: *They named us* (direct object) *the winners* (object predicative). See also **subject predicative.** 3.7

compound. A compound is a word from a combination of two or more words (strictly speaking, two or more **bases**). Compounds may be written solid (*turncoat, mouthpiece*), hyphenated (*mother-in-law*, *cook-chill*), or as separate orthographic words (*smart card*, *junk food*). Noun compounds generally have their main stress on the first word. 2.1.2.1

compound noun phrase a unit consisting of two coordinated noun phrases. 10.12

compound quantifier see **quantifier**. 6.13.2.2

compound sentence. A compound sentence is a sentence that consists of two or more **main clauses** (each of which could be an independent sentence) that are linked by co-ordination, the coordinator generally being *and, but,* or *or* ('It has only been a week *and* I feel lonesome without you'). 2.3.2

concessive clause a clause which indicates that the situation in the host clause is un-expected in view of what is said in the concessive clause. 14.5.7

concrete noun a noun used to refer to an entity that is typically perceptible and tangible. 5.5.3

conditional clause. Most conditional clauses are introduced by the subordinator *if.* Con-ditions may be open (or real), leaving completely open whether the condition will be fulfilled (*You're going to be in trouble if you've infected me*). Or they may be hypothetical (or unreal or closed), expressing that the condition has not been fulfilled (for past condi-tions), is not fulfilled, or will not be fulfilled. Hypothetical conditions take backshifted tenses: for present and future conditions, the past is used in the conditional clause and a past modal (generally *would*) in the host clause ('If I had my dictionary, I *would look* up the word'); for past conditions, the **past perfect** is used in the conditional clause and a past perfect modal (generally *would have*) in the host clause ('If I *had seen* them, I *would have invited* them to eat with us'). Subjunctive *were* is sometimes used instead of indica-tive *was* in the conditional clause, particularly in formal style ('If she *were* here, you would not need me'). Conditional clauses may also have **subject–operator inversion** without a subordinator, generally when the operator is *had, were,* or *should* ('*Had* I known, I would have told you'). See also **backshifting, alternative condition, *wh*-conditional clause.** 14.5.3

conditional subordinator e.g. *if.* 14.5.3.4

conjoin a unit (which may be a clause; the main verb (finite or non-finite) with its comple-ments; or various kinds of phrase (including those consisting of just one word)) linked by a coordinator to another unit. 9.1.1

conjunct. Conjuncts are sentence adverbials that indicate logical relationships between sentences or between clauses. They are mainly adverbs (e.g. *therefore, however, neverthe-less*) or prepositional phrases (e.g. *on the other hand, in consequence, in conclusion*). See also **disjunct.** 8.7.1

conjunction. Conjunctions are either coordinators (or coordinating conjunctions) or sub-ordinators (or subordinating conjunctions). The central coordinators are *and, or,* and *but.* Coordinators link units of equal status, which may be clauses or phrases (including single words): *I recognized them, but they didn't remember me; out of work and in trouble; soft or hard.* Often considered as marginal coordinators are *nor* and *for.* The coordination may be emphasized by a correlative expression: *both ... and; either ... or; not (only) ... but (also); neither ... nor.* Subordinators link subordinate clauses to their host clauses. Among the many subordinators are *if, since, because, although: I can lend you some money if you have none on you.* Subordinators are sometimes emphasized by a correlative expression in the following clause: *if ... then; because ... therefore; although ... nevertheless; whether ... or; as ... so.* 9.1

conjunctive adverb a **conjunct**

constituent any of the units that constitute the structure of a sentence, i.e. subject, verb, direct, object, indirect object, subject predicative, object predicative, and the optional constituent, adverbial. 2.3.1, 3.1.5

content disjunct a type of disjunct which may be modal (commenting on the truth-value) or evaluative (making a value judgement). 8.7.2.2

content word see **closed class**.

contracted describing an operator that has been shortened, usually by the loss of the vowel and sometimes the initial consonant. 4.2

coordinated clause a clause linked to another clause at the same grammatical level. 13.2

coordinated phrase a phrase linked to another clause at the same grammatical level. 10.12

coordination. Coordination is the linking of two or more units that would have the same function if they were not linked. When coordinators such as *and* are present, the coordination is syndetic: *I enjoy classical music, jazz, and pop music*. When coordinators are not present but are implied, the coordination is asyndetic: '*Distinguished guests, colleagues, friends*, I welcome you all.' If three or more units are coordinated and the coordinator is repeated between each unit, the coordination is polysyndetic: 'The cake contains *eggs and flour and cheese and honey and spices*.' Coordination of noun phrases may be segregatory or combinatory. In segregatory combination each noun phrase could function separately in a paraphrase involving the coordination of the clauses: '*Bomb warnings and drugs courier baggage* were mentioned' →; '*Bomb warnings* were mentioned and *drugs courier baggage* was mentioned.' This is not possible in combinatory coordination: '*Peter and Laura* first met at a dance'. Combinatory coordination is also found with adjectives: 'a *red, white, and blue* flag.' See also **conjunction**. 13.2, 4.5.1

coordinative apposition. In coordinative apposition the two noun phrases that are in apposition are linked by the coordinator *and* or *or*: *egg or electroencephalogram*; *She is the book's author and Mr. Deng's youngest daughter*. 4.5.2

coordinator a conjunction linking units of equal status. 4.5.1, 9.1.1

copular verb. A copular (or linking) verb is complemented by a **subject predicative** in sentence or clause structure. The most common copular verb is *be*; others include *become* (*my friend*), *feel* (*tired*), *get* (*ready*), *seem* (*happy*). A copular prepositional verb is a prepositional verb (combination of verb plus preposition) that is complemented by a subject predicative: *sound like* (*you*), *turn into* (*a monster*), *serve as* (*mitigating circumstances*). 3.6

co-refer (with) have the same reference (as)

correlative see **conjunction**.

count noun. A count (or countable) noun is a noun that has both singular and plural forms (*book* / *books*) and can be take determiners (as appropriate) that accompany distinctions in number (*a* / *this book*, *many* / *these books*). 5.5.1

countable noun a **count noun**

dangling describing an adverbial participle or verbless clause whose understood subject is not identical with the subject of the host clause. 14.4.2

declarative. A declarative (or declarative sentence) is the most common sentence type, typically used in the expression of statements and generally requiring subject–verb order: *It was raining last night*; *Nobody saw us*; *Cindy is the best candidate*. The other sentence types, with which it is contrasted, are interrogative, imperative, and exclamative. 2.4

declarative question a declarative that has the force of a question, in speech ending with rising intonation, and in writing with a question mark: *You accept their word?*. 2.9

definite. A definite noun phrase conveys the assumption that the hearer can identify what it refers to. Identification may be assumed when (for example) the phrase refers to something previously mentioned or uniquely identifiable from general knowledge or from the particular context. Definite reference is associated with the use of the definite article *the*,

the personal pronouns, the demonstratives, and proper names. Definite reference contrasts with indefinite reference, commonly signalled by the indefinite article *a / an* ('I bought *a* used car last week for the family, but *the* car (or *it*) is giving me a lot of trouble'). 10.16.1

definite article. The definite article is *the*. With singular noun phrases it contrasts with the indefinite article *a / an* (*a house, the house*). With plural noun phrases it contrasts with the zero article, i.e. the absence of an article or other determiner (*the houses, houses*), or with the indefinite determiner *some* (*the houses, some houses*). 6.2

deictic relating to **deixis**.

deixis. Deixis may be situational or textual. Situational deixis denotes the use of expressions to point to some feature of the situation, typically persons or objects in the situation and temporal or locational features. For example, the pronoun *I* is necessarily deictic, referring to the speaker and writer and shifting its reference according to who is speaking or writing. Similarly, *here* and *now* may be situationally bound as is the use of tenses that take as their point of reference the time of speaking or writing. Textual deixis denotes the use of expressions to point to other expressions in the linguistic context. References to what comes earlier are anaphoric, whereas references to what comes later are cataphoric. See also **anaphoric**. 15.2.2

demonstrative. The demonstrative pronouns and determiners are singular *this* and *that* and their respective plurals *these* and *those*. 4.3.2.1, 6.14

deontic. Deontic (or root or intrinsic) meanings of the modals refer to some kind of human control over the situation, such as permission or obligation (*may* in *You may sit down now* or *must* in *I must tell you about it*). Deontic meanings contrast with epistemic meanings, which refer to some kind of evaluation of the truth-value of the proposition such as possibility or necessity (*may* in *It may rain later* or *must* in *That must be your sister*). Each of the modals has both kinds of meaning. See also **auxiliary**. 11.8

dependent genitive see **genitive**. 5.10.4

dependent possessive a possessive pronoun that is dependent on a noun. 4.3.2.3

descriptive genitive a genitive phrase used as a modifier. 5.12.7

determiner. Determiners introduce noun phrases. They convey various pragmatic and semantic contrasts relating to the type of reference of the noun phrase and to notions such as number and quantity. In their positional potentialities they fall into three sets: predeterminers (e.g. *all, both*), central determiners (e.g. *a / an, the, my, this*), and postdeterminers (e.g. *two, many, several*). Most of the words that function as determiners also function as pronouns (e.g. *this, some, all*). 6.1, 10.4

direct condition a condition expressed by a conditional clause indicating that the truth of the host clause (or apodosis) is dependent on the fulfilment of the condition in the conditional clause (or protasis). 14.5.3

direct object. A direct object is a **complement** of a transitive verb. It generally follows the verb in a declarative sentence (*my car* in *Norman has borrowed my car*). It can be made the subject of a corresponding passive sentence (*My car has been borrowed by Norman*) and can be elicited by a question with *who(m)* or *what* in company with the subject and the verb (*What did Norman borrow? My car*). The direct object is typically the entity affected by the action. 3.1.3

direct speech. Direct speech quotes the actual words used by somebody, and in writing it is enclosed by quotation marks: (*Charles asked me,*) '*What shall I do next?*'. Indirect speech reports the substance of what was said or written: (*Charles asked me*) *what he should do next*. 15.1

disjunct. Disjuncts are sentence adverbials, either style disjuncts or content disjuncts. Style disjuncts comment on the act of speaking or writing, and may be adverbs (*bluntly*, *honestly, personally*), prepositional phrases (*in all fairness, in short, between you and me*), non-finite clauses (*frankly speaking, putting it bluntly, to be truthful*), and finite clauses (*if I may say so, since you ask me*): '*Honestly,* I didn't do it'; '*Since you ask me,* I wouldn't mind a drink'. Content disjuncts comment on the truth-value of what is said (*possibly, undoubtedly, in all probability*) or evaluate it (*unfortunately, to my delight, what is more disappointing*): 'Our side will *undoubtedly* win'; '*Unfortunately,* the deadline has passed'. 8.7.2

ditransitive see **transitive verb**. 3.5

double genitive see **genitive**. 5.10.4

doubly transitive phrasal-prepositional verb a **phrasal-prepositional verb** which has two objects. See **phrasal-prepositional verb**. 11.21.2

doubly transitive prepositional verb a prepositional verb with two objects, the first object being a direct object and the second object a prepositional object, introduced by a preposition. See **prepositional verb**. 11.20.2

dummy operator. Auxiliary *do* is a dummy operator, since it functions as an operator in the absence of any other auxiliary when an operator is required to form questions (*My sister likes them* → *Does my sister like them?*), to make the sentence negative (*My sister doesn't like them*), or to form an abbreviated clause (*My sister likes them, and I do too*). 11.1

dynamic describing a verb used in referring to a happening. 3.9.5.2

-ed participle see **participle**. 4.2.4, 7.2.5

ellipsis. Ellipsis is the omission of a part of a normal structure. The ellipted part can be understood from the situational context (ellipsis of *have you* in *Got any suggestions?*) or the textual context, where it may be anaphoric (dependent on what precedes: *May I drive? Yes, you may*) or cataphoric (dependent on what follows: *If you don't want to, I'll drive*). See also **anaphoric**. 3.11, 13.1.2

elliptical sentence an incomplete sentence that is perfectly normal and acceptable because rule-governed. 13.1.2.3

embedded describing a grammatical unit that is nested inside another unit. 2.1.2.1

emphasis special importance or prominence attached to a certain part of a sentence. 11.2.3

emphatic reflexive a **reflexive pronoun** used in addition to another nominal to emphasize that nominal. See **reflexive pronoun**. 6.10

empty *it* the same as **prop *it***.

enclitic see **clitic**. 5.10.5

end focus. The principle of end focus requires that the most important information comes at the end of the sentence or clause. 5.11, 10.7

end weight. The principle of end weight requires that a longer unit follow a shorter unit if the choice is available. See also **extraposed postmodifier**.

epistemic meaning. Epistemic meaning, in a modal auxiliary, is meaning which refers to some kind of judgement of the truth-value of the proposition, such as its possibility or necessity. See also **deontic**. 11.8

event present perfect a use of the present perfect to refer to one or more events that have taken place in a period that precedes the present time of speaking or writing. 11.11.3

event progressive a use of the progressive aspect to indicate that an event is or was in progress. 11.15

eventive role a semantic role referring to an event. 3.9.1.5, 3.9.2.1

exclamative. An exclamative (or exclamative sentence) is a sentence type in which the exclamative element is fronted, introduced by *what* (followed by the rest of the noun phrase) or by *how* (otherwise): *What a good time we had*; *How kind you are.* 2.4, 2.8

exclusive adverb a type of focusing adjunct that emphasizes that what is said is restricted entirely to the focused part. 8.7.3.4

exclusive *we* excludes the person or persons addressed. 6.4.1.3

existential sentence a sentence in which the subject is postponed and replaced by existential *there*, which is followed by a verb phrase (generally with *be* as the main verb). 3.10.3, 6.8

existential *there* Existential *there* is used in a rearrangement of the sentence in which the subject is postponed, the effect being to present the postponed (notional) subject as new information: *Too many cars are ahead of us* → *There are too many cars ahead of us.* If the sentence consists only of the subject and the verb *be*, then only the existential sentence is normally possible: *There's still time.* 6.8

experiencer role a semantic role which refers to someone who has experienced a sensation, an emotion, or cognition. 3.9.1.3

extraposed postmodifier. An extraposed postmodifier is a postmodifier in a noun phrase (generally a noun phrase functioning as subject) that is postponed to a later position in the sentence in accordance with the principle of **end weight**: *A tape recording in which a huge ransom was demanded was received* → *A tape recording was received in which a huge ransom was demanded.* 3.10.2

extrinsic meaning the same as **epistemic meaning**. See also **deontic**.

factual (of a finite or *-ing* participle clause) referring to some situation that has existed. 14.7.8

fall a nuclear pitch change from high to low. 2.6

finite. A verb is finite if it displays tense, the distinction between present and past tense: *cares / cared*, *take / took*. A verb phrase is finite if the first (or only) verb in the phrase is finite, all other verbs being non-finite: *is caring / was caring*, *has taken / had taken*. A clause is finite if its verb is finite: *I cared about what they thought of me*; *I generally take a nap after lunch.* The non-finite verb forms are the infinitive, the *-ing* participle, and the *-ed* participle. See also **aspect, clause, infinitive, participle**. 11.3, 14.1.1.1

first person the category of person in a pronoun or verb which includes the speaker or speakers (in written language, the writer or writers). 6.4.1

focusing adjunct a type of adjunct that focuses on a particular unit in a sentence or clause. 8.7.3.4

formal describing language that is characterized by a relatively impersonal attitude and adherence to certain social conventions

fraction a numeral referring to a quantity less than one. 6.15.3

fronting the presence of an element at the front of a clause rather than in its more typical position. 12.9.3

full verb a **main verb**. 7.1

function word a **grammatical word**. See also **word class**.

gapping a type of ellipsis that sometimes occurs in the middle of a coordinated clause, affecting the second clause and subsequent clauses, by which the main verb and/or an auxiliary is ellipted, possibly with any preceding auxiliaries and a following verb complement, such as a direct object, and an adverbial. 3.11.2.1, 13.2.5

gender. Gender is a grammatical category in which contrasts are made within a word class (in present-day English restricted to certain pronouns and determiners) such as personal/non-personal, masculine/feminine/neuter. The most conspicuous gender contrasts in present-day English are found in the third person singular personal pronouns *he/she/it*. 5.9, 6.4.3

gender-neutral describing a pronoun that makes no gender distinction. 6.3.3.4

generic. In generic reference, noun phrases are used in generalizations to refer to all members of the class denoted by the phrases that are relevant in the context: '*Coffee* contains *caffeine*'; '*The poor* are always with us'; '*Apples* are good for you'; 'An apple a day keeps *the doctor* away'. 6.5, 10.16.3

generic pronoun the pronoun *one* used with generic reference. 6.5

genitive. The genitive (or possessive) can applies to nouns and some pronouns. the genitives for *child* are singular *child's* and plural *children's*, and for *girl* they are singular *girl's* and plural *girls'*. Genitives may be dependent or independent. A phrase with a dependent genitive is dependent on a following noun phrase: 'the child's parents', parallel with 'her parents'. The independent genitive is not dependent in this way, though a following noun may be implied: 'I'm going to my cousin's.' The double genitive is a combination of a genitive and an *of*-phrase: 'that article of Estelle's.' The group genitive applies not just to the noun to which it is attached: 'an hour and a half's sleep'; 'the president of the company's resignation'. See also **case**. 5.10.2

gerund. The gerund is an *-ing* participle that shares characteristics of a noun and a verb. *Finding* is a gerund in 'It depends on Algeria's *finding* more efficient ways to run its factories'. Like a noun it is preceded by a genitive (*Algeria's*) that is dependent on it, but like a verb it takes a direct object (*finding more efficient ways to run its factories*). The genitive is often replaced by a noun in the common case (*Algeria*). In the same context, possessive pronouns (*their* in *their finding*) are often replaced by pronouns in the objective case (*them finding*). 14.7.6

gradability. Gradable words allow intensification and comparison. *Clever* is gradable because we can intensify it up or down on a scale of cleverness (*very clever, quite clever, somewhat clever*) and it can be compared (*cleverer, cleverest, as clever, more clever*). On the other hand, *animate* is not gradable.

gradable describing an adjective or adverb which can be viewed as on a scale. 4.4, 8.4

grammatical conforming to the rules of grammar. 1.10

grammatical word a word, generally a closed-class word, which plays a role in the grammatical relations between words or higher units. 5.1.5

group genitive see **genitive**

head the principal word in a phrase. 2.1.1.2

historic present a use of the simple present tense to refer to past time. 11.6.2.3

host clause see **subordinate clause**

host phrase see **subordinate clause**

hypotaxis. Hypotaxis is in contrast with parataxis. Parataxis is a relationship between two or more units that are of equal grammatical status, as in coordination (*books and magazines*), whereas hypotaxis is a relationship between two units, one of which is dependent on the other, as in modification (the relationship between the relative *that-* clause and its noun head *books* in *books that I have read*). 13.5

hypothetical condition see **conditional clause**. 14.5.3.2

hypothetical past a use of the past tense mainly in hypothetical conditions that relate to present or future time, conveying belief in the non-fulfilment of the condition. 11.6.1.3

hypothetical past perfect a use of the past perfect in hypothetical conditions that relate to past time, indicating the knowledge or belief that the condition was not fulfilled. 11.12

hypothetical subjunctive see **subjunctive**. 11.10

identified role a semantic role which refers to someone or something identified through the subject predicative, which has the identifying role. 3.9.1.2, 3.9.4.2

imperative An imperative is a sentence (or clause) type. The verb is in the **base form**, and typically the subject is absent, though *you* is implied as subject: *Look over there*. The term 'imperative' is also used for the verb functioning in the imperative sentence (*look* in *Look over there*, *be* in *Be quiet*). 2.4, 2.7, 4.2.1

inclusive we the use of *we* to include also the person or persons addressed. 6.4.1.2

indefinite article. The indefinite article is *a* before consonant sounds (a house) and *an* before vowel sounds (an hour). See also **definite article**. 6.2

indefinite determiner/pronoun. Indefinite determiners and indefinite pronouns have indefinite reference. Some indefinite determiners and pronouns have the same form (*some, any, either, neither, all, both*), but *no* is only a determiner and others (e.g. *none, someone*) are only pronouns. See also **definite**. 6.13

indefinite reference see **definite**.

independent genitive see **genitive**. 5.10.4

independent possessive a possessive pronoun that can function independently (i.e. is not dependent on a noun). 4.3.2.3

indicative a mood of the verb which applies to most verbs used in declaratives, and to verbs used in interrogatives and exclamatives. See **mood**. 4.2.1

indirect condition a condition expressed by some conditional clauses that is related to the speech act. 14.5.3

indirect object. An indirect object is a **complement** of a transitive verb. It normally comes between the verb and the **direct object** (*Jean* in *I gave Jean the old computer*). It can be elicited by a question introduced by *who(m)* (*Who did you give the old computer (to)?—Jean*), and can be made subject of a corresponding passive sentence (*Jean was given the old computer*). The indirect object typically has the role of recipient or beneficiary of the action. 3.1.3, 3.5

indirect speech see **direct speech**. 15.1

infinitive. The infinitive has the **base form** of the verb. It may be preceded by infinitival *to* (*to be, to say*), but the bare infinitive (without *to*) is used after modals (*can say*), the dummy operator *do* (*did say, doesn't know*), and the imperative auxiliary *do* (*Do tell us*).

infinitive clause. An infinitive clause is a clause whose verb is an infinitive ('I want *to learn Chinese*').

inflection. An inflection is an **affix** that expresses a grammatical relationship, such as the plural *-s* in candidates and the *-ed* ending in wanted. In English, inflections are always suffixes. 2.2.2, 5.2.2

-*ing* participle see **participle**. 4.2.4

initial correlative expression a correlative expression emphasizing coordination, e.g. *both ... and*; *either ... or*; *not (only) ... but (also)*. 9.1.1.2

instantaneous present a use of the present tense to refer to a single event that occurs simultaneously with the time of speaking or writing. 11.5.2.3

intensifier a type of focusing adjunct that denotes a place on a scale of intensity, either upward or downward. 8.7.3.4

interjection. An interjection is an exclamatory emotive word that is loosely attached to the sentence or used as an utterance by itself, such as *oh* and *boo*. 8.9

interrogative. An interrogative (or interrogative sentence) is a sentence type in which there is **subject–operator inversion** (the operator coming before the subject), as in *Do you know them?* (in contrast to the **declarative** word order in *You know them*). The exception is if the subject is a *wh*-item in *wh*-questions, in which case the subject retains its position, as in

Who knows them? (in contrast to *Who do they know?*). Interrogatives are typically used to ask questions. 2.4

interrogative adverb. The interrogative adverbs are *how, when, where,* and *why.* They are used to form *wh*-questions: *How did you find it? When did you last see her?*

interrogative determiner/pronoun. The interrogative pronouns are *who, whom, whose, which,* and *what.* The interrogative determiners are *which, what,* and *whose.* Like the interrogative adverbs, they are used to form *wh*-questions: *Who wants to play? Whose desk is this?.* 4.3.2.6, 6.12.1.1

intransitive phrasal verb see **phrasal verb**. 11.19.1

intransitive verb. An intransitive verb is a verb that does not have a **complement**. 3.4

intrinsic meaning the same as **deontic meaning**

irregular verb a verb which does not follow the general pattern of adding *-ed* to form the past and past participle. 7.6

juxtaposed clauses paratactically related clauses that do not imply coordination. 13.5.2.3

left dislocation. In left dislocation, an anticipatory noun phrase ('a phrase dislocated to the left') is followed by a pronoun that occupies the normal position for the phrase: '*Your mother, she* was just misunderstood'. In right dislocation, an anticipatory pronoun is in the normal position and an explanatory phrase appears later: '*They*'re not great social animals, *computer scientists.*' 3.10.4, 10.11

lexical verb a **main verb**

lexical word see **closed class**. 5.1.5

linking verb a **copular verb**

locative role a semantic role that designates the place of the subject or object. 3.9.4.3

main clause. A main clause is a clause that is not subordinate to another clause. It may be coextensive with the sentence or it may be coordinated with one or more other main clauses. 2.3.2, 13.2

main verb. The main (or lexical) verb is the head of the verb phrase (*smoking* in *may have been smoking*) and is sometimes preceded by one or more other main clauses. 3.1.2, 7.1, 11.1

mandative subjunctive see **subjunctive**. 11.9.3

manner clause a clause referring to the manner of the action expressed by the verb. 14.5.11

marginal auxiliary. A verb that is used both as an auxiliary and as a main verb. See **auxiliary**. 7.9

mass noun a **non-count noun**

metalinguistic describing language used to speak about language

modal, modal auxiliary see **auxiliary**. 11.1, 11.8

modal perfect a combination of a modal with the perfect auxiliary *have* in the infinitive. 11.13

modality a semantic category that deals with two types of judgement: those referring to the factuality of what is said (its certainty, probability, or possibility), and those referring to human control over the situation (ability, permission, intention, obligation). 4.2.2

modification the presence or role of a modifier

modifier. A modifier is an element within the noun phrase which usually adds information characterizing more specifically what the head refers to. A **premodifier** precedes the head and a **postmodifier** follows it: in *the first opportunity to deal with it, first* is the premodifier and *to deal with it* is the postmodifier. 10.2

monotransitive see **transitive**. 3.5

monotransitive phrasal-prepositional verb see **phrasal-prepositional verb**. 11.21.1

monotransitive prepositional verb see **prepositional verb**. 11.20.1

mood. One of the formal categories into which verb forms are classified, indicating whether the verb is expressing fact, command, wish, hypothesis, etc. English has three moods: **indicative, imperative**, and **subjunctive**. The indicative applies to most verbs in **declarative** sentences and to verbs in **interrogatives** and **exclamatives**. The imperative and the present subjunctive have the base form of the verb, and the past subjunctive is confined to *were*. See also **subjunctive**. 4.2.1

morpheme. A morpheme is an abstract unit established for the analysis of word structure. It is a basic unit in the vocabulary. A word can be analysed as consisting of one morpheme (*sad*) or two or more morphemes (*unluckily*; compare *luck, lucky, unlucky*), each morpheme usually expressing a distinct meaning. When a morpheme is represented by a segment, that segment is a morph. If a morpheme can be represented by more than one morph, the morphs are **allomorphs** of the same morpheme: the prefixes *in-* (*insane*), *il-* (*illegible*), *im-* (*impossible*), *ir-* (*irregular*) are allomorphs of the same negative morpheme. A portmanteau morph represents more than one morph: *men* is a combination of the morpheme for *man* plus the plural morpheme. An empty morph is a morph that lacks meaning; for example the *-o-* in combining forms such as *psychology*. A suppletive morph is a morph from a different root that is used in a grammatical set; for example *went* is the suppletive past of the verb *go*. A zero morph is postulated where a morpheme is expected in the grammatical system but is not represented; for example, the zero relative pronoun in *a letter I wrote* (compare *a letter that I wrote*). A free morph is one that occurs independently as a word, whereas a bound morph is always combined with one or more other morphs to form a word: inflections such as the plural *-s* are bound morphs, as are the suffix *-ness* in *goodness* and the bound morph *cran-* in *cranberry*. 2.2.2

morphological relating to the structure of a word

multiplier a subclass of determiner comprising *once, twice, thrice, double, treble, quadruple*, and multiplying expressions headed by *times* (e.g. *ten times*). 10.4.1.1

multi-word verb. A multi-word verb is a combination of a verb with one or more other words to form an idiomatic unit. The most common multi-word verbs are **phrasal verbs** (e.g. *give in*) and **prepositional verbs** (e.g. *rely on*). 11.18, 12.10.6

mutation change in the root vowel of a word associated with inflection. 5.7.2

negation the grammatical means of denying the truth of an affirmative clause or sentence. 2.11

negative expressing negation. 2.11

neutral term the **unmarked term**. 8.5

nominal a word or phrase functioning as a noun phrase

nominal adjective. A nominal adjective is an adjective that functions as the head of a noun phrase. Like adjectives in general, nominal adjectives may be modified by an adverb (*very sick* in *They looked after the very sick*) and take comparative and superlative forms (*poorer* in *She employed the poorer among them, best* in *The best is yet to come*). 8.3

nominal clause. Nominal clauses have a range of functions similar to those of noun phrases. For example, they can be the subject of a sentence: the *that*-clause in *That they believe him is doubtful*, and the *whether*-clause in *Whether or not I am invited is irrelevant*. 14.2.1, 14.3

nominal relative clause. A nominal relative clause (or independent relative clause or free relative clause) is a clause whose introductory *wh*-word is a fusion of **relative pronoun** or **relative determiner** with an implied **antecedent**: *Whoever said that* ('Any person who …') *needs his head examining*; *What you want* ('The thing that you want') *is too expensive*;

They don't know how to behave ('the way in which they should behave'). See also **relative clause**. 6.12.4, 14.3.4

nominal relative determiner/pronoun. Nominal relative pronouns and determiners introduce **nominal relative clauses**. There are twelve nominal relative pronouns: *who, whom, whoever, whomever, whosoever, whomsoever, which, whichever, whichsoever, what, whatever, whatsoever. Which* and *what* and their compounds can also be determiners. 6.12.4

non-assertive determiner, pronoun a determiner or pronoun which has a negative force, tending to occur in non-assertive contexts, particularly in negative, interrogative, and conditional clauses. 6.13.1.1

non-count noun. A non-count (or uncountable or mass) noun does not have a plural form; for example: *furniture, happiness, information*. Many nouns that are generally non-count can be treated as count when they are used to refer to different kinds (*French wines*) or to quantities (*two coffees*, 'two cups of coffee'). See also **count noun**. 5.5.2

non-factual (of an infinitive clause) referring to a situation that may come into existence. 14.7.8

non-finite see **finite**. 11.3

non-finite clause a clause whose verb is a non-finite verb. 14.1.1.2

non-generic see **generic**.

non-past tense the **simple present tense**. 11.5

non-personal referring to an entity which is not a person. 4.3.2.5

non-restrictive see **restrictive**. 10.8

non-standard see **standard English**.

notional based on meaning.

noun. A noun is a word that (alone or with modifiers) is capable of functioning as subject (*rice* in '*Rice* is grown in this country'), or direct object ('I like *rice*'), or complement of a preposition ('This is made from *rice*'). 4.3.1

noun of speaking a noun such as *statement, assertion, question,* or *explanation*. 15.1.2

noun phrase. A noun phrase is a phrase whose head (possibly its only word) is a noun (*coffee* in 'I prefer *black coffee*'), a pronoun (*that* in 'I prefer *that*'), or a nominal adjective (*elderly* in 'I prefer catering for *the elderly*'). See also **nominal adjective**. 2.1.1.2, 10.2

NP the **noun phrase**. 10.2

nuclear tone. A nuclear tone is the most prominent movement of pitch within a tone unit, a segment in an utterance that contains a distinct sequence of tones. The most common nuclear tones are falls (or falling tones) and rises (or rising tones). 2.6, 11.2.3

number a grammatical category which distinguishes between singular and plural. 4.2.6–7, 4.3.1.1.

numeral a closed word class with the subclasses **cardinal, ordinal**, and **fraction**. 6.15

O symbol for **object**. 3.1.3

object see **direct object, indirect object**. 9.2

object predicate see **subject predicate**. 3.1.3

objective case see **case**. 4.3.2.2, 6.4.4

objective genitive a genitive phrase whose relationship to the second noun phrase corresponds to that between an object and a verb. 5.12.2

oblique object a **prepositional object**. 11.20.1 Note

open condition a condition which leaves completely open whether the condition will be fulfilled. 14.5.3.1

open word class   a word class which readily admits new members. 4.1.2, 5.1.1

operator.   The operator is a verb that is being used for negation, interrogation, emphasis, and abbreviation. When the **main verb** *be* is the only verb in the verb phrase, it can function as operator (*is* in *He isn't in* and *Is he in?*). In British English in particular, the main verb *have* can similarly function as operator (*has* in *Has he any children?*). Otherwise, the operator is the first (or only) auxiliary in the verb phrase (*may* in *May I come in?* and *is* in *Is it raining?*). In the absence of another potential operator, the **dummy operator** *do* is introduced (*did* in *Did you see them?*).

optative subjunctive   see **subjunctive**. 11.9.1

ordinal, ordinal numeral   a numeral that refers to a position in a sequence. 6.15.2

P   symbol for **predicative**

paradigm.   A paradigm is a set of grammatically related forms, such as the five forms of the irregular verb *drive*: *drive, drives, driving, drove, driven*.

parataxis   see **hypotaxis**. 13.4

parenthetic clause   a clause inserted as an explanation or elaboration into a sentence which is grammatically complete without it. 13.5.2.4

part of speech   another term for **word class**

participle.   There are two participles: the *-ing* participle (or present participle) and the *-ed* participle (or past participle). Both are non-finite forms of verbs. The *-ing* participle always ends in *-ing* (*shouting, singing, writing*). The *-ed* participle ends in *-ed* in regular verbs (*shouted*), where it is identical with the simple past (*They shouted at him, He was shouted at*), but it need not have an *-ed* ending in irregular verbs (*sung, written*). The *-ing* participle is used to form the progressive aspect (*He was shouting*), and the *-ed* participle is used to form the perfect aspect (*She has written*) and the passive (*It was sung beautifully*). Both participles function as the verb in non-finite clauses: *-ing* participle clauses ('*Writing letters* is a chore') and *-ed* participle clauses ('*Written in an unknown script*, the inscription posed a challenge to scholars'). See also **aspect, passive**. 7.4, 7.5

particle.   A particle is a word that does not take inflections and does not fit into the traditional word classes; for example, the negative particle *not* and infinitival *to*. Particles also include the words that are used to form **multi-word verbs** (*in* in *give in*, *at* in *look at*, *up* and *with* in *put up with*), though further analysis may differentiate them as adverbs and prepositions. 11.18

particularizer adverb   a type of focusing adjunct that emphasizes that what is said is restricted chiefly to the focused part. 8.7.3.4

partitive expression   an expression of part to whole, such as *a piece of cheese*. 5.5.4

passive voice.   Passive voice is contrasted with active voice. Voice applies only to transitive verbs (those taking an object). The active is the norm. An active sentence will generally take the order subject-verb-object (or possibly two objects, the indirect followed by the direct): *Most students take the examination; Sandra took all the money*. The corresponding passive sentence will have the active object (*the examination; all the money*) as subject, the active subject (*Most students; Sandra*) will optionally appear after the verb in a *by*-phrase, and the active verb phrase will be turned into a passive phrase by the introduction of the auxiliary *be* followed by the *-ed* participle of the main verb: *The examination is taken (by most students); All the money was taken (by Sandra)*. For all regular verbs and for many irregular verbs the *-ed* participle is identical with the simple past: *Paul invited all the teachers → All the teachers were invited (by Paul)*. See also **direct object, indirect object**. 2.12, 4.2.5

past   see **tense**. 4.2.3

past participle   the *-ed* participle

past perfect. The past perfect is a combination of the past tense of the perfect auxiliary *have* with the *-ed* participle: *had revealed, had made, had seen, had been* (*crying*). See also **aspect**. 11.4, 11.12

past progressive. The past progressive is a combination of the past of the progressive auxiliary *be* with the *-ing* participle of the following verb: *was phoning, were having, were being examined.* See also **aspect**. 11.4

past subjunctive see **subjunctive**.

perfect see **aspect**. 4.2.4, 11.4

perfect participle the *-ed* participle

performative verb. A performative verb is a verb used to perform the **speech act** it denotes. For examples: *I apologize* constitutes an apology.

peripheral describing a member of a word class which does not conform to all the characteristics of that class. 5.1.3

person. Three persons are distinguished. The first person indicates the speaker(s) or writer(s); the second person indicates the hearer(s) or reader(s); the third person indicates any others. The distinctions apply to noun phrases and verbs. For example: *I* is the first person singular of the personal pronoun, and *am* is the corresponding first person singular of the present tense of *be*. In the plural, the first person *we* may be inclusive (including hearer(s)/reader(s)) or exclusive (including others). Similarly, the second person *you* may include others, though not speakers or writers. 4.2.6–7, 6.4.1

personal pronoun. The personal pronouns are *I/me, you, he/him, she/her, it, we/us, they/them.* 4.3.2.2

phrasal verb. A phrasal verb is a **multi-word verb** in which a verb is combined with an adverb to form an idiomatic unit. The phrasal verb may be intransitive, without an object (*shut up* 'keep quiet', *give in* 'surrender'), or transitive ('*point out* something', '*make up* something'). With transitive phrasal verbs the adverb may precede or follow the object ('find *out* the truth', 'find the truth *out*') though if the object is a pronoun the adverb generally follows the object ('find it *out*'). 11.19

phrasal-prepositional verb. A phrasal-prepositional verb is a **multi-word verb** in which a verb combines with an adverb and a preposition to form an idiomatic unit. Monotransitive phrasal-prepositional verbs have just one object, a prepositional object ('*look down on* somebody', meaning 'despise'). Doubly transitive phrasal-prepositional verbs take two objects ('*let* somebody *in on* something'). 11.21

phrase. The phrase comes between the word and the clause in the hierarchy of grammatical units. Five phrase types are distinguished: **noun phrase, verb phrase, adjective phrase, adverb phrase, prepositional phrase**. 2.1.1, 10.1

place clause an adverbial clause referring to position or direction. 14.5.1

pluperfect the **past perfect**

plural denoting more than one. 5.6.1

polysyndetic coordination see **coordination**. 13.8.1

possessive genitive the use of the genitive to express a relationship between two nouns where the verbs *have* or *possess* could be used in a paraphrase. 5.12.1

possessive pronoun. The possessive pronouns are the possessives of the **personal pronouns**. They may be dependent (*my, your, his, her, its, our, their*) or independent (*mine, yours, his, hers, its, ours, theirs*). 4.3.2.3, 6.3

postdeterminer see **determiner**.

postmodification the presence or role of a postmodifier

postmodifier see **modifier**. 10.5

postmodify act as postmodifier to

PP a **prepositional phrase.** 2.1.2.1

pragmatics. Pragmatics is the study of the use of the language and its interpretation in situational contexts.

predeterminer see **determiner.** 10.4.1.1

predicate. Sentences and clauses are often divided into the subject and the predicate. The predicate consists of the verb and its **complements** and **adverbials** that are functioning as **adjuncts.** In the sentence *I met a girl on the train today,* *I* is the subject and the rest of the sentence is the predicate. Excluded from the predicate are sentence adverbials: **conjuncts** such as *therefore* and *however,* and **disjuncts** such as *perhaps* and *on the other hand.* 3.1.2, 3.1.4

predicative describing an adjective which can be used as subject predicative. 8.2

prefix see **affix.**

premodification the presence or role of a premodifier

premodifier see **modifier.** 10.6

premodify act as premodifier to

preposition. A preposition is a word that introduces a prepositional phrase, which consists of a preposition and the prepositional complement. In *for your sake, for* is a preposition and the noun phrase *your sake* is its complement. Prepositional complements may also be *-ing* participle clauses (*trying harder* in *by trying harder*) and *wh-*clauses (*whether I will be available* in *about whether I will be available*). 9.2

prepositional complement see **preposition.** 12.9.1

prepositional object. A prepositional object is the object of a **prepositional verb** (*the painting* in *I looked closely at the painting*) or the object of a **phrasal-prepositional verb** (*your insults* in *I've put up with your insults for too long*). In both instances, the object is introduced by a preposition. 11.20.1

prepositional phrase see **preposition.** 2.1.2.1, 9.2, 10.1, 12.9

prepositional verb. A prepositional verb is a **multi-word verb** in which a verb combines with a **preposition** to form an idiomatic unit. Monotransitive prepositional verbs take one object, a **prepositional object** (*a grant* in *I applied for a grant*). Doubly transitive verbs take two objects: a **direct object** and a **prepositional object.** In *Nobody will blame you for the mistake, you* is the direct object and *the mistake* is the prepositional object (introduced by the preposition *for*). A copular prepositional verb takes a **subject predicative** as its complement, a *waste of time* in *It looks like a waste of time* (compare *It looks wasteful,* where *looks* is a **copular verb**). 11.20

present one of the two tense categories indicated by verb inflections. See **tense.** 4.2.3

present participle the *-ing* participle

present perfect. The present perfect is a combination of the present tense of the perfect auxiliary *have* with the *-ed* participle of the following verb: *has seen, have owned.* See also **aspect.** 11.4, 11.11

present progressive. The present progressive is a combination of the progressive auxiliary *be* with the *-ing* participle of the following verb: *am saying is taking, are eating.* See also **aspect.** 11.4

present subjunctive see **subjunctive.**

primary pronouns a set of pronouns including the personal, possessive, and reflexive pronouns. 6.3

primary reflexive a reflexive pronoun used in place of a personal pronoun to signal that it co-refers with another nominal in the same sentence or clause

principal parts. The principal parts of a main verb are the three forms of a verb that are sufficient for deriving a list of all forms of the verb. The principal parts are the **base form**

(*sail, see, drink, put*), the past (*sailed, saw, drank, put*), and the *-ed* participle (*sailed, seen, drunk, put*). From the base form we can derive the *-s* form (*sails, sees, drinks, puts*) and the *-ing* participle (*sailing, seeing, drinking, putting*). 7.6

process adjunct a type of adjunct that relates to the process conveyed by the verb and its complements. 8.7.3.3

pro-clause a word substituting for a clause. 14.3.1

proclitic see **clitic**.

progressive see **aspect**. 4.2.4, 11.4, 11.15

progressive participle the present participle used with the auxiliary *be* to form the progressive aspect. 11.15

pronoun. Pronouns are a closed class of words that have a range of functions similar to those of nouns; for example they can serve as subject (*I* in *I know Paula*) or direct object (*me* in *Paula knows me*). Typically they point to entities in the situation or to linguistic units in the previous or following context. Many pronouns have the same form as corresponding determiners: *some* is a pronoun in *I have some with me*, whereas it is a **determiner** in *I have some money with me*. See also **demonstrative, indefinite determiner/pronoun, interrogative determiner/pronoun, nominal relative determiner/pronoun, personal pronoun, possessive pronoun, quantifier, reciprocal pronoun, reflexive pronoun, relative pronoun, wh-pronoun.** 4.3.2, 6.1

pronoun shifting the shifting of personal pronouns, possessive pronouns, and reflexives to take account of the reporting situation (typically from first person to third person). 15.2.2.1

proper noun. Proper nouns contrast with common nouns. Proper nouns have unique reference. They name specific people, places, etc. (*Esther, New York*). 5.4

prop *it* *it* used to fill the place of a required function, generally the subject. 6.7.4

proportion clause an adverbial clause expressing the proportion of one situation to another. 14.5.12

prototypical the same as **central**

purpose clause an adverbial clause referring to a situation that is intended to take place. 14.5.9

putative *should* a use of *should* in contexts that suggest that some situation may exist now or in the future. 11.8.8

quantifier. The primary quantifiers can function either as **pronouns** or as **determiners**: *many, more, most, a few, fewer, fewest, several, enough, much, more, most, a little, less, least, enough, few, little*. There are also compound quantifiers that function only as pronouns; for example: *a bit, a lot, a couple*. 6.13.2.

real condition an **open condition**

reason clause an adverbial clause which expresses such notions as reason and cause for what is conveyed in the host clause. 14.5.8

reciprocal pronoun. A reciprocal pronoun is a pronoun that co-refers with a noun phrase that is plural in form or meaning. The reciprocal pronouns are *each other* and *one another*. 6.11

recurrent present a use of the present tense for events that happen repeatedly. 11.5.2.2

recurrent present perfect a use of the present perfect to refer to a period extending from the past to the present time of speaking or writing, with reference to recurrent events (not to an unbroken state). 11.11.2

recurrent progressive a use of the progressive aspect to refer to a set of recurrent events that are viewed as in progress over a limited period of time. 11.15

reduced relative clause see **relative clause**.

referential shifts changes in the use of pronouns, tense, etc., resulting from the change of direct speech to indirect speech. 15.2.2

referring *it* the pronoun *it* used to refer back to a linguistic unit in the previous context. 6.7.1

reflexive pronoun. In standard English the reflexive pronouns are *myself, ourselves, yourself, yourselves, himself, herself, itself, themselves.* Singular *ourself* and *themself* are also used sometimes. 4.3.2.4

reflexive verb a verb which requires a reflexive pronoun as object. 6.9.3.3

register. A register is a variety of the language that relates to the type of activity for which the language is used. Major registers at the highest level of abstraction include exposition, narration, instruction, argumentation. More specific registers include news reports, personal letters, legal language, advertising.

relative adverb. Relative adverbs are used to introduce **relative clauses**. The relative adverbs are *when, where,* and *why*: 'the hotel *where* I stayed', 'the occasion *when* we first met', 'the reason *why* he did it'.

relative clause. Relative clauses postmodify nouns ('the house *that I own*'), pronouns ('those *who trust me*'), and nominal adjectives ('the elderly *who* are sick'). Sentential relative clauses relate not to any of those items but to a sentence, a clause, or a part of a clause: 'I missed them, *which is a pity*'. Relative clauses may be **restrictive** or non-restrictive, but sentential relative clauses are only non-restrictive. Relative clauses are introduced by a relative item—a **relative adverb**, a **relative determiner**, or a **relative pronoun**. Reduced relative clauses are non-finite clauses that correspond to the full (finite) relative clauses: 'the person *to see*' ('the person *that you should see*'), 'the patient *waiting in the next room*', 'the work *set for tomorrow*'.

relative determiner. Relative determiners are used to introduce **relative clauses**. The relative determiners are *whose* and *which*: 'the patient *whose* records were misplaced', 'The complaint has been formally lodged, in *which* case I'd like a copy'.

relative pronoun. Relative pronouns are used to introduce relative clauses. The relative pronouns are *who, whom, which, that,* and zero: 'the candidate *who* was rejected', 'the meal *which* I prepared', 'a book *that I've just read*'. When *that* is omitted, the relative is the zero relative: 'a book I've just read'. 4.3.2.5

reported clauses a clause containing reported speech. 13.5.2.6

reported speech conveys reports of acts of communication, including those of the reporters themselves. 15

reporting clause a clause indicating the speaker. 13.5.2.6, 15.1.1

restrictive. Modification may be either restrictive or non-restrictive. Modification is restrictive when the modifier is intended to restrict the reference of the noun phrase. In *hair that grows slowly*, the postmodifying relative clause *that grows slowly* distinguishes that type of hair from other types. In 'This is Peter West, *who edits a men's magazine*', the relative clause *who edits a men's magazine* is non-restrictive, since it does not restrict the reference of *Peter West* but instead contributes information about Peter West. 10.8

resultant role a semantic role that refers to something that comes into existence as a result of the action of the verb. 3.9.2.3

result clause a clause which refers to a situation that is or was in effect, the result of the situation described in the host clause. 14.5.10

rhetorical question a sentence type having the form of a question but the communicative function of a statement. 2.9

right dislocation see **left dislocation**. 3.10.5, 10.11

rise a nuclear pitch change from low to high. 2.6

root see **base**.

root meaning the same as **deontic meaning**.

S symbol for **subject**.

second person the category of person in a pronoun or verb which includes the person or persons addressed but excludes the speaker. 6.4.1

segregatory coordination see **coordination**. 10.13

semantic relating to meaning.

semantic role the role played by a constituent of a sentence or clause in the description of a situation by the sentence or clause. 3.9

semi-auxiliary see **auxiliary**. 11.1

semi-auxiliary sentence adverbial term sometimes used to comprise **conjunct** and **disjunct**. 8.7.1

sentence. The canonical sentence consists of one or more grammatically complete clauses. See **clause, orthographic**. 2.1.1, 13.1.2

sentence adverbial a type of adverbial which points to logical links with what precedes or expresses a comment by the speaker or writer, and is excluded from the predicate. 3.1.4

sentential relative clause. A sentential relative clause is a relative clause whose antecedent is the whole or part of what comes before it in the sentence. See **relative clause**. 10.10

sequence of tenses. Sequence of tenses applies to indirect speech. It is the relationship between the tenses of the verbs in the reporting clause and the reported clause as a result of backshift of the verb in the reported clause. See **direct speech, backshifting, tense**. 11.6.1.1, 15.2.2.2

-s form the form of the verb, ending in -s, used for the third person singular present. 10.14

similarity clause an adverbial clause expressing the similarity of one situation to another. 14.5.12

simple past see **tense**. 11.5.1

simple preposition a preposition consisting of one word. 9.2.1

simple present see **tense**. 11.5.2

simple sentence. A simple sentence consists of one **main clause**, without any subordinate clauses: *No fingerprints were found anywhere in the house.* 2.3.1, 3.1, 13.4

singular denoting one. 4.3.1.1, 5.6.1

situational deixis see **deixis**.

situational ellipsis see **ellipsis**. 3.11.1, 13.1.2.1.

source genitive a genitive phrase that denotes such relationships as authorship and origin. 5.12.5

space adjunct a type of adjunct that indicates position and direction. 8.7.3.1

specific A noun phrase has specific reference when it refers to a specific person, thing, place, etc. The reference in *a novel* is non-specific in 'I have always wanted to write *a novel*', since it does not refer to a particular novel. 10.16.2

speech act. A speech act is the performance of an utterance (spoken or written) in a particular context with a particular intention is a speech act. The intention is the illocutionary force of the speech act. The illocutionary force of *You may smoke in here* is (for one plausible interpretation) permission and for *You mustn't smoke in here* it is prohibition. See also **performative verb**. 2.10

split infinitive. A split infinitive is the separation between infinitival *to* and the infinitive verb by the insertion of one or more words. For example *really* splits the infinitive in 'to *really* understand'. See **infinitive**. 7.2.1.4

388 GLOSSARY OF GRAMMATICAL TERMS

standard English. Standard English is the national variety of English in countries such as the United States and England and is not restricted to any region within the country. It is to be distinguished from accents with which it may be pronounced. Standard English is preeminently the language of printed matter, and is the dialect of English that is taught in the education system. Other dialects of English used in the country are non-standard.

state present a use of the present tense that refers to a state that remains unaltered throughout. 11.5.2.1

state present perfect a use of the present perfect tense to refer to a state that began before the present time of speaking or writing and continues until that time. 11.11.1

stative describing a verb used in referring to a state of affairs. 3.9.5.1

stranded preposition. A preposition is stranded when it is left by itself, without a follow-ing prepositional complement. *With* is a stranded preposition in 'It will be dealt *with* at once'. It is followed by the prepositional complement *it* in 'I will deal *with it* at once'. See **preposition**. 12.9.2.

stranding the occurrence of a construction in which the preposition is stranded.

style disjunct a type of disjunct which can be paraphrased by a clause with a verb of speak-ing. 8.7.2.1

subject. The subject of a sentence (or clause) is the constituent that normally comes before the verb in a **declarative** sentence (*They* in '*They* have told you about it') and changes positions with the operator (**subject–operator inversion**) in an **interrogative** sentence ('*Have they* told you about it?'). Where applicable, the verb agrees in number and person with the subject: '*I am* ready' (the subject *I* is first person singular and so is *am*), '*He cares* about you' (the subject *he* is third person singular and so is *cares*). 3.3

subject–operator inversion. In subject-operator inversion, the subject and the **operator** change places. For example, the declarative sentence '*You have* spent all of it' has the normal word order, whereas the corresponding interrogative sentence '*Have you* spent all of it?' exhibits subject–operator inversion: the operator *have* comes before the subject *you*. 3.10.7

subject predicative. A subject predicative is the **complement** of a **copular verb** such as *be* or *seem*. It may be an adjective phrase, and adverb phrase, or a prepositional phrase as well as a noun phrase or a **nominal clause**: 'Paula feels *very self-conscious*' (adjective phrase), 'Norman is *outside*' (adverb), 'I am *out of breath*' (prepositional phrase), 'Amanda is *my best friend*' (noun phrase), 'My advice is *to say nothing*' (nominal clause). A complex-transitive verb has two complements: a direct object and an object predicative. In 'I made *my position clear*', *my position* is the direct object and *clear* is the object complement. The predicative relationship between the object and its complement is analogous to that between the subject and the subject predicative in '*My position* is *clear*'. 3.6

subject–verb agreement see **subject**. 10.14

subject–verb inversion reversal of the order of the subject and verb. 3.10.6

subjective case see **case**. 4.3.2.2, 6.4.4

subjective genitive a genitive phrase whose relationship to the second noun phrase corresponds to that between a subject and a verb. 5.12.2

subjunctive. There are two subjunctives: the present subjunctive and the past subjunctive. The present subjunctive has the **base form** of the verb, and the past subjunctive is re-stricted to *were*. The present subjunctive has three uses. The optative subjunctive ex-presses a wish: 'God *help* the Republic'; contrast the indicative *helps* in 'God *helps* the Republic'. The suppositional subjunctive expresses a supposition, and is used chiefly with conditional and concessive clauses: 'I can teach him, even though it *be* inconvenient for me'. The mandative subjunctive is used in *that*-clauses that convey and order, request, or intention: 'They demanded that he *appear* before them for interrogation.' The past subjunctive *were* is the hypothetical subjunctive, used in hypothetical **conditional clauses** and some other hypothetical constructions: 'If I *were* you, I wouldn't go.' 4.2.1, 11.9–10

subordinate clause. Subordinate clauses are grammatically dependent on a host (or superordinate) clause or host phrase and generally function as a constituent of their host. In the sentence (coterminous with a **main clause**) 'I wonder *whether they are at home*', the *whether*-clause is a subordinate clause. In the noun phrase 'the lunch *that I've just finished*', the relative clause *that I've just finished* is a subordinate clause. 2.3.3, 13.3, 14.1

subordinating conjunction a subordinator

subordination the presence or role of a subordinate clause. 13.3

subordinator see **conjunction**. 9.1.2, 13.9.1

substitute pronoun the pronoun *one* used as a substitute for an indefinite noun phrase or for the head of a noun phrase. 6.6

suffix see **affix**.

superlative see **adjective, adverb, comparison**. 4.4, 8.4

suppletion. Suppletion is the use of a word from a different root to complete a **paradigm**, a grammatically related set of forms. Suppletive *went* (from the verb *wend*) is the past of the verb *go*. See also **morpheme**.

suppositional subjunctive an occasional use of the present subjunctive in adverbial clauses, particularly in conditional and concessive clauses. 11.9.2

syndetic coordination see **coordination**. 4.5.1, 13.2.3

syntax the ways in which words combine into structures of phrases, clauses, and sentences. 1.7

tag question. Tag questions are attached to sentences that are not **interrogatives**. Typically, they are abbreviated *yes–no* questions: 'You can do it, *can't you?*', 'It hasn't reached you yet, *has it?*'. 2.6

temporal clause an adverbial clause referring to the time of a situation. 14.5.2

temporal genitive a genitive phrase that denotes a period of time or a duration of time. 5.12.4

tense. Tense is a grammatical category referring to the time of a situation. English has two tenses that are signalled by the form of the verb: present and past. The tense distinction is made on the first or only verb in the verb phrase: *sings/ sang, is/ was crying, has/ had made*. The simple present is the present tense when there is only one verb (the **main verb**): *sings, shows, writes, catches*. Analogously, the simple past is the past tense when there is only one verb: *sang, showed, wrote, caught*. 4.2.3, 11.4

tense shifting see **backshifting**. 15.2.2.2

textual deixis see **deixis**. 3.11.2, 13.1.2.2.

textual ellipsis see **ellipsis**. 3.11.2, 13.1.2.2.

third person the category of person in a pronoun or verb which excludes the speaker and the person or persons addressed. 6.4.1

time adjunct a type of adjunct that indicates position in time, duration, and frequency. 8.7.3.2

***to*-infinitive** see **infinitive**. 7.2.1.4

***to*-infinitive clause** see **infinitive**. 14.3.2.3

transferred negation the transfer of negation from the subordinate clause to the host clause. 14.3.1.1 Note

verb phrase. A verb phrase is a phrase whose head is a **main verb** (or lexical verb). The main verb may be preceded within the verb phrase by one or more **auxiliaries** or **semi-auxiliaries**: *speaks, is speaking, is going to speak.* 2.1.1.2, 3.1.2

vocative. A vocative is an optional addition to the basic sentence (or clause) structure, and is used to address directly the person or persons spoken to: 'You have a smudge on your nose, *Robin*.' 3.8, 10.15

voice. Voice is a grammatical category which distinguishes between active and passive. The distinction applies to both clauses and verb phrases. See **passive**. 4.2.5

voicing the change of an unvoiced consonant such as *f* to its voiced equivalent *v* associated with the plural inflection of certain nouns. 5.7.1

***wh*-adverb.** The *wh*-adverbs are used (1) for questions and interrogative clauses: *how, when, where, why*; (2) for exclamative sentences and clauses: *how*; (3) for relative clauses: *when, where, why, whereby, whereupon*, and the two archaic adverbs *whence, wherein*; (4) for nominal relative clauses: *how, when, why, where*; (5) for *wh*-conditional clauses: *however, whenever, wherever.* 8.7.3.3

***wh*-clause** a subordinate interrogative clause introduced by a *wh*-word. 14.3.2.2

***wh*-conditional clause.** A *wh*-conditional clause leaves open the number of possible conditions: '*Whatever you've been doing*, you've been doing the right thing' ('if you've been doing X, if you've been doing Y, . . .'). 6.12.5, 14.5.6

***wh*-conditional determiner, pronoun** a determiner or pronoun which introduces a *wh*-conditional clause. 6.12.5

***wh*-determiner.** The *wh*-determiners are (1) for questions and interrogative clauses: *which, what, whose*; (2) for **exclamative** sentences and clauses: *what*; (3) for **relative clauses**: *whose, which*; (4) for **nominal relative clauses**: *which, what*; (5) for ***wh*-conditional** clauses: *whatever, whichever.* See **determiner**. 6.12

***wh*-pronoun.** The *wh*-pronouns are used (1) for questions and interrogative clauses: *whom, whom, whose, which, what*; (2) for **relative clauses**: *who, whom, which*; (3) for **nominal relative clauses**: *who, whom, whoever, whomever, whosoever, whomsoever, which, whichever, whichsoever, what, whatever, whatsoever*; (4) for ***wh*-conditional** clauses: *whoever, whomever, whosoever, whomsoever, whatever, whichever.* 6.12

***wh*-question.** *Wh*-questions and *wh*-interrogative clauses are introduced by a *wh*-word, which may be alone or within a phrase: '*Who* is next?'; '*To what* do I owe this visit?'; 'They asked me *which way* they should go'. 2.5.2

***wh*-relative pronoun** see ***wh*-pronoun**. 4.3.2.5, 10.9.1

wh*-word.** *Wh*-words are words beginning with *wh*- (wh*-adverbs, *wh*-determiners**, and ***wh*-pronouns**), but they also include *how* and its compounds (such as *however*). 2.5.2

word class. A word class (or part of speech) is a class of words, such as noun and verb, that share characteristics. Word classes may be **open classes** (open to new words) or **closed classes** (which generally do not admit new words). Classes may be divided into subclasses; for example, within nouns the distinction between common nouns and proper nouns. 5.1

word-formation. Word-formation refers to the process of forming new words from existing words or segments of words.

***yes–no* clause** a subordinate interrogative clause corresponding to a *yes–no* question. 14.3.2.1

***yes–no* question.** A *yes–no* question is a question that typically may be appropriately answered by *yes* or *no*. *Yes–no* questions have **subject-operator inversion**, in which the **operator** comes before the subject: '*Are* (operator) *you* (subject) ready?'; '*Have* (operator) *they* (subject) finished their breakfast?'; '*Do* (operator) *we* (subject) pay for ourselves?' 2.5.1

zero article. A zero article (or zero determiner) is postulated for noun phrases where no article (or other determiner) is present. It is a device for simplifying the grammar by assuming a contrast that is elsewhere present in the singular: the contrast between the definite article *the* and the indefinite article *a/an* is extended to the plural, as in *a student, the student,* (zero article) *students, the students.* See also **definite article, morpheme.** 5.5.2

zero plural a noun plural form that is identical with the singular form. 5.7.3

zero relative. The zero relative (or zero relative pronoun) is postulated at the beginning of a relative clause when no **relative pronoun** is overtly present. For example, the relative pronouns *which* and *that* introduce the relative clauses in 'computer games *which* I enjoy'; 'the car *that* they have just bought'. The same clauses are said to be introduced by a zero relative when these pronouns are omitted: 'computer games I enjoy'; 'the car they have just bought'. See also **morpheme.** 6.12.3.3, 10.9.3, 13.9.1

zero *that* the subordinator *that* regarded as having been omitted (when its clause is not functioning as subject). 13.9.1

Index

All references are to sections, chapters, or notes. A reference to a chapter number is followed by *passim*, indicating that the topic is dealt with throughout the chapter. A reference to a note is presented as a section number followed by *note*.

References for a section within the same chapter are separated by commas. Sets of references for sections within different chapters are separated by semicolons. Major references are given in **bold**.